Lecture Notes in Computer Science 8711

Commenced Publication in 1973
Founding and Former Series Editors:
Gerhard Goos, Juris Hartmanis, and Jan van Leeuwen

Editorial Board

Axel Legay   Marius Bozga (Eds.)

Formal Modeling
and Analysis
of Timed Systems

12th International Conference, FORMATS 2014
Florence, Italy, September 8-10, 2014
Proceedings

 Springer

Volume Editors

Axel Legay
Inria, Bâtiment C
Campus Universitaire de Beaulieu
35042 Rennes Cedex, France
E-mail: axel.legay@inria.fr

Marius Bozga
VERIMAG, Distributed and Complex Systems Group
Centre Equation, 2 Avenue de Vignate
38610 Gieres, France
E-mail: marius.bozga@imag.fr

ISSN 0302-9743   e-ISSN 1611-3349
ISBN 978-3-319-10511-6   e-ISBN 978-3-319-10512-3
DOI 10.1007/978-3-319-10512-3
Springer Cham Heidelberg New York Dordrecht London

Library of Congress Control Number: 2014946204

LNCS Sublibrary: SL 1 – Theoretical Computer Science and General Issues

Typesetting: Camera-ready by author, data conversion by Scientific Publishing Services, Chennai, India

Printed on acid-free paper

Springer is part of Springer Science+Business Media (www.springer.com)

Preface

This volume contains the proceedings of the 2014 International Conference on Formal Modeling and Analysis of Timed Systems (FORMATS 2014), held in Florence, Italy, during September 8–10, 2014.

FORMATS 2014 was the 12th of a series dedicated to the advancement of modeling and analysis techniques for timed systems. This year, FORMATS was part of FLORENCE 2014 – a one-week scientific event with conferences and workshops in the areas of formal and quantitative analysis of systems.

FORMATS 2014 attracted 36 submissions in response to the call for papers. Each submission was assigned to at least three members of the Program Committee. The Program Committee discussed the submissions electronically, judging them on their perceived importance, originality, clarity, and appropriateness to the expected audience. The Program Committee selected 16 papers for presentation, leading to an acceptance rate of 44%.

Complementing the contributed papers, the program of FORMATS 2014 included an invited lecture by Sanjoy Baruah on the "Modeling and Analysis of Mixed-Criticality Systems."

The chairs would like to thank the authors for submitting their papers to FORMATS 2014. We are grateful to the reviewers who contributed to nearly 140 informed and detailed reports and discussions during the electronic Program Committee meeting. We also sincerely thank the Steering Committee for their advice. Finally, we would like to thank the organizers of FLORENCE 2014 for taking care of both the local organization and the website for FORMATS. FORMATS 2014 was sponsored by Verimag and Inria.

June 2014

Axel Legay
Marius Bozga

Organization

Program Committee

Parosh Aziz Abdulla	Uppsala University, Sweden
Erika Abraham	RWTH Aachen University, Germany
Eugene Asarin	LIAFA, University Paris Diderot, France
Luca Bortolussi	University of Trieste, Italy
Marius Bozga	Verimag/CNRS, Grenoble, France
Alexandre David	CISS/Aalborg University, Denmark
Alexandre Donzé	UC Berkeley, USA
Georgios Fainekos	Arizona State University, USA
Goran Frehse	Université Joseph Fourier Grenoble 1, Verimag, France
Martin Fränzle	Carl von Ossietzky Universität Oldenburg, Germany
Gilles Geeraerts	Université Libre de Bruxelles, Belgium
Marcin Jurdzinski	University of Warwick, UK
Joost-Pieter Katoen	RWTH Aachen University, Germany
Kai Lampka	Uppsala University, Sweden
Laurent Fribourg	LSV/CNRS, Paris, France
Axel Legay	IRISA/Inria, Rennes, France
Didier Lime	École Centrale de Nantes, France
Nicolas Markey	LSV, CNRS ENS Cachan, France
Thiagarajan P.S.	National University of Singapore
David Parker	University of Birmingham, UK
Ocan Sankur	ENS Cachan, France
Ana Sokolova	University of Salzburg, Austria
Oleg Sokolsky	University of Pennsylvania, USA
Louis-Marie Traonouez	Inria Rennes, France
Ashutosh Trivedi	Indian Institute of Technology, Bombay, India
Frits Vaandrager	Radboud University Nijmegen, The Netherlands
Enrico Vicario	Università di Firenze, Italy
Sergio Yovine	CONICET, Argentina

Additional Reviewers

Abdullah, Syed Md. Jakaria	Bogomolov, Sergiy
Akshay, S.	Bouyer, Patricia
Bartocci, Ezio	Casagrande, Alberto
Berthomieu, Bernard	Chatain, Thomas

Chen, Sanjian
Chen, Xin
Craciunas, Silviu
Desai, Ankush
Doyen, Laurent
Dreossi, Tommaso
Eggers, Andreas
Estiévenart, Morgane
Feng, Lu
Guha, Shibashis
Haddad, Serge
Hagemann, Willem
Helms, Domenik
Jansen, Nils
Jonsson, Bengt
King, Andrew
Lampka, Kai
Lippautz, Michael
Martos-Salgado, María

Massart, Thierry
Nellen, Johanna
Ouaknine, Joel
Paulevé, Loïc
Piazza, Carla
Rezine, Othmane
Rodriguez, Cesar
Roux, Olivier H.
Ruemmer, Philipp
S., Krishna
Sangnier, Arnaud
Schupp, Stefan
Sharma, Arpit
Stainer, Amelie
Stigge, Martin
Swaminathan, Mani
Wojtczak, Dominik
Yu, Huafeng

Table of Contents

The Modeling and Analysis of Mixed-Criticality Systems
(Extended Abstract) 1
  Sanjoy Baruah

Modeling Bitcoin Contracts by Timed Automata..................... 7
  Marcin Andrychowicz, Stefan Dziembowski, Daniel Malinowski,
  and Lukasz Mazurek

Data-Driven Statistical Learning of Temporal Logic Properties......... 23
  Ezio Bartocci, Luca Bortolussi, and Guido Sanguinetti

Finding Best and Worst Case Execution Times of Systems Using
Difference-Bound Matrices 38
  Omar Al-Batainch, Mark Reynolds, and Tim French

Delay-Dependent Partial Order Reduction Technique for Time
Petri Nets.. 53
  Hanifa Boucheneb, Kamel Barkaoui, and Karim Weslati

On MITL and Alternating Timed Automata over Infinite Words 69
  Thomas Brihaye, Morgane Estiévenart, and Gilles Geeraerts

Time Petri Nets with Dynamic Firing Dates:
Semantics and Applications 85
  Bernard Berthomieu, Silvano Dal Zilio, Lukasz Fronc,
  and François Vernadat

Verification and Performance Evaluation of Timed Game Strategies 100
  Alexandre David, Huixing Fang, Kim Guldstrand Larsen,
  and Zhengkui Zhang

The Power of Proofs: New Algorithms for Timed Automata Model
Checking 115
  Peter Fontana and Rance Cleaveland

Anonymized Reachability of Hybrid Automata Networks 130
  Taylor T. Johnson and Sayan Mitra

Combined Global and Local Search for the Falsification
of Hybrid Systems 146
  Jan Kuřátko and Stefan Ratschan

Weak Singular Hybrid Automata 161
    Shankara Narayanan Krishna, Umang Mathur, and Ashutosh Trivedi

Non-convex Invariants and Urgency Conditions on Linear Hybrid
Automata.. 176
    Stefano Minopoli and Goran Frehse

Time-Bounded Reachability for Initialized Hybrid Automata with
Linear Differential Inclusions and Rectangular Constraints 191
    Nima Roohi and Mahesh Viswanathan

Virtual Integration of Real-Time Systems Based on Resource
Segregation Abstraction 206
    Ingo Stierand, Philipp Reinkemeier, and Purandar Bhaduri

Timed Pattern Matching.. 222
    Dogan Ulus, Thomas Ferrère, Eugene Asarin, and Oded Maler

Interval Abstraction Refinement for Model Checking
of Timed-Arc Petri Nets 237
    Sine Viesmose Birch, Thomas Stig Jacobsen, Jacob Jon Jensen,
    Christoffer Moesgaard, Niels Nørgaard Samuelsen, and Jiří Srba

Author Index.. 253

The Modeling and Analysis
of Mixed-Criticality Systems
Extended Abstract

Sanjoy Baruah*

Department of Computer Science,
The University of North Carolina
Chapel Hill, NC 27599, USA
baruah@cs.unc.edu

Abstract. Methodologies that are currently widely used in the design
and implementation of safety-critical real-time application systems are
primarily focused on ensuring correctness. This, in conjunction with the
trend towards implementing such systems using COTS components, may
lead to very poor utilization of the implementation platform resources
during run-time. Mixed-criticality implementations have been proposed
as one means of achieving more efficient resource utilization upon such
platforms. The real-time scheduling community has been developing a
theory of mixed-criticality scheduling that seeks to solve resource alloca-
tion problems for mixed-criticality systems. There is a need for the formal
methods and analysis community to work on developing methodologies
for the design and analysis of mixed-criticality systems; such methodologies, in conjunction with the work on mixed-criticality scheduling
currently being done in the real-time scheduling community, has the potential to significantly enhance our ability to design and implement large,
complex, real-time systems in a manner that is both provably correct and
resource-efficient.

Correctness and Efficiency Considerations

The discipline of real-time computing has its origins in the application domains
of defense, space, and aviation. These are all highly safety-critical domains that
place a great premium on correctness, since the consequences of incorrect system
behavior is potentially very severe. Furthermore, early systems in these application domains had limited computational capabilities upon which to implement
the desired functionalities. Early real-time systems were therefore required to
both be *correct*, and have *resource-efficient implementations*.

In the early years of the discipline, these twin goals of correctness and efficiency were achieved by keeping things very simple: safety-critical computer
systems were restricted to being very simple, responsible for very simple, highly

* Supported in part by NSF grants CNS 1016954, CNS 1115284, and CNS 1218693;
and ARO grant W911NF-09-1-0535.

A. Legay and M. Bozga (Eds.): FORMATS 2014, LNCS 8711, pp. 1–6, 2014.

repetitive, functionalities. They were typically implemented as carefully hand-crafted code executing upon very simple and predictable processors. Run-time behavior was therefore very predictable, and hence correctness could be demonstrated in a fairly straightforward manner.

Choosing Correctness Over Efficiency

However, things soon became far more complicated. The requirements placed upon safety-critical computer systems increased significantly in size and complexity, and continue to increase at a very rapid pace. This meant that safety-critical systems could no longer be implemented upon simple and predictable processors; instead, advanced modern processors that offer far greater computational capabilities but exhibit less predictable run-time behavior increasingly came to be used in implementing even highly safety-critical real-time systems. As a consequence of this increase in the complexity and diversity of real-time application system requirements and implementation platforms, it soon became impossible for a single system developer, or a small group of developers, to keep all details in mind while reasoning about a system design and implementation. Instead, it became necessary to introduce *abstractions* that would highlight the relevant aspects of a system's behavior while concealing the less important aspects.

In devising these abstractions, the real-time systems research community was deeply influenced by the increasingly central role that computer systems are coming to play in the control of safety-critical devices and systems. The increasing criticality of these systems, coupled with their increasing complexity and diversity, meant that correctness was becoming both more important, and more difficult to achieve. In contrast, ensuring efficiency of implementation became less important as Moore's Law, compounded over decades, made it possible to provide larger amounts of computing capabilities at relatively low cost.

Given this state of affairs — correctness becoming increasingly both more important and more difficult to achieve, and efficiency mattering less — the real-time systems community made the rational decision to focus on abstractions that facilitate the correct construction of systems, letting efficiency considerations recede to the background. An important advance here was the introduction of the *synchrony assumption* [2], which separated functional and temporal correctness concerns by introducing the concept of logical time. Time considerations were re-integrated into a functionally correct design by the use of abstractions and mechanisms such as logical execution time, timed automata, etc. These abstractions, which are sometimes collectively referred to by the umbrella term *model-based design* for timed systems, have proved extremely popular; supported by powerful tools and rigorous proof and design formalisms, such model-based design methodologies are widely used today in developing systems in safety-critical industrial domains such as automotive, aviation, etc.

But it is important to realize that the end-product of the process of designing a system using these model-based design methodologies is a *model* of the system, not its physical realization upon an implementation platform. We do not currently know how to implement such models upon modern advanced platforms in a resource-efficient manner; instead, current practice is to use ad hoc techniques to obtain an implementation of a model that is developed using a model-based design process (and thereby rigorously proved to be correct), without worrying too much about efficiency, compensating for this lack of efficiency by an over-provisioning of computational and other resources upon the implementation platform.

The Problem of Modern Platforms

As safety-critical systems became ever more complex and computationally demanding, it became necessary to implement them upon the most advanced computing platforms available. Due to cost and related reasons, such platforms are increasingly coming to be built using commercial off-the-shelf (COTS) processors and other components. COTS processors are generally developed with the objective of providing improved "typical" or average-case performance rather than better worst-case guarantees; they therefore incorporate advanced architectural features such as multi-level cache memories, deep pipelining, speculative out-of-order execution, etc., that do indeed significantly improve average performance but also lead to very large *variances* in run-time behavior. For example, it is known [1] that the simple operation of adding two integer variables and storing the result in a third may take from as few as 3 to as many as 321 cycles on the Motorola PowerPC-755 (by contrast, the earlier Motorola 68K processor, which was state-of-the art in the 1990's, always executes this operation in exactly 20 cycles). In order to predict the precise behavior that will be experienced by a particular process during run-time, extensive knowledge of the run-time situation –the inputs to the process at run-time; the states of the other processes that are executing concurrently; etc.– must be known; since such knowledge is not usually obtainable during system design time, the run-time behavior is *unpredictable* beforehand.

The Move towards Mixed-Criticality Systems

Summarizing the points made above:

- Safety-critical system requirements have become vastly more complex, and more computation-intensive.
- They must therefore be implemented upon advanced modern computing platforms, which offer increased computing capabilities but are unpredictable and exhibit great variance between average-case and worst-case behavior.
- Given the extremely safety-critical nature of the applications, though, their correctness must nevertheless be validated to extremely high levels of assurance.

Since the systems are so complex and the implementation platforms so unpredictable, system correctness at the desired high levels of assurance is guaranteed during the system design process by tremendous over-provisioning of computational and other platform resources during system design time. However, the very conservative assumptions that must be made during validation in order to ensure correctness at the desired levels of assurance are highly unlikely to occur during the typical run; hence, much of the over-provisioned resources are unlikely to actually be used during run-time. As a consequence, such system implementations will see extremely low resource utilization during run-time. **SWaP** concerns (the Size, and Weight of the implementation platform, and the Power, or rather, the energy, that is consumed by it) make such resource under-utilization increasingly unacceptable. One approach towards improving run-time resource usage is by moving towards *mixed-criticality* implementations, in which the highly safety-critical functionalities are implemented upon the same platform as less critical functionalities. This approach has proved very popular in safety-critical application domains, as is evident in industry-driven initiatives such as Integrated Modular Avionics (IMA) [4] in aerospace and AUTOSAR[1] in the automotive industry. Informally speaking, the idea is that the resources that are provisioned to highly critical functionalities during design time, but are likely to remain unused by these functionalities at run-time, can be "re-claimed" and used to make performance guarantees, albeit at lower levels of assurance, to the less critical functionalities.

Mixed-Criticality Scheduling Theory

The recently emergent field of mixed-criticality scheduling theory (see, e.g., [3] for a current survey) is concerned with the study of resource-allocation, scheduling, and synchronization in such mixed-criticality systems. Two related but distinct approaches have been widely investigated: one focused primarily on run-time robustness, and the other on verification.

Run-time robustness is a form of fault tolerance that allows graceful degradation to occur in a manner that is mindful of criticality levels: informally speaking, in the event that all functionalities implemented upon a shared platform cannot be serviced satisfactorily the goal is to ensure that less critical functionalities are denied their requested levels of service before more critical functionalities are. Approaches in mixed-criticality scheduling theory that seek to ensure such run-time robustness are centered upon identifying, during run-time, when cumulative resource demand exceeds the available supply, and triggering a *mode change* [6] when this happens. Real-time scheduling theory has a rich history of results towards obtaining resource-efficient implementations of mode changes (see [5] for a survey); these techniques may be adapted to ensure run-time robust mixed-criticality systems.

Static verification of mixed-criticality systems is closely related to the problem of *certification* in safety-critical application domains. The accelerating trend in safety-critical application domains such as automotive and avionics systems towards computerized control of an ever-increasing range of functionalities, both

---

[1] AUTomotive Open System ARchitecture — see www.autosar.org

safety-critical and non-critical, means that even in highly safety-critical systems, typically only a relatively small fraction of the overall system is actually of critical functionality and needs to be certified. In order to certify a system as being correct, the certification authority (CA) may mandate that certain assumptions be made about the worst-case behavior of the system during run-time. CA's tend to be very conservative, and hence it is often the case that the assumptions required by the CA are far more pessimistic than those the system designer would typically use during the system design process if certification was not required. However, while the CA is only concerned with the correctness of the safety-critical part of the system the system designer wishes to ensure that the entire system is correct, including the non-critical parts. Vestal [7] first identified the challenge of obtaining certification for integrated system implementations in which different functionalities need to have their correctness validated to different levels of assurance, while simultaneously ensuring efficient resource-utilization. The real-time scheduling community has since produced a vast amount of work that builds upon Vestal's seminal idea; see [3] for a survey.

A Need for Participation by the FORMATS Community

These advances in mixed-criticality scheduling theory point to a promising approach towards reintegrating efficiency considerations into the design and implementation of provably correct safety-critical real-time application systems. However, much of this work is based upon relatively low-level and simple workload models, such as collections of independent jobs, or systems represented as a finite collection of recurrent (e.g., periodic and sporadic) tasks. Prior experience has shown that such simple models are inadequate for building truly complex systems – more powerful models, at higher levels of abstraction and possessing greater expressive power, are needed. The development of such models, along with accompanying design methodologies, proof formalisms, and tool support, is one of the prime strengths of the formal methods and modeling community. There is therefore a pressing need for the formal methods and modeling community to take a close look at mixed-criticality systems, to develop more powerful models for representing such systems, and to extend the mixed-criticality scheduling theories to become applicable to these more advanced models. It is my belief that such work is best conducted in co-ordinated, cooperative efforts between the formal methods and the real-time scheduling communities.

Acknowledgements. The ideas discussed in this extended abstract are based upon discussions with a number of colleagues and research collaborators, Alan Burns in particular. Others include (in alphabetical order) Jim Anderson, Saddek Bensalem, Vincenzo Bonifaci, Pontus Ekberg, Gerhard Fohler, Laurent George, Nan Guan, Alberto Marchetti-Spaccamela, Joseph Sifakis, Leen Stougie, Lothar Thiele, Steve Vestal, and Wang Yi.

References

1. Slide-show: Introduction to aiT, http://www.absint.com/ait/slides/4.htm (accessed on June 23, 2014)
2. Benveniste, A., Berry, G.: The synchronous approach to reactive and real-time systems. Proceedings of the IEEE 79(9), 1270–1282 (1991)
3. Burns, A., Davis, R.: Mixed-criticality systems: A review (2013), http://www-users.cs.york.ac.uk/~burns/review.pdf
4. Prisaznuk, P.J.: Integrated modular avionics. In: Proceedings of the IEEE 1992 National Aerospace and Electronics Conference (NAECON 1992), vol. 1, pp. 39–45 (May 1992)
5. Real, J., Crespo, A.: Mode change protocols for real-time systems: A survey and a new proposal. Real-Time Syst. 26(2), 161–197 (2004)
6. Sha, L., Rajkumar, R., Lehoczky, J., Ramamritham, K.: Mode change protocols for priority-driven preemptive scheduling. Real-Time Systems 1, 243–264 (1988)
7. Vestal, S.: Preemptive scheduling of multi-criticality systems with varying degrees of execution time assurance. In: Proceedings of the Real-Time Systems Symposium, pp. 239–243. IEEE Computer Society Press, Tucson (2007)

Modeling Bitcoin Contracts by Timed Automata⋆

Marcin Andrychowicz, Stefan Dziembowski⋆⋆,
Daniel Malinowski, and Łukasz Mazurek

University of Warsaw
Cryptology and Data Security Group, Poland
www.crypto.edu.pl

Abstract. Bitcoin is a peer-to-peer cryptographic currency system. Since its introduction in 2008, Bitcoin has gained noticeable popularity, mostly due to its following properties: (1) the transaction fees are very low, and (2) it is not controlled by any central authority, which in particular means that nobody can "print" the money to generate inflation. Moreover, the transaction syntax allows to create the so-called *contracts*, where a number of mutually-distrusting parties engage in a protocol to jointly perform some financial task, and the fairness of this process is guaranteed by the properties of Bitcoin. Although the Bitcoin contracts have several potential applications in the digital economy, so far they have not been widely used in real life. This is partly due to the fact that they are cumbersome to create and analyze, and hence risky to use.

In this paper we propose to remedy this problem by using the methods originally developed for the computer-aided analysis for hardware and software systems, in particular those based on the timed automata. More concretely, we propose a framework for modeling the Bitcoin contracts using the timed automata in the UPPAAL model checker. Our method is general and can be used to model several contracts. As a proof-of-concept we use this framework to model some of the Bitcoin contracts from our recent previous work. We then automatically verify their security in UPPAAL, finding (and correcting) some subtle errors that were difficult to spot by the manual analysis. We hope that our work can draw the attention of the researchers working on formal modeling to the problem of the Bitcoin contract verification, and spark off more research on this topic.

1   Introduction

Bitcoin is a digital currency system introduced in 2008 by an anonymous developer using a pseudonym "Satoshi Nakamoto" [22]. Despite of its mysterious origins, Bitcoin became the first cryptographic currency that got widely adopted — as of January 2014 the Bitcoin capitalization is over € 7 bln. The enormous success of Bitcoin was also widely covered by the media (see e.g. [15,5,24,20,21]) and even attracted the attention of several governing bodies and legislatures, including the US Senate [20]. Bitcoin owes its popularity mostly to the fact that it has no central authority, the transaction fees are very low, and the amount of coins in the circulation is restricted, which in particular

---

⋆ This work was supported by the WELCOME/2010-4/2 grant founded within the framework of the EU Innovative Economy (National Cohesion Strategy) Operational Programme.
⋆⋆ On leave from the *Sapienza* University of Rome.

A. Legay and M. Bozga (Eds.): FORMATS 2014, LNCS 8711, pp. 7–22, 2014.

means that nobody can "print" money to generate inflation. The financial transactions between the participants are published on a public ledger maintained jointly by the users of the system.

One of the very interesting, but slightly less known, features of the Bitcoin is the fact that it allows for more complicated "transactions" than the simple money transfers between the participants: very informally, in Bitcoin it is possible to "deposit" some amount of money in such a way that it can be claimed only under certain conditions. These conditions are written in the form of the *Bitcoin scripts* and in particular may involve some timing constrains. This property allows to create the so-called *contracts* [26], where a number of mutually-distrusting parties engage in a Bitcoin-based protocol to jointly perform some task. The security of the protocol is guaranteed purely by the properties of the Bitcoin, and no additional trust assumptions are needed. This Bitcoin feature can have several applications in the digital economy, like creating the assurance contracts, the escrow and dispute mediation, the rapid micropayments [26], the multi-party lotteries [8]. It can also be used to add some extra properties to Bitcoin, like the certification of the users [16], or creating the secure "mixers" whose goal is to enhance the anonymity of the transactions [18]. Their potential has even been noticed by the media (see, e.g., a recent enthusiastic article on the *CNN Money* [21]).

In our opinion, one of the obstacles that may prevent this feature from being widely used by the Bitcoin community is the fact that the contracts are tricky to write and understand. This may actually be the reason why, despite of so many potential applications, they have not been widely used in real life. As experienced by ourselves [6,7,8], developing such contracts is hard for the following reasons. Firstly, it's easy to make subtle mistakes in the scripts. Secondly, the protocols that involve several parties and the timing constraints are naturally hard to analyze by hand. Since mistakes in the contracts can be exploited by the malicious parties for their own financial gain, it is natural that users are currently reluctant to use this feature of Bitcoin.

In this paper we propose an approach that can help designing secure Bitcoin contracts. Our idea is to use the methods originally developed for the computer-aided analysis for hardware and software systems, in particular the timed automata [1,2]. They seem to be the right tool for this purpose due to the fact that the protocols used in the Bitcoin contracts typically have a finite number of states and depend on the notion of time. This time-dependence is actually two-fold, as (1) it takes some time for the Bitcoin transactions to be confirmed (1 hour, say), and (2) the Bitcoin transactions can come with a "time lock" which specifies the time when a transaction becomes valid.

Our Contribution. We propose a framework for modeling the Bitcoin contracts using timed automata in the UPPAAL model checker [9,17] (this is described in Sec. 2). Our method is general and can be used to model a wide class of contracts. As a proof-of-concept, in Sec. 3 we use this framework to model two Bitcoin contracts from our previous work [8,6]. This is done manually, but our method is quite generic and can potentially be automatized. In particular, most of the code in our implementation does not depend on the protocol being verified, but describes the properties of Bitcoin system. To model a new contract it is enough to specify the transactions used in the contract, the knowledge of the parties at the beginning of the protocol and the protocol followed by the parties. We then automatically verify the security of our contracts in UPPAAL (in Sec. 3.1). The UPPAAL code for the contracts modeled and verified by us is available at the web page http://crypto.edu.pl/uppaal-btc.zip.

Future Work. We hope that our work can draw the attention of the researchers working on formal modeling to the problem of the Bitcoin contracts verification, and spark off more research on this topic. What seems especially interesting is to try to fully automatize this process. One attractive option is to think of the following workflow: (1) a designer of a Bitcoin contract describes it in UPPAAL (or, possibly, in some extension of it), (2) he verifies the security of this idealized description using UPPAAL, and (3) if the idealized description verifies correctly, then he uses the system to "compile" it into a real Bitcoin implementation that can be deployed in the wild. Another option would be to construct a special tool for designing the Bitcoin contracts, that would produce two outputs: (a) a code in the UPPAAL language (for verification) and (b) a real-life Bitcoin implementation.

Of course, in both cases one would need to formally show the soundness of this process (in particular: that the "compiled" code maintains the properties of the idealized description). Hence, this project would probably require both non-trivial theoretical and engineering work.

Preliminaries. Timed automata were introduced by Alur and Dill [1,2]. There exist other model checkers based on this theory, like Kronos [29] and Times [4]. It would be interesting to try to implement our ideas also in them. Other formal models that involve the notion of the real time include the timed Petri nets [10], the timed CSP [25], the timed process algebras [28,23], and the timed propositional temporal logic [3]. One can try to model the Bitcoin contracts also using these formalisms. For the lack of space, a short introduction to UPPAAL was moved to Appendix (see the full version of the paper[1]). The reader may also consult [9,17] for more information on this system.

We assume reader's familiarity with the public-key cryptography, in particular with the signature schemes (an introduction to this concept can be found e.g. in [19,12]). We will frequently denote the key pairs using the capital letters (e.g. A), and refer to the private key and the public key of A by: $A.sk$ and $A.pk$, respectively. We will also use the following convention: if $A = (A.sk, A.pk)$ then $\text{sig}_A(m)$ denotes a signature on a message m computed with $A.sk$ and $\text{ver}_A(m, \sigma)$ denotes the result (true or false) of the verification of a signature σ on message m with respect to the public key $A.pk$. We will use the "Ƀ" symbol to denote the Bitcoin currency unit.

1.1 A Short Description of Bitcoin

Since we want the exposition to be self-contained, we start with a short description of Bitcoin, focusing only on the most relevant parts. For the lack of space we do not describe how the coins are created, how the transaction fees are charged, and how the Bitcoin "ledger" is maintained. A more detailed description of Bitcoin is available on the *Bitcoin wiki* site [11]. The reader may also consult the original Nakamoto's paper [22].

---

[1] The full version of this paper is available at http://arxiv.org/abs/1405.1861

Introduction. In general one of the main challenges when designing a digital currency is the potential double spending: if coins are just strings of bits then the owner of a coin can spend it multiple times. Clearly this risk could be avoided if the users have access to a trusted ledger with the list of all the transactions. In this case a transaction would be considered valid only if it is posted on the board. For example suppose the transactions are of a form: "user X transfers to user Y the money that he got in some previous transaction T_p", signed by the user X. In this case each user can verify if money from transaction T_p has not been already spent by X. The main difficulty in designing the fully-distributed peer-to-peer currency systems is to devise a system where the users jointly maintain the ledger in such a way that it cannot be manipulated by an adversary and it is publicly-accessible.

In Bitcoin this problem is solved by a cryptographic tool called *proofs-of-work* [14]. We will not go into the details of how this is done, since it is not relevant to this work. Let us only say that the system works securely as long as no adversary controls more computing power than the combined computing power of all the other participants of the protocol[2]. The Bitcoin participants that contribute their computing power to the system are called the *miners*. Bitcoin contains a system of incentives to become a miner. For the lack of space we do not describe it here.

Technically, the ledger is implemented as a chain of blocks, hence it is also called a "block chain". When a transaction is posted on the block chain, it can take some time before it appears on it, and even some more time before the user can be sure that this transaction will not be cancelled. However, it is safe to assume that there exists an upper bound on this waiting time (1-2 hours, say). We will denote this time by MAX_LATENCY.

As already highlighted in the introduction, the format of the Bitcoin transactions is in fact quite complex. Since it is of a special interest for us, we describe it now in more detail. The Bitcoin currency system consists of *addresses* and *transactions* between them. An address is simply a public key pk[3]. Normally every such key has a corresponding private key sk known only to one user, which is an *owner* of this address. The private key is used for signing the transactions, and the public key is used for verifying the signatures. Each user of the system needs to know at least one private key of some address, but this is simple to achieve, since the pairs (sk, pk) can be easily generated offline.

Simplified Version. We first describe a simplified version of the system and then show how to extend it to obtain the description of the real Bitcoin. Let $A = (A.sk, A.pk)$ be a key pair. In our simplified view a transaction describing the fact that an amount v (called the *value* of a transaction) is transferred from an address $A.pk$ to an address $B.pk$ has the following form $T_x = (y, B.pk, v, \text{sig}_A(y, B.pk, v))$, where y is an index of a previous transaction T_y. We say that $B.pk$ is the recipient of T_x, and that the transaction T_y

---

[2] It is currently estimated [24] that the combined computing power of the Bitcoin participants is around 64 exaFLOPS, which exceeds by factor over 200 the total computing power of world's top 500 supercomputers, hence the cost of purchasing the equipment that would be needed to break this system is huge.

[3] Technically an address is a *cryptographic hash* of pk. In our informal description we decided to assume that it is simply pk. This is done only to keep the exposition as simple as possible, as it improves the readability of the transaction scripts later in the paper.

is an *input* of the transaction T_x, or that it is *redeemed* by this transaction (or redeemed by the address $B.pk$). More precisely, the meaning of T_x is that the amount v of money transferred to $A.pk$ in transaction T_y is transferred further to $B.pk$. The transaction is valid only if (1) $A.pk$ was a recipient of the transaction T_y, (2) the value of T_y was at least v (the difference between the value of T_y and v is called the *transaction fee*), (3) the transaction T_y has not been redeemed earlier, and (4) the signature of A is correct. Clearly all of these conditions can be verified publicly.

The first important generalization of this simplified system is that a transaction can have several "inputs" meaning that it can accumulate money from several past transactions $T_{y_1}, \ldots, T_{y_\ell}$. Let $A_1, \ldots, A_\ell$ be the respective key pairs of the recipients of those transactions. Then a multiple-input transaction has the following form: $T_x = (y_1, \ldots, y_\ell, B.pk, v, \mathrm{sig}_{A_1}(y_1, B.pk, v), \ldots, \mathrm{sig}_{A_\ell}(y_\ell, B.pk, v))$, and the result of it is that $B.pk$ gets the amount v, provided it is at most equal to the sum of the values of transactions $T_{y_1}, \ldots, T_{y_\ell}$. This happens only if *none* of these transactions has been redeemed before, and *all* the signatures are valid.

Moreover, each transaction can have a *time lock t* that tells at what time in the future the transaction becomes valid. The lock-time t can refer either to a measure called the "block index" or to the real physical time. In this paper we only consider the latter type of time-locks. In this case we have $T_x = (y_1, \ldots, y_\ell, B.pk, v, t, \mathrm{sig}_{A_1}(y_1, B.pk, v, t), \ldots, \mathrm{sig}_{A_\ell}(y_\ell, B.pk, v, t))$. Such a transaction becomes valid only if time t is reached and if none of the transactions $T_{y_1}, \ldots, T_{y_\ell}$ has been redeemed by that time (otherwise it is discarded). Each transaction can also have several outputs, which is a way to divide money between several users and to divide transactions with large value into smaller portions. We ignore this fact in our description since we will not use it in our protocols.

More Detailed Version. The real Bitcoin system is significantly more sophisticated than what is described above. First of all, there are some syntactic differences, the most important being that each transaction T_x is identified not by its index, but by its hash $H(T_x)$. Hence, from now on we will assume that $x = H(T_x)$.

The main difference is, however, that in the real Bitcoin the users have much more flexibility in defining the condition on how the transaction T_x can be redeemed. Consider for a moment the simplest transactions where there is just one input and no time-locks. Recall that in the simplified system described above, in order to redeem a transaction, its recipient $A.pk$ had to produce another transaction T_x signed with his private key $A.sk$. In the real Bitcoin this is generalized as follows: each transaction T_y comes with a description of a function (*output-script*) π_y whose output is Boolean. The transaction T_x redeeming the transaction T_y is valid if π_y evaluates to true on input T_x. Of course, one example of π_y is a function that treats T_x as a pair (a message m_x, a signature σ_x), and checks if σ_x is a valid signature on m_x with respect to the public key $A.pk$. However, much more general functions π_y are possible. Going further into details, a transaction looks as follows: $T_x = (y, \pi_x, v, \sigma_x)$, where $[T_x] = (y, \pi_x, v)$ is called the *body*[4] of T_x and σ_x is a "witness" that is used to make the script π_y evaluate to

---

[4] In the original Bitcoin documentation this is called "simplified T_x". Following our earlier work [8,6,7] we chosen to rename it to "body" since we find the original terminology slightly misleading.

true on T_x (in the simplest case σ_x is a signature on $[T_x]$). The scripts are written in the Bitcoin scripting language [27], which is stack-based and similar to the Forth programming language. It is on purpose not Turing-complete (there are no loops in it), since the scripts need to evaluate in (short) finite time. It provides basic arithmetical operations on numbers, operations on stack, if-then-else statements and some cryptographic functions like calculating hash function or verifying a signature.

The generalization to the multiple-input transactions with time-locks is straightforward: a transaction has a form: $T_x = (y_1, \ldots, y_\ell, \pi_x, v, t, \sigma_1, \ldots, \sigma_\ell)$, where the body $[T_x]$ is equal to $(y_1, \ldots, y_\ell, \pi_x, v, t)$, and it is valid if (1) time t is reached, (2) *every* $\pi_i([T_x], \sigma_i)$ evaluates to true, where each π_i is the output script of the transaction T_{y_i}, and (3) none of these transac-

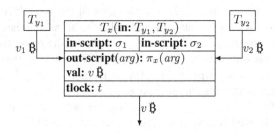

Fig. 1. A graphical representation of a transaction $T_x = (y_1, y_2, \pi_x, v, t, \sigma_1, \sigma_2)$

tions has been redeemed before. We will present the transactions as boxes. The redeeming of transactions will be indicated with arrows (the arrows will be labelled with the transaction values). An example of a graphical representation of a transaction is depicted in Fig. 1.

The transactions where the input script is a signature, and the output script is a verification algorithm are the most common type of transactions. We will call them *standard transactions*. Currently some miners accept only such transactions, due to the fact that writing more advanced scripts is hard and error-prone, and anyway the vast majority of users does not use such advanced features of Bitcoin. Fortunately, there exist other miners that do accept the non-standard (also called *strange*) transactions, one example being a big mining pool[5] called *Eligius* (that mines a new block on average once per hour). We also believe that in the future accepting the general transaction will become standard, maybe at a cost of a slightly increased fee. Actually, popularizing the Bitcoin contracts, by making them safer to use, is one of the goals of this work.

2 Modeling the Bitcoin

To reason formally about the security of the contracts we need to describe the attack model that corresponds to the Bitcoin system. The model used in [8,6] was inspired by the approach used in the complexity-based cryptography. This way of modeling protocols, although very powerful, is not well-suited for the automatic verification of cryptographic protocols. In this section we present the approach used in this paper, based on timed-automata, using the syntax of the UPPAAL model checker.

In our model each party executing the protocol is modeled as a timed automaton with a structure assigned to it that describes the party's knowledge. States in the automaton

---

[5] Mining pools are coalitions of miners that perform their work jointly and share the profits.

describe which part of the protocol the party is performing. The transitions in the automaton contain conditions, which have to be satisfied for a transition to be taken and actions, which are performed whenever a transition is taken.

The communication between the parties may be modeled in a number of various ways. It is possible to use synchronization on channels offered by UPPAAL and shared variables representing data being sent between the parties. In all protocols verified by us, the only messages exchanged by the parties were signatures. We decided to model the communication indirectly using shared variables — each party keeps the set of known signatures, and whenever a sender wants to send a signature, he simply adds it to the recipient's set.

The central decision that needs to be made is how to model the knowledge of the honest parties and the adversary. Our representation of knowledge is symbolic and based on Dolev-Yao model [13], and hence we assume that the cryptographic primitives are perfectly secure. In our case it means, for example, that it is not possible to forge a signature without the knowledge of the corresponding private key, and this knowledge can be modeled in a "binary" way: either an adversary knows the key, or not. The hash functions will be modeled as random oracles, which in particular implies that they are collision-resilient and hard to invert. We also assume that there exists a secure and authenticated channel between the parties, which can be easily achieved using the public key cryptography. Moreover, we assume that there is a fixed set of variables denoting the private/public pairs of Bitcoin keys. A Bitcoin protocol can also involve secret strings known only to some parties. We assume that there is a fixed set of variables denoting such strings. For each private key and each secret string there is a subset of parties, which know them, but all public keys and hashes of all secret strings are known to all the parties (if this is not the case then they can be broadcast by parties knowing them).

A block chain is modelled using a shared variable (denoted bc) keeping the status of all transactions and a special automaton, which is responsible for maintaining the state of bc (e.g. confirming transactions).

In the following sections we describe our model in more details.

2.1 The Keys, the Secret Strings, and the Signatures

We assume that the number of the key pairs in the protocol is known in advance and constant. Therefore, key pairs will be simply referred by consecutive natural numbers (type **Key** is defined as an integer from a given range). Secret strings are modelled in the same way. As already mentioned we assume that all public keys and hashes of all secrets are known to all parties.

```
typedef struct {
    Key key;
    TxId tx_num;
    Nonce input_nonce;
} Signature;
```

Fig. 2. The signatures type

Moreover, we need to model the signatures over transactions (one reason is that they are exchanged by the parties in some protocols). They are modelled by structures containing a transaction being signed, the key used to compute a signature and an input_nonce, which is related to the issue of transaction malleability and described in Appendix *Malleability of transactions* in the full version of this paper.

2.2   The Transactions

We assume that all transactions that can be created by the honest parties during the execution of the protocol comes from a set, which is known in advance and of size T. Additionally, the adversary can create his own transactions. As explained later (see Sec. 2.4 below) we can upper-bound the number of adversarial transactions by T. Hence the total upper bound on the number of transactions is $2T$.

For simplicity we refer to the transactions using fixed identifiers instead of their hashes. We can do this because we know all the transactions, which can be broadcast in advance (compare Sec.2.4 for further discussion). A single-input and single-output transaction is a variable of a record type **Tx** defined in Fig. 3. The num field is the identifier of the transaction, and the input field is the identifier of its input transaction. The value field denotes the value of the transaction (in ฿). The timelock field indicates the time lock of the transaction, and the timelock_passed is a boolean field indicating whether the timelock has passed.

```
typedef struct {
        TxId num;
        TxId input;
        int value;
        int timelock;
        bool timelock_passed;
     Status status;
      Nonce nonce;
        bool reveals_secret;
      Secret secret_revealed;
OutputScript out_script;
} Tx;
```

Fig. 3. The transactions type

The status field is of a type **Status** that contains following values: UNSENT (indicating that transaction has not yet been sent to the block chain), SENT (the transaction has been sent to the block chain and is waiting to be confirmed), CONFIRMED (the transaction is confirmed on the block chain, but not spent), SPENT (the transaction is confirmed and spent), and CANCELLED (the transaction was sent to the block chain, but while it was waiting for being included in the block chain its input was redeemed by another transaction).

The out_script denotes the output script. In case the transaction is standard it simply contains a public key of the recipient of the transaction. Otherwise, it refers to a hard-coded function which implements the output script of this transaction (see Sec. 2.5 for more details).

The inputs scripts are modelled only indirectly (the fields reveals_secret and secret_revealed). More precisely, we only keep information about which secrets are included in the input script.

The above structure can be easily extended to handle multiple inputs and outputs.

2.3   The Parties

The parties are modelled by timed automata describing protocols they follow. States in the automata describe which part of the protocol the party is performing. The transitions in the automata contain conditions, which have to be satisfied for a transition to be taken and actions, which are performed whenever a transition is taken. An example of such automaton appears in Fig. 7. and is described in more details in Appendix UPPAAL *syntax* in the full version of the paper. The adversary is modelled by a special automaton described in Sec. 2.4.

Moreover, we need to model the knowledge of the parties (both the honest users and the adversary) in order to be able to decide whether they can perform a specific action in a particular situation (e.g. compute the input script for a given transaction). Therefore for each party, we define a structure describing its knowledge. More technically: this knowledge is modelled by a record type **Party** defined in Fig. 4.

```
typedef struct {
                bool know_key[KEYS_NUM];
                bool know_secret[SECRETS_NUM];
        int[0,KNOWN_
SIGNATURES_SIZE] known_signatures_size;
            Signature known_signatures
                    [KNOWN_SIGNATURES_SIZE];
} Party;
```

Fig. 4. The parties type

The boolean tables know_key[KEYS_NUM] and know_secret[SECRETS_NUM] describe the sets of keys and secrets (respectively) known to the party: know_key[i] = true if and only if the party knows the i-th secret key, and know_secret[i] = true if and only if the party knows the i-th secret string. The integer known_signatures_size describes the number of the additional signatures known to the party (i.e. received from other parties during the protocol), and the array known_signatures contains these signatures.

2.4 The Adversary

The real-life Bitcoin adversary can create an arbitrary number of transactions with arbitrary output scripts, so it is clear that we need to somehow limit his possibilities, so that the space of possible states is finite and of a reasonable size. We show that without loss of generality we can consider only scenarios in which an adversary sends to the block chain transactions only from a finite set depending only on the protocol.

The knowledge of an adversary is modeled in the similar way to honest parties, but we do not specify the protocol that he follows. Instead, we use a generic automaton, which (almost) does not depend on the protocol being verified and allows to send to the block chain any transaction at any time assuming some conditions are met, e.g. that the transaction is valid and that the adversary is able to create its input script.

We observe that the transactions made by the adversary can influence the execution of the protocol only in two ways: either (1) the transaction is identical to the transaction from the protocol being verified or (2) the transaction redeems one of the transactions from the protocol. The reason for above is that honest parties only look for transactions of the specific form (as in the protocol being executed), so the only thing an adversary can do to influence this process is to create a transaction, which looks like one of these transactions or redeem one of these. Notice that we do not have to consider transactions with multiple inputs redeeming more than one of the protocol's transactions, because there is always an interleaving in which the adversary achieves the same result using a number of transactions with single inputs. The output scripts in the transactions of type (2) do not matter, so we may assume that an adversary always sends them to one particular key known only to him.

Therefore, without loss of generality we consider only the transactions, which appear in the protocol being verified or transactions redeeming one of these transactions. Hence, the total number of transactions, which are modeled in our system is twice as big as the number of transactions in the original protocol.

The adversary is then a party, that can send an arbitrary transaction from this set if only he is able to do so (e.g. he is able to evaluate the input script and the transaction's input is confirmed, but not spent). If the only actions of the honest parties is to post transactions on the block chain, then one can assume that this is also the only thing that the adversary does. In this case his automaton, denoted `Adversary` is very simple: it contains one state and one loop, that simply tries to send an arbitrary transaction from the mentioned set. This is depicted in Fig. 5 (for a moment ignore the left loop).

Fig. 5. The automaton for the Adversary

In some protocols the parties besides of posting the transactions on the block chain, also exchange messages with each other. This can be exploited by the adversary, and hence we need to take care of this in our model. This is done by adding more actions in the `Adversary` automaton. In our framework, this is done manually. For example in the protocol that we analyze in Sec. 3 Alice sends a signature on the *Fuse* transaction. This is reflected by the left loop in the `Adversary` automaton in Fig. 5, which should be read as follows: if the adversary is able to create a signature on the *Fuse* transaction and Bob did not receive it yet, then he can send it to Bob.

Of course, our protocols need to be analyzed always "from the point of view of an honest Alice" (assuming Bob is controlled by the adversary) and "from the point of view of an honest Bob" (assuming Alice is controlled by the adversary). Therefore, for each party we choose whether to use the automaton describing the protocol executed by the parties or the already mentioned special automaton for an adversary.

2.5   The Block Chain and the Notion of Time

In Bitcoin whenever a party wants to post a transaction on the block chain she broadcasts it over a peer-to-peer network. In our model this is captured as follows. We model the block chain as a shared structure denoted bc containing the information about the status of all the transactions and a timed automaton denoted `BlockChainAgent` (see Fig. 6), which is responsible for maintaining the state of bc. One of the duties of `BlockChainAgent` is ensuring that the transactions which were broadcast are confirmed within appropriate time frames.

In order to post a transaction t on the block chain, a party p first runs the `try_to_ send( Party p, Tx t)` function, which broadcasts the transaction if it is legal. In particular, the `can_send` function checks if (a) the transaction has not been already sent, (b) all its inputs are confirmed and unredeemed and (c) a given party p can create the corresponding input script. The only non-trivial part is (c) in case of non-standard transactions, as this check is protocol-dependent. Therefore, the exact condition on when the party p can create the appropriate input script, has to be extracted manually from the description of the protocol. If all these tests succeed, then the function communicates the fact of broadcasting the transaction using the shared structure bc.

Fig. 6. The BlockChainAgent automaton

Once a transaction t has been broadcast, the BlockChainAgent automaton attempts to include it in the block chain (lower loop in Fig. 6). The BlockChainAgent automaton also enforces that every transaction gets included into the block chain in less than MAX_LATENCY time, which is a constant that is defined in the system. This is done by the invariant on the right state in Fig. 6 that guarantees that every transaction is waiting for confirmation less than MAX_LATENCY.

Eavesdropping on the Network. The other issue with the block chain is that the peers in the network can see transactions before they are confirmed. Therefore if a transaction t contains (e.g. in its input script) a secret string x then an adversary can learn the value of x before t is confirmed and for example use it to create a different transaction redeeming the input of t (a similar scenario is possible for a two-party lottery protocol from [8], which is only secure in a "private channel model"). To take such possibilities into account, broadcasting a transaction results in disclosure of the secret string x, what in our model corresponds to setting appropriate knowledge flags for all parties.

Malleability of Transactions. BlockChainAgent automaton is also responsible for choosing the nonces, which imitate the attacks involving the malleability of transactions. This is described in details in Appendix *Malleability of transactions* in the full version of the paper.

3   Modeling the Bitcoin-Based Timed Commitment Scheme from [8]

In this section we describe the "contract-dependent" part of our model. Our method of modeling and verifying Bitcoin contracts as timed automata is generic and can be applied to a large class of Bitcoin contracts (and even possibly automatized as described in the paragraph "Future work" on page 9). However, it is easier to describe it using a concrete example. As a proof-of-concept we constructed the automata corresponding to a very simple contract called the "Bitcoin-based timed commitment scheme" from [8]. For the lack of space we only sketch informally what the protocol is supposed to do. In the protocol one of the parties (called Alice) commits herself to a secret string s. A key difference between this protocol and classic commitment schemes is that Alice is forced to open the commitment (i.e. reveal the string s) until some agreed moment of time (denoted PROT_TIMELOCK) or pay 1 Ƀ to Bob. The full description can be found in Appendix *Bitcoin-based timed commitment scheme* in the full version of the paper. Although the verification of correctness is quite straightforward in this case, we would like to stress that our method is applicable to more complicated contracts, like the NewSCS protocol from [8] (see Section 3.2), for which the correctness is much less obvious.

3.1   The Results of the Verification

Before running the verification procedure in UPPAAL it is necessary to choose, which parties are honest and which are malicious.

In UPPAAL it is done by selecting an automaton following the protocol or the malicious automaton for an adversary described in Sec. 2.4 for each of the parties. We started with verification of the security from the point of view of honest Bob. To this end we used an honest automaton for Bob (see Fig. 7) and an adversary automaton described before for Alice (see Fig. 5).

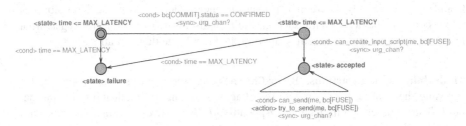

Fig. 7. The automaton for an honest Bob in timed-commitment scheme

The property that we checked is the following:

```
A[] (time >= PROT_TIMELOCK+MAX_LATENCY) imply
        (hold_bitcoins(parties[BOB]) == 1 or parties[BOB].know_secret[0]
                                or BobTA.failure),
```

which, informally means: "after time PROT_TIMELOCK + MAX_LATENCY one of the following cases takes place: either (a) Bob earned 1 ฿, or (b) Bob knows the committed
secret, or (c) Bob rejected the commitment in the commitment phase". This is exactly
the security property claimed in [8], and hence the verification confirmed our belief that
the protocol is secure. We verified the security from the point of view of Alice in the
similar way.

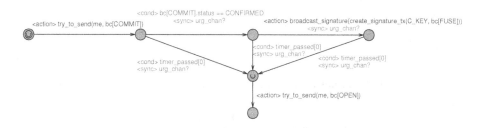

Fig. 8. The automaton for an honest Alice in timed-commitment scheme

The property we verified means that Alice does not lose any bitcoins in the execution
of the protocol (even if Bob is malicious).

As a test we also run the verification procedure on the following two statements:

```
A[] (time >= PROT_TIMELOCK) imply (parties[BOB].know_secret[0])
A[] (time >= PROT_TIMELOCK) imply (hold_bitcoins(parties[ALICE]) == 1).
```

The first one states that after time PROT_TIMELOCK Bob knows the secret (which can be
not true, if Alice refused to send it). The second one states that after time PROT_TIME-
LOCK Alice holds 1 ฿ (which occurs only if Alice is honest, but not in general). The
UPPAAL model checker confirmed that these properties are violated if one of the parties is malicious, but hold if both parties follow the protocol (i.e. when honest automata
are used for both parties). Moreover, UPPAAL provides diagnostic traces, which are
interleavings of events leading to the violation of the property being tested. They allow to immediately figure out, why the given property is violated and turned out to be
extremely helpful in debugging the automata.

3.2   The NewSCS Protocol from [8]

We also modeled and verified the Simultaneous Commitment Scheme (NewSCS) protocol from [8], which is relatively complicated as it contains 18 transactions. To understand it fully the reader should probably look in the [8], but as reference we included
the description of these contracts in Appendix *Simultaneous commitment scheme* in the

full version of the paper. Informally speaking, the NewSCS scheme is a protocol that allows two parties, Alice and Bob, to simultaneously commit to their secrets (s_A and s_B, respectively) in such a way that each commitment is valid only if the other commitment was done correctly. Using UPPAAL we automatically verified the following three conditions, which are exactly the security statements claimed in [6]:

- After the execution of the protocol by two honest parties, they both know both secrets and hold the same amount of coins as at the beginning of the protocol, which in UPPAAL syntax was formalized as:

```
A[] (time >=  PROT_TIMELOCK+MAX_LATENCY) imply
    (parties[ALICE].know_secret[SB_SEC] and parties[BOB].know_secret[SA_SEC]
      and hold_bitcoins(parties[ALICE]) == 2
      and hold_bitcoins(parties[BOB]) == 2)
```

(here SA_SEC and SB_SEC denote the secrets of Alice and Bob, respectively, and 2 is the value of the deposit).
- An honest Bob cannot lose any coins as a result of the protocol, no matter how the dishonest Alice behaves:

```
2) A[] (time >= PROT_TIMELOCK) imply hold_bitcoins(parties[BOB]) >= 2
```

- If an honest Bob did not learn Alice's secret then he gained Alice's deposit as a result of the execution.

```
3) A[] ((time >= PROT_TIMELOCK+2*MAX_LATENCY) imply
        ((parties[ALICE].know_secret[SB_SEC]
            and !parties[BOB].know_secret[SA_SEC])
        imply hold_bitcoins(parties[BOB]) >= 3))
```

The analogous guarantees hold for Alice, when Bob is malicious. The verification of each of the mentioned properties took less than a minute on a dual-core 2.4 GHz notebook. We confirmed that the protocol NewSCS is correct, but there are some implementation details, which are easy to miss and our first implementation (as an automaton) turned out to contain a bug, which was immediately found due to the verification process and diagnostic traces provided by UPPAAL. Moreover UPPAAL turned out to be very helpful in determining the exact time threshold for the time locks, for example we confirmed that the time at which the parties should abort the protocol claimed in [7] ($t - 3MAX\_LATENCY$) is strict.

These experiments confirmed that the computer aided verification and in particular UPPAAL provides a very good tool for verifying Bitcoin contracts, especially since it is rather difficult to assess the correctness of Bitcoin contracts by hand, due to the distributed nature of the block chain and a huge number of possible interleavings. Therefore, we hope that our paper would encourage designers of complex Bitcoin contracts to make use of computer aided verification for checking the correctness of their constructions.

References

1. Alur, R., Dill, D.L.: Automata for modeling real-time systems. In: Paterson, M. (ed.) ICALP 1990. LNCS, vol. 443, pp. 322–335. Springer, Heidelberg (1990)
2. Alur, R., Dill, D.L.: A theory of timed automata. Theoretical Computer Science (1994)
3. Alur, R., Henzinger, T.A.: A really temporal logic. Journal of the ACM (1994)

4. Amnell, T., Fersman, E., Mokrushin, L., Pettersson, P., Yi, W.: TIMES - A tool for modelling and implementation of embedded systems. In: Katoen, J.-P., Stevens, P. (eds.) TACAS 2002. LNCS, vol. 2280, p. 460. Springer, Heidelberg (2002)

5. Andreessen, M.: Why Bitcoin Matters. The New York Times (January 2013), http://dealbook.nytimes.com/2014/01/21/why-bitcoin-matters/ (accessed on January 26, 2014)

6. Andrychowicz, M., Dziembowski, S., Malinowski, D., Mazurek, Ł.: Fair two-party computations via the bitcoin deposits. Cryptology ePrint Archive, Report 2013/837 (2013), http://eprint.iacr.org/2013/837, accepted to the 1st Workshop on Bitcoin Research

7. Andrychowicz, M., Dziembowski, S., Malinowski, D., Mazurek, Ł.: How to deal with malleability of Bitcoin transactions. ArXiv e-prints (December 2013)

8. Andrychowicz, M., Dziembowski, S., Malinowski, D., Mazurek, Ł.: Secure Multiparty Computations on Bitcoin. Cryptology ePrint Archive (2013), http://eprint.iacr.org/2013/784, accepted to the 35th IEEE Symposium on Security and Privacy, Oakland (2014)

9. Behrmann, G., David, A., Larsen, K.G.: A tutorial on uppaal 4.0 (2006)

10. Berthomieu, B., Diaz, M.: Modeling and verification of time dependent systems using time Petri nets. IEEE Trans. Softw. Eng. 17(3), 259–273 (1991)

11. Bitcoin. Wiki, http://en.bitcoin.it/wiki/

12. Delfs, H., Knebl, H.: Introduction to Cryptography: Principles and Applications. Information Security and Cryptography. Springer (2007)

13. Dolev, D., Yao, A.C.: On the security of public key protocols. IEEE Transactions on Theory (1983)

14. Dwork, C., Naor, M.: Pricing via processing or combatting junk mail. In: Brickell, E.F. (ed.) CRYPTO 1992. LNCS, vol. 740, pp. 139–147. Springer, Heidelberg (1993)

15. The Economist. The Economist explains: How does Bitcoin work? (April 2013), http://www.economist.com/blogs/economist-explains/2013/04/economist-explains-how-does-bitcoin-work (accessed on January 26, 2014)

16. Ateniese, G., et al.: Certified bitcoins. Cryptology ePrint Archive, Report 2014/076

17. Bengtsson, J., Larsen, K., Larsson, F., Pettersson, P., Yi, W.: UPPAAL - a tool suite for automatic verification of real-time systems. In: Alur, R., Sontag, E.D., Henzinger, T.A. (eds.) HS 1995. LNCS, vol. 1066, pp. 232–243. Springer, Heidelberg (1996)

18. Barber, S., Boyen, X., Shi, E., Uzun, E.: Bitter to better — how to make bitcoin a better currency. In: Keromytis, A.D. (ed.) FC 2012. LNCS, vol. 7397, pp. 399–414. Springer, Heidelberg (2012)

19. Katz, J., Lindell, Y.: Introduction to Modern Cryptography. Chapman & Hall/Crc Cryptography and Network Security Series. Chapman & Hall/CRC (2007)

20. Lee, T.B.: Here's how Bitcoin charmed Washington, http://www.washingtonpost.com/blogs/the-switch/wp/2013/11/21/heres-how-bitcoin-charmed-washington (accessed on January 26, 2014)

21. Morris, D.Z.: Bitcoin is not just digital currency. It's Napster for finance. CNN Money (January 2014), http://finance.fortune.cnn.com/2014/01/21/bitcoin-platform (accessed on January 26, 2014)

22. Nakamoto, S.: Bitcoin: A peer-to-peer electronic cash system (2008)

23. Nicollin, X., Sifakis, J.: The algebra of timed processes, atp: Theory and application. Inf. Comput. 114(1), 131–178 (1994)

24. Cohen, R.: Global Bitcoin Computing Power Now 256 Times Faster Than Top 500 Supercomputers, Combined! Forbes, http://www.forbes.com/sites/reuvencohen/2013/11/28/global-bitcoin-computing-power-now-256-times-faster-than-top-500-supercomputers-combined/

25. Reed, G.M., Roscoe, A.W.: A timed model for communicating sequential processes. Theor. Comput. Sci. 58(1-3), 249–261 (1988)
26. Bitcoin wiki. Contracts, http://en.bitcoin.it/wiki/Contracts (accessed on January 26, 2014)
27. Bitcoin wiki. Script, https://en.bitcoin.it/wiki/Script (accessed on January 26, 2014)
28. Yi, W.: CCS + time = an interleaving model for real time systems. In: Leach Albert, J., Monien, B., Rodríguez-Artalejo, M. (eds.) ICALP 1991. LNCS, vol. 510, pp. 217–228. Springer, Heidelberg (1991)
29. Yovine, S.: Kronos: a verification tool for real-time systems. Journal on Software Tools for Technology Transfer 1 (October 1997)

Data-Driven Statistical Learning
of Temporal Logic Properties*

Ezio Bartocci[1], Luca Bortolussi[2,3], and Guido Sanguinetti[4,5]

[1] Faculty of Informatics, Vienna University of Technology, Austria
[2] DMG, University of Trieste, Italy
[3] CNR/ISTI, Pisa, Italy
[4] School of Informatics, University of Edinburgh, UK
[5] SynthSys, Centre for Synthetic and Systems Biology, University of Edinburgh, UK

Abstract. We present a novel approach to learn logical formulae characterising the emergent behaviour of a dynamical system from system observations. At a high level, the approach starts by devising a data-driven statistical abstraction of the system. We then propose general optimisation strategies for selecting formulae with high satisfaction probability, either within a discrete set of formulae of bounded complexity, or a parametric family of formulae. We illustrate and apply the methodology on two real world case studies: characterising the dynamics of a biological circadian oscillator, and discriminating different types of cardiac malfunction from electro-cardiogram data. Our results demonstrate that this approach provides a statistically principled and generally usable tool to logically characterise dynamical systems in terms of temporal logic formulae.

1 Introduction

Dynamical systems are among the most widely used modelling frameworks, with important applications in all domains of science and engineering. Much of the attraction of dynamical systems modelling lies in the availability of effective simulation tools, enabling predictive modelling, and in the possibility of encoding complex behaviours through the interaction of multiple, simple components. This leads naturally to the notion of *emergent properties*, i.e. properties of the system trajectories which are a nontrivial consequence of the local interaction rules of the system components. Emergent properties of deterministic dynamical systems can often be easily verified through simulations. Quantitatively identifying the emergent properties of a stochastic system, instead, is a much harder problem.

In the simplest scenario, one assumes that a mathematical model of the system of interest is already available (e.g. as a continuous time Markov chain, or a stochastic differential equation), generally thanks to the availability of domain expertise. This problem is often termed *mining requirements*: this is an active field of research, with many recent contributions extending its scalability and applicability [18,27]. This approach

---

* L.B. acknowledges partial support from the EU-FET project QUANTICOL (nr. 600708) and by FRA-UniTS. G.S. acknowledges support from the ERC under grant MLCS306999. E.B. acknowledges the support of the Austrian FFG project HARMONIA (nr. 845631).

A. Legay and M. Bozga (Eds.): FORMATS 2014, LNCS 8711, pp. 23–37, 2014.

is predicated on two premises: first, a trustworthy model of the system must be available, and, secondly, efficient model checking algorithms must be available for the class of properties/models under consideration. These two conditions are often onerous in many scientific applications, where models can be both complex and highly uncertain. However, data generation is becoming increasingly cheap for many complex systems, raising the possibility that emergent properties may be formally identified from data.

This problem, although clearly of considerable practical relevance, has received comparatively little attention in the literature. Early work by [10] proposed a greedy algorithm to identify formulae with high support directly from data, with the ultimate aim of unravelling the logical structure underpinning observed dynamics in systems biology. More recently, Asarin et al. in [4] proposed a geometric construction to identify the formula (within a specified parametric family) which fitted observations best. In both cases, the methods work directly with the raw data, and are hence potentially vulnerable to noise in the data. Furthermore, both sets of authors remark that the identifiability of formulae is severely limited by the quantity of data available, which hampers the applicability of the methods in many practical circumstances.

Here, we aim to address both identifiability and robustness problems by taking an alternative, statistical approach, which brings back a model-based perspective to the data-driven approach. We consider a variation of the property learning problem, where we observe trajectories from two distinct processes and the aim is to identify properties that best discriminate between two observed processes, i.e. are satisfied with high probability by trajectories from one process and with low probability by trajectories from the second. At the core of our method is a *statistical abstraction*, a flexible, data driven statistical model which provides a compact representation of the dynamics of the system. The choice of the statistical model is performed using statistical model selection techniques, combining domain expertise with data driven methods; in this paper, we will illustrate our approach on two contrasting applications: a systems biology application where considerable prior knowledge permits the use of a rather restricted and complex family of candidate models, and a biomedical application where such knowledge is unavailable, and hence we use a more black box model. Once a suitable model is selected, the satisfaction probability of a formula can be evaluated quantitatively (using a model checking tool), enabling rational selection of formulae with high support or that best discriminate two models obtained from two datasets. This *property learning* problem can be further broken down into two subproblems: learning the structure of the formula, and learning parameters involved in the formula. These optimisation problems can be tackled in many ways: here, we use a local search algorithm for structure learning, and a recently proposed, provably convergent algorithm [25] for learning the parameters of the formula. Figure 1 illustrates schematically the modular structure of our approach.

The rest of the paper is organised as it follows: in the next section we give an overview of the proposed approach, reviewing the relevant statistical and logical concepts. We then present results on the two case studies, briefly describing the procedure through which the statistical model was devised in each case, and illustrating the capabilities of the approach to infer non-trivial properties from the data. We conclude the paper by discussing the implications of our contribution, both from the practical and the methodological aspect.

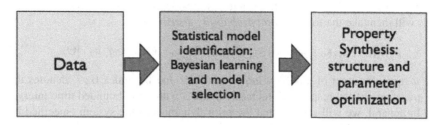

Fig. 1. Schematic workflow of our approach: starting from data, a suitable statistical model is chosen (within a family of models) via Bayesian learning methods. That enables us to evaluate the probability of formulae in a suitable logic, which can then be maximised as a function of the formula structure or formula parameters

2 Problem Statement and Methodology

The property synthesis problem can have many flavours. One can be interested in finding the properties that best characterise a single set of observations, or find properties that discriminate between a good and a bad set of observed scenarios. The examples discussed in this paper fall into this second class, but a similar machinery can be used for finding properties with high support. The discrimination problem is the following:

Given two sets of signals/time traces (the good and the bad set), find a temporal logic formula that best discriminates between them, i.e. such that it is satisfied with high probability by the good set and with low probability by the bad one.

Essentially, this problem can be seen as a temporal logic version of a classification problem, in which we look for temporal patterns separating two sets of observed signals.

At a high level, our approach is made up of two distinct modules: a model selection step, where a suitable statistical model is learnt from the data, and a property synthesis step, where we perform learning of formulae with high discriminating power. The advantage of the statistical generalisation performed in the first phase, which distinguishes our approach from other related work (see also Section 4) is that it offers a statistically sound treatment of noise and the ability of generating simulated data, avoiding the data shortage problem in the second phase.

In this section we describe the methods we use for performing these steps in this paper, as well as providing some background on the specific logic we will use to encode emergent properties. We emphasize however that, while we believe the choices we made in performing the two steps are state-of-the-art, the concept of our approach is entirely modular, so that any other model selection/optimisation method could be employed towards the same goal.

2.1 Statistical Modelling of Data: Learning and Model Selection

Our statistical methodologies will be embedded within the *probabilistic machine learning* framework [8]. Let $\mathbf{x}$ denote the state variables associated with our system, and let

$\hat{\mathbf{x}}_1, \ldots, \hat{\mathbf{x}}_N$ denote observations of the system at times $0 \leq t_1, \ldots, t_N \leq T$. Our statistical models will then take the form of *joint probability distributions*

$$p\left(\hat{\mathbf{x}}_1, \ldots, \hat{\mathbf{x}}_N, \mathbf{x}_{0:T}, \mu_{0:T} | \Theta\right) = p\left(\hat{\mathbf{x}}_1, \ldots, \hat{\mathbf{x}}_N | \mathbf{x}_{0:T}, \Theta\right) p\left(\mathbf{x}_{0:T}, \mu_{0:T} | \Theta\right)$$

where μ represent a set of auxiliary *latent variables* and the index $0 : T$ denotes the *whole trajectory* of the respective stochastic process within the bounded time interval $[0, T]$. In general, we will assume that the prior dynamics of the system (specified by $p\left(\mathbf{x}_{0:T}, \mu_{0:T} | \Theta\right)$) are Markovian, and that the observation noise is independent and identically distributed at different time points. Additionally, the models are parametrised by a family of parameters Θ which may enter both the noise model (probability of the observations given the true state of the system $\mathbf{x}$) and the prior dynamics $p\left(\mathbf{x}_{0:T}, \mu_{0:T} | \Theta\right)$. The introduction of the latent variables can be justified in several ways: in some cases, the latent variables represent physically relevant unobserved quantities (e.g., promoter occupancy state as in Section 3.1); otherwise, they may be a convenient device to represent a more rich dynamics in a compact way (as in the heart modelling example in Section 3.2). We stress that Hidden Markov Models, Continuous-Time Markov Chains, (Stochastic) Differential Equations and Hybrid Systems all fall into the class of models considered here.

The general principle for learning in probabilistic models is based on the concept of *evidence maximisation*, whereby one seeks to determine the value of parameters Θ that maximises the evidence or marginal likelihood

$$p\left(\hat{\mathbf{x}}_1, \ldots, \hat{\mathbf{x}}_N | \Theta\right) = \int d\mu_{0:T} d\mathbf{x}_{0:T} \, p\left(\hat{\mathbf{x}}_1, \ldots, \hat{\mathbf{x}}_N, \mathbf{x}_{0:T}, \mu_{0:T} | \Theta\right)$$

where the integral sign is used generically to denote marginalisation (it is replaced by a sum in the case of discrete variables). In general, the marginalisation procedure is computationally problematic, and much research in machine learning is devoted to find efficient marginalisation algorithms for specific classes of models.

The evidence at the optimal value of the parameters provides a measure of the goodness of fit of a model to a data set. However, models with different numbers of parameters will not necessarily be comparable in terms of evidence: richer models with more parameters tend to have higher evidence. One therefore needs to penalise the complexity of the model. There exist several information criteria which combine the maximum value of the likelihood with a penalty on the number of parameters. Here we use the *Akaike Information Criterion (AIC)* [1], which penalises the likelihood by subtracting a term containing the logarithm of the number of parameters. Explicitly, the AIC score is defined as

$$AIC = 2k - 2\log L$$

where k is the number of parameters of the model, and L is the optimised value of the marginal likelihood. This simple score can be shown to approach asymptotically, in the large sample limit, the information lost by using the model as a proxy for the (unknown) data generating process. Therefore minimisation of the AIC score across a finite number of models is often used as a criterion for model selection.

2.2   Learning Properties

The second module of our approach consists of algorithms for optimising the probability of a formula being true within a discrete set of parametric formulae. This difficult hybrid optimisation problem is naturally broken down in a discrete and a continuous optimisation problem, which can be interleaved. Before describing the algorithms we use, we briefly review the logic we consider, the Metric Interval Temporal Logic (MITL).

Metric Interval Temporal Logic. Temporal logic [22] provides a very elegant framework to specify in a compact and formal way an emergent behaviour in terms of *time-dependent* events. Among the myriads of temporal logic extensions available, Metric Interval Temporal Logic [3] (MITL) is very suitable to characterise properties of (real-valued) signals evolving in continuous time. The syntax of MITL is as follows.

Definition 1 (MITL syntax). *The syntax of MITL is given by*

$$\varphi := \top \mid q \mid \neg\varphi \mid \varphi_1 \wedge \varphi_2 \mid \mathbf{X}_{[a,b]}\varphi \mid \varphi_1 \, \mathbf{U}_{[a,b]} \, \varphi_2,$$

where $\top$ *is a true formula (*$\bot = \neg\top$ *is false),* q *is an atomic proposition which is either true or false in each state* $\mathbf{x}$ *(we denote with* $\mathcal{L}(\mathbf{x})$ *the set of atomic propositions true in* $\mathbf{x}$*), conjunction and negation are the standard boolean connectives,* $[a,b]$ *is a dense-time interval with* $0 \leq a < b$*,* $\mathbf{X}_{[a,b]}$ *is the* next *operator and* $\mathbf{U}_{[a,b]}$ *is the until operator.*

The (bounded) until operator $\varphi_1 \, \mathbf{U}_{[a,b]} \, \varphi_2$ requires φ_1 to hold from now until, in a time between a and b time units, φ_2 becomes true, while the (bounded) next operator $\mathbf{X}_{[a,b]}\varphi$ requires φ to hold in the next state, to be reached between a and b units of time. The *eventually* operator $\mathbf{F}_{[a,b]}$ and the *always* operator $\mathbf{G}_{[a,b]}$ can be defined as usual: $\mathbf{F}_{[a,b]}\varphi := \top\mathbf{U}_{[a,b)}\varphi$, $\mathbf{G}_{[a,b]}\varphi := \neg\mathbf{F}_{[a,b]}\neg\varphi$. More precisely, MITL can be given a semantics based on boolean signals, which are functions of time to $\{\top, \bot\}$. Boolean signals corresponding to atomic propositions are obtained from a (real-valued) input signal $\mathbf{x}(t)$ by point-wise lifting: $q(t) := q \in \mathcal{L}(\mathbf{x}(t))$. The extension of MITL that deals with real-valued signals is known as Signal Temporal Logic, see [19] for further details on the logic and the monitoring algorithm.

MITL is a logic that is interpreted over traces, and a formula φ identifies the subset of traces that satisfy it, $\{\mathbf{x} \models \varphi\}$. A stochastic model $\mathcal{M}$, however, is a probability distribution on the space of traces, and as such we can measure how much $\mathcal{M}$ satisfies φ by computing the probability $p(\varphi|\mathcal{M}) = Prob_{\mathcal{M}}\{\mathbf{x} \models \varphi\}$. This probability is notoriously difficult to calculate analytically even for simple models [11], hence, we resort to Monte Carlo methods, applying statistical model checking (SMC) [15] to estimate the probability of a MITL formula in a generative model.

Discrimination Function. In order to set up a proper learning problem, we need to consider a score function to optimise, encoding the criterion to discriminate between two models. Here we choose a simple score function, namely the log odds ratio between the satisfaction probabilities. More precisely, let $\mathcal{M}_1$ and $\mathcal{M}_2$ be the two models learnt from the two datasets and φ a candidate MITL formula. The log odds ratio score R_φ is defined as

$$R_\varphi = \log \frac{p(\varphi_1 \mid \mathcal{M}_1)}{p(\varphi_2 \mid \mathcal{M}_2)}, \tag{2.1}$$

and it is maximised when the probability of the first model is close to one and the probability in the second model is close to zero.

Structure Learning. Identifying the structure of a MITL formula which is satisfied with high probability by the model is a difficult combinatorial optimisation problem. Combinatorial optimisation algorithms exist but we are aware of few theoretical convergence guarantees. In this paper we do not tackle the problem in its full generality, but we set up a greedy search scheme which requires some basic knowledge of the domain at hand.

More specifically, we assume to have a fixed set of *basic* template formulae $\mathcal{T}$. First, we search exhaustively in $\mathcal{T}$ by optimising the continuous parameters of each $\varphi \in \mathcal{T}$, and thus computing its best score (i.e the log odds ratio). Then, we rank the formulae in $\mathcal{T}$ and select the subset of higher score. If in this way we find a few good candidate formulae, we proceed to the second phase, otherwise we enlarge the set $\mathcal{T}$, and try again. The choice of the thresholds to select good candidates is delicate and problem dependent. In the second phase, we take the best formulae $\mathcal{T}_{best}$ and combine them using some predefined combination rules (for instance, boolean combinations), and run again the continuous optimisation on the parameters, ranking again the formulae and selecting those with highest score. As the set $\mathcal{T}_{best}$ is expected to be small, we will be searching exhaustively a reasonably small set of formulae. At this stage, we expect this greedy optimisation to have found some good formula. If not, we can proceed to combine together the best formulae of this second round, possibly with another set of combinators, or reconsider the choice of the basic templates $\mathcal{T}$.

Parameter Learning. We now turn to the issue of tuning the parameters of (a set of) formulae to maximise their satisfaction probability. More specifically, we assume that we have a MITL formula φ_θ which depends on some continuous parameters θ. We aim to maximise its discriminative power $R_\varphi(\theta)$ defined in equation (2.1). Naturally, this quantity is an intractable function of the formula parameters; its value at a finite set of parameters can be noisily estimated using an SMC procedure. The problem is therefore to identify the maximum of an intractable function with as few (approximate) function evaluations as possible. This problem is closely related to the central problem of reinforcement learning of determining the optimal policy of an agent with as little exploration of the space of actions as possible. We therefore adopt a provably convergent stochastic optimisation algorithm, the GP-UCB algorithm [25], to solve the problem of continuous optimisation of formula parameters. Intuitively, the algorithm interpolates the noisy observations using a stochastic process (a procedure called emulation in statistics) and uses the uncertainty in this fit to determine regions where the true maximum can lie. This algorithm has already been used in a formal modelling scenario in [9].

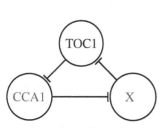
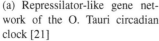

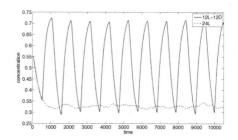

(a) Repressilator-like gene net-   (b) O. Tauri circadian clock: average.
work of the O. Tauri circadian
clock [21]

Fig. 2. The repressilator-like model of the O.Tauri circadian clock (left) is a cyclic negative-feedback loop composed of three repressor genes: TOC_1, CCA_1, and an unknown gene X. The comparison of the average evolution (right) of the circadian clock for the 12h light/12h dark model (blue solid line) and the 24h light model (red dashed line) shows that light plays a crucial role in stabilising the oscillatory period. Parameters of the simulation are as in [21].

3   Results

3.1   Logical Characterisation of a Biological Oscillator

Our first case study is the circadian clock in *Ostreococcus Tauri*, a simple unicellular alga often used as a minimal plant model organism [21]. The circadian clock is an important regulator of the metabolism of the plant and is controlled by the mutually repressive interaction of three genes, TOC1, CCA1 and one expressing a not yet characterized protein (denoted as X here), see Fig. 2 left for a scheme of the genetic circuit. Gene repression of the TOC1 gene is further modulated by light, which plays the role of an external input and acts as a stabiliser of the oscillatory pattern.

   In this example, a parametrised statistical model was already learned from data in [21]. The stochastic hybrid models we consider couple Stochastic Differential Equations (SDEs) for protein dynamics with a two-state model of gene promoter, which can be either free or bound to the repressor. In the latter case, the protein expression is reduced. More precisely, the protein dynamics is given by the SDE

$$dX_i = (A_i\mu_i + b_i - \lambda_i X_i)dt + \sigma dW,$$

where μ_i denotes the state of the promoter gene i (with $\mu_i = 1$ denoting the repressed state and $\mu_i = 0$ the active state), b_i is the basal production rate, $A_i < 0$ reduces it in case of repression, and λ_i is the degradation rate. The dynamics of the promoter is a two-state Markov chain with switch rates given by

$$f_{bind,i}(\mathbf{X}) = k_{p_i} \exp(k_{e_i} X_j), \quad f_{unbind,i}(\mathbf{X}) = k_u,$$

i.e. with constant unbinding rate and with binding rate depending on the repressor concentration. To model the influence of light on the protein TOC1, we modify the binding and unbinding rates of its regulatory protein X as follows:

Table 1. Statistics for six runs of the optimization of parameter $\theta \in [0.05, 0.35]$. The algorithm was initialised by sampling the function (2.1) 16 times from 100 simulation runs of each mode, and terminated with less than 4 additional samples on average. The variability of the results is due to the noisy nature of the function evaluation.

Av. θ	Av. log odds ratio	Av. sat. prob. 12L-12D	Av. sat. prob. 24L
0.148	4.295	0.83	0.008
Range θ	Range log odds ratio	Range sat. prob. 12L-12D	Range sat. prob. 24L
$[0.138, 0.157]$	$[3.689, 4.522]$	$[0.77, 0.87]$	$[0.004, 0.012]$

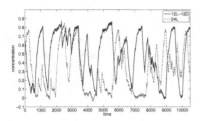

(a) O. Tauri circadian clock: single trace.

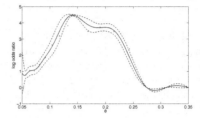

(b) Log odd ratio: emulation function

Fig. 3. Left: Single trace of TOC1 protein evolution for the O. Tauri model, with parameters as in [21]. Right: Emulated log odds ratio as a function of the threshold θ of MITL Formula 3.2 (blue solid line) and 95% error bounds (black dashed lines). The green points are the estimated values of the function.

$$f_{bind,TOC1}(\mathbf{X}) = (1-\gamma)\left(k_{p_i}\exp(k_{e_i}X_j)\right) + \gamma \cdot k_{light}^b(t), \quad f_{unbind,i}(\mathbf{X}) = (1-\gamma)k_u + \gamma \cdot k_{light}^u(t),$$

where γ is set to 0.20 and the values of $k_{light}^{b/u}(t)$ depend on the light conditions.

As an example of our property learning procedure, we seek a temporal logic formula which discriminates system trajectories between the following two conditions: the system is *entrained*, i.e. is receiving a 12h light/12h dark input signal (12L-12D), or it is being kept in constant light (24L). These conditions are encountered by *O. tauri* at high latitudes, and it is a scientifically important question how clock regulation can withstand such extreme environmental changes. In this example, we will *fix a template* and limit ourselves to learn parameters with the Bayesian continuous optimisation scheme discussed in Section 2. The key difference between the 12L-12D model and the 24L model is that oscillations in the 12L - 12D regime should maintain phase coherence with the input. This is indeed true, as can be seen from Figure 2(b), where we show the average of 500 trajectories. Detecting phase coherence on single trajectories is however a much tougher proposition, as subtle phase shifts can be easily masked by irregularities due to the intrinsic stochasticity of the processes, see Figure 3(a).

We therefore use the approach of [12], converting the signal from the time domain to the frequency domain using the Short Time Fourier Transform (STFT) [2]. This technique is generally employed to analyse non-stationary signals, whose statistic characteristics vary with time. STFT consists of reading the samples of the signals using fixed window of time where to apply the standard Fourier transform. The result is a spectrogram where is possible to observe for each region of time the characteristic frequencies of the signal. Since we know the oscillation frequency ω_o of the 12L-12D model, by fixing a time window of $T_o = 10/\omega_o$, we expect to find a peak in the STFT at frequency ω_o in the 12L-12D model, but not in the 24L model. Using the STFT (with rectangular window), we can require this peak to persist for a certain amount of time T, leading to the formula

$$\varphi_{FFT,\theta} = G_{[0,T]}(f(\omega_0, \cdot) \geq \theta), \tag{3.2}$$

where $f(\omega_0, t)$ is the absolute value of the STFT at frequency ω_0 for the window of length T_o starting at time t, and T is fixed to 1000. The goal therefore becomes to find the best discriminating θ. In Table 1, we report the results of 6 runs of the optimization algorithm, searching for the best $\theta \in [0.05, 0.35]$, while the functional dependency of log odds ratio on θ, as emulated by the Bayesian optimisation procedure, is shown in Figure 3(b). We find an optimal value (the median from the 6 runs) of 0.1492, corresponding to a satisfaction probability in the 12L-12D model of approximatively 0.84 and a satisfaction probability in the 24L model of approximatively 0.01, confirming that this formula has a good discriminatory power.

3.2 Logical Discrimination of Cardiac Arrhythmias

Basic cardiac physiology - Arrhythmias are electrophysiological cardiac malfunctions which cause significant mortality and morbidity. The most common, non-invasive diagnostic tool to monitor the heart's electrophysiological function is the electrocardiogram (ECG). An ECG machine is able to record the electrical activity of the heart through a set of electrodes (called ECG leads) placed by the physician on the chest wall and limbs of the patient. As Figure 4 b) illustrates, in a healthy patient the ECG signal consists of three main consecutive waves: **the P wave** corresponding to the depolarization and the consequent contraction of the atria, **the QRS complex** representing the rapid depolarization and contraction of the ventricles and **the T wave** identifying the recovery or depolarization of the ventricles.

ECG signals are interpreted by physicians through a hierarchy of annotations. The fundamental unit in the ECG is the heartbeat (or, simply, beat) defined as the interval between two consecutive **R peaks**. The beats are annotated using a symbol characterizing the type of beat observed (some of them shown in Figure 4 a-d). Beats are usually machine annotated through pattern recognition algorithms such as support vector machines. In this work, we will use directly an annotated version of the ECG signals as a sequence of beat symbols with associated beat durations.

A higher level annotation of ECG data is given by the *rhythms*, sequences of beats exhibiting a coherent pattern. Figure 5 a) shows an example of an ECG pattern for a normal sinus rhythm. Even in this case some abnormal heartbeats (such as a premature ventricular contraction in Figure 5 d)) can sporadically occur without medical significance. We present here initial results on annotated ECG data from the MIT-BIH Arrhythmia Database [20]. We restricted our attention to a subset of possible rhythms which were more prevalent in the data: bigeminy, trigeminy, ventricular tachycardia and the normal rhythm. These signals are predominantly composed of **V** and **N** symbols, often with a similar frequency, hence discrimination is more challenging.

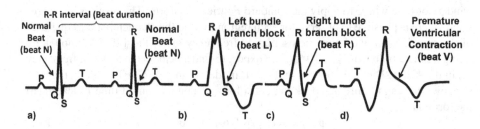

Fig. 4. a) ECG pattern for two normal beats; b-c) Left /Right bundle branch block is an abnormal beat where one ventricle is delayed and contracts later than the other; d) Premature ventricular contraction is characterized by a premature wider QRS complex, not preceded by a P wave and followed by an usually large T wave with an opposite concavity than in the normal beat.

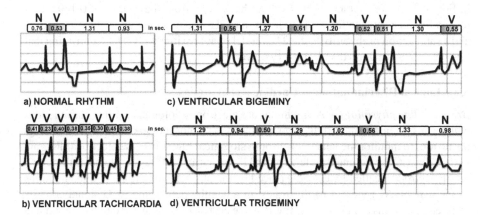

Fig. 5. Some ECG patterns: a) normal sinus rhythm; b) ventricular tachycardia, b) ventricular bigeminy, c) ventricular trigeminy. On the top of each signal is reported the annotation for each beat and its duration in seconds, while on the bottom is reproduced the electrical signal. The ECG data was obtained from the MIT-BIH Arrhythmia Database [20]

Statistical modelling - Due to the discrete time nature of the signal, we selected Hidden Markov Models (HMMs) as a class of statistical models that could provide a suitable statistical abstraction of the data. HMMs [23] are a workhorse of statistics and signal processing and have been previously employed in the context of formal modelling of heart function in [6]. Briefly, an HMM is a tuple $H = \langle S,A,O,B,\pi \rangle$ containing a finite set S of states, a transition probability matrix A, a set O of observation symbols, an observation probability distribution B, and an initial state distribution π. In our case, we have hybrid observations consisting of pairs o_s, o_t where o_s is the emitted symbol (type of beat) and o_t the beat duration (in seconds). We therefore assume the observation probability to factorise as a product of a discrete probability on the beat types and a Gaussian on the observation times. HMM models were learnt using the Baum-Welch algorithm [23] and selected using the AIC score defined in Section 2.

Summary of experimental procedure - Due to space restrictions, we present results on a single patient (patient 233); other patients yielded similar results. Code to recreate the experimental results is available for academic use from the authors upon request. The experimental procedure can be summarised as follows

- For each rhythm, we learn HMM models with 2 to 6 states, and select the one with best AIC score. We learn the model simultaneously on all segments annotated as a certain rhythm (e.g. bigeminy).
- For each pair of abnormal/ normal rhythm, we learn template formulae starting from the basic set of formulae $\mathcal{T}_2$, corresponding to possible patterns of length 2 of symbols V and N: $\mathcal{T}_2 = \{\mathbf{FG}_{\leq T}\varphi_{NN}, \mathbf{FG}_{\leq T}\varphi_{NV}, \mathbf{FG}_{\leq T}\varphi_{VN}, \mathbf{FG}_{\leq T}\varphi_{VV}\}$, where $\varphi_{YZ} = Y \wedge (\mathbf{X}_{[0,b_Y]}(Z \wedge \mathbf{X}_{[0,b_Z]}(\top)))$ and we optimise the continuous parameters (T, b_N, b_V) to obtain the maximum discriminative power [1].
- If after the optimisation phase no highly supported formula was found, i.e. a formula with high log-odd ratio of abnormal versus normal signal and high satisfaction probability, we rerun the procedure increasing the pattern length of one (hence, first for $\mathcal{T}_3$, then $\mathcal{T}_4$, and so on).
- We then selected the most supported formulae of $\mathcal{T}_k$ to further combine them, as discussed in the previous section. We run the continuous optimisation also for these formulae, and chose the ones having both high log-odd ratio and satisfaction probability for the abnormal rhythm.

We now present results on discrimination of the three abnormal rhythms in more detail.

Bigeminy - Learning formula templates for the discrimination of bigeminy against normal heart behaviour proceeded as follows: in the first optimisation run, the two formulae with highest log-odd ratio where $\mathbf{FG}_{\leq T}\varphi_{NV}$ and $\mathbf{FG}_{\leq T}\varphi_{VN}$, scoring more than 5, with a satisfaction probability in bigeminy of about 0.8.

The other two formulae, instead, have a log-odd ratio zero or less. Hence, we selected these two formulae for the second phase of the discrete search, obtaining $\mathbf{FG}_{\leq T}(\varphi_{NV} \vee \varphi_{VN})$ as the only candidate for the second round. This formula clearly codes for the pattern VN repeated many times (for as long as T units of time). Running the continuous optimisation, we find a log-odd ratio of 4.08, which is lower than in the previous case, but it corresponds to a satisfaction probability of 0.9994 in the abnormal rhythm, and a probability of 0.016 in the normal one, corresponding to a sensitivity of $> 99\%$ and a specificity of approximately 98%. Hence, this formula turns to have a good discriminative power, and its relatively low log-odd ratio depends on its high sensitivity to small values of the denominator. The upper bound of time T is optimally set to 3.8, close to the maximum of 4. Upper bounds on beat duration are also close to their maximum. Note that the alternation of V and N is precisely what characterises bigeminy: our method learned the correct pattern used by physicians, and additionally quantitated the time such a pattern persists for.

---

[1] We search in the following space: maximal duration of symbols is constrained between 0 and 2.5 seconds, while the lower bound was set to zero. The total duration T varies between 0 and an upper bound depending on the signal, equal to 4 for bigeminy, 7 for trigeminy, 2 for tachycardia. We generate signals of fifteen seconds. The choice of bounds for T is consistent with the duration of raw signals in the training set.

Table 2. Average log-odd ratio and satisfaction probability of abnormal and normal signals for the best discriminating formulae learned from patient 223, as tested on other three patients (per type of abnormality). The fourth row reports the number of signals in the training set to learn each model of the abnormal signals in patient 223. The formulae learnt were tested on patients: 119, 213, and 233 for bigeminy; 119, 201,208 for trigeminy; 213, 215, 233 for ventricular tachycardia. The fifth row shows the number of signals considered in the testing set per type of abnormality.

	Bigeminy	Trigeminy	V. Tachycardia
Av. log-odd ratio	3.32	2.99	7.68
Av. prob. abnormal	0.99	0.99	0.99
Av. prob. normal	0.06	0.08	0.0005
Learning Set (num. of signals)	7	3	7
Testing Set (num. of signals)	84	75	10

Trigeminy - To discriminate trigeminy vs normal rhythm, we proceeded analogously as for bigeminy, starting with the same set $\mathcal{T}_2$ of formulae. In this case, however, no formula of length 2 was found to have a high support in discriminating trigeminy (less than 3.5), hence we considered basic templates corresponding to patterns of length 3. The analysis in this case gave high log-odd ratio (4 or greater) to three formulae: $\mathbf{FG}_{\leq T}\varphi_{VNN}$, $\mathbf{FG}_{\leq T}\varphi_{NVN}$, and $\mathbf{FG}_{\leq T}\varphi_{NNV}$, with for a small duration T for all three cases. We then took all possible combination of at least two of those formula using disjunction, and found the most discriminating formula (log-odd ratio 7.8, satisfaction probability for trigeminy 0.9968, and for normal signal of 0.004) to be $\mathbf{FG}_{\leq T}(\varphi_{VNN} \vee \varphi_{NVN} \vee \varphi_{NNV})$, corresponding to the pattern VNN repeating in time for approximatively $T = 4.25$ seconds. Again in this case, the method found the hallmark pattern of trigeminy and additionally quantified its persistent behaviour. We also tested that this formula works well in discriminating trigeminy versus bigeminy (log-odd ratio of 8.5).

Ventricular tachycardia - This case turned out to be the simplest one. A good discriminating formula was found already in the set $\mathcal{T}_2$, corresponding to the pattern VV. In particular, the continuous optimisation returned a log-odd ratio of 2.9, corresponding to a satisfaction probability in the abnormal rhythm of 0.9998 and of 0.05 in the normal rhythm, with the global validity time T set approximatively to 1.25 seconds. This corresponds to tachycardia being characterised by a stretch of about 3 to 4 V beats.

Discrimination on other patients - So far, we considered discriminative power as applied to the same patient on which the models were learnt. We now consider the much harder task of assessing whether estimated formulae remain discriminative when also applied to other patients' ECG data. We considered three other patients for each arrhythmia, and obtained an high discriminative power, as reported in Table 2. We also tested the formulae on raw signals taken from the database[2], obtaining the following results, in terms of satisfaction probability: 0.954 for bigeminy versus 0.038 for normal rhythms (on the same patients); and 0.918 for trigeminy versus 0.287 for normal rhythms. The high satisfaction probability on normal rhythms for this last case is almost entirely

---

[2] 22 signals for bigeminy of length at least 4.5, 49 for trigeminy of length at least 5, and about 80 for normal rhythms. We did not treat tachycardia because there were too few signals.

explained by the presence, in the extended data set, of several patients with slow heart beats. The relatively low duration of the pattern learnt on the training patient, 4.25s, can be matched in the slow beat patients by patterns consisting of a single V preceded and followed by two Ns, which are very common in normal rhythm. Increasing the time bound to 7s reduced the satisfaction probability in normal rhythms to 0.014, while the satisfaction probability for trigeminy remained stable to 0.906.

4   Related Work

Mining temporal logic specifications from data is an emerging field of computer aided verification [4,10,18,14,27,28]. Generally, this task is predicated on the availability of a fully specified and deterministic model, enabling a quantitative evaluation of the probability that a certain formula will hold. This enables the deployment of optimisation based machine learning techniques, such as decision trees [14] or stochastic optimisation methods [28,27]. Learning temporal logic specifications directly from observed traces of the system is considerably more challenging. In general, solving the full structure and parameter learning problem is infeasible, due to the intractability resulting from a hybrid combinatorial/continuous optimisation problem. Heuristic search approaches have been proposed in [10]; while these may prove effective in specific modelling problems, they generally do not offer theoretical guarantees, and can be prone to over-fitting/vulnerable to noise. Geometric approaches such as the one proposed in [4] rest on solid mathematical foundations but can also be vulnerable to noise, and require potentially very large amounts of data to permit identification. While preparing this manuscript, we became aware of a work of imminent publication [17] which employs a notion of robustness of satisfiability of a formula to guide an optimisation based mining procedure. While this approach can be applied also in a model-free scenario, empirical estimation of the robustness of a formula may require the observation of a large number of traces of the system; for example, one of the case studies in [17] used 600 independent realisations of the system, a number that far exceeds the experimental capabilities in many applications such as systems biology.

Our strategy of constructing a statistical model of data ameliorates this issue, at the price of an increased complexity of the mining problem, which we tackle by combining statistical modelling ideas from machine learning with formal verification methods. In this respect, our work is related to a number of other recent attempts to deploy machine learning tools within a verification context [7,26,16]. Similar ideas to the ones used in this paper have been deployed on the parameter synthesis problem in [9,5], where the GP-UCB algorithm was used to identify the parameters of a model which maximised the satisfaction/robustness of a formula. Statistical abstractions draw their roots in the *emulation* field in statistics: within the context of dynamical systems, emulation has been recently used in [13] to model compactly the interface between subsystems of complex gene regulatory networks.

5   Conclusions

Modern science is increasingly becoming data intensive, with vast amounts of data being produced across disciplines as diverse as economics, physics and biology. Marrying formal computational modelling with statistical, data-modelling techniques is therefore a pressing priority to advance the applicability of computational thinking to real world problems. In this paper, we exploit concepts from formal modelling and machine learning to develop methodologies which can identify temporal logic formulae which discriminate different stochastic processes based on observations. While we aim to be guided by the data, our approach is not entirely data driven: approaches which rely directly on induction from data, such as [10,4], often need very long time series, which are not available in many applications such as systems biology. Rather, we use a statistical abstraction, i.e. a family of stochastic models, to represent the data, and use machine learning methods to select an optimal model based on the data. This procedure brings back a model based perspective, with considerable advantages in terms of interpretability of the underlying dynamics. Furthermore, it enables us to deploy advanced machine learning methods to statistically optimise the temporal logic formulae we are seeking.

While we believe our machine learning perspective brings some distinctive novel ideas to the problem, several major avenues remain open for further research. Our approach focussed primarily on parametrising temporal logic formulae, rather than determining also a template for the formula structure. This combinatorial optimisation problem is intrinsically computationally hard, and may require directly imposing restrictions on the logic as in [17]. Scaling our approach to high dimensional spaces of parameters could also be problematic, as Bayesian optimisation methods severely suffer from the curse of dimensionality. In this respect, sparse approximation may be beneficial [24] but are so far untested in a Bayesian optimisation context. Finally, our experimental section demonstrated the applicability of our approach to a potentially wide class of problems. We hope this may lead to more focussed interdisciplinary studies in emerging application fields such as synthetic biology.

References

1. Akaike, H.: A new look at the statistical model identification. IEEE Trans. Aut. Control 19(6), 716–723 (1974)
2. Allen, J.B.: Short term spectral analysis, synthesis, and modification by discrete fourier transform. IEEE Transactions on Acoustics, Speech, and Signal Processing 3, 235–238
3. Alur, R., Feder, T., Henzinger, T.A.: The benefits of relaxing punctuality. J. ACM 43(1), 116–146 (1996)
4. Asarin, E., Donzé, A., Maler, O., Nickovic, D.: Parametric Identification of Temporal Properties. In: Khurshid, S., Sen, K. (eds.) RV 2011. LNCS, vol. 7186, pp. 147–160. Springer, Heidelberg (2012)
5. Bartocci, E., Bortolussi, L., Nenzi, L., Sanguinetti, G.: On the robustness of temporal properties for stochastic models. In: Proc. of HSB 2013, pp. 3–19 (2013)
6. Bartocci, E., Corradini, F., Di Berardini, M.R., Smolka, S.A., Grosu, R.: Modeling and simulation of cardiac tissue using hybrid I/O automata. Theor. Comput. Sci. 410(33-34), 3149–3165 (2009)
7. Bartocci, E., Grosu, R., Karmarkar, A., Smolka, S.A., Stoller, S.D., Zadok, E., Seyster, J.: Adaptive runtime verification. In: Qadeer, S., Tasiran, S. (eds.) RV 2012. LNCS, vol. 7687, pp. 168–182. Springer, Heidelberg (2013)
8. Bishop, C.M.: Pattern Recognition and Machine Learning. Springer (2006)
9. Bortolussi, L., Sanguinetti, G.: Learning and Designing Stochastic Processes from Logical Constraints. In: Joshi, K., Siegle, M., Stoelinga, M., D'Argenio, P.R. (eds.) QEST 2013. LNCS, vol. 8054, pp. 89–105. Springer, Heidelberg (2013)

10. Calzone, L., Chabrier-Rivier, N., Fages, F., Soliman, S.: Machine learning biochemical networks from temporal logic properties. In: Priami, C., Plotkin, G. (eds.) Trans. on Comp. Sys. Bio. VI. LNCS (LNBI), vol. 4220, pp. 68–94. Springer, Heidelberg (2006)

11. Chen, T., Diciolla, M., Kwiatkowska, M., Mereacre, A.: Time-bounded verification of CTMCs against real-time specifications. In: Fahrenberg, U., Tripakis, S. (eds.) FORMATS 2011. LNCS, vol. 6919, pp. 26–42. Springer, Heidelberg (2011)

12. Donzé, A., Maler, O., Bartocci, E., Nickovic, D., Grosu, R., Smolka, S.A.: On temporal logic and signal processing. In: Chakraborty, S., Mukund, M. (eds.) ATVA 2012. LNCS, vol. 7561, pp. 92–106. Springer, Heidelberg (2012)

13. Georgoulas, A., Clark, A., Ocone, A., Gilmore, S., Sanguinetti, G.: A subsystems approach for parameter estimation of ode models of hybrid systems. In: Proc. of HSB 2012. EPTCS, vol. 92 (2012)

14. Grosu, R., Smolka, S.A., Corradini, F., Wasilewska, A., Entcheva, E., Bartocci, E.: Learning and detecting emergent behavior in networks of cardiac myocytes. Commun. ACM 52(3), 97–105 (2009)

15. Jha, S.K., Clarke, E.M., Langmead, C.J., Legay, A., Platzer, A., Zuliani, P.: A Bayesian approach to model checking biological systems. In: Degano, P., Gorrieri, R. (eds.) CMSB 2009. LNCS, vol. 5688, pp. 218–234. Springer, Heidelberg (2009)

16. Kalajdzic, K., Bartocci, E., Smolka, S.A., Stoller, S.D., Grosu, R.: Runtime Verification with Particle Filtering. In: Legay, A., Bensalem, S. (eds.) RV 2013. LNCS, vol. 8174, pp. 149–166. Springer, Heidelberg (2013)

17. Kong, Z., Jones, A., Ayala, A.M., Gol, E.A., Belta, C.: Temporal Logic Inference for Classification and Prediction from Data. In: Proc. of HSCC 2014, pp. 273–282. ACM (2014)

18. Lee, C., Chen, F., Roşu, G.: Mining parametric specifications. In: Proc. of ICSE 2011, pp. 591–600. ACM (2011)

19. Maler, O., Nickovic, D.: Monitoring temporal properties of continuous signals. In: Lakhnech, Y., Yovine, S. (eds.) FORMATS/FTRTFT 2004. LNCS, vol. 3253, pp. 152–166. Springer, Heidelberg (2004)

20. Moody, G.B., Mark, R.G.: The impact of the MIT-BIH arrhythmia database. IEEE Eng. Med. Biol. Mag. 20(3), 45–50 (2001)

21. Ocone, A., Millar, A.J., Sanguinetti, G.: Hybrid regulatory models: a statistically tractable approach to model regulatory network dynamics. Bioinformatics 29(7), 910–916 (2013)

22. Pnueli, A.: The temporal logic of programs. In: IEEE Annual Symposium on Foundations of Computer Science, pp. 46–57 (1977)

23. Rabiner, L.R.: A tutorial on hidden Markov models and selected applications in speech recognition. Proceedings of the IEEE 77(2), 257–286 (1989)

24. Rasmussen, C.E., Williams, C.K.I.: Gaussian Processes for Machine Learning. MIT Press (2006)

25. Srinivas, N., Krause, A., Kakade, S.M., Seeger, M.W.: Information-theoretic regret bounds for gaussian process optimization in the bandit setting. IEEE Transactions on Information Theory 58(5), 3250–3265 (2012)

26. Stoller, S.D., Bartocci, E., Seyster, J., Grosu, R., Havelund, K., Smolka, S.A., Zadok, E.: Runtime Verification with State Estimation. In: Khurshid, S., Sen, K. (eds.) RV 2011. LNCS, vol. 7186, pp. 193–207. Springer, Heidelberg (2012)

27. Xiaoqing, J., Donzé, A., Deshmukh, J.V., Seshia, S.A.: Mining Requirements from Closed-loop Control Models. In: Proc. of HSCC 2013, pp. 43–52. ACM (2013)

28. Yang, H., Hoxha, B., Fainekos, G.: Querying Parametric Temporal Logic Properties on Embedded Systems. In: Nielsen, B., Weise, C. (eds.) ICTSS 2012. LNCS, vol. 7641, pp. 136–151. Springer, Heidelberg (2012)

Finding Best and Worst Case Execution Times of Systems Using Difference-Bound Matrices

Omar Al-Bataineh, Mark Reynolds, and Tim French

The University of Western Australia, Perth, Australia

Abstract. The paper provides a solution to the fundamental problems of computing the shortest and the longest time taken by a run of a timed automaton from an initial state to a final state. It does so using the difference-bound matrix data structure to represent zones, which is a state-of-the-art heuristic to improve performance over the classical (and somewhat brute-force) region graph abstraction. The solution provided here is conceptually a marked improvement over some earlier work on the problems [16,9], in which repeated guesses (guided by binary search) and multiple model checking queries were effectively but inelegantly and less efficiently used; here only one run of the zone construction is sufficient to yield the answers. The paper then reports on a prototype implementation of the algorithms using Difference Bound Matrices (DBMs), and presents the results of its application on a realistic automatic manufacturing plant.

1 Introduction

Real-time systems are systems that designed to run applications and programs with very precise timing and a high degree of reliability. These systems can be said to be failed if they can not guarantee response within strict time constraints. The success of a real-time system depends on whether all the scheduled tasks can be guaranteed to complete their executions before their deadlines. Usually, best-case execution time (BCET) and worst-case execution time (WCET) are used for schedulability analysis of real-time systems. Recently, there has been a considerable interest in using formal methods and, in particular (timed automata) model checking [8] for computing BCET and WCET since it gives precise answers to these questions in an automatic way [16,4].

As a first contribution of this paper, we give an efficient zone-based algorithms for computing BCET and WCET using *Difference Bound Matrices* (DBMs). Similar to [7,18,15] the solution goes by adding an extra global clock that acts as an observer and then computing the zone graph of the automaton, by means of a standard forward analysis using DBMs. One of the outcomes of the analysis is that the correctness of the computation of BCET and WCET depends mainly on the way we normalise (abstract) the zones in the resulting zone graph. It is well-known that normalisation is a necessary step in order to guarantee termination in timed automata [17,5]. However, the standard approaches for analysing a timed automaton that depend on computing the zone graph of the automaton while normalising zones at each step of the successor computation [5], will give abstract

A. Legay and M. Bozga (Eds.): FORMATS 2014, LNCS 8711, pp. 38–52, 2014.

zones and hence result in abstract values of the execution times. Therefore, the direct application of these approaches is inconvenient for the analysis of WCET.

To get precise and accurate values of execution times we choose to work with search trees whose nodes are unapproximated or real zones. The algorithms follow a new paradigm where zones are not abstracted, hence preserving the value of extra clock. Instead, abstraction is used to detect when a zone has already been explored, that is, when two non-abstracted zones have the same abstraction. When a final state is reached, the constraints on the extra clock in the zone yield expected BCET and WCET values. The proposed algorithms can successfully handle acyclic TA and TA containing cycles given that the automaton under analysis has no run of infinite length. Note that even on a TA without cycles, a WCET of infinity is still possible if not every reachable location is guarded by an invariant containing an upper bound on some clock. We then report on a prototype implementation of the algorithms using the model checker opaal [10] and present the results of its application by computing the BCET/WCET of a realistic automatic manufacturing plant taken from [11] when analysing it under different configurations. We show that the proposed algorithms can outperform the conventional binary search approach used in [16,9] by several orders of magnitude.

Related Work. It is claimed in [19] that model checking is inadequate for WCET analysis. However, in [16] Metzner has shown that model checking can be used efficiently for WCET analysis. He used model checking to improve WCET analyses for hardware with caching. The work in [9] has used model checking to measure WCET of real-world, modern processors with good performance. However, in these works, the user needs to verify repeatedly temporal formulas while guessing values for the WCET and using model checking to determine whether the right value has been found.

Closest to our work is [3] which uses a variant of timed automata called "priced timed automata" and the DBM data structure to compute the minimum cost of reaching a goal state in the model. A priced timed automata can associate costs with locations, where the costs are multiplied by the amount of time spent in a location. An automata may be designed so that the total cost corresponds to the execution time, and thus this approach may be used to calculate the best case execution time problem. The optimisation algorithm uses a similar approach to Dijkstra's algorithm to search the state space, and the state space is optimised via partial normalisation. In our work we provide a robust approach that maintains real zones, and can be applied to solve both the best and worst case execution time problems.

2 Preliminaries

2.1 Timed Automata

Timed automata are an extension of the classical finite state automata with clock variables to model timing aspects [1]. Let X be a set of clock variables, the clock interpretation v for the set X is a mapping from X to $\mathbb{R}^+$ where $\mathbb{R}^+$ denotes the set of nonnegative real numbers.

Definition 1. *A timed automaton $\mathcal{A}$ is a tuple $(\Sigma, L, L_0, L_F, X, I, E)$, where*

- *Σ is a finite set of actions.*
- *L is a finite set of locations.*
- *$L_0 \subseteq L$ is a finite set of initial or starting locations.*
- *$L_F \subseteq L$ is a finite set of final locations.*
- *X is a finite set of clocks.*
- *$I : L \rightarrow \mathcal{C}(X)$ is a mapping from locations to clock constraints, called the location invariant.*
- *$E \subseteq L \times L \times \Sigma \times 2^X \times \Phi(X)$ is a finite set of transitions. An edge $(l, l', a, \lambda, \sigma)$ represents a transition from location l to location l' after performing action a. The set $\lambda \subseteq X$ gives the clocks to be reset with this transition, and σ is a clock constraint over X.*

Note that we assume that the automaton can not perform actions after reaching its corresponding final locations. The semantics of a timed automaton $(\Sigma, L, L_0, L_F, X, I, E)$ is defined by associating a transition systems with it. With each transition a clock constraint called a guard is associated and with each location a clock constraint called its invariant is associated. Since transitions are instantaneous, time can elapse in a location. A state of a timed automaton is of the form (l_i, v_i) which consists of two different parts, the current location and the current values of all clocks. The initial states are of the form $(l_0 \in L_0, v_0)$ where the valuation $v_0(x) = 0$ for all $x \in X$.

Definition 2. *Transitions of an automaton may include clock resets and guards which give conditions on the interval in which a transition can be executed and whose syntax is:*

$$\phi ::= t \prec c \mid \phi_1 \wedge \phi_2$$

where $t \in X$, $c \in \mathbb{N}$, and $\prec \in \{<, \leq, =, >, \geq\}$.
There are two types of transitions in timed automata:

1. *delay transitions that model the elapse of time while staying at some location: for a state (l, v) and a real-valued time increment $\delta \geq 0$, $(l, v) \xrightarrow{\delta} (l, v + \delta)$ if for all v' with $v \leq v' \leq v + \delta$, the invariant $I(l)$ holds.*
2. *action transitions that execute an edge of the automata: for a state (l, v) and a transition $(l, l', a, \lambda, \sigma)$ such that $v \models \sigma$, $(l, v) \xrightarrow{a} (l', v[\lambda := 0])$.*

So for an automaton to move from a location to another a delay transition followed by an action transition must be performed. We write this as $\xrightarrow{d_i} \xrightarrow{a_i}$.

A timed action is a pair (t, a) where $a \in \Sigma$ is an action performed by an automaton $\mathcal{A}$ after $t \in \mathbb{R}^+$ time units since $\mathcal{A}$ has been started.

Definition 3. *A run of a timed automaton* $\mathcal{A} = (\Sigma, L, L_0, L_F, X, I, E)$ *with an initial state* (l_0, v_0) *over a timed trace* $\zeta = (t_1, a_1), ..., (a_n, t_n)$ *is a sequence of transitions of the form.*

$$\langle l_0, v_0 \rangle \xrightarrow{d1, a1} \langle l_1, v_1 \rangle \xrightarrow{d2, a2} \langle l_2, v_2 \rangle, ..., \xrightarrow{dn, an} \langle l_n, v_n \rangle$$

satisfying the condition $t_i = t_{i-1} + d_i$ *for all* $i \geq 1$ *and that* $l_0 \in L_0$, $l_n \in L_F$, *and* $l_i \notin L_F$ *for all* $i < n$.

Since the locations of an automaton are decorated with a delay-quantity and that transitions between locations are instantaneous, the delay of a timed execution is simply the sum of the delays spent in the visited locations. Recall that the amount of time that can be spent in a certain location is described by means of invariants on a number of clock variables.

Definition 4. *(Delay of a run.) Let* $r = \langle l_0, v_0 \rangle \xrightarrow{d_1, a_1} \langle l_1, v_1 \rangle \ ... \ \xrightarrow{d_n, a_n} \langle l_n, v_n \rangle$ *be a timed run in the set of runs* $\mathcal{R}$. *The delay of* r, $delay(r)$, *is the sum* $\sum_{i=1}^{n} d_i$. *Hence, the problem of computing the BCET and WCET of* $\mathcal{A}$ *can be formalized as follows.*

$$BCET(\mathcal{A}) = \inf_{\forall r \in \mathcal{R}} (delay(r))$$

$$WCET(\mathcal{A}) = \sup_{\forall r \in \mathcal{R}} (delay(r))$$

2.2   The Zone Approach

In the original work of Alur and Dill [1], they proposed an abstraction technique by which an infinite timed transition system (i.e. timed automata) can be converted into an equivalent finitely symbolic transition system called region graph where reachability is decidable. However, it has been shown that the region automaton is highly inefficient to be used for implementing practical tools. Instead, most real-time model checking tools like UPPAAL, Kronos and RED apply abstractions based on so-called zones, which is much more practical and efficient for model checking real-time systems. In a zone graph [12], zones are used to denote symbolic states. A state is a pair (l, Z), where l is a location in the TA model and Z is a clock zone that represents sets of clock valuations at l. Formally a clock zone is a conjunction of inequalities that compare either a clock value or the difference between two clock values to an integer. In order to have a unified form for clock zones we introduce a reference clock x_0 to the set of clocks X in the analysed model that is always zero. The general form of a clock zone can be described by the following formula.

$$(x_0 = 0) \wedge \bigwedge_{0 \leq i \neq j \leq n} ((x_i - x_j) \prec c_{i,j})$$

where $x_i, x_j \in X$, $c_{i,j}$ bounds the difference between them, and $\prec \in \{\leq, <\}$. Considering a timed automaton $\mathcal{A} = (\Sigma, L, L_0, L_F, X, I, E)$, with a transition

$e = (l, a, \psi, \lambda, l')$ in E we can construct an abstract zone graph $\mathcal{Z}(\mathcal{A})$ such that states of $\mathcal{Z}(\mathcal{A})$ are zones of $\mathcal{A}$. The clock zone $succ(Z, e)$ will denote the set of clock valuations Z' for which the state (l', Z') can be reached from the state (l, Z) by letting time elapse and by executing the transition e. The pair $(l', succ(Z, e))$ will represent the set of successors of (l, Z) under the transition e. Since every constraint used in the invariant of an automaton location or in the guard of a transition is a clock zone, we can use zones for various state reachability analysis algorithms for timed automata.

The most important property of zones is that they can be represented as matrices. Several algorithms based on the notion of zones are implemented using the difference bound matrices (DBMs), which is the most commonly used data structure for the representation of zones.

2.3   The Difference Bound Matrices

A DBM [12] is a two-dimensional matrix that records the difference upper bounds between clock pairs up to a certain constant. In order to have a unified form for clock constraints in DBM we introduce a reference clock x_0 with the constant value 0 ($X = X \cup \{x_0\}$). The matrix is indexed by the clocks in X together with the special clock x_0. The element in a DBM D is of the form $(D_{i,j}, \prec)$ where $D_{i,j}$ bounds the difference between $x_i - x_j$, and $\prec \in \{\leq, <\}$. Each row in the matrix represents the bound difference between the value of the clock x_i and all the other clocks in the zone, thus a zone can be represented by at most $|X|^2$ atomic constraints. The first column in the matrix encodes the upper bounds of the clocks since the constraints in that column are of the form $x_i - x_0 \prec c$. On the other hand, the first row in the matrix encodes the lower bounds of the clocks where the constraints on that row are of the form $x_0 - x_i \prec c$.

Since entries of DBM represent bound differences between the values of the clocks in the model, it is possible sometimes to derive some constraints using the other constraints. For example, the sum of the upper bounds on the difference $x_i - x_j$ and $x_j - x_k$ is an upper bound on the difference $x_i - x_k$. That is, $D_{i,k} \prec D_{i,j} + D_{j,k}$. This observation can be used to tighten the DBM.

Deriving the tightest constraint on a pair of clocks in a DBM is equivalent to finding the shortest path between their nodes in the graph interpretation of the zone. Therefore, most model checking tools for timed automata use the Floyd-Warshall algorithm [13] to compute the canonical form of DBMs. In fact, canonical forms make easier some operations over DBMs like the test for inclusion between zones. For example, when comparing whether two zones are equivalent we need to verify whether the corresponding canonical DBMs of these zones are identical. It is interesting to mention that for zone-based timed automata model checking, termination is ensured by normalising all zones with respect to a maximum constant k. That is, if the clock is never compared to a constant greater than k, then the value of the clock will have no impact on the computation of the automaton $\mathcal{A}$ once it exceeds k [5].

Definition 5. *Let Z be a zone represented by a DBM in a canonical form $D = (D_{i,j}, \prec_{i,j})_{i,j=0,..n}$ and k be a clock ceiling. We can compute the k-normalization of the DBM $D' = (D'_{i,j}, \prec'_{i,j})_{i,j=0,..n}$ as follows:*

$$(D'_{i,j}; \prec'_{i,j}) = \begin{cases} (\infty, <) & \text{if } D_{i,j} > k, \\ (\text{-}k, <) & \text{if } D_{i,j} < -k, \\ (D_{i,j}, \prec_{i,j}) & \text{otherwise.} \end{cases}$$

However, in the last few years, there has been a considerable development in the normalization procedure [5,2,14] for the purpose of providing coarser abstractions of TA. It is well-known that for diagonal-free TA (i.e. a class of TA in which the test of the form $(x - y \prec c)$ is disallowed) if we take α_A associating to each clock x_i the maximal constant c such that $x \prec c$ appears in some guard of A (i.e. $\alpha = (\max_x)_{x \in X}$), then the resulting abstract graph preserves the reachability properties [5]. However, since these approaches normalise the zones at each step of the successor computation, they will give abstract zones and hence result in abstract values of the execution times. To solve the problem we choose to maintain real zones when computing the zone graph and use normalization just for inclusion checking as described in the following section.

3 Zone-Based Algorithms For Calculating BCET and WCET

An algorithmic solution to the BCET/WCET problem can be given by adding an additional global clock (let us call it x_i) to the automaton under analysis that acts as an observer in the sense that x_i does not participate in the invariants or guards of the automaton. Then one computes the zone graph of the automaton (involving x_i), by means of a standard forward analysis using DBMs. To get the BCET and WCET, the algorithm needs to look at the value of the constraints $(D_{0,i}, \prec_{0,i})$ and $(D_{i,0}, \prec_{i,0})$ respectively in the DBM D obtained in the final states, where $\prec \in \{<, \leq\}$ and i is the index of the global clock x_i.

3.1 The Zone-Based Algorithms

Before discussing how one can solve the BCET/WCET problems it is necessary first to summarise how the zone graph of a given automaton can be constructed using the new paradigm. Let D be a DBM in canonical form. We want to compute the successor of D w.r.t to a transition $e = (l, l', a, \lambda, \phi)$. can be obtained using a number of elementary DBM operations which can be described as follows.

1. Intersect D with the invariant of location l to find the set of possible clock assignments for the current state.
2. Canonize the resulting DBM and check the consistency of the matrix.
3. Let an arbitrary amount of time elapse on all clocks. In a DBM this means all elements $D_{i,0}$ are set to ∞.

4. Take the intersection with the invariant of location l again to find the set of possible clock assignments that still satisfy the invariant.
5. Take the intersection with the guard ϕ to find the clock assignments that are accepted by the transition.
6. Canonize the resulting DBM and check the consistency of the matrix.
7. Set all the clocks in λ that are reset by the transition to 0.
8. Take the intersection with the location invariant of the target location l'.
9. Canonize the resulting zone at the target location l' and check the consistency of the matrix.

Combining all of the above steps into one formula, we obtain

$$succ(D, e) = \texttt{canon}(\texttt{canon}((\texttt{canon}(D \wedge I(l))^{\Uparrow} \wedge I(l)) \wedge \phi)[\lambda := 0])) \wedge I(l'))$$

where $\texttt{canon}$ represents a canonization function that takes as input a DBM and returns a canonized matrix in the sense that each atomic constraint in the matrix is in the tightest form, $I(l)$ is the invariant at location l, and $\Uparrow$ denotes the elapse of time operation. Note that intersection does not preserve canonical form [5], so we should canonize $(D \wedge I(l))$ before opening the zone up using the elapse of time operation. Similarly, we should canonize $((\texttt{canon}(D \wedge I(l))^{\Uparrow} \wedge I(l)) \wedge \phi)$ before resetting any clock (if any). Since after executing the transition e all the clocks in the automaton have to advance at the same rate. Recall that when opening a zone up the upper bound of the clocks are set to ∞, and when resetting a particular clock the lower and upper bounds of that clock are set to 0. So canonization is indeed necessary at steps 2 and 6. The resulting zone at step 7 needs to be intersected with the clock invariant at the target location l' and canonizing afterwards. This is necessary in order to ensure that the guard ϕ and the reset operation ($[\lambda := 0]$) implies invariant at the target location, as the transition to l' would be disabled otherwise, and one could erroneously reach a final state with such a transition, resulting in a wrong WCET or BCET. After applying the guard and the target invariant, the matrix must be checked for consistency. Checking the consistency of a DBM is done by computing the canonical form and then checking the diagonal for negative entries.

The algorithms depicted in Figures 1 and 2 represent respectively the zone-based algorithms for calculating the BCET and WCET of real-time distributed systems. The algorithms takes as input an automaton $\mathcal{M}$ for the system to be analysed. The algorithm consists of three basic steps, computing the state space of the automaton $\mathcal{M}$, searching for the set of final states in $\mathcal{M}$, and then performing some operations on that set in order to determine the minimum and the maximum value that the additional clock x_i can reach at that set of states. Each node in the computed tree is of the form (l_i, Z_i) where l_i is a location in the automaton and Z_i is the corresponding *unapproximated* zone. It uses two data structures WAIT and PASSED to store symbolic states waiting to be examined, and the states that are already examined, respectively. The WAIT set is instantiated with the initial symbolic state (l_0, Z_0). The global variable BCET holds the currently best known shortest execution time of reaching the final location; initially it is ∞. Similarly, the global variable WCET holds the currently

best known longest execution time of reaching the final location; initially it is
0. The global clock x_i keeps track of the execution time of the system. In each
iteration of the **while** loop, the algorithm selects a symbolic state from WAIT,
checking if the state is a final state. If the state does not evolve to any new state
then we consider it as a final state of some branch in the graph. If the state
$s = (l_i, Z_i)$ is a final state we update the best known BCET to the lower bound of
x_i at Z_i if it is smaller than the current value of BCET. On the other hand, if the
state is not a final state and the lower bound of the clock x_i in the successors of
that state is less than the intermediate BCET, we add these successors to WAIT
and continue to the next iteration. Note that the algorithm computes the state
space of $\mathcal{M}$ step by step using the operation $post_a(l_i, Z_i)$ which computes the
successors of the given symbolic state (l_i, Z_i). The operation $\texttt{lowerBound}(Z, x_i)$
returns the lower bound of the clock x_i in the zone Z which is equivalent to the
value of $(-D_{0,x_i})$ in the corresponding DBM. The operation $\texttt{upperBound}(Z, x_i)$
returns the upper bound of the clock x_i in the zone Z which is equivalent to the
value of $(D_{x_i,0})$ in the corresponding DBM.

It is worth mentioning here that we treat BCET and WCET differently when
computing them. Since the computation of BCET can be improved during the
analysis. That is, during the state space exploration, if a non-final state has a lower
bound greater than the intermediate BCET, this state does not need to be explored
any further and hence we do not add its successors to the WAIT list. On the other
hand, if the WCET algorithm encounters a reachable state with unconstrained
location then the search can stop immediately since the WCET will be infinity.

Input: $(\mathcal{M})$
Output: BCET $:= \infty$
clock x_i
PASSED $:= \emptyset$, WAIT $:= \{(l_0, Z_0)\}$
while WAIT $\neq \emptyset$
 select (l, Z) from WAIT
 //Check if (l, Z) is a final node on some branch of the tree
 if for all $a \in \Sigma$ $post_a((l, Z)) = \emptyset$ **then**
  if $\texttt{lowerBound}(Z, x_i) <$ BCET **then**   BCET $:= \texttt{lowerBound}(Z, x_i)$
  add (l, Z) to PASSED
  for all (l', Z') such that $(l, Z) \rightsquigarrow (l', Z')$ **do**
 // check if lower bound of x_i in the new zone is less than the best known BCET
  if $\texttt{lowerBound}(Z', x_i) <$ BCET
   if $(Z' \setminus UC) \not\subseteq closure_\alpha(Z'' \setminus UC)$ for all $(l', Z'') \in$ PASSED
    then add (l', Z') to WAIT
return BCET

Algorithm 1. Zone-base algorithm for Computing Best-Case Execution Time

---

Efficient inclusion testing. The test of the form $Z \subseteq closure_\alpha(Z')$ used in the
proposed algorithm, where $closure_\alpha(Z')$ is the region closure of a set of valua-

---

Input: ($\mathcal{A}$)
Output: WCET := 0
clock x_i
PASSED := $\emptyset$, WAIT := $\{(l_0, Z_0)\}$
while WAIT $\neq \emptyset$
  select (l, Z) from WAIT
  //Check if (l, Z) is a final node on some branch of the tree
  if for all $a \in \Sigma$ $post_a((l, Z)) = \emptyset$ **then**
    if upperBound$(Z, x_i) >$ WCET   **then** WCET := upperBound(Z, x_i)
  add (l, Z) to PASSED
  for all $(l^{'}, Z^{'})$ such that $(l, Z) \rightsquigarrow (l^{'}, Z^{'})$ **do**
  // if the location of the new state is not guarded with an invariant
    if $upperBound(Z^{'}, x) = \infty$ **then** $\{$WCET := ∞; $WAIT := \emptyset$; break$\}$
  // Check inclusion between zones
    if $(Z^{'} \setminus UC) \not\subseteq closure_\alpha(Z^{''} \setminus UC)$ for all $(l^{'}, Z^{''}) \in$ PASSED
      then add $(l^{'}, Z^{'})$ to WAIT
return WCET

Algorithm 2. Zone-base algorithm for Computing Worst-Case Execution Time

tions $Z^{'}$, is the key difference with respect to the other standard algorithms for TA that make use the tests of the form $Approx_\alpha(Z) \subseteq Approx_\alpha(Z^{'})$. The idea is that instead of considering nodes $(l, Approx_\alpha(Z))$ with set of approximated valuations $Approx_\alpha(Z)$, one considers a union of the parts (regions) of $\mathbb{R}^X_{\geq 0}$ that intersect Z. The closure by regions of a zone Z with respect to a set of regions R is defined as the smallest set of regions from R that have a non-empty intersection with Z (i.e. $closure_R(Z) = \{m \in R \mid Z \cap m \neq \emptyset\}$) [6]. It is important to note that $Approx_\alpha(Z)$ is different than $closure_\alpha(Z)$: $Approx_\alpha(Z)$ is an approximation of a zone which can be computed using the standard normalization procedures like k-normalization and hence it is a convex whereas $closure_\alpha(Z)$ is a region closure of a zone and hence it can be non-convex [6]. As observed in [14] to decide whether a region R intersects a zone Z it is enough to verify that the projection on every pair of variables is nonempty (see proposition 1). The proofs given in [6,14] have shown that the inclusion test $Z \subseteq closure_\alpha(Z^{'})$ is sound for some operator α and is as efficient as the test $Approx_\alpha(Z) \subseteq Approx_\alpha(Z^{'})$, and hence the overall complexity for inclusion checking is still $O(|X|^2)$, where $|X|$ is the number of clocks. The advantages of this are twofold: (1) it allows us to maintain real zones which is necessary for the correctness of our analysis, and (2) it guarantees the correct termination of the search without increasing the computational complexity. Note also that the algorithm for checking $Z \subseteq closure_\alpha(Z^{'})$ neither need to represent nor to compute the closure which may not be a zone (see Theorem 1). Before adding a new state (l, Z) to WAIT we check if $(Z \setminus UC) \subseteq closure_\alpha(Z^{'} \setminus UC)$ for any state $(l, Z^{'}) \in$ WAIT since when $(Z \setminus UC) \subseteq closure_\alpha(Z^{'} \setminus UC)$ then all states reachable from (l, Z) are also reachable from $(l, Z^{'})$, and thus we only need to explore $(l, Z^{'})$, where the set UC represents the set of constraints in the zones involving the extra clocks x_i. Note that it is necessary to check inclusion between zones with respect only to the automaton clocks.

Definition 6. *Suppose we have a bound function that assigns to each clock x_i in $\mathcal{A}$ a bound $\alpha_x \in \mathbb{N}$. A region [1] with respect to α is the set of valuations specified as follows:*

1. for each clock $x \in X$, one constraint from the set: $\{x = c \mid c = 0, ..., \alpha_x\} \cup \{c - 1 < x < c \mid c = 1, ..., \alpha_x\} \cup \{x > \alpha_x\}$
2. for each pair of clocks x, y having interval constraints: $c - 1 < x < c$ and $d - 1 < y < d$, it is specified if $fract(x)$ is less than, equal or greater than $fract(y)$.

Proposition 1. *[14] Let R be a region and Z be a zone. The intersection $R \cap Z$ is empty iff there exist variables x, y such that $Z_{yx} + R_{xy} \leq (<, 0)$.*

where R_{xy} is the weight of the edge $x \xrightarrow{\prec_{xy} D_{xy}} y$ in the canonical distance graph representing R. Similarly for Z_{xy}.

Theorem 1. *[14] Let Z, Z' be zones in canonical form. Then $Z \not\subseteq closure_\alpha(Z')$ iff there exists variables x, y, both different than x_0, such that one of the following conditions holds:*

1. $Z'_{0,x} < Z_{0,x}$ and $Z'_{0,x} \leq (\alpha_x, \leq)$, or
2. $Z'_{x,0} < Z_{x,0}$ and $Z'_{x,0} \geq (-\alpha_x, \leq)$, or
3. $Z_{x,0} \geq (-\alpha_x, \leq)$ and $Z'_{x,y} < Z_{x,y}$ and $Z'_{x,y} \leq (\alpha_y, \leq) + \lfloor Z_{x,0} \rfloor$.

where $\lfloor Z_{x,0} \rfloor$ is the integral part of the entry $Z_{x,0}$ in the zone Z and α_x is the corresponding normalization constant of the clock x. Recall that the entry $Z_{x,0}$ has the form $(\lfloor Z_{x,0} \rfloor, \prec_{x,0})$. However, to implement the inclusion test given in Theorem 1 two operations on bounds are needed: comparison and addition. We define that $(n, \prec_1) < (m, \prec_2)$ if $n < m$ and $(n, <) < (n, \leq)$. Further we define addition as $n + \infty = \infty$, $(n, \leq) + (m, \leq) = (n + m, \leq)$, and $(n, <) + (m, \prec) = (n + m, <)$.

Theorem 2. *The zone-based Algorithms 1and 2 compute correctly the minimum and maximum execution times of an automaton $\mathcal{A}$ and guarantee termination.*

Note that the algorithm computes the transitive closure of $\rightsquigarrow$ step by step using the operation $post_a(l_i, Z_i)$ (while normalization is disabled) until it reaches the final state of the explored path and then checks whether the lower-bound value of the clock x_i is smaller than the best known value of BCET, therefore the algorithm guarantees to return with a correct answer. Termination is ensured since there are finitely many sets of the form $closure_{\alpha \mathcal{A}}(Z)$. Also the algorithm is guaranteed to terminate because $\rightsquigarrow$ is finite since the algorithm is working on a finite structure.

We now turn to discuss the complexity of the DBM-based algorithms. In Table 1 we summarise the necessary DBM operations used by the algorithms with their complexity. All required operations can be implemented on DBMs with satisfactory efficiency. Given the time complexity of each DBM operation performed by the algorithms we end up with a polynomial time complexity of the form given in Theorem 3, where d is the number of states in the WAIT list that have the same discrete part with the new generated state that results from executing the operation $post_a(l_i, Z_i)$, we use this for the inclusion test operation. Note that the value of d is bounded by the number of generated zones ($|Z|$) of the automaton under analysis.

Table 1. Complexity of BCET/WCET algorithms in terms of DBM operations

DBM-operation	Complexity
Inclusion test (i.e. $Z \subseteq closure_\alpha(Z')$)	$O(|X|^2)$
Consistency test	$O(|X|^2)$
Constraint satisfaction	$O(|X|^2)$
Delay	$O(|X|)$
Resetting Clocks	$O(|X|)$
Constraint intersection	$O(|X|^2)$
Canonization	$O(|X|^3)$
Clock-lower/upper bound test	$O(1)$

Theorem 3. *The BCET/WCET zone-based algorithms have a polynomial time complexity of* $O((|X|^3 + d.|X|^2).|E|.|Z|)$.

4   Implementation

In this section we briefly summarise our prototype implementation of the model checking algorithms given in Section 3.1. The prototype implementation has been developed using the opaal tool [10] which has been designed to rapidly prototype new model checking algorithms. The opaal tool is implemented in Python and is a standalone model checking engine. Models are specified using the UPPAAL XML format. The main step in the implementation of the algorithms is the representation of sets of symbolic state and the operations required on them. We use the open source UPPAAL DBM library for the internal symbolic representation of time zones in the algorithms.

5   Case Studies

We consider here a simple realistic automatic manufacturing plant taken from Daws and Yovine [11]. We first give an informal description of the case study then we give the timed automata model of the entire system in UPPAAL, and finally report on the results obtained from running the BCET/WCET algorithms on the case study when considering it under different configurations.

The manufacturing plant that we consider consists of a conveyor belt that moves from left to right, a processing or service station, and two robots that move boxes between the station and the belt. The first robot called D-Robot takes a box from the station and put it on the left end of the belt. The second robot called G-Robot picks the box from the right end of the belt and transfers it to the station to be processed. We are then interested in verifying the minimum and maximum amount of time a box can take to be processed when considering the manufacturing plant under different configurations.

The timed automaton for the D-Robot is given in Figure 1. Initially, the robot waits until a box is ready indicated by the synchronisation label **s-ready**. Next, it picks the box up, turns right and puts the box on the moving belt. It then turns left and returns to its initial position.

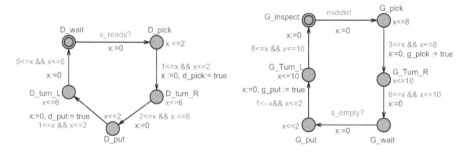

Fig. 1. The D-Robot template   **Fig. 2.** The G-Robot template

The timed automaton for the G-Robot is given in Figure 2. This robot waits at the inspection point at the right end of the belt until a box passes this point. The G-Robot must pick up the box before it falls off the end of the belt. Next, it turns right, waits for the station to finish processing the previous box and then puts the box at the station. Finally, it turns left back to the inspection point. Note that picking the box up by the robot, turning left or right takes time which depends mainly on the speed of the robot.

The timed automaton for the processing station is given in Figure 4. The station is initially empty. Once a box arrives at the station it takes around 8-10 time units to be processed. The box is then ready to be picked up by the D-Robot.

The timed automaton for the box is given in Figure 3. The box initially moves from the left end of the belt to the inspection point. It takes between 133-134 time units for the box to reach the inspection point from the left end of the belt. Then it will be picked up by the G-Robot.

Using the zone-based algorithms we could analyse the manufacturing system up to 9 processes (automata) (6 boxes, G-Robot, D-Robot, and a service station). All experiments are conducted on a PC with 32-bit Redhat Linux 7.3 with Intel (R) core CPU at 2.66 GHz and with 4 GB RAM. In Table 2 we verify the performance of the system under the following time constraints: the time required for the box to reach the inspection point is within $[133, 134]$, and the time required

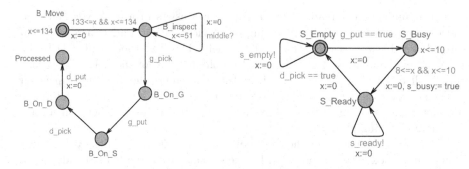

Fig. 3. The Box template   **Fig. 4.** The processing station template

Table 2. The BCET/WCET of the manufacturing system for different number of boxes where the two robots move at different speeds

No. of processes	Run-time/Memory (BCET)	Run-time/Memory (WCET)	BCET	WCET
4	0.011s/33,042KB	0.015s/38,072KB	158	171
6	0.435s/39,470KB	0.922s/45,860KB	158	185
9	55s/469,463KB	72s/524,096KB	158	215
14	205s/469,463KB	280s/524,096KB	158	325

Table 3. The BCET/WCET of the manufacturing system for different number of boxes where the two robots move at the same speed

No. of processes	Run-time/Memory (BCET)	Run-time/Memory (WCET)	BCET	WCET
4	0.01s/33,042KB	0.015s/38,072KB	149	153
6	0.435s/39,470KB	0.922s/45,860KB	149	174
9	55s/469,463KB	70s/524,096KB	149	204
14	205s/469,463KB	280s/524,096KB	149	255

to process a box at the station is within $[8, 10]$. In this configuration, we assume that the D-Robot is faster than the G-Robot in the sense that the D-Robot can turn left and right and pick up and put boxes faster than the G-Robot as shown in Figures 1 and 2. As we expect when we increase the number of boxes in the model the value of WCET varies which implies that the number of boxes in the model impacts directly the WCET. However, it is not the case for the BCET since the value of BCET does not depend on the number of boxes in the model. The reason why the BCET does not change as we increase the number of boxes is because in the best case scenario the box will be processed immediately once it arrives the service station so that there will not be any queuing delay.

In Table 3 we verify the system under the same settings used in Table 2 except that we increase the speed of the two robots and assume that both robots move at the same speed. In this configuration the time the robot takes to pick the box up or to put it down is within $[1, 2]$ time units, and the time it takes to turn left or right is within $[2, 6]$ time units. As shown in Table 3 the performance of the system under this configuration has been improved where the values of BCET and WCET decreased under this configuration.

We now compare the performance of our approach with the classical binary search approach used in [16,9] in which the user needs to repeatedly verify some parametrised temporal formulas until they hold. For example, one can use the temporal formula $\mathbf{AG}(x_i \leq p)$ to verify the upper bound for termination of the models, where $\mathbf{AG}$ are temporal operators that mean for each reachable state in the model the value of the extra clock x_i can not exceed the bound p. Using the binary search approach we could analyse the manufacturing system up to 9 processes (6 boxes, G-Robot, D-Robot, and a service station). As shown in Table 4 the binary search approach is quite competitive to our approach when considering small instances of the system. However, when considering instances with large number of processes the proposed approach outperforms the binary search approach by several order of magnitude, enabling models involving large number of processes to be model checked efficiently.

Table 4. The BCET/WCET of the manufacturing system using binary search approach for different number of boxes where the two robots move at different speeds

No. of processes	Run-time/Memory (BCET)	Run-time/Memory (WCET)	BCET	WCET
4	0.031s/58,05KB	0.055s/65,82KB	158	171
6	0.635s/256,47KB	2.922s/465,96KB	158	185
9	285s/896,463KB	425s/1026,096KB	158	215

6 Conclusion

In this work we proposed algorithms for determining the best and worst case "execution time" in timed automata by modifying the underlying model-checking algorithm, rather than analyzing those times by augmenting the models with clock variables and querying those. The proposed algorithms can successfully handle acyclic TA and TA containing cycles given that the automaton under analysis has no run of infinite length. The algorithms avoid the extra computations and the extra canonization steps that may be needed if normalization is applied at each step of the successor computation. For future work we intend to extend the algorithms to be able to correctly handle arbitrary timed automata.

References

1. Alur, R., Dill, D.: A theory of timed automata. TCS, 183–235 (1994)
2. Behrmann, G., Bouyer, P., Larsen, K.G., Radek, P.: Lower and upper bounds in zone-based abstractions of timed automata. Int. J. Softw. Tools Technol. Transf., 204–215 (2006)
3. Behrmann, G., Fehnker, A., Hune, T., Larsen, K.G., Pettersson, P., Romijn, J.: Efficient Guiding Towards Cost-Optimality in UPPAAL. In: Margaria, T., Yi, W. (eds.) TACAS 2001. LNCS, vol. 2031, pp. 174–188. Springer, Heidelberg (2001)

4. Behrmann, G., Larsen, K.G., Rasmussen, J.I.: Beyond liveness: Efficient parameter synthesis for time bounded liveness. In: Pettersson, P., Yi, W. (eds.) FORMATS 2005. LNCS, vol. 3829, pp. 81–94. Springer, Heidelberg (2005)
5. Bengtsson, J.E., Yi, W.: Timed automata: Semantics, algorithms and tools. In: Desel, J., Reisig, W., Rozenberg, G. (eds.) ACPN 2003. LNCS, vol. 3098, pp. 87–124. Springer, Heidelberg (2004)
6. Bouyer, P.: Forward analysis of updatable timed automata. Form. Methods Syst. Des. 24, 281–320 (2004)
7. Bryans, J., Bowman, H., Derrick, J.: Model checking stochastic automata. ACM Transactions on Computational Logic (TOCL) 4(4), 452–492 (2003)
8. Clarke, E.M., Grumberg, O., Peled, D.: Model checking. MIT Press (2001)
9. Dalsgaard, A.E., Olesen, M.C., Toft, M., Hansen, R.R., Larsen, K.G.: METAMOC: Modular Execution Time Analysis using Model Checking. In: WCET 2010, pp. 113–123 (2010)
10. Dalsgaard, A.E., Hansen, R.R., Jørgensen, K.Y., Larsen, K.G., Olesen, M.C., Olsen, P., Srba, J.: opaal: A lattice model checker. In: Bobaru, M., Havelund, K., Holzmann, G.J., Joshi, R. (eds.) NFM 2011. LNCS, vol. 6617, pp. 487–493. Springer, Heidelberg (2011)
11. Daws, C., Yovine, S.: Two examples of verification of multirate timed automata with kronos. In: Proceedings of the 16th IEEE Real-Time Systems Symposium, RTSS 1995. IEEE Computer Society (1995)
12. Dill, D.L.: Timing assumptions and verification of finite-state concurrent systems. In: Proceedings of the International Workshop on Automatic Verification Methods for Finite State Systems, pp. 197–212. Springer-Verlag New York, Inc. (1990)
13. Floyd, R.W.: Algorithm 97: Shortest path. Communications of the ACM (1962)
14. Herbreteau, F., Kini, D., Srivathsan, B., Walukiewicz, I.: Using non-convex approximations for efficient analysis of timed automata. In: FSTTCS (2011)
15. Horváth, A., Paolieri, M., Ridi, L., Vicario, E.: Transient analysis of non-markovian models using stochastic state classes. Performance Evaluation 69(7), 315–335 (2012)
16. Metzner, A.: Why model checking can improve WCET analysis. In: Alur, R., Peled, D.A. (eds.) CAV 2004. LNCS, vol. 3114, pp. 334–347. Springer, Heidelberg (2004)
17. Rokicki, T.G.: Representing and Modeling Digital Circuits. PhD thesis, Stanford University (1993)
18. Traonouez, L.-M., Lime, D., Roux, O.H.: Parametric model-checking of time petri nets with stopwatches using the state-class graph. In: Cassez, F., Jard, C. (eds.) FORMATS 2008. LNCS, vol. 5215, pp. 280–294. Springer, Heidelberg (2008)
19. Wilhelm, R.: Why AI + ILP is good for WCET, but MC is not, nor ILP alone. In: Steffen, B., Levi, G. (eds.) VMCAI 2004. LNCS, vol. 2937, pp. 309–322. Springer, Heidelberg (2004)

Delay-Dependent Partial Order Reduction Technique for Time Petri Nets

Hanifa Boucheneb[1,2], Kamel Barkaoui[2], and Karim Weslati[1]

[1] Laboratoire VeriForm, Department of Computer Engineering and Software Engineering,
École Polytechnique de Montréal,
P.O. Box 6079, Station Centre-ville, Montréal, Québec, H3C 3A7, Canada
hanifa.boucheneb@polymtl.ca
[2] Laboratoire CEDRIC, Conservatoire National des Arts et Métiers,
192 rue Saint Martin, Paris Cedex 03, France
kamel.barkaoui@cnam.fr

Abstract. Partial order reduction techniques aim at coping with the state explosion problem by reducing, while preserving the properties of interest, the number of transitions to be fired from each state of the model. For (time) Petri nets, the selection of these transitions is, generally, based on the structure of the (underlying) Petri net and its current marking. This paper proposes a partial order reduction technique for time Petri nets (TPN in short), where the selection procedure takes into account the structure, including the firing intervals, and the current state (i.c., the current marking and the firing delays of the enabled transitions). We show that our technique preserves non-equivalent firing sequences of the TPN. Therefore, its extension to deal with LTL_{-X} properties is straightforward, using the well established methods based on the stuttering equivalent sequences.

1 Introduction

A time Petri net (TPN in short) is a Petri net, where each transition is labelled with an interval specifying, relatively to its enabling date, its minimal and maximal firing delays. Time Petri nets are definitely established as a powerful formalism for formal verification of real time systems. The verification techniques, such as reachability analysis, are based on the so-called state space abstraction, where states reachable by the same firing sequence, but at different dates, are grouped in the same set and considered modulo some relation of equivalence (abstract states, state classes or state zones) [5,7,10,8,25]. However, for highly concurrent systems, these verification techniques face a severe problem of state space explosion. To alleviate this problem, partial order approaches are proposed in the literature for time Petri nets such as: partial order unfolding [12,13,23] and partial order reduction [14,20,19,24,26]. The idea of the unfolding techniques is to translate a TPN model into an acyclic Petri net with firing time constraints, respecting the partial order of the originate model. The available unfolding techniques are however limited to 1-safe TPNs[1]. The common characteristics of the partial order reduction methods is that they explore a subset of firing sequences (representative firing sequences) from each (abstract) state. These subsets are sufficient to verify the properties of interest.

---

[1] A 1-safe time Petri net is a 1-bounded time Petri net (i.e., each place can contain at most one token).

A. Legay and M. Bozga (Eds.): FORMATS 2014, LNCS 8711, pp. 53–68, 2014.
© Springer International Publishing Switzerland 2014

Among the TPN state space abstractions in the literature, we consider the Contracted State Class Graph (CSCG in short) [10] and investigate partial order reduction techniques, which preserve non-equivalent firing sequences of the TPN (i.e., there is no maximal firing sequence[2] in the TPN with no equivalent sequence[3] in the reduced space and vice-versa). Since the CSCG preserves markings and firing sequences of the TPN, the purpose is to select a subset of firable transitions to be explored from each state class, so as to cover all and only all non-equivalent firing sequences of the CSCG.

In almost all partial order reduction techniques, the selection procedure of representative transitions is based on an independence relation over transitions. Intuitively, two transitions are independent, if they can neither disable nor enable each other and their firings in both orders lead to the same state. If a transition is selected to be fired from a state, then all its dependent and firable transitions are selected too. Various sufficient conditions, guaranteeing an effective selection of an over-approximation of dependent transitions, are proposed in the literature such as persistent sets [14], ample sets [19,20] and stubborn sets [24]. However, in the context of the TPN state space abstractions such as the CSCG, the different interleavings of the same set of transitions lead, in general, to different abstract states and then the relation of independency is difficult to meet. To overcome this limitation, two main techniques are used in the literature: the local time semantics [3,15,18] and Partially Ordered Sets (POSETs) of transitions or events [1,16,17,26].

The local time semantics approaches suppose that the model consists of a set of components, each one is represented by a timed model (timed automaton, TPN, etc.) and has, in addition to its clocks, a reference clock. The reference clocks evolve asynchronously and are synchronized when needed (i.e., when an action of synchronization is executed). Such approaches need additional clocks and the differences between reference clocks may diverge leading to an infinite state space [17].

The partial order reduction approaches based on POSETs aim to force the independency relation by fixing partially the firing order of transitions or events [1,16,17,26]. The idea is to compute, by exploring one sequence of transitions, the convex hull of abstract states reachable by some of its equivalent sequences. However, unlike timed automata [22], for TPNs, including 1-safe TPNs, this convex hull is not necessarily the union of the abstract states reached by equivalent sequences of transitions [6]. In [26], to deal with this issue, the authors use the notion of *truth parents* and compute the union of abstract states reachable by equivalent sequences obtained by permuting some independent transitions (in the sense of stubborn sets). The notion of truth parent involves to keep, in each abstract state, in addition to time constraints of the enabled transitions, those of their parents. All the different possible parents of the enabled transitions are considered when computing successors of abstract states, as the firing delay of a transition is relative to the firing date of its parent. Moreover, the selection procedure of independent transitions takes into account neither the static nor the dynamic timing information of the model. In [16], the authors have defined a state space abstraction

---

[2] A maximal firing sequence is either infinite or finite ending up in a deadlock state (i.e., a state with no enabled transitions).

[3] Two sequences ω and ω' are equivalent (denoted $\omega \equiv \omega'$) iff ω' can be obtained from ω by successive permutations of its transitions. By convention, it holds that $\omega \equiv \omega'$.

where the firing order constraints between non-related transitions[4] are totally ignored when computing successors. The subset of transitions explored from each abstract state is a persistent set [16]. However, the state space abstraction proposed in [16] preserve neither markings nor the firing sequences of the TPN. The counterexample is given by the TPN at Fig.1.a.

In this paper, we propose a partial order reduction technique based on POSETs and whose selection procedure of representative transitions takes into account the static and dynamic firing intervals of transitions. We show that the resulting reduced graph preserves non-equivalent sequences of the TPN. So, the extension of the verification approach proposed here to LTL_{-X}[5] properties over markings could be achieved as shown in [24].

The rest of the paper is organized as follows. Section 2 is devoted to TPN, its semantics and its CSCG. Section 3 defines the notions of partial order successor and reduced state class graph. Section 4 is devoted to our reduced state class graph and the proof that it preserves the non-equivalent firing sequences of the TPN. Section 5 reports some experimental results. Finally, the conclusion is presented in Section 6.

2   Time Petri Nets

2.1   Definition and Semantics

Let P be a nonempty set. A multi-set over P is a function $M : P \longrightarrow \mathbb{N}$, $\mathbb{N}$ being the set of natural numbers, defined also by the formal sum: $\sum_{p \in P} M(p) \bullet p$ [6].

We denote P_{MS} and 0 the set of all multi-sets over P and the empty multi-set, respectively. Let $M_1 \in P_{MS}$, $M_2 \in P_{MS}$ and $\prec \in \{\leq, =, <, >, \geq\}$. Operations on multi-sets are defined as usual:

1) $\forall p \in P$, $p \in M_1$ iff $M_1(p) > 0$;
2) $M_1 + M_2 = \sum_{p \in P} (M_1(p) + M_2(p)) \bullet p$;

3) $M_1 \prec M_2$ iff $\forall p \in P, M_1(p) \prec M_2(p)$;
4) $M_1 \nprec M_2$ iff not $(M_1 \prec M_2)$;

5) $M_1 \times M_2 = \sum_{p \in P} Min(M_1(p), M_2(p)) \bullet p$;

If the multi-sets M_1 and M_2 are s.t. $M_1 \leq M_2$, then $M_2 - M_1$ is the multi-set defined by: $\sum_{p \in P} (M_2(p) - M_1(p)) \bullet p$.

Let $\mathbb{Q}^+$ and $\mathbb{R}^+$ be the sets of non-negative rational and real numbers, respectively, and $INT_{\mathbb{X}} = \{[a, b] | (a, b) \in \mathbb{X} \times (\mathbb{X} \cup \{\infty\})\}$, for $\mathbb{X} \in \{\mathbb{Q}^+, \mathbb{R}^+\}$, the set of intervals whose lower and upper bounds are in $\mathbb{X}$ and $\mathbb{X} \cup \{\infty\}$, respectively.

Definition 1. *A time Petri net is a tuple $\mathcal{N} = (P, T, pre, post, M_0, Is)$ where P and T are finite and nonempty sets of places and transitions s.t. $P \cap T = \emptyset$; pre and post are the backward and forward incidence functions (pre, post : $T \longrightarrow P_{MS}$); $M_0 \in P_{MS}$ is the initial marking; Is is the static firing function (Is : $T \to INT_{Q^+}$). $\downarrow Is(t)$ and $\uparrow Is(t)$ denote the lower and upper bounds of the static firing interval of transition t.*

---

[4] Transitions are non-related if no one is enabled by the others.
[5] LTL_{-X} properties are LTL properties where the next operator X is forbidden.
[6] The symbol $\bullet$ is an optional separator between elements of M and their occurrence numbers.

For $t \in T$, $Adj(t) = \{t' \in T \mid (pre(t) + post(t)) \times (pre(t') + post(t')) \neq 0\}$ denotes the set of transitions connected with t via some place (adjacent transitions).

Several semantics are proposed in the literature for the TPN model [4,9,11]. An overview and a classification of the TPN semantics can be found in [9]. They differ mainly in the interpretation of the notion of newly enabled transition, the characterization of states and the server policy. The notion of newly enabled transitions may refer to the intermediate markings (markings resulting from the consumption of tokens) or the markings before or after firings (intermediate or atomic firing semantics) [4]. The timing information is either associated with transitions represented by clocks or delays (threshold semantics) or tokens represented by clocks giving their ages (age semantics) [11]. The service policy specifies whether several enabling instances of the same transition may be handled simultaneously (multiple-server semantics) or not (single-server semantics). We consider here the classical and widely used semantics (i.e., the threshold, intermediate and single-server semantics).

Each marking of $\mathcal{N}$ is a multi-set over P. Let M be a marking of $\mathcal{N}$ and $t \in T$ a transition. The transition t is enabled at marking M, denoted $M[t\rangle$ iff all required tokens for firing t are present in M, i.e., $M \geq pre(t)$. In case t is enabled at M, its firing leads to the marking $M' = M - pre(t) + post(t)$. The notation $M[t\rangle M'$ means that t is enabled at M and M' is the marking reached from M by t. We denote by $En(M)$ the set of transitions enabled at M, i.e., $En(M) = \{t \in T \mid M \geq pre(t)\}$.

For $t \in En(M)$, we denote by $CF(M, t)$ the set of transitions enabled at M but in conflict with t, i.e., $CF(M, t) = \{t' \in En(M) \mid t' = t \vee M \not\geq pre(t) + pre(t')\}$.

For any sequence $t_1 t_2 ... t_n \in T^+$, the usual notation $M[t_1 t_2 ... t_n\rangle$ means that there are markings $M_1, ..., M_n$ so that $M_1 = M$ and $M_i[t_i\rangle M_{i+1}$, for $i \in [1, n-1]$ and $M_n[t_n\rangle$. The notation $M[t_1 t_2 ... t_n\rangle M'$ gives, in addition, the marking reached by the sequence.

Let M' be the successor marking of M by t. We denote by $Nw(M, t)$ the set of transitions newly enabled at the marking M' reached from M by firing t. Formally, $Nw(M, t)$ contains t, if t is enabled at M', and also all transitions enabled at the marking M' but not enabled at the intermediate marking $M - pre(t)$, i.e.,
$Nw(M, t) = \{t' \in En(M') \mid t' = t \vee M - pre(t) \not\geq pre(t')\}$.

Starting from the initial marking M_0, the marking of $\mathcal{N}$ evolves by firing transitions at irregular intervals of time. When a transition t is newly enabled, its firing interval is set to its static firing interval. Bounds of its interval decrease synchronously with time until it is fired or disabled by a conflicting firing. Transition t is firable, if the lower bound of its firing interval reaches 0. It must fire immediately, without any additional delay, when the upper bound of its firing interval reaches 0, unless it is disabled by another firing. The firing of a transition takes no time but leads to a new marking.

Syntactically, in the context of $\mathcal{N}$, a state is defined as a pair $s = (M, I)$, where M is a marking and I is a firing interval function ($I: En(M) \rightarrow INT_{R+}$). The initial state of $\mathcal{N}$ is $s_0 = (M_0, I_0)$, where $I_0(t) = Is(t)$, for all $t \in En(M_0)$.

Let $\mathcal{S} = \{(M, I) \mid M \in P_{MS} \wedge I: En(M) \rightarrow INT_{R+}\}$ be the set of all syntactically correct states, $s = (M, I)$ and $s' = (M', I')$ two states of $\mathcal{S}$, $dh \in \mathbb{R}^+$ a nonnegative real number, $t \in T$ a transition and $\rightarrow$ the transition relation defined by:

- $s \xrightarrow{dh} s'$ (s' is also denoted $s + dh$) iff the state s' is reachable from state s by dh time units, i.e., $\forall t \in En(M), dh \leq \uparrow I(t), M' = M$ and
$\forall t' \in En(M'), I'(t') = [Max(0, \downarrow I(t') - dh), \uparrow I(t') - dh]$.
- $s \xrightarrow{t} s'$ iff t is immediately firable from s and its firing leads to s', i.e.,
$t \in En(M), \quad \downarrow I(t) = 0, \quad M' = M - pre(t) + post(t)$, and

$$\forall t' \in En(M'), I'(t') = \begin{cases} Is(t') & \text{if } t' \in Nw(M, t) \\ I(t') & \text{otherwise.} \end{cases}$$

The semantics of $\mathcal{N}$ is defined by the transition system $(S, \rightarrow, s_0)$, where $S \subseteq \mathcal{S}$ is the set of all states reachable from s_0 by $\xrightarrow{*}$ (the reflexive and transitive closure of $\rightarrow$).

A *run* in $(S, \rightarrow, s_0)$, starting from a state s_1 of S, is a maximal sequence $\rho = s_1 \xrightarrow{dh_1} s_1 + dh_1 \xrightarrow{t_1} s_2 \xrightarrow{dh_2} s_2 + dh_2 \xrightarrow{t_2} s_3....$ By convention, for any state s_i, relation $s_i \xrightarrow{0} s_i$ holds. Sequences $dh_1 t_1 dh_2 t_2...$ and $t_1 t_2...$ are called the timed trace and firing sequence (untimed trace) of ρ, respectively. The total elapsed time during the run ρ, denoted $time(\rho)$, is $\sum_{i=1,|\rho|} dh_i$, where $|\rho|$ is the length of the firing sequence of ρ.

An infinite run ρ is diverging if $time(\rho) = \infty$, otherwise it is said to be zeno. Runs of $\mathcal{N}$ are all runs of the initial state s_0. A TPN model is said to be non-zeno if all its runs are non-zeno. We consider here only non-zeno TPNs. This restriction ensures that each enabled transition will eventually become firable in the future, unless it is disabled by a conflicting transition. The *timed language* of $\mathcal{N}$ is the set of its timed traces. A marking M is reachable in $\mathcal{N}$ iff $\exists s \in S$ s.t. the marking of s is M.

2.2   Contracted State Class Graph

Let $\mathcal{N} = (P, T, pre, post, M_0, Is)$ be a TPN. Several state space abstractions have been proposed in the literature for $\mathcal{N}$: the *State Class Graph (SCG)* [5], the *Contracted State Class Graph (CSCG)* [10], the *Geometric Region Graph (GRG)* [25], the *Strong State Class Graph (SSCG)* [5], the *Zone Based Graph (ZBG)* [7] and the *Atomic State Class Graphs (ASCGs)* [5,8,25]. In such abstractions, all states grouped in the same node share the same marking and the union of their time domains is represented by a consistent conjunction of atomic constraints[7]. From the practical point of view, every conjunction of atomic constraints is represented by means of a *Difference Bound Matrix* (DBM) [2]. Although the same nonempty domain may be encoded by different conjunction of atomic constraints, their DBMs have a canonical form. The canonical form of a DBM is the representation with tightest bounds on all differences between variables, computed by propagating the effect of each entry through the DBM. Two conjunctions of atomic constraints are equivalent (i.e., represent the same domain) iff their DBMs have the same canonical form. Canonical forms make operations over formulas much simpler [2].

Among these abstractions, we consider the CSCG. The CSCG is the quotient graph of the SCG [5] w.r.t. some relation of equivalence over state classes of the SCG [10]. Intuitively, this relation groups together all state classes, which have the same marking

---

[7] An atomic constraint is a constraint of the form $x \prec c, -x \prec c$ or $x - y \prec c$, where x, y are real-valued variables, $\prec \in \{<, =, \leq, \geq, >\}$ and $c \in \mathbb{Q} \cup \{\infty, -\infty\}$ is a rational number.

and triangular constraints[8], but not necessarily the same simple atomic constraints[9]. The CSCG and SCG have the same reachable markings and firing sequences [10]. In other words, the CSCG preserves markings and firing sequences of the SCG, which, in turn, preserves markings and firing sequences of $\mathcal{N}$ [5]. The CSCG of $\mathcal{N}$ is finite iff $\mathcal{N}$ is bounded (i.e. has a finite number of reachable markings).

Syntactically, a CSCG state class is defined as a pair $\alpha = (M, F)$, where M is a marking and F is a consistent conjunction of triangular atomic constraints over firing delays of transitions enabled at M. The formula F characterizes the union of firing time domains of all states within α. By convention, $F = true$ if the number of enabled transitions at M is less than 2 (i.e., there is no triangular atomic constraint in F). A state $s' = (M', I')$ belongs to α iff $M = M'$ and its firing time domain (i.e.,
$\bigwedge_{t \in En(M')} \downarrow I'(t) \leq t \leq \uparrow I'(t)$) is included in the firing time domain of α (i.e., F).

The CSCG initial state class is $\alpha_0 = (M_0, F_0)$, where

$$F_0 = \bigwedge_{t,t' \in En(M_0) \text{ s.t. } t \neq t'} t - t' \leq \uparrow Is(t) - \downarrow Is(t'),$$

t and t' being real-valued variables representing firing delays of transitions t and t', respectively. It keeps only the triangular atomic constraints of the SCG initial state class.

Let $\mathcal{C}_S$ be the set of all syntactically correct CSCG state classes and $succ$ a successor function from $\mathcal{C}_S \times T$ to $\mathcal{C}_S \cup \{\emptyset\}$ defined by: $\forall \alpha \in \mathcal{C}_S, \forall t_f \in T$,

- $succ(\alpha, t_f) \neq \emptyset$ (i.e., t_f is firable from α) iff $t_f \in En(M)$ and the following formula is consistent (its domain is not empty): $F \wedge (\bigwedge_{t \in En(M)} t_f - t \leq 0)$.
  Intuitively, this formula, called the firing condition of t_f from α, means that t_f is firable from α before all other transitions enabled at M. In other words, there is at least a valuation of firing delays in F s.t. t_f has the smallest firing delay.
- If $succ(\alpha, t_f) \neq \emptyset$ then $succ(\alpha, t_f) = (M', F')$, where:
  $M' = M - pre(t_f) + post(t_f)$ and F' is computed in three steps:
  1) Set F' to $F \wedge \bigwedge_{t \in En(M)} t_f - t \leq 0 \wedge \bigwedge_{t' \in Nw(M,t_f)} \downarrow Is(t') \leq t'^f - t_f \leq \uparrow Is(t')$
  (Variables t'^f for $t' \in Nw(M, t_f)$ are new variables introduced for representing the firing delays of the newly enabled transitions. The notation t'^f allows to deal with the situation where t' is enabled before firing t_f and newly enabled by t_f (i.e. $t' \in CF(M, t_f) \cap Nw(M, t_f)$). The new instance of t' is temporally represented by t'^f, in this step);
  2) Put F' in canonical form[10] and eliminate all transitions of $CF(M, t_f)$;
  3) Rename each t'^f into t'.

Let $\alpha = (M, F) \in \mathcal{C}_S$. We denote by $Fr(\alpha) = \{t \in T \mid succ(\alpha, t) \neq \emptyset\}$ the set of transitions firable from α. The function $succ$ is extended to sequences of transitions as follows: $\forall \omega \in T^*$, $succ(\alpha, \omega) = succ(succ(\alpha, \omega_1), \omega_2)$, where $\omega = \omega_1 \omega_2$ and, by

---

[8] A triangular atomic constraint is an atomic constraint of the form $x - y \prec c$.

[9] A triangular atomic constraint is an atomic constraint of the form $x \prec c$ or $-x \prec c$.

[10] The canonical form of F' is the formula corresponding to the canonical form of its DBM.

convention, $succ(\alpha, \epsilon) = \alpha$, ϵ being the empty sequence. We denote by $||\omega|| \subseteq T$ the set of transitions appearing in ω.

The CSCG of $\mathcal{N}$ is the structure $\mathbb{C} = (\mathcal{C}, succ, \alpha_0)$, where α_0 is the initial CSCG state class of $\mathcal{N}$ and $\mathcal{C}$ is the set of state classes accessible from α_0 by applying repeatedly the successor function $succ$, i.e., $\mathcal{C} = \{\alpha \in \mathcal{C}_S | \exists \omega \in T^*, \alpha = succ(\alpha_0, \omega) \neq \emptyset\}$. A sequence $\omega \in T^+$ is a firing sequence of $\mathbb{C}$ iff $succ(\alpha_0, \omega) \neq \emptyset$.

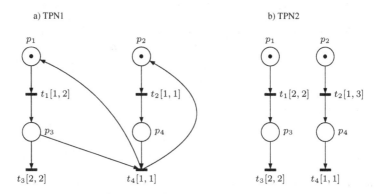

Fig. 1. Two simple TPNs

Example 1. Consider the model $TPN2$ at Fig.1.b. Its CSCG initial state class is: $\alpha_0 = (p_1 + p_2, -1 \leq t_1 - t_2 \leq 1)$. There are two enabled transitions t_1 and t_2, which are also firable from α_0, since their firing conditions $-1 \leq t_1 - t_2 \leq 1 \wedge t_1 \leq t_2$ and $-1 \leq t_1 - t_2 \leq 1 \wedge t_2 \leq t_1$ are consistent. For instance, let us compute the successor of α_0 by t_1. The firing of t_1 leads to the state class $\alpha_1 = (p_2 + p_3, -2 \leq t_2 - t_3 \leq -1)$. Its marking is computed as usual. Its formula is computed in three steps:

1) Set the formula to the firing condition of t_1 from α_0 augmented with time constraints of transition t_3 newly enabled by t_1: $-1 \leq t_1 - t_2 \leq 1 \wedge t_1 \leq t_2 \wedge t_3^1 - t_1 = 2$;
2) Put the formula in canonical form and eliminate t_1: $-2 \leq t_2 - t_3^1 \leq -1$;
3) Rename t_3^1 in t_3: $-2 \leq t_2 - t_3 \leq -1$.

Following the same procedure, we obtain $succ(\alpha, t_1 t_2) = (p_3 + p_4, 0 \leq t_3 - t_4 \leq 1)$ and $succ(\alpha, t_2 t_1) = (p_3 + p_4, 1 \leq t_3 - t_4 \leq 2)$.

3 Partial Order Reduction Based on POSETs

3.1 Partial Order Successors and Reduced State Class Graphs

The idea of partial order successors is to relax the firing condition of a transition by eliminating some firing order constraints when computing successors of state classes. The aim is to handle concisely the equivalent sequences of transitions, obtained by permuting some independent transitions (i.e., partially ordered sets of transitions). As a result, the union of state classes reached by all these sequences is computed by exploring only one of them.

Definition 2. *Let* $\alpha = (M, F)$ *be a state class of* C_S, $t_f \in T$ *a transition and* $X \subseteq$ *T a subset of transitions. The partial order successor of* α *by* t_f *w.r.t.* X, *denoted* $succ_X(\alpha, t_f)$, *is either equal* $\emptyset$ *or a state class of* C_S *defined by:*

$$succ_X(\alpha, t_f) \neq \emptyset \text{ iff } X \subseteq En(M) \wedge succ(\alpha, t_f) \neq \emptyset.$$

If $succ_X(\alpha, t_f) \neq \emptyset$ *then the state class* $\alpha' = succ_X(\alpha, t_f)$ *is computed as* $succ(\alpha, t_f)$, *except that the firing condition, used in step 1, is replaced with:* $F \wedge \bigwedge\limits_{t \in X} t_f \leq t$.

Formally, If $succ_X(\alpha, t_f) \neq \emptyset$ *then* $succ_X(\alpha, t_f) = (M', F')$, *where* $M' = M - pre(t_f) + post(t_f)$ *and* F' *is computed in three steps:*
1) Set F' *to* $F \wedge \bigwedge\limits_{t \in X} t_f \leq t \wedge \bigwedge\limits_{t' \in Nw(M, t_f)} \downarrow Is(t') \leq t'^f - t_f \leq \uparrow Is(t')$;
2) Put F' *in canonical form and eliminate all transitions of* $CF(M, t_f)$;
3) Rename each t'^f *in* t'.
The formula used in step 1, called the processing formula of $succ_X(\alpha, t_f)$, *does not impose any firing order between* t_f *and transitions of* $En(M) - X$. *Therefore, it holds that* $\forall t_f \in T, succ(\alpha, t_f) \subseteq succ_X(\alpha, t_f)$ *and* $succ_{En(M)}(\alpha, t_f) = succ(\alpha, t_f)$.

Example 2. Consider the model $TPN2$ at Fig.1.b and its initial state class $\alpha_0 = (p_1 + p_2, -1 \leq t_1 - t_2 \leq 1)$. Transitions t_1 and t_2 are both enabled and firable from α_0. Therefore, $succ_{\{t_1\}}(\alpha_0, t_1) \neq \emptyset$ and $succ_{\{t_2\}}(\alpha_0, t_2) \neq \emptyset$. For instance, $succ_{\{t_1\}}(\alpha_0, t_1)$ is the state class $\alpha'_1 = (M'_1, F'_1)$, where $M_1 = p_2 + p_3$ and F'_1 is computed in three steps:
1) Set F'_1 to $-1 \leq t_1 - t_2 \leq 1 \wedge t_3^n - t_1 = 2$;
2) Put the formula in canonical form and eliminate t_1: $-3 \leq t_2 - t_3^n \leq -1$;
3) Rename t_3^n in t_3: $-3 \leq t_2 - t_3 \leq -1$.
The partial order successor of α'_1 by t_2 w.r.t. $\{t_2\}$ is $\alpha'_2 = (p_3 + p_4, 0 \leq t_3 - t_4 \leq 2)$, where its formula F'_2 is computed in three steps:
1) Set F'_2 to $-3 \leq t_2 - t_3 \leq -1 \wedge t_4^n - t_2 = 1$;
2) Put the formula in canonical form and eliminate t_1: $0 \leq t_3 - t_4^n \leq 2$;
3) Rename t_4^n in t_4: $0 \leq t_3 - t_4 \leq 2$.
Note that $succ_{\{t_2\}}(succ_{\{t_1\}}(\alpha_0, t_1), t_2) = succ(\alpha_0, t_1 t_2) \cup succ(\alpha_0, t_2 t_1)$. Therefore, $succ(succ_{\{t_2\}}(succ_{\{t_1\}}(\alpha_0, t_1), t_2), t_3)$ gives the union of state classes reached by sequences $t_1 t_2 t_3$ and $t_2 t_1 t_3$. The union of these sequences can be represented by the partially ordered set $(\{t_1, t_2, t_3\}, t_1 \leq t_3 \wedge t_2 \leq t_3)$.

We provide, in the following, some relationships between successors and partial order successors of state classes, which will be helpful to establish a partial order reduction technique and prove that it preserves the non-equivalent firing sequences of the TPN. Let us first define the notion of *effect-independent* transitions used in our partial order reduction technique (instead of the notion of truth parent [26]).

Definition 3. *Let* $\alpha = (M, F) \in C_S$ *be a state class,* $t_i \in Fr(\alpha)$ *and* $t_j \in Fr(\alpha)$ *two transitions firable from* α. *Let* M_i *and* M_j *be the successor markings of* M *by* t_i *and* t_j, *respectively. Transitions* t_i *and* t_j *are effect-independent in* α, *denoted* $t_i \|_\alpha t_j$ *iff their effects are independent of their firing order, i.e.,*

$$CF(M, t_i) = CF(M_j, t_i) \wedge CF(M, t_j) = CF(M_i, t_j) \wedge$$
$$Nw(M, t_i) = Nw(M_j, t_i) \wedge Nw(M, t_j) = Nw(M_i, t_j).$$

Note that the relation $\|_\alpha$ is symmetric (i.e., $t_i\|_\alpha t_j$ iff $t_j\|_\alpha t_i$).

Lemma 1. *Let $\alpha = (M, F) \in \mathcal{C}_S$, $t_i \in Fr(\alpha)$, M_i the successor marking of M by t_i, and $X \subseteq En(M)$ s.t. $CF(M, t_i) \subseteq X$.*
(i) $\forall t_j \in X \cap En(M_i)$, $succ(succ_X(\alpha, t_i), t_j) = succ(\alpha, t_i t_j)$ and
(ii) $\forall t_j \in Fr(\alpha) - X$, s.t. $X \cap CF(M, t_j) = \emptyset \wedge t_i\|_\alpha t_j$,
$$succ(succ_X(\alpha, t_i), t_j) = succ(\alpha, t_i t_j) \cup succ_X(succ(\alpha, t_j), t_i)$$

Proof. The transition t_i is firable from α. Then, $succ(\alpha, t_i) \neq \emptyset$ and $succ_X(\alpha, t_i) \neq \emptyset$.
(i) The processing formula of $succ(succ_X(\alpha, t_i), t_j)$, denoted ϕ, is:

$$(F \wedge \bigwedge_{t \in X} t_i \le t \wedge \bigwedge_{t' \in Nw(M, t_i)} \downarrow Is(t') \le t'^i - t_i \le\uparrow Is(t')) \wedge$$
$$(\bigwedge_{t \in En(M_i) - Nw(M, t_i)} t_j \le t \wedge \bigwedge_{t' \in Nw(M, t_i)} t_j \le t'^i \wedge \bigwedge_{t' \in Nw(M_i, t_j)} \downarrow Is(t') \le t'^j - t_j \le\uparrow Is(t')).$$

By assumption, $t_j \in X \cap En(M_i)$. There are two cases: $t_j \in X \cap Nw(M, t_i)$ (i.e., t_j is newly enabled at M_i) and $t_j \in (En(M) - CF(M, t_i)) \cap X$ (i.e., t_j is not newly enabled at M_i but belongs to X). In both cases, it holds that $(\phi \wedge t_i \le t_j) \equiv \phi$. By definition, $En(M_i) = (En(M) - CF(M, t_i)) + Nw(M, t_i)$. Therefore, the following constraints of ϕ: $t_i \le t_j \wedge t_j \le t$, for $t \in En(M) - CF(M, t_i)$ imply $t_i \le t$ for $t \in En(M) - CF(M, t_i)$. Adding these redundant constraints to ϕ does not affect its domain. Since $CF(M, t_i) \subseteq X$, $En(M) = (En(M) \cap X) \cup (En(M) - CF(M, t_i))$ and then ϕ is equivalent to:

$$(F \wedge \bigwedge_{t \in En(M)} t_i \le t \wedge \bigwedge_{t' \in Nw(M, t_i)} \downarrow Is(t') \le t'^i - t_i \le\uparrow Is(t')) \wedge$$
$$(\bigwedge_{t \in En(M_i) - Nw(M, t_i)} t_j \le t \wedge \bigwedge_{t' \in Nw(M, t_i)} t_j \le t'^i \wedge \bigwedge_{t' \in Nw(M_i, t_j)} \downarrow Is(t') \le t'^j - t_j \le\uparrow Is(t')).$$

Therefore, $succ(succ_X(\alpha, t_i), t_j) = succ(\alpha, t_i t_j)$.
(ii) By assumption, $t_i \in Fr(\alpha)$, $t_j \in Fr(\alpha) - X$ and $CF(M, t_i) \subseteq X$. Then, $succ(\alpha, t_i t_j) \neq \emptyset$ and $succ(\alpha, t_i t_j) \subseteq succ(succ_X(\alpha, t_i), t_j) \neq \emptyset$. Consider now the processing formula above ϕ of $succ(succ_X(\alpha, t_i), t_j)$. It holds that $\phi \equiv ((\phi \wedge t_i \le t_j) \vee (\phi \wedge t_j \le t_i))$. Following the same steps as in (i), we show that $(\phi \wedge t_i \le t_j)$ is equivalent to the firing condition of $succ(\alpha, t_i t_j)$. For $(\phi \wedge t_j \le t_i)$, by definition, $En(M_i) = (En(M) - CF(M, t_i)) + Nw(M, t_i)$ and, by assumption, $X \cap CF(M, t_j) = \emptyset$. Therefore, the following constraints of ϕ: $t_j \le t_i \wedge t_i \le t$, for $t \in X$ imply $t_j \le t$ for $t \in X$. Adding these redundant constraints to $\phi \wedge t_j \le t_i$ does not affect its domain. Since $CF(M, t_i) \subseteq X \subseteq En(M)$, $En(M) = (En(M) - CF(M, t_i)) \cup X$, we can state that $\phi \wedge t_j \le t_i$ is equivalent to:

$$(F \wedge \bigwedge_{t \in X} t_i \le t \wedge \bigwedge_{t' \in Nw(M, t_i)} \downarrow Is(t') \le t'^i - t_i \le\uparrow Is(t')) \wedge$$
$$(\bigwedge_{t \in En(M)} t_j \le t \wedge \bigwedge_{t' \in Nw(M_i, t_j)} \downarrow Is(t') \le t'^j - t_j \le\uparrow Is(t')).$$

Let M_j be the successor marking of M by t_j. By assumption, $t_i \|_\alpha t_j$ and $X \subseteq (En(M) - CF(M, t_j))$. It follows that $X \subseteq En(M_j)$ and then $\phi \wedge t_j \le t_i$ is equivalent to the processing formula of $succ_X(succ(\alpha, t_j), t_i)$. Consequently, $succ(succ_X(\alpha, t_i), t_j) = succ(\alpha, t_i t_j) \cup succ_X(succ(\alpha, t_j), t_i)$. □

Intuitively, given a selection procedure (over state classes) of the representative transitions, a reduced state class graph based on POSETs is generated by first computing the partial order successors of the initial state class, by its selected transitions w.r.t. themselves, and then repeating the procedure for each computed but not processed state class.

Definition 4. *Let* $\mathbb{C} = (\mathcal{C}, succ, \alpha_0)$ *be the CSCG of a TPN* $\mathcal{N}$ *and* G *a function from* $\mathcal{C}_S$ *to* 2^T *called a partial order generator. The reduced state class graph (RSCG for short) generated by* G *is the tuple* $\mathbb{R} = (G, \mathcal{C}_G, succ_G, \alpha_0)$, *where* $\mathcal{C}_G = \{\alpha | \alpha_0 \xrightarrow{*}_G \alpha\}$ *is the set of reachable state classes in* $\mathbb{R}$ *and* $\xrightarrow{*}_G$ *is the reflexive and transitive closure of the transition relation* $\longrightarrow_G$ *defined by:* $\forall \alpha, \alpha' \in \mathcal{C}_S, \forall t_f \in T,$

$$\alpha \xrightarrow{t_f}_G \alpha' \text{ iff } t_f \in G(\alpha) \wedge succ(\alpha, t_f) \neq \emptyset \wedge \alpha' = succ_{G(\alpha)}(\alpha, t_f).$$

Let $\alpha \in \mathcal{C}_G$ *and* $\omega = t_1 t_2 ... t_n$ *be a sequence of transitions. We write* $\alpha \xrightarrow{\omega}_G \alpha_n$ *iff* $\exists \alpha_1, \alpha_2, ..., \alpha_n \in \mathcal{C}_G$ *s.t.* $\alpha \xrightarrow{t_1}_G \alpha_1 \xrightarrow{t_2}_G \alpha_2 ... \xrightarrow{t_n}_G \alpha_n$, *with* $\alpha_n = succ_G(\alpha, \omega).$

The RSCG $\mathbb{R}$ *preserves the non-equivalent sequences of the CSCG* $\mathbb{C}$ *iff for each maximal sequence of* $\mathbb{R}$, *there is an equivalent sequence in* $\mathbb{C}$ *and vice-versa.*

4   RSCG Preserving Non-equivalent Sequences of $\mathcal{N}$

We propose, in the following, a partial order generator G and show that it results in a RSCG preserving non-equivalent sequences of the CSCG. The proposed generator takes into account the structure of the TPN, including the static firing intervals of transitions, the marking and the firing domain of the current state class. The timing information derived from the structure of the TPN is captured in a matrix called the delay lower bound matrix.

4.1   Delay Lower Bound Matrix of $\mathcal{N}$

According to the TPN semantics, when a transition t_j is fired, the conflicting transitions are disabled and new transitions may be enabled. The firing delay interval of each newly enabled transition t_i refers to its enabling date (i.e., the firing date of t_j). The lower bound of the firing delay of transition t_i relatively to the firing date of t_j is $\downarrow Is(t_i)$. We define the delay lower bound matrix L as a square matrix over the set of transitions T, where: $\forall t_i, t_j \in T,$

$$l_{ij} = \begin{cases} 0 & \text{if } t_i = t_j \\ \downarrow Is(t_i) & \text{if } t_i \neq t_j \wedge pre(t_i) \times post(t_j) \neq 0 \\ \infty & \text{otherwise.} \end{cases}$$

We denote by $\bar{L}$ the canonical form of L obtained by applying the Floyd-Warshall's shortest path algorithm. This algorithm converges, as the lower bounds of the static firing intervals are non-negative finite rational numbers. Intuitively, $\bar{l}_{ij}$ is a lower bound of the firing delay of the transition t_i, relatively to the firing date of the transition t_j, for the case where t_i is not enabled when t_j is fired. Note that $\bar{l}_{ij} = \infty$ means that there is no path connecting t_j to t_i and then t_i cannot be enabled directly or indirectly by t_j.

Table 1. Firing delay lower bound matrix of the TPN1 at Fig.1.a and its canonical form

L	t_1	t_2	t_3	t_4		$\bar{L}$	t_1	t_2	t_3	t_4
t_1	0	∞	∞	1		t_1	0	2	∞	1
t_2	∞	0	∞	2		t_2	2	0	∞	1
t_3	1	∞	0	∞		t_3	2	4	0	3
t_4	2	2	∞	0		t_4	1	1	∞	0

Example 3. Table 1 reports the matrices L and $\bar{L}$ of the TPN at Fig.1.a. For instance, the value 2 of $\bar{l}_{21}$ is a lower bound of the firing delay of t_2, relatively to the firing date of t_1, in case t_2 is not enabled when t_1 is fired. It corresponds to the potential situation where t_1 enables t_4, which, in turn, enables t_2 (i.e., $\bar{l}_{21} = l_{24} + l_{41} = \downarrow Is(t_2) + \downarrow Is(t_4)$). Note that a lower bound of the enabling delay of t_2 relatively to the firing date of t_1, in case t_2 is not enabled when t_1 is fired, is $\bar{l}_{21} - \downarrow Is(t_2) = 1$.

4.2 Computing a Partial Order Generator G

Several algorithms have been proposed in the literature to compute partial order generator G for the RSCG preserving different kinds of properties such as deadlocks and LTL_{-X} properties. In general, these algorithms infer G from the static structure of the model, without taking into account the timing information. We propose here an algorithm for computing G inspired from the stubborn sets method [24,26], but does not use the notion of truth parent [26]. It uses instead the notion of effect-independent transitions and the (static and dynamic) timing information of the model. For each state class, the idea is to select a firable transition and recursively select all enabled transitions which may affect directly/indirectly the effects of the selected ones, until reaching a fix point. Formally, let $\alpha = (M, F)$ be a state class, D the canonical form of F (i.e., $d_{ij} = Max(t_i - t_j | F)$, for $t_i, t_j \in En(M)$). The set $G(\alpha)$ is the smallest set of transitions of $En(M)$, which satisfies all the following conditions:

C0: $Fr(\alpha) \neq \emptyset \Leftrightarrow G(\alpha) \cap Fr(\alpha) \neq \emptyset$.
C1: $\forall t_i \in G(\alpha), CF(M, t_i) \subseteq G(\alpha)$.
C2: $\forall t_i \in G(\alpha), \forall t_j \in En(M),$
     $\forall t_k \in Adj(t_i) - En(M), \bar{l}_{kj} - \downarrow Is(t_k) \leq d_{ij} \Rightarrow t_j \in G(\alpha),$
C3: $\forall t_i \in G(\alpha), \forall t_j \in Fr(\alpha), \ not(t_i \|_\alpha t_j) \Rightarrow t_j \in G(\alpha)$ and
C4: $\forall t_i \in G(\alpha), \forall t_j \in En(M), \ t_i \notin Fr(\alpha) \wedge t_j \in Fr(\alpha) \Rightarrow t_j \in G(\alpha)$.

We denote by **SC** the conjunction $C0 \wedge C1 \wedge C2 \wedge C3 \wedge C4$. Intuitively, C0 ensures that $G(\alpha)$ is empty only for deadlock state classes. Condition C1 means that there is no transition outside $G(\alpha)$ in conflict, in M, with a transition of $G(\alpha)$. Therefore, the firing of any transition outside $G(\alpha)$ will not disable any transition of $G(\alpha)$. Condition C2 ensures that during the enabledness of any transition t_i of $G(\alpha)$, no transition t_j outside $G(\alpha)$ may enable directly/indirectly a transition which is adjacent to t_i. Conditions C2 and C3 implies that the effect of t_i will not be affected by firing any transition outside $G(\alpha)$. They ensure that $succ_G$ handles all equivalent sequences resulting from permuting transitions of $G(\alpha)$ with other firable transitions [6]. Condition C4 states that there is no transition t_j outside $G(\alpha)$, which must be fired before some transition of $G(\alpha)$.

4.3   Does G Preserve the Non-equivalent Firing Sequences of $\mathcal{N}$?

The proof that G preserves the non-equivalent firing sequences of $\mathcal{N}$ is stated in Theorem 1. It is based on some useful conditions established in Lemma 2.

Lemma 2. *Let* $\alpha = (M, F)$ *be a state class. Then:*
$G(\alpha) \models SC \Rightarrow \forall \omega \in (T - G(\alpha))^+,$
$\qquad succ(\alpha, \omega) \neq \emptyset \Rightarrow \forall t_i \in G(\alpha), (i)\ succ(\alpha, \omega t_i) \neq \emptyset \wedge\ (ii)\ succ(\alpha, t_i \omega) \neq \emptyset.$

Proof. By assumption $succ(\alpha, \omega) \neq \emptyset$. Since the first transition of ω is firable from α and does not belong to $G(\alpha)$, then C0 of SC implies that $G(\alpha) \neq \emptyset$; C4 of SC imposes that t_i is firable from α; C1 of SC states that $CF(M, t_i) \subseteq G(\alpha)$.

(i): Suppose that for some $t_i \in G(\alpha)$, $succ(\alpha, \omega t_i) = \emptyset$. As $t_i \in Fr(\alpha)$ and $CF(M, t_i) \subseteq G(\alpha)$, this assumption implies that there are at least two transitions t_j and t_k in $\|\omega\|$ s.t. t_j is enabled and not conflict with t_i in M (i.e., $t_j \in En(M) - CF(M, t_i)$), and t_k is enabled directly or indirectly by t_j but in conflict with t_i, which implies that $t_k \in Adj(t_i) - En(M)$. The delay between the firing date of t_j and the enabling date of t_k can at least be equal to $\bar{L}_{kj} - \downarrow Is(t_k)$. From the fact that $t_j \notin G(\alpha)$ and $t_k \in Adj(t_i) - En(M)$, by construction of $G(\alpha)$ (i.e., C2 of SC), it holds that $\bar{L}_{kj} - \downarrow Is(t_k) > d_{ij}$. By definition, d_{ij} is the maximal delay between the firing dates of transitions t_j and t_i (i.e., maximal value of $t_i - t_j$ in the firing domain of α). Therefore, $\bar{L}_{kj} - \downarrow Is(t_k) > d_{ij}$ implies that, after firing t_j, t_i will reach its maximal firing delay before that t_k becomes enabled and then $succ(\alpha, \omega) = \emptyset$, which contradicts the assumption. Therefore, $succ(\alpha, \omega) \neq \emptyset \Rightarrow succ(\alpha, \omega t_i) \neq \emptyset$.

(ii): Conditions C1, C2 and C3 of SC imply that the firing of transitions of ω does not affect the effect of t_i. Let $\omega = t_1 ... t_n$, $n \geq 1$. The effect of t_i from α and $succ(\alpha, t_1)$ is the same. Since from M, sequences $t_1 t_i$ and $t_i t_1$ lead to the same marking, it follows that t_1 and t_i are effect-independent in α. Sequences $t_1 t_i$ and $t_i t_1$ are then both firable from α. We repeat recursively the same process on $succ(\alpha, t_1)$ and the first transition of $t_2 ... t_n$ until processing all transitions of ω. Therefore, t_i is effect-independent of all transitions of ω and then $succ(\alpha, t_i \omega) \neq \emptyset$. $\qquad \square$

Theorem 1. *Let* $\mathcal{N}$ *be a TPN with no unbounded static firing intervals. Then:*
$\mathbb{G} \models SC \Rightarrow$ *the RSCG preserves non-equivalent sequences of the CSCG.*

Proof. Let M be a marking and ω a firing sequence of M (i.e., $M[\omega >)$. The sequence ω of M is maximal iff it is infinite or leads to a deadlock marking. Let $\Omega(M)$ be a set of maximal firing sequences of M. To prove that the RSCG preserves the non-equivalent firing sequences of the CSCG, it suffices to show that: $\forall \alpha = (M, F) \in \mathcal{C}_S$,

(i) $\forall \omega \in \Omega(M), succ(\alpha, \omega) \neq \emptyset \Rightarrow \exists \omega' \in T^+, \omega \equiv \omega' \wedge succ_G(\alpha, \omega') \neq \emptyset$ and

(ii) $\forall \omega \in \Omega(M), succ_G(\alpha, \omega) \neq \emptyset \Rightarrow \exists \omega' \in T^+, \omega \equiv \omega' \wedge succ(\alpha, \omega') \neq \emptyset$.

(i) : By assumption, ω is a maximal sequence of M and $succ(\alpha, \omega) \neq \emptyset$. Then, $Fr(\alpha) \neq \emptyset$. According to C0 of SC, $G(\alpha) \neq \emptyset$. From the fact that the TPN has no unbounded intervals, the non-zenoness, assumed here, guarantees that each enabled transition will eventually fire in the future, unless it is disabled by another firing. Transitions outside $G(\alpha)$ cannot disable any transition of $G(\alpha)$. We can then state that ω contains at least a transition of $G(\alpha)$, i.e., $\exists t_f \in G(\alpha), \exists \omega_1 \in (T - G(\alpha))^*, \exists \omega_2 \in T^*$, s.t. $\omega = \omega_1 t_f \omega_2$. According to Lemma 2, $succ(\alpha, \omega_1) \neq \emptyset \Rightarrow succ(\alpha, \omega_1 t_f) \neq \emptyset \wedge succ(\alpha, t_f \omega_1) \neq \emptyset$. Since $succ(\alpha, t_f \omega_1) \subseteq succ(succ_{G(\alpha)}(\alpha, t_f), \omega_1)$, it follows that $succ(succ_{G(\alpha)}(\alpha, t_f), \omega_1 \omega_2) \neq \emptyset$.

Let $\alpha_1 = succ_{G(\alpha)}(\alpha, t_f) = (M_1, F_1)$. The sequence $\omega_1 \omega_2$ is a maximal sequence of M_1. We repeat the same process on α_1 and $\omega_1 \omega_2$ until reaching a deadlock or a state class already processed. Therefore, $\exists \omega' \in T^+, \omega' \equiv \omega \wedge succ_G(\alpha, \omega') \neq \emptyset$.

(ii) : 1) For $\omega = t_1$, by definition, $succ_{G(\alpha)}(\alpha, t_1) \neq \emptyset$ iff $succ(\alpha, t_1) \neq \emptyset$.

2) For $\omega = t_1 t_2$, $succ_{G(\alpha)}(\alpha, t_1 t_2) \neq \emptyset$ iff $succ(succ_{G(\alpha)}(\alpha, t_1), t_2) \neq \emptyset$. If $t_2 \in G(\alpha)$ or $t_2 \notin Fr(\alpha)$, according to Lemma 1, $succ(succ_{G(\alpha)}(\alpha, t_1), t_2) = succ(\alpha, t_1 t_2) \neq \emptyset$. Otherwise, from C3 of SC and Lemma 1, it follows that $t_1 \| _\alpha t_2$, sequences $t_1 t_2$ and $t_2 t_1$ are firable from α, and $succ(succ_{G(\alpha)}(\alpha, t_1) = succ(\alpha, t_1 t_2) \cup succ_{G(\alpha)}(succ(\alpha, t_2), t_1)$.

3) For $\omega = t_1...t_n$, with $n > 2$, $succ_G(\alpha, \omega) \neq \emptyset$ iff $succ(succ_G(\alpha, t_1...t_{n-1}), t_n) \neq \emptyset$. Let $\alpha_{n-1} = succ_G(\alpha, t_1...t_{n-2})$. If $t_n \in G(\alpha_{n-1})$ or $t_n \notin Fr(\alpha_{n-1})$, according to Lemma 1, $succ(succ_G(\alpha, t_1...t_{n-1}), t_n) = succ(succ_G(\alpha, t_1...t_{n-2}), t_{n-1} t_n)$. Otherwise, using C3 of SC and Lemma 1, we state that $t_{n-1} \| _\alpha t_n$, sequences $t_{n-1} t_n$ and $t_n t_{n-1}$ are firable from $succ_G(\alpha, t_1...t_{n-2})$, and $succ(succ_G(\alpha, t_1...t_{n-1}), t_n) = succ(succ_G(\alpha, t_1...t_{n-2}), t_{n-1} t_n) \cup succ_{G(\alpha}(succ(succ_G(\alpha, t_1...t_{n-2}), t_n), t_{n-1})$.

Now, it suffices to repeat the same development process until reaching terms where $succ$ is directly applied on α. Each time two adjacent transitions are permuted, they are firable in both order and effect-independent. Therefore, $succ_G(\alpha, \omega) \neq \emptyset \Rightarrow \exists \omega' \equiv \omega, succ(\alpha, \omega') \neq \emptyset$. □

For a TPN with unbounded firing intervals, the non-zenoness, assumed here, guarantees that each enabled transition will become firable in the future, unless it is disabled by another firing. However, the firing of a transition, with an unbounded static firing interval, may be delayed indefinitely to lead in the reduced graph to some cycle such that the transition is firable from all state classes of the cycle but does not belong to their G (unfair sequence). The fairness criterion (we must not indefinitely neglect some transition) is not guaranteed by SC. To deal with the fairness criterion, G has to satisfy, in addition to SC, the Cycle closing condition, i.e., for every cycle in the reduced state class graph, there is at least one state class s.t. its G is equal to its set of firable transitions (fully expanded node) considered in [20] to address the same problem. With this additional condition, Theorem 1 is also valid for TPNs with unbounded static firing intervals.

Table 2. Some experimental results

TPN	RSCG	RSCG'	CSCG	TPN	RSCG	RSCG'	CSCG		Is of HC	Is of FMS
$SH(1)$				$SH(3)$					$t_1[1,2]$	$tp_1[3,3]$
NSC	230	888	1011	NSC	1524	71591	79231		$t_2[2,3]$	$tp_2[3,3]$
NCSC	303	1494	1816	NCSC	2030	228182	265362		$t_3[3,3]$	$tp_3[3,3]$
CPU (s)	0	0	0	CPU (s)	0	690	976		$t_4[1,1]$	$tm_1[1,1]$
$HC(2)$				$HC(3)$					$t_5[1,2]$	$tm_2[1,1]$
NSC	236	398	889	NSC	1294	4165	10654		$t_6[1,2]$	$tp_3 m_2[1,2]$
NCSC	306	560	2021	NCSC	1842	7864	35554		$t_7[3,3]$	$tp_3 s[1,2]$
CPU (s)	0	0	0	CPU (s)	0	2	8		$t_8[2,2]$	$tp_1 m1[2,2]$
$HC(4)$				$HC(5)$					$t_9[1,1]$	$tp_2 m_2[1,1]$
NSC	10447	39822	102265	NSC	59468	? > 151090	? > 140823		$t_{10}[1,1]$	$tp_1 e[1,1]$
NCSC	15284	100749	446242	NCSC	93614	> 494987	> 579023		$t_{11}[1,2]$	$tp_1 j[1,1]$
CPU (s)	15	202	2221	CPU (s)	367	> 3600	> 3600		$t_{12}[2,3]$	$tp_2 j[2,2]$
$FMS(2)$				$FMS(3)$					$t_{13}[1,1]$	$tp_2 e[1,1]$
NSC	3434	7791	7824	NSC	6839	29164	29235		$t_{14}[1,1]$	$tp_1 s[1,2]$
NCSC	4862	20908	21254	NCSC	9496	86485	90017		$t_{15}[1,1]$	$tp_{12}[1,2]$
CPU (s)	1	2	2	CPU (s)	4	77	71		$t_{16}[1,2]$	$tp_2 s[1,1]$
$FMS(4)$				$FMS(5)$					$t_{17}[1,1]$	$tm_3[1,1]$
NSC	31330	107307	117316	NSC	68506	? > 197144	? > 187677		$t_{18}[1,4]$	$tp_{12} m_3[2,2]$
NCSC	45337	330480	396066	NCSC	99816	> 551688	> 583206			$tp_{12} s[1,2]$
CPU (s)	60	1248	1908	CPU (s)	270	> 3600	> 3600			$tx[2,2]$

5   Experimental Results

We have tested our partial order technique on several small TPNs, the model of dependent task scheduling taken from [21][11] and the extension with static firing intervals of two models taken from the MCC (Model Checking Contest) held within Petri Nets 2013[12]: HouseConstruction (HC in short) and FMS (see Table 2 for their static firing intervals). Table 2 reports the number of state classes (NSC), the number of computed state classes (NCSC) and the CPU time in seconds of the RSCG, RSCG' and CSCG for SH, HC and FMS. The graph RSCG' is a variant of the RSCG, where C2 of SC is replaced with C2': $\forall t_i \in G(\alpha), \forall t_j \in En(M), \forall t_k \in Adj(t_i) - En(M), \bar{l}_{kj} \neq \infty \Rightarrow t_j \in G(\alpha)$. Intuitively, C2' means that $G(\alpha)$ includes all enabled transitions which may enable directly / indirectly any transition adjacent to some transition of $G(\alpha)$. In other words, unlike C2, C2' does not consider the firing delays of transitions. An interrogation mark indicates a situation where the computation has not been completed after 1 hour. Note that for a state class α, $G(\alpha)$ is computed by choosing randomly a firable transition t_f from $Fr(\alpha)$, setting $G(\alpha)$ to $CF(M, t_f)$, and then applying recursively, C1, C2, C3 and C4 until a fix point is reached. Its size is dependent on the first selected transition. The model $HC(n)$ is a free-choice and connected TPN[13], n being the initial marking of the source place p_1. The model $FMS(n)$ is a strongly-connected TPN[14], n being the initial marking of places p_1, p_2 and p_3. For all tested models, the RSCG shows a significant reduction in time and number of computed state classes, compared to the CSCG and the RSCG'. The gain (in time and space) of the RSCG' over the CSCG is much more significant for the connected TPN ($HC(n)$) than the strongly-connected TPN ($FMS(n)$). The reason is that in strongly-connected TPNs, every transition is reachable from any other one and then $C2'$ will always hold. Furthermore, we obtain further reduction, when we increase the marking, as it results in increasing the number of concurrent enabled transitions.

6   Conclusion

In this paper, we have considered the TPN model and proposed, using its CSCG, a partial order reduction technique, which preserves non-equivalent firing sequences of the TPN. Our technique is inspired from the stubborn sets [24,26] but takes into account the (static and dynamic) timing information of the model. For the tested models, the proposed technique allows a significant gain in time and space, in comparison with its "untimed" version and the CSCG.

---

[11] The model is referred here as $SH(n)$, n being the number of tokens in place $pstart$.

[12] http://mcc.lip6.fr

[13] A free-choiceTPN is a TPN, where for every transition t, $pre(t)$ and $post(t)$ are sets of places, and the sets of input places of any pair of transitions are either equal or disjoint. In a strongly-connected TPN, there is a directed path between every two nodes (places or transitions).

[14] In a connected TPN, there is a undirected path between every two nodes.

References

1. Belluomini, W., Myers, C.J.: Timed state space exploration using POSETs. IEEE Transactions on Computer-Aided Design of Integrated Circuits 19(5), 501–520 (2000)
2. Bengtsson, J.: Clocks, DBMs and States in Timed Systems. PhD thesis, Dept. of Information Technology, Uppsala University (2002)
3. Bengtsson, J.E., Jonsson, B., Lilius, J., Yi, W.: Partial order reductions for timed systems. In: Sangiorgi, D., de Simone, R. (eds.) CONCUR 1998. LNCS, vol. 1466, pp. 485–500. Springer, Heidelberg (1998)
4. Bérard, B., Cassez, F., Haddad, S., Lime, D., Roux, O.H.: The expressive power of time Petri nets. Theoretical Computer Science 474, 1–20 (2013)
5. Berthomieu, B., Vernadat, F.: State class constructions for branching analysis of time Petri nets. In: Garavel, H., Hatcliff, J. (eds.) TACAS 2003. LNCS, vol. 2619, pp. 442–457. Springer, Heidelberg (2003)
6. Boucheneb, H., Barkaoui, K.: Reducing interleaving semantics redundancy in reachability analysis of time Petri nets. ACM Transactions on Embedded Computing Systems (TECS) 12(1), 259–273 (2013)
7. Boucheneb, H., Gardey, G., Roux, O.H.: TCTL model checking of time Petri nets. Logic and Computation 19(6), 1509–1540 (2009)
8. Boucheneb, H., Hadjidj, R.: CTL* model checking for time Petri nets. Theoretical Computer Science TCS 353(1-3), 208–227 (2006)
9. Boucheneb, H., Lime, D., Roux, O.H.: On multi-enabledness in time Petri nets. In: Colom, J.-M., Desel, J. (eds.) PETRI NETS 2013. LNCS, vol. 7927, pp. 130–149. Springer, Heidelberg (2013)
10. Boucheneb, H., Rakkay, H.: A more efficient time Petri net state space abstraction useful to model checking timed linear properties. Fundamenta Informaticae 88(4), 469–495 (2008)
11. Boyer, M., Diaz, M.: Multiple-enabledness of transitions in time Petri nets. In: 9th IEEE International Workshop on Petri Nets and Performance Models, pp. 219–228 (2001)
12. Chatain, T., Jard, C.: Complete finite prefixes of symbolic unfoldings of safe time Petri nets. In: Donatelli, S., Thiagarajan, P.S. (eds.) ICATPN 2006. LNCS, vol. 4024, pp. 125–145. Springer, Heidelberg (2006)
13. Delfieu, D., Sogbohossou, M., Traonouez, L.M., Revol, S.: Parameterized study of a time Petri net. In: Cybernetics and Information Technologies, Systems and Applications: CITSA, pp. 89–90 (2007)
14. Godefroid, P.: Partial-Order Methods for the Verification of Concurrent Systems. LNCS, vol. 1032, pp. 1–142. Springer, Heidelberg (1996)
15. Håkansson, J., Pettersson, P.: Partial order reduction for verification of real-time components. In: Raskin, J.-F., Thiagarajan, P.S. (eds.) FORMATS 2007. LNCS, vol. 4763, pp. 211–226. Springer, Heidelberg (2007)
16. Lilius, J.: Efficient state space search for time Petri nets. In: MFCS Workshop on Concurrency - Algorithms and Tools. ENTCS, vol. 8, pp. 113–133 (1998)
17. Lugiez, D., Niebert, P., Zennou, S.: A partial order semantics approach to the clock explosion problem of timed automata. Theoretical Computer Science TCS 345(1), 27–59 (2005)
18. Minea, M.: Partial order reduction for model checking of timed automata. In: Baeten, J.C.M., Mauw, S. (eds.) CONCUR 1999. LNCS, vol. 1664, pp. 431–446. Springer, Heidelberg (1999)
19. Peled, D.: All from one, one for all: on model checking using representatives. In: Courcoubetis, C. (ed.) CAV 1993. LNCS, vol. 697, pp. 409–423. Springer, Heidelberg (1993)
20. Peled, D., Wilke, T.: Stutter invariant temporal properties are expressible without the next-time operator. Information Processing Letters 63(5), 243–246 (1997)

21. Romulo, F., Raimundo, B., Paulo, M.: Analysis of real-time scheduling problems by single step and maximal step semantics for time petri net models. In: 3rd Brazilian Symposium on Computing Systems Engineering (SBESC), pp. 107–112 (2013)
22. Ben Salah, R., Bozga, M., Maler, O.: On interleaving in timed automata. In: Baier, C., Hermanns, H. (eds.) CONCUR 2006. LNCS, vol. 4137, pp. 465–476. Springer, Heidelberg (2006)
23. Semenov, A., Yakovlev, A.: Verification of asynchronous circuits using time Petri net unfolding. In: 33rd Annual Conference on Design Automation (DAC), pp. 59–62 (1996)
24. Valmari, A., Hansen, H.: Can stubborn sets be optimal? In: Lilius, J., Penczek, W. (eds.) PETRI NETS 2010. LNCS, vol. 6128, pp. 43–62. Springer, Heidelberg (2010)
25. Yoneda, T., Ryuba, H.: CTL model checking of time Petri nets using geometric regions. EICE Trans. Inf. & Syst. E99-D(3), 297–306 (1998)
26. Yoneda, T., Schlingloff, B.H.: Efficient verification of parallel real-time systems. Formal Methods in System Design 11(2), 187–215 (1997)

On MITL and Alternating Timed Automata over Infinite Words*

Thomas Brihaye[1], Morgane Estiévenart[1,**], and Gilles Geeraerts[2,***]

[1] Université de Mons, Belgium
[2] Université libre de Bruxelles, Belgium

Abstract. *One clock alternating timed automata* (OCATA) have been introduced as natural extension of (one clock) timed automata to express the semantics of MTL [15]. In this paper, we consider the application of OCATA to the problems of model-checking and satisfiability for MITL (a syntactic fragment of MTL), interpreted over infinite words. Our approach is based on the *interval semantics* (recently introduced in [5] in the case of finite words) extended to infinite words. We propose region-based and zone-based algorithms, based on this semantics, for MITL model-checking and satisfiability. We report on the performance of a prototype tool implementing those algorithms.

1 Introduction

Model-checking [7] is today one of the most prominent and successful techniques to establish *automatically* the correctness of a computer system. The system designer provides a *model-checker* with a *model* of the system and a *formal property* that the system must respect. The model-checker either proves that the system respects the property, or outputs an error trace that can be used for debugging. For their implementation, many model-checkers rely on the so-called *automata-based approach*, where the behaviours of the system and the set of *bad behaviours* are represented by the languages $L(B)$ and $L(A_{\neg\varphi})$ of Büchi automata B and $A_{\neg\varphi}$ respectively. Then, the model-checker performs automata-based manipulations to check whether $L(B) \cap L(A_{\neg\varphi}) = \emptyset$. While Büchi automata are adequate for modeling systems, properties are more easily expressed by means of logical sentences. The linear temporal logic (LTL for short) is arguably one of the most studied logic to express such requirements. Algorithms to turn an LTL formula φ into a Büchi automaton A_φ recognising the same language are well-known, thereby enabling its use in model-checkers.

Yet, this classical theory is not adequate for reasoning about *real-time* properties of systems, because Büchi automata and LTL can only express *sequence of events*, but have no notion of (time) *distance* between those events. Introduced by Alur and Dill in 1994 [1], *timed automata* (an extension of Büchi automata

---

* The research leading to these results has received funding from the European Union Seventh Framework Programme (FP7/2007-2013) under Grant Agreement n°601148 (CASSTING).

** This author has been supported by a FRIA scholarship.

*** Supported by a 'Crédit aux chercheurs' number 1808881 of the F.R.S./FNRS.

A. Legay and M. Bozga (Eds.): FORMATS 2014, LNCS 8711, pp. 69–84, 2014.

with clocks, i.e. real variables that evolve synchronously) are today the best accepted model for those real-time systems. Symmetrically, several logics have been introduced to specify real-time properties of systems. Among them, MITL (a syntactic fragment of MTL [11]) is particularly appealing, because it combines expressiveness [3] and tractability (MTL is mostly undecidable [3], while model-checking and satisfiability are EXPSPACE-c in MITL). A comprehensive and efficient automata-based framework to support MITL model-checking (and other problems such as satisfiability) is thus highly desirable. In a recent work [5] we made a first step towards this goal in the restricted case of *finite words semantics*. We rely on *one-clock alternating timed automata* (OCATA for short), in order to avoid the direct, yet involved, translation from MITL to timed automata first introduced in [3]. The translation from MITL to OCATA – which has been introduced by Ouaknine and Worrell in the general case of MTL [15] – is straightforward. However, the main difficulty with alternating timed automata is that they cannot, in general, be converted into an equivalent timed automaton, even in the one-clock case. Indeed, a run of an alternating automaton can be understood as several copies of the same automaton running in parallel on the same word. Unfortunately, the clock values of all the copies are not always synchronised, and one cannot bound, a priori, the number of different clock values that one must track along the run. Hence, contrary to the untimed word case, subset construction techniques cannot be directly applied to turn an OCATA into a timed automaton (with finitely many clocks).

Our solution [5] amounts to considering an alternative semantics for OCATA, that we call the *interval semantics*, where clock valuations are not punctual values but intervals with real endpoints. One of the features of this semantic is that several clock values can be grouped into intervals, thanks to a so-called *approximation function*. For instance, consider a configuration of an OCATA with three copies of the automaton currently in the same location ℓ, and with clock values 0.42, 1.2 and 5.7 respectively. It can be approximated by a single interval $[0.42, 5.7]$, meaning: 'there are two copies with clock values 0.42 and 5.7, and there are *potentially* several copies with clock values in the interval $[0.42, 5.7]$'. This technique allows to reduce the number of variables needed to track the clock values of the OCATA. While this grouping yields an under-approximation of the accepted language, we have showed [5] that, in the case of finite words, and for an OCATA A_φ obtained from an MITL formula φ, one can always define an approximation function s.t. the language of A_φ is preserved and the number of intervals along all runs is bounded by a constant $M(\varphi)$ depending on the formula. Using classical subset construction and tracking the endpoints of each interval by means of a pair of clocks, we can then translate the OCATA into a Büchi TA accepting the same language.

In the present work, we continue this line of research and demonstrate that our techniques carry on to the infinite words case. Achieving this result is not straightforward because OCATA on infinite words have not been studied as deeply as in the finite words case, probably because infinite words language emptiness of OCATA is decidable only on restricted subclasses [15,17].

Hence, to reach our goal, we make several technical contributions regarding infinite words OCATA, that might be of interest outside this work. First, in Section 3 we adapt the interval semantics of [5] to the infinite words case. Then, in Section 4, we introduce *tree-like* OCATA (TOCATA for short), a subclass of OCATA that exhibit some structure akin to a tree (in the same spirit as the Weak and Very Weak Alternating Automata [12,10]). For every MTL formula φ, we show that the OCATA A_φ obtained by the Ouaknine and Worrell construction [15] recognises the language of φ (a property that had never been established in the case of infinite words, as far as we know[1]), is in fact a TOCATA. This shows in particular that TOCATA are semantically different from the 'weak OCATA' introduced in [17] (where 'weak' refers to weak accepting conditions), and whose emptiness problem is decidable. We prove specific properties of TOCATA that are important in our constructions (for instance, TOCATA on infinite words can be easily complemented), and we adapt the classical Miyano and Hayashi construction [14] to obtain a procedure to translate any TOCATA A_φ obtained from an MITL formula into an equivalent timed Büchi automaton B_φ. Equipped with these theoretical results, we propose in Section 6 algorithms to solve the *satisfiability* and *model-checking* problems of MITL. We define region-based and zone-based [2] versions of our algorithms. Our algorithms work *on-the-fly* in the sense that they work directly on the structure of the OCATA $\mathcal{A}_\varphi$ (whose size is linear in the size of φ), and avoid building B_φ beforehand (which is, in the worst case, exponential in the size of φ). Finally in Section 6, we present prototype tools implementing those algorithms. To the best of our knowledge, these are the first tools solving those problems for the full MITL. We report on and compare their performance against a benchmark of MITL formulas whose sizes are parametrised. While still preliminary, the results are encouraging. Missing proofs can be found in the full version of this paper [6].

2 Preliminaries

Basic notions. Let $\mathbb{R}$, $\mathbb{R}^+$ and $\mathbb{N}$ denote the sets of real, non-negative real and natural numbers respectively. We call **interval** a convex subset of $\mathbb{R}$. We rely on the classical notation $\langle a, b \rangle$ for intervals, where $\langle$ is (or [, $\rangle$ is) or], $a \in \mathbb{R}$ and $b \in \mathbb{R} \cup \{+\infty\}$. For an interval $I = \langle a, b \rangle$, we let $\inf(I) = a$ be the *infimum* of I, $\sup(I) = b$ be its *supremum* (a and b are called the *endpoints* of I) and $|I| = \sup(I) - \inf(I)$ be its *length*. We note $\mathcal{I}(\mathbb{R})$ the set of all intervals. We note $\mathcal{I}(\mathbb{R}^+)$ (resp. $\mathcal{I}(\mathbb{N}^{+\infty})$) the set of all intervals whose endpoints are in $\mathbb{R}^+$ (resp. in $\mathbb{N} \cup \{+\infty\}$). Let $I \in \mathcal{I}(\mathbb{R})$ and $t \in \mathbb{R}$, we note $I + t$ for $\{i + t \in \mathbb{R} \mid i \in I\}$.

Let Σ be a finite alphabet. An *infinite word* on a set S is an infinite sequence $s = s_1 s_2 s_3 \ldots$ of elements in S. An infinite time sequence $\bar{\tau} = \tau_1 \tau_2 \tau_3 \ldots$ is an infinite word on $\mathbb{R}^+$ s.t. $\forall i \in \mathbb{N}, \tau_i \leq \tau_{i+1}$. An *infinite timed word* over Σ is a pair $\theta = (\bar{\sigma}, \bar{\tau})$ where $\bar{\sigma}$ is an infinite word over Σ, $\bar{\tau}$ an infinite time sequence. We also note θ as $(\sigma_1, \tau_1)(\sigma_2, \tau_2)(\sigma_3, \tau_3) \ldots$. We denote by $T\Sigma^\omega$ the set of all infinite timed words. A *timed language* is a (possibly infinite) set of infinite timed words.

---

[1] Even in [15] where the authors consider a fragment of MTL over infinite words, but consider only safety properties that are reduced to questions on finite words.

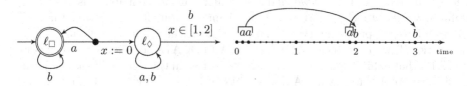

Fig. 1. (left) OCATA $\mathcal{A}_\varphi$ with $\varphi = \Box(a \Rightarrow \Diamond_{[1,2]}b)$. (right) The grouping of clocks.

Metric Interval Temporal Logic. Given a finite alphabet Σ, the formulas of MITL are defined by the following grammar, where $\sigma \in \Sigma$, $I \in \mathcal{I}(\mathbb{N}^{+\infty})$ is non-singular:

$$\varphi := \top \mid \sigma \mid \varphi_1 \wedge \varphi_2 \mid \neg\varphi \mid \varphi_1 U_I \varphi_2.$$

We adopt the following shortcuts: $\Diamond_I \varphi$ stands for $\top U_I \varphi$, $\Box_I \varphi$ for $\neg\Diamond_I \neg\varphi$, $\varphi_1 \tilde{U}_I \varphi_2$ for $\neg(\neg\varphi_1 U_I \neg\varphi_2)$, $\Box\varphi$ for $\Box_{[0,\infty)}\varphi$ and $\Diamond\varphi$ for $\Diamond_{[0,\infty)}\varphi$. Given an MITL formula φ, we note $Sub(\varphi)$ the set of all subformulas of φ. We let $|\varphi|$ denote the *size of* φ, defined as the *number* of U and $\tilde{U}$ modalities it contains. Given an infinite timed word $\theta = (\bar\sigma, \bar\tau)$ over Σ, a position $i \in \mathbb{N}_0$ and an MITL formula φ, we write $(\theta, i) \models \varphi$ when θ *satisfies* φ from position i. This satisfaction relation is defined in the usual way (see appendix [6]), let us only recall the semantics of the Until (which is *non strict* in our setting): $(\theta, i) \models \varphi_1 U_I \varphi_2$ iff $\exists j \geq i$: $(\theta, i) \models \varphi_2$, $\tau_j - \tau_i \in I \wedge \forall i \leq k < j$: $(\theta, k) \models \varphi_1$. We say that θ *satisfies* φ, written $\theta \models \varphi$, iff $(\theta, 1) \models \varphi$. We note $[\![\varphi]\!]$ the timed language $\{\theta \mid \theta \models \varphi\}$. Observe that we can transform any MITL formula in an equivalent *negative normal form* formula (i.e., negation can only be present on letters $\sigma \in \Sigma$) using the operators: $\wedge, \vee, \neg, U_I$ and $\tilde{U}_I$.

Alternating timed automata. One-clock alternating timed automata (OCATA for short) have been introduced by Ouaknine and Worrell to define the language of MTL formulas [16]. We will rely on OCATA to build our automata based framework for MITL. Let $\Gamma(L)$ be a set of formulas of the form $\top$, or $\bot$, or $\gamma_1 \vee \gamma_2$ or $\gamma_1 \wedge \gamma_2$ or ℓ or $x \bowtie c$ or $x.\gamma$, with $c \in \mathbb{N}$, $\bowtie \in \{<, \leq, >, \geq\}$, $\ell \in L$. We call $x \bowtie c$ a *clock constraint*. Then, a *one-clock alternating timed automaton* (OCATA) [16] is a tuple $\mathcal{A} = (\Sigma, L, \ell_0, F, \delta)$ where Σ is a finite alphabet, L is a finite set of locations, ℓ_0 is the initial location, $F \subseteq L$ is a set of accepting locations, $\delta : L \times \Sigma \to \Gamma(L)$ is the transition function. Intuitively, disjunctions in $\delta(\ell)$ model non-determinism, conjunctions model the creation of several automaton copies running in parallel (that must all accept for the word to be accepted) and $x.\gamma$ means that the clock x is reset when taking the transition.

Example 1. Fig. 1 (left) shows an OCATA $\mathcal{A}_\varphi = \{\Sigma, \{\ell_\Box, \ell_\Diamond\}, \ell_\Box, \{\ell_\Box\}, \delta\}$, over the alphabet $\Sigma = \{a, b\}$, and with transition function: $\delta(\ell_\Box, a) = \ell_\Box \wedge x.\ell_\Diamond$, $\delta(\ell_\Box, b) = \ell_\Box$, $\delta(\ell_\Diamond, a) = \ell_\Diamond$ and $\delta(\ell_\Diamond, b) = \ell_\Diamond \vee (x \geq 1 \wedge x \leq 2)$. We depict a conjunctive transition such as $\delta(\ell_\Box, a) = \ell_\Box \wedge x.\ell_\Diamond$ by an arrow splitting in two branches connected to $\ell_\Box$ and $\ell_\Diamond$ (they might have different resets: the reset of clock x is depicted by $x := 0$). Intuitively, when reading an a from $\ell_\Box$ with clock value v, the automaton starts *two copies of itself*, the former in location $\ell_\square$, with clock value v, the latter in location $\ell_\lozenge$ with clock value 0. Both copies should accept the suffix for the word to be accepted. The edge labeled by $b, x \in [1,2]$ from $\ell_\lozenge$ has no target location: it depicts the fact that, when the automaton has a copy in location $\ell_\lozenge$ with a clock valuation in $[1,2]$, the copy accepts all further suffixes and can thus be *removed* from the automaton.

3 The Intervals Semantics for OCATA on Infinite Words

In this section, we adapt to infinite timed words the intervals semantics introduced in [5]. In this semantics, *configurations* are sets of *states* (ℓ, I), where ℓ is a location of the OCATA and I is an *interval* (while in the standard semantics states are pairs (ℓ, v), where v is the valuation of the clock). Intuitively, a state (ℓ, I) is an abstraction of a set of states of the form (ℓ, v) with $v \in I$.

Formally, a *state* of an OCATA $\mathcal{A} = (\Sigma, L, \ell_0, F, \delta)$ is a pair (ℓ, I) where $\ell \in L$ and $I \in \mathcal{I}(\mathbb{R}^+)$. We note $S = L \times \mathcal{I}(\mathbb{R}^+)$ the state space of $\mathcal{A}$. When $I = [v, v]$ (sometimes denoted $I = \{v\}$), we shorten (ℓ, I) by (ℓ, v). A *configuration* of an OCATA $\mathcal{A}$ is a (possibly empty) finite set of states of $\mathcal{A}$ in which all intervals associated with a same location are disjoint. In the rest of the paper, we sometimes see a configuration C as a function from L to $2^{\mathcal{I}(\mathbb{R}^+)}$ s.t. for all $\ell \in L$: $C(\ell) = \{I \mid (\ell, I) \in C\}$. We note $\mathsf{Config}(\mathcal{A})$ the set of all configurations of $\mathcal{A}$. The *initial configuration* of $\mathcal{A}$ is $\{(\ell_0, 0)\}$. For a configuration C and a delay $t \in \mathbb{R}^+$, we note $C + t$ the configuration $\{(\ell, I + t) \mid (\ell, I) \in C\}$. Let E be a finite set of intervals from $\mathcal{I}(\mathbb{R}^+)$. We let $\|E\| = |\{[a, a] \in E\}| + 2 \times |\{I \in E \mid \inf(I) \neq \sup(I)\}|$ denote the number of *individual clocks* we need to encode all the information present in E, using one clock to track singular intervals, and two clocks to retain $\inf(I)$ and $\sup(I)$ respectively for non-singular intervals I. For a configuration C, we let $\|C\| = \sum_{\ell \in L} \|C(\ell)\|$.

Interval semantics. Let $M \in \mathsf{Config}(\mathcal{A})$ be a configuration of an OCATA $\mathcal{A}$, and $I \in \mathcal{I}(\mathbb{R}^+)$. We define the satisfaction relation "$\models_I$" on $\Gamma(L)$ as:

$$M \models_I \top$$
$$M \models_I \gamma_1 \wedge \gamma_2 \text{ iff } M \models_I \gamma_1 \text{ and } M \models_I \gamma_2$$
$$M \models_I \gamma_1 \vee \gamma_2 \text{ iff } M \models_I \gamma_1 \text{ or } M \models_I \gamma_2$$

$$M \models_I \ell \quad \text{iff } (\ell, I) \in M$$
$$M \models_I x \bowtie c \text{ iff } \forall x \in I, x \bowtie c$$
$$M \models_I x.\gamma \quad \text{iff } M \models_{[0,0]} \gamma$$

We say that a configuration M is a *minimal model* of the formula $\gamma \in \Gamma(L)$ wrt $I \in \mathcal{I}(\mathbb{R}^+)$ iff $M \models_I \gamma$ and there is no $M' \subsetneq M$ such that $M' \models_I \gamma$. Intuitively, for $\ell \in L, \sigma \in \Sigma$ and $I \in \mathcal{I}(\mathbb{R}^+)$, a minimal model of $\delta(\ell, \sigma)$ wrt I represents a (minimal) configuration the automaton can reach from state (ℓ, I) by reading σ. Observe that the definition of $M \models_I x \bowtie c$ only allows to take a transition $\delta(\ell, \sigma)$ from state (ℓ, I) if all the values in I satisfy the clock constraint $x \bowtie c$ of $\delta(\ell, \sigma)$. We denote $\mathsf{Succ}((\ell, I), \sigma) = \{M \mid M \text{ is a minimal model of } \delta(\ell, \sigma) \text{ wrt } I\}$. We lift the definition of Succ to configurations C as follows: $\mathsf{Succ}(C, \sigma)$ is the set of all configurations C' of the form $\cup_{s \in C} M_s$, where, for all $s \in C$: $M_s \in \mathsf{Succ}(s, \sigma)$. That is, each $C' \in \mathsf{Succ}(C, \sigma)$ is obtained by choosing one minimal model M_s in $\mathsf{Succ}(s, \sigma)$ for each $s \in C$, and taking the union of all those M_s.

Example 2. Let us consider again the OCATA of Fig. 1 (left), and let us compute the minimal models of $\delta(\ell_\Diamond, b) = \ell_\Diamond \vee (x \geq 1 \wedge x \leq 2)$ wrt to $[1.5, 2]$. A minimal model of $\ell_\Diamond$ wrt $[1.5, 2]$ is $M_1 = \{(\ell_\Diamond, [1.5, 2])\}$. A minimal model of $(x \geq 1 \wedge x \leq 2)$ is $M_2 = \emptyset$ since all values in $[1.5, 2]$ satisfy $(x \geq 1 \wedge x \leq 2)$. As $M_2 \subseteq M_1$, M_2 is the unique minimal model of $\delta(\ell_\Diamond, b)$ wrt $[1.5, 2]$: $\mathsf{Succ}((\ell_\Diamond, [1.5, 2]), b) = \{M_2\}$.

Approximation functions. Let us now recall the notion of *approximation functions* that associate with each configuration C, a set of configurations that *approximates* C *and contains less states than* C. Formally, for an OCATA $\mathcal{A}$, an *approximation function* is a function $f : \mathrm{Config}\,(\mathcal{A}) \mapsto 2^{\mathrm{Config}(\mathcal{A})}$ s.t. for all configurations C, for all $C' \in f(C)$, for all locations $\ell \in L$: (i) (i) $\|C'(\ell)\| \leq \|C(\ell)\|$; (ii) for all $I \in C(\ell)$, there exists $J \in C'(\ell)$ s.t. $I \subseteq J$; and (iii) for all $J \in C'(\ell)$, there are $I_1, I_2 \in C(\ell)$ s.t. $\inf(J) = \inf(I_1)$ and $\sup(J) = \sup(I_2)$. We note $APP_\mathcal{A}$ the set of approximation functions for $\mathcal{A}$. We lift all approximation functions f to sets $\mathcal{C}$ of configurations in the usual way: $f(\mathcal{C}) = \cup_{C \in \mathcal{C}} f(C)$. In the rest of the paper we will rely mainly on approximation functions that enable to *bound* the number of clock copies in all configurations along all runs of an OCATA $\mathcal{A}$. Let $k \in \mathbb{N}$, we say that $f \in APP_\mathcal{A}$ is a *k-bounded approximation function* iff for all $C \in \mathrm{Config}\,(\mathcal{A})$, for all $C' \in f(C)$: $\|C'\| \leq k$.

f-Runs of OCATA. We can now define formally the notion of *run* of an OCATA in the interval semantics. This notion will be parametrised by an approximation function f, that will be used to reduce the number of states present in each configuration along the run. Each new configuration in the run is thus obtained in three steps: letting time elapse, performing a discrete step, and applying the approximation function. Formally, let $\mathcal{A}$ be an OCATA of state space S, $f \in APP_\mathcal{A}$ be an approximation function and $\theta = (\sigma_1, \tau_1)(\sigma_2, \tau_2) \ldots (\sigma_i, \tau_i) \ldots$ be an infinite timed word. Let us note $t_i = \tau_i - \tau_{i-1}$ for all $i \geq 1$, assuming $\tau_0 = 0$. An *f-run of $\mathcal{A}$ on θ* is an infinite sequence $C_0, C_1, \ldots, C_i, \ldots$ of configurations s.t.: $C_0 = \{(\ell_0, 0)\}$ and for all $i \geq 1$: $C_i \in f(\mathsf{Succ}(C_{i-1} + t_i, \sigma_i))$. Observe that for all pairs of configurations C, C' s.t. $C' \in f(\mathsf{Succ}(C + t, \sigma))$ for some f, t and σ, each $s \in C$ can be associated with a unique set $\mathsf{dest}(C, C', s) \subseteq C'$ containing all the 'successors' of s in C' and obtained as follows. Let $\overline{C} \in \mathsf{Succ}(C + t, \sigma)$ be s.t. $C' \in f(\overline{C})$. Thus, by definition, $\overline{C} = \cup_{\overline{s} \in C} M_{\overline{s}}$, where each $M_{\overline{s}} \in \mathsf{Succ}(\overline{s}, \sigma)$ is the minimal model that has been chosen for $\overline{s}$ when computing $\mathsf{Succ}(C, \sigma)$. Then, $\mathsf{dest}(C, C', s) = \{(\ell', J) \in C' \mid (\ell', I) \in M_s$ and $I \subseteq J\}$. Remark that $\mathsf{dest}(C, C', s)$ is well-defined because intervals are assumed to be disjoint in configurations. The function dest allows to define a DAG representation of runs, as is usual with alternating automata. We regard a run $\pi = C_0, C_1, \ldots, C_i, \ldots$ as a rooted DAG $G_\pi = (V, \rightarrow)$, whose vertices V correspond to the states of the OCATA (vertices at depth i correspond to C_i), and whose set of edges $\rightarrow$ expresses the OCATA transitions. Formally, $V = \cup_{i \geq 0} V_i$, where for all $i \geq 0$: $V_i = \{(s, i) \mid s \in C_i\}$ is the set of all vertices of depth i. The root of G_π is $((\ell_0, 0), 0)$. Finally, $(s_1, i_1) \rightarrow (s_2, i_2)$ iff $i_2 = i_1 + 1$ and $s_2 \in \mathsf{dest}(C_{i-1}, C_i, s_1)$. From now on, we will mainly rely on the DAG characterisation of *f*-runs.

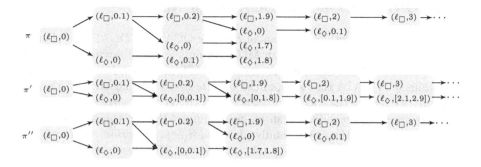

Fig. 2. Several OCATA run prefixes

Example 3. Fig. 2 displays three DAG representation of run prefixes of $\mathcal{A}_\varphi$ (Fig. 1), on the word $(a, 0.1)(a, 0.2)(a, 1.9)(b, 2)(b, 3)\dots$ (grey boxes highlight the successive configurations). π only is an *Id*-run and shows why the number of clock copies cannot be bounded in general: if $\mathcal{A}_\varphi$ reads n a's between instants 0 and 1, n copies of the clock are created in location $\ell_\Diamond$.

f-language of OCATA. We can now define the accepted language of an OCATA, parametrised by an approximation function f. A *branch* of an f-run G is a (finite or) infinite path in G_π. We note $Bran^\omega(G)$ the set of all *infinite* branches of G_π and, for a branch β, we note $Infty(\beta)$ the set of locations occurring infinitely often along β. An f-run is *accepting* iff $\forall \beta \in Bran^\omega(G), Infty(\beta) \cap F \neq \emptyset$ (i.e. we consider Büchi acceptance condition). We say that an infinite timed word θ is f-accepted by $\mathcal{A}$ iff there exists an accepting f-run of $\mathcal{A}$ on θ. We note $L_f^\omega(\mathcal{A})$ the language of all infinite timed words f-accepted by $\mathcal{A}$. We close the section by observing that a standard semantics for OCATA (where clock valuations are punctual values instead of intervals) is a particular case of the interval semantics, obtained by using the approximation function Id s.t. $Id(C) = \{C\}$ for all C. We denote by $L^\omega(\mathcal{A})$ the language $L_{Id}^\omega(\mathcal{A})$. Then, the following proposition shows the impact of approximation functions on the accepted language of the OCATA: they can only lead to *under-approximations* of $L^\omega(\mathcal{A})$.

Proposition 4. *For all OCATA $\mathcal{A}$, for all $f \in APP_\mathcal{A}: L_f^\omega(\mathcal{A}) \subseteq L^\omega(\mathcal{A})$.*

Proof (Idea). In *Id*-runs, all clock values are punctual, while in f-runs, clock values can be non-punctual intervals. Consider a set $(\ell, v_1), \dots, (\ell, v_n)$ of states in location ℓ and with punctual values $v_1 \leq \dots \leq v_n$, and consider its approximation $s = (\ell[v_1, v_n])$. Then, if a σ-labeled transition is firable from s, it is also firable from all (ℓ, v_i). The converse is not true: there might be a set of σ-labeled transitions that are firable from each (ℓ, v_i), but no σ-labeled transition firable from s, because *all clock values* in I must satisfy the transition guard. $\square$

4   TOCATA: A Class of OCATA for MITL

In this section, we introduce the class of *tree-like* OCATA (TOCATA for short), and show that, when applying, to an MITL formula φ, the construction defined by Ouaknine and Worrell [16] in the setting of MTL interpreted on *finite words*, one obtains a TOCATA that accepts the *infinite words* language of ϕ. To prove this result, we rely on the specific properties of TOCATA (in particular, we show that their acceptance condition can be made simpler than in the general case). Then, we show that there is a family of *bounded approximation functions* $f_\varphi^\star$, s.t., for every MITL formula φ, $L_{f_\varphi^\star}^\omega(\mathcal{A}_\varphi) = L^\omega(\mathcal{A}_\varphi)$. This result will be crucial to the definition of our on-the-fly model-checking algorithm in Section 5. We also exploit it to define a natural procedure that builds, for all MITL formula φ, a *Büchi timed automaton* $\mathcal{B}_\varphi$ accepting $[\![\varphi]\!]$.

From MITL to OCATA. We begin by recalling the syntactic translation from MTL (a superset of MITL) to OCATA, as defined by Ouaknine and Worrell [16]. Observe that it has been defined in the setting of *finite words*, hence we will need to prove that it is still correct in the infinite words setting. Let φ be an MITL formula (in negative normal form). We let $\mathcal{A}_\varphi = (\Sigma, L, \ell_0, F, \delta)$ where: L is the set containing the initial copy of φ, noted 'φ_{init}', and all the formulas of $Sub(\varphi)$ whose outermost connective is 'U' or '$\tilde{U}$'; $\ell_0 = \varphi_{init}$; F is the set of the elements of L of the form $\varphi_1 \tilde{U}_I \varphi_2$. Finally δ is defined by induction on the structure of φ:

- $\delta(\varphi_{init}, \sigma) = x.\delta(\varphi, \sigma)$
- $\delta(\varphi_1 \vee \varphi_2, \sigma) = \delta(\varphi_1, \sigma) \vee \delta(\varphi_2, \sigma)$; $\delta(\varphi_1 \wedge \varphi_2, \sigma) = \delta(\varphi_1, \sigma) \wedge \delta(\varphi_2, \sigma)$
- $\delta(\varphi_1 U_I \varphi_2, \sigma) = (x.\delta(\varphi_2, \sigma) \wedge x \in I) \vee (x.\delta(\varphi_1, \sigma) \wedge \varphi_1 U_I \varphi_2 \wedge x \leq sup(I))$
- $\delta(\varphi_1 \tilde{U}_I \varphi_2, \sigma) = (x.\delta(\varphi_2, \sigma) \vee x \notin I) \wedge (x.\delta(\varphi_1, \sigma) \vee \varphi_1 \tilde{U}_I \varphi_2 \vee x > sup(I))$
- $\forall \sigma_1, \sigma_2 \in \Sigma$: $\delta(\sigma_1, \sigma_2) = \begin{cases} \text{true if } \sigma_1 = \sigma_2 \\ \text{false if } \sigma_1 \neq \sigma_2 \end{cases}$ and $\delta(\neg\sigma_1, \sigma_2) = \begin{cases} \text{false if } \sigma_1 = \sigma_2 \\ \text{true if } \sigma_1 \neq \sigma_2 \end{cases}$
- $\forall \sigma \in \Sigma$: $\delta(\top, \sigma) = \top$ and $\delta(\bot, \sigma) = \bot$.

Example 5. As an example, consider again the OCATA $\mathcal{A}_\varphi$ in Fig. 1. It accepts exactly $[\![\Box(a \Rightarrow \Diamond_{[1,2]} b)]\!]$. It has been obtained by means of the above construction (trivial guards such as $x \leq +\infty$, and the state φ_{init} have been omitted).

Tree-like OCATA. Let us now define a strict subclass of OCATA that captures all the infinite words language of MTL formulas, but whose acceptance condition can be made simpler. An OCATA $\mathcal{A} = (\Sigma, L, \ell_0, F, \delta)$ is a TOCATA iff there exists a partition $L_1, L_2, \ldots, L_m$ of L and a partial order $\preccurlyeq$ on the sets $L_1, L_2, \ldots, L_m$ s.t.: (i) each L_i contains either only accepting states or no accepting states: $\forall 1 \leq i \leq m$ either $L_i \subseteq F$ or $L_i \cap F = \emptyset$; and (ii) the partial order $\preccurlyeq$ is compatible with the transition relation and yields the 'tree-like' structure of the automaton in the following sense: $\preccurlyeq$ is s.t. $L_j \preccurlyeq L_i$ iff $\exists \sigma \in \Sigma$, $\ell \in L_i$ and $\ell' \in L_j$ such that ℓ' is present in $\delta(\ell, \sigma)$. In particular, OCATA built from *MTL* formulas, such as $\mathcal{A}_\varphi$ in Fig. 1, are TOCATA. Since MTL is a superset of MITL, this proposition is true in particular for MITL formulas:

Proposition 6. *For every MTL formula φ, $\mathcal{A}_\varphi$ is a TOCATA.*

Proof. Let $L = \{\ell_1, \ell_2, \ldots, \ell_m\}$ be the locations of $\mathcal{A}_\varphi$. We consider the partition $\{\ell_1\}, \{\ell_2\}, \ldots, \{\ell_m\}$ of L and the order $\preccurlyeq$ s.t. $\{\ell_j\} \preccurlyeq \{\ell_i\}$ iff ℓ_j is a subformula of ℓ_i. It is easy to check that they satisfy the definition of TOCATA.   □

Properties of TOCATA. Let us now discuss two peculiar properties of TOCATA that are not enjoyed by OCATA. The first one is concerned with the acceptance condition. In the general case, a run of an OCATA is accepting iff all its branches visit accepting states infinitely often. Thanks to the partition characterising a TOCATA, this condition can be made simpler: a run is now accepting iff each branch eventually visits accepting states *only*, because it reaches a partition of the locations that are all accepting.

Proposition 7. *An Id-run G_π of a TOCATA $\mathcal{A}$ with set of accepting locations F is accepting iff $\forall \beta = \beta_0 \beta_1 \ldots \beta_i \ldots \in Bran^\omega(G_\pi)$, $\exists n_\beta \in \mathbb{N}$ s.t. $\forall i > n_\beta$: $\beta_i = ((\ell, v), i)$ implies $\ell \in F$.*

The second property of interest for us is that TOCATA can be easily complemented. One can simply swap accepting and non-accepting locations, and 'dualise' the transition relation, *without changing the acceptance condition*[2] (as in the case of OCATA on finite words [16]). Formally, the dual of a formula $\varphi \in \Gamma(L)$ is the formula $\overline{\varphi}$ defined inductively as follows. $\forall \ell \in L$, $\overline{\ell} = \ell$; $\overline{false} = true$ and $\overline{true} = false$; $\overline{\varphi_1 \vee \varphi_2} = \overline{\varphi_1} \wedge \overline{\varphi_2}$; $\overline{\varphi_1 \wedge \varphi_2} = \overline{\varphi_1} \vee \overline{\varphi_2}$; $\overline{x.\varphi} = x.\overline{\varphi}$; the dual of a clock constraint is its negation (for example: $\overline{x \leq c} = x > c$). Then, for all TOCATA $\mathcal{A} = (\Sigma, L, \ell_0, F, \delta)$, we let $\mathcal{A}^C = (\Sigma, L, \ell_0, L \setminus F, \overline{\delta})$ where $\overline{\delta}(\ell, \sigma) = \overline{\delta(\ell, \sigma)}$. Thanks to Proposition 7, we prove that $\mathcal{A}^C$ accepts the complement of $\mathcal{A}$'s language:

Proposition 8. *For all TOCATA $\mathcal{A}$, $L^\omega(\mathcal{A}^C) = T\Sigma^\omega \setminus L^\omega(\mathcal{A})$.*

TOCATA and MITL. Equipped with those results we can now expose the two main results of this section. First, the translation from MTL to OCATA introduced in [16] carries on to infinite words (to the best of our knowledge this had not been proved before and does not seem completely trivial since our proof requires the machinery of TOCATA developed in this paper). Second, for every MITL formula φ, we can devise an $M(\varphi)$-bounded[3] approximation function $f_\varphi^\star$ to bound the number of intervals needed along all runs of the intervals semantics of the TOCATA $\mathcal{A}_\varphi$, while retaining the semantics of φ. Notice that this second property fails when applied to formulae φ of MTL.

Theorem 9. *(i) For every MTL formula φ, $L^\omega(\mathcal{A}_\varphi) = \llbracket \varphi \rrbracket$.*
(ii) For every MITL formula φ, there is an $M(\varphi)$-bounded approximation function $f_\varphi^\star$ s.t. $L_{f_\varphi^\star}^\omega(\mathcal{A}_\varphi) = \llbracket \varphi \rrbracket$.

---

[2] In general, applying this construction yields an OCATA *with co-Büchi acceptance condition* for the complement of the language.

[3] $M(\varphi) \leq |\varphi| \times \max\limits_{I \in \mathcal{I}_\varphi} \left(4 \times \left\lceil \frac{\inf(I)}{|I|} \right\rceil + 2, 2 \times \left\lceil \frac{\sup(I)}{|I|} \right\rceil + 2 \right)$, where $\mathcal{I}_\varphi$ is the set of all the intervals that occur in φ.

Proof (Ideas). Point (i) has been proved in the finite words case in [16, Prop. 6.4]. This proof relies crucially on the fact that OCATA can be complemented in this case. Thanks to Proposition 8, we can adapt the proof of [16]. The proof of (ii) can be adapted from [5, Th. 13], thanks to Proposition 7.   □

Example 10. Let us illustrate the idea behind the approximation function $f_\varphi^\star$ by considering again the run prefixes on $\theta = (a, 0.1)(a, 0.2)(a, 1.9)(b, 2)(b, 3)(b, 4) \ldots$ in Fig. 2. The two first positions (with $\sigma_1 = \sigma_2 = a$) of θ satisfy $\Diamond_{[1,2]}b$, *thanks to the b in position 4* (with $\tau_4 = 2$), while position 3 (with $\sigma_3 = a$) satisfies $\Diamond_{[1,2]}b$ *thanks to the b in position 5* (with $\tau_5 = 3$), see Fig. 1 (right). Hence, $f_\varphi^\star$ groups the two clock copies created in $\ell_\Diamond$ when reading the two first a's, but keeps the third one apart. This yields the $f_\varphi^\star$-run π'' in Fig. 2. On the other hand, the strategy of grouping all the clock copies present in each location, which yields π', is not a good solution. This prefix cannot be extended to an accepting run because of the copy in state $(\ell_\Diamond, [2.1, 2.9])$ in the rightmost configuration, that will never be able to visit an accepting location.

From MITL to Büchi timed automata. Thanks to the bound $M(\varphi)$ on the number of clock copies and the approximation function $f_\varphi^\star$, given by Theorem 9, it is now easy to build a timed automaton with Büchi acceptance condition[4] [1] accepting $[\![\varphi]\!]$ for every MITL formula φ. To explain the construction, we first associate with all OCATA $\mathcal{A} = (\Sigma, L, \ell_0, F, \delta)$ and approximation function f the *timed transition system* $\mathsf{TTS}(\mathcal{A}, f) = (\Sigma, S^{\mathsf{TTS}}, s_0^{\mathsf{TTS}}, \to^{\mathsf{TTS}})$ where $S^{\mathsf{TTS}} = \mathsf{Config}(\mathcal{A})$, $s_0^{\mathsf{TTS}} = \{(\ell_0, [0, 0])\}$ and $(s_1, t, \sigma, s_2) \in \to^{\mathsf{TTS}}$ iff $s_2 \in f(\mathsf{Succ}(s_1 + t, \sigma))$ for some $t \geq 0$ and $\sigma \in \Sigma$. Notice that the non-determinism of the transition also chooses the approximation (among the propositions allowed by the function f). Then, we associate with $\mathsf{TTS}(\mathcal{A}, f)$ a Büchi acceptance condition by adapting the classical construction due to Miyano and Hayashi [14] to our setting. Formally, we let $\mathsf{MHTS}(\mathcal{A}, f)$ be the timed transition system $(\Sigma, S^{\mathsf{MH}}, s_0^{\mathsf{MH}}, \to^{\mathsf{MH}}, \alpha)$ obtained from $\mathsf{TTS}(\mathcal{A}, f)$ by labeling all $\mathcal{A}$ states in all configurations with a marker which is either $\top$ or $\bot$. Intuitively, a state is marked by $\top$ iff all the branches it belongs to have visited a final location of $\mathcal{A}$ since the last accepting state of $\mathsf{MHTS}(\mathcal{A}, f)$ (i.e., a state where all markers are $\top$). Formally, (i) $S^{\mathsf{MH}} = 2^{L \times \mathcal{I}(\mathbb{R}^+) \times \{\top, \bot\}}$. Each state s is thus of the form $\{(\ell_1, I_1, m_1), \ldots, (\ell_n, I_n, m_n)\}$ where $\{(\ell_1, I_1), \ldots, (\ell_n, I_n)\}$ is a state of $\mathsf{TTS}(\mathcal{A}, f)$, denoted $\mathsf{conf}(s)$, and the m_i are the markers; (ii) $s_0^{\mathsf{MH}} = \{(\ell_0, [0, 0], \bot)\}$; (iii) α is the set of accepting states of $\mathsf{MHTS}(\mathcal{A})$ and contains all states of the form $\{(\ell_1, I_1, m_1), \ldots, (\ell_n, I_n, m_n)\}$ s.t. $m_i = \top$ for all $1 \leq i \leq n$; and (iv) $\to^{\mathsf{MH}} \subseteq S \times \mathbb{R}^+ \times \Sigma \times S$ is the transition relation s.t. $(s_1, t, \sigma, s_2) \in \to^{\mathsf{MH}}$ iff $(\mathsf{conf}(s_1), t, \sigma, \mathsf{conf}(s_2)) \in \to^{\mathsf{TTS}}$, and the markers in s_2 are updated from the markers in s_1 in the following way. If $s_1 \in \alpha$, then the markers of all $\mathcal{A}$-states (ℓ, I) in s_1 are $\top$ iff $\ell \in F$. Otherwise, if $\mathsf{conf}(s_1) \notin \alpha$, then $s = (\ell, I, \top) \in s_2$ iff either $\ell \in F$ or for all $(\ell', I', m) \in s_1$ s.t. $(\ell, I) \in \mathsf{dest}(\mathsf{conf}(s_1), \mathsf{conf}(s_2), (\ell', I'))$, we have $m = \top$. We associate with $\mathsf{MHTS}(\mathcal{A}, f)$ the language $L(\mathsf{MHTS}(\mathcal{A}, f))$

---

[4] See Appendix [6] for a formal definition.

obtained by interpreting α as a Büchi acceptance condition, i.e., a timed word $\theta = (\bar{\sigma}, \bar{\tau}) \in L(\mathsf{MHTS}\,(\mathcal{A}, f))$ iff there is an infinite path of $\mathsf{MHTS}\,(\mathcal{A}, f)$ visiting α infinitely often and labeled by $(\bar{\tau}_1, \sigma_1)(\bar{\tau}_2 - \bar{\tau}_1, \sigma_2) \cdots (\bar{\tau}_i - \bar{\tau}_{i-1}, \sigma_i) \cdots$. Clearly, $L(\mathsf{MHTS}\,(\mathcal{A}, f)) = L_f^\omega(\mathcal{A})$ [14].

Building on this formalisation, one can define a timed automaton with Büchi acceptance condition $\mathcal{B}_\varphi = (\Sigma, B, b_0, X, F^\mathcal{B}, \delta^\mathcal{B})$ that simulates $\mathsf{MHTS}\,(\mathcal{A}_\varphi, f_\varphi^\star)$, and thus accepts $[\![\varphi]\!]$, for every MITL formula φ. Locations of $\mathcal{B}_\varphi$ associate with each location ℓ of $\mathcal{A}_\varphi$ a sequence of triples (x, y, m), where x and y are clocks that store the infimum and supremum of an interval respectively, and m is a Miyano-Hayashi marker. Formally, for a set of clocks X, we let $\mathsf{loc}(X)$ be the set of functions S that associate with each $\ell \in L$ a finite sequence $(x_1, y_1, m_1), \ldots, (x_n, y_n, m_n)$ where, for $1 \leq i \leq n$, $m_i \in \{\top, \bot\}$ and (x_i, y_i) is a pair of clocks from X s.t. each clock only occurs once in $S(L)$. Then:

- X is the set of clocks of $\mathcal{B}_\varphi$ s.t. $|X| = M(\varphi)$;
- $B = \{S \in \mathsf{loc}(X)\}$ is the set of locations of $\mathcal{B}_\varphi$. Thus, a configuration (S, v) of $\mathcal{B}_\varphi$ (where S is the location and v the valuation of the clocks X) encodes the labeled configuration $C = \{(\ell, [v(x), v(y)], m) \mid (x, y, m) \in S(\ell)\}$;
- $b_0 = S_0$ is the initial location of $\mathcal{B}_\varphi$ and is s.t. $\forall \ell \in L \setminus \{\ell_0\}$, $S_0(\ell) = \emptyset$, and $S_0(\ell_0) = (x, y, \bot)$, where x and y are two clocks arbitrarily chosen from X;
- $F^\mathcal{B} = \{S \subset B \mid (x, y, m) \in S(L) \Rightarrow m = \top\}$ is the set of final locations of $\mathcal{B}_\varphi$.

We skip the (mathematically heavy) definition of the transition function $\delta^\mathcal{B}$. It follows the intuitions given above (see the technical report for further details [6]). Because the number of clock copies along all runs in the $f_\varphi^\star$ semantics of $\mathcal{A}_\varphi$ is bounded, this TA simulates faithfully $\mathcal{A}_\varphi$ and accepts the same language:

Theorem 11. $L^\omega(\mathcal{B}_\varphi) = L_{f_\varphi^\star}^\omega(\mathcal{A}_\varphi)$.

5   MITL Model-Checking and Satisfiability with TOCATA

In this section, we fix an MITL formula φ and a TA $\mathcal{B} = (\Sigma, B, b_0, X, \delta^\mathcal{B}, F^\mathcal{B})$, and we consider the two following problems: (i) the *model-checking problem* asks whether $L(\mathcal{B}) \subseteq [\![\varphi]\!]$; (ii) the *satisfiability problem* asks whether $[\![\varphi]\!] \neq \emptyset$. The construction of the TA $\mathcal{B}_{\neg\varphi}$ from φ of the previous section allows to solve those problems using classical algorithms [1]. Unfortunately, building $\mathcal{B}_{\neg\varphi}$ can be prohibitive in practice. To mitigate this difficulty, we present an efficient *on-the-fly* algorithm to perform MITL model-checking, which takes as input the TA $\mathcal{B}$ and the TOCATA $\mathcal{A}_{\neg\varphi}$ (whose size is linear in the size of φ). It consists in exploring symbolically the state space of the timed transition system $\mathcal{S}_{\mathcal{B}, \neg\varphi}$ which is obtained by first taking the synchronous product of $\mathsf{TTS}\,(\mathcal{A}_{\neg\varphi}, f_{\neg\varphi}^\star)$ and the transition system[5] $\mathsf{TTS}\,(\mathcal{B})$ of $\mathcal{B}$ [1], and then associating Miyano-Hayashi markers with its states, by adapting the construction of $\mathsf{MHTS}\,(\mathcal{A}, f)$ given above to cope

---

[5] See appendix [6] for a formal definition.

with the configurations of $\mathcal{B}$. Namely[6], we associate a Miyano-Hayashi marker with the configurations of $\mathcal{B}$ too, and a state of $\mathcal{S}_{\mathcal{B},\neg\varphi}$ is accepting iff all markers (including the one on the $\mathcal{B}$ configuration) are $\top$. Obviously, $L(\mathcal{B}) \subseteq [\![\varphi]\!]$ iff $\mathcal{S}_{\mathcal{B},\neg\varphi}$ has no accepting run (i.e., no run visiting accepting states infinitely often). Symmetrically, we can solve the *satisfiability problem* by looking for accepting run in MHTS $(\mathcal{A}_\varphi, f_\varphi^\star)$ (since the techniques are similar for model-checking and satisfiability, we will only detail the former in this section).

Region-based algorithms. Since $\mathcal{S}_{\mathcal{B},\neg\varphi}$, we adapt the region abstraction of [16] in order to cope with: 1. the valuations of the clocks that are now *intervals*; and 2. the Miyano-Hayashi markers. Following the approach of [16] we represent each region by a unique word. Let $c_{\max}$ be the maximal constant of automata $\mathcal{B}$ and $\mathcal{A}_{\neg\varphi}$. Let $\mathsf{Reg}\,(c_{\max})$ denote the set of one-clock regions up to $c_{\max}$, i.e. $\mathsf{Reg}\,(c_{\max}) = \{\{i\} \mid i = 0,1,\ldots,c_{\max}\} \cup \{(i,i+1) \mid i = 0,1,\ldots,c_{\max}-1\} \cup \{(c_{\max},+\infty)\}$. Then, we encode regions of $\mathcal{S}_{\mathcal{B},\neg\varphi}$ by finite words whose letters are finite sets of tuples of the form (ℓ, r, m, k), where $\ell \in L \cup B$, $r \in \mathsf{Reg}\,(c_{\max})$, $m \in \{\top, \bot\}$ and $0 \leq k \leq M(\varphi)/2$. For a state $s = (C, (\ell^{\mathcal{B}}, v, m))$ of $\mathcal{S}_{\mathcal{B},\neg\varphi}$, we let its *region* be the word $H(s) = H_1 H_2 \cdots H_m$, s.t. the H_i's are built as follows:

1. For each location ℓ, let $C(\ell) = \{(\ell', I, m) \in C \mid \ell' = \ell\}$. Assume $C(\ell) = \{(\ell_1, I_1, m_1),\ldots,(\ell_k, I_k, m_k)\}$, with $I_1 \leq \cdots \leq I_k$. Then, we first build $E_\ell = \{(\ell_i, \inf(I_i), m_i, i), (\ell_i, \sup(I_i), m_i, i) \mid 1 \leq i \leq k\}$. We treat $(\ell^{\mathcal{B}}, v, m)$ symmetrically, and let $E^{\mathcal{B}} = \{(\ell^{\mathcal{B}}, v(x_1), m, 1),\ldots,(\ell^{\mathcal{B}}, v(x_n), m, n)\}$. We let $\mathcal{E} = E^{\mathcal{B}} \cup_{\ell \in L} E_\ell$. That is, all elements in $\mathcal{E}$ are tuples (ℓ, v, m, i), where ℓ is a location (of $\mathcal{A}_\varphi$ or $\mathcal{B}$), v is a real value (interval endpoint or clock value), m is a Miyano-Hayashi marker and i is bookkeeping information that links v to an interval (if ℓ is a location of $\mathcal{A}_\varphi$), or to a clock (ℓ is a location of $\mathcal{B}$).
2. We partition $\mathcal{E}$ into $\mathcal{E}_1,\ldots,\mathcal{E}_m$ s.t. each $\mathcal{E}_i$ contains all elements from $\mathcal{E}$ with the same fractional part to their second component (assuming $frac(u) = 0$ for all $u > c_{\max}$). We assume the ordering $\mathcal{E}_1, \mathcal{E}_2,\ldots, \mathcal{E}_m$ reflects the increasing ordering of the fractional parts.
3. For all $1 \leq i \leq m$, we obtain H_i from $\mathcal{E}_i$ by replacing the second component of all elements in $\mathcal{E}_i$ by the region from $\mathsf{Reg}\,(c_{\max})$ they belong to.

Example 12. Consider a TA $\mathcal{B}$ with 1 clock, let $c_{\max} = 2$, and let $s = \{\{(\ell_1, [0, 1.3], \bot), (\ell_1, [1.8, 2.7], \top)\}, (\ell^{\mathcal{B}}, 1.3, \bot)\}$. The first step of the construction yields the set $\mathcal{E} = \{(\ell_1, 0, \bot, 1), (\ell_1, 1.3, \bot, 1), (\ell_1, 1.8, \top, 2), (\ell_1, 2.7, \top, 2), (\ell^{\mathcal{B}}, 1.3, \bot, 1)\}$. Then, we have $H(s) = \{(\ell_1, \{0\}, \bot, 1), (\ell_1, (2, +\infty), \top, 2)\} \{(\ell_1, (1, 2), \bot, 1), (\ell^{\mathcal{B}}, (0, 1), \bot, 1)\} \{(\ell_1, (1, 2), \top, 2)\}$.

We extend the function H to set of states in the usual way. Then, assuming $\mathcal{S}_{\mathcal{B},\neg\varphi} = (\Sigma, S, s_0, \rightarrow, \alpha)$ we let $\mathcal{H}_{\mathcal{B},\neg\varphi} = (H(S), H(s_0), \rightarrow^{\mathcal{H}}, H(\alpha))$ be the untimed transition system which is the quotient of $\mathcal{S}_{\mathcal{B},\neg\varphi}$ by H, with $W_1 \rightarrow^{\mathcal{H}} W_2$

---

[6] Details omitted. Observe that $\mathcal{S}_{\mathcal{B},\neg\varphi}$ cannot be obtained by taking the synchronous product of MHTS $(\mathcal{A}_{\neg\varphi}, f_{\neg\varphi}^\star)$ and TTS $(\mathcal{B})$, because the Miyano-Hayashi markers need to be synchronised, and must thus be added *after* the synchronous product.

iff there are s_1, s_2 s.t. $W_1 = H(s_1)$, $W_2 = H(s_2)$ and $(s_1, t, \sigma, s_2) \in \rightarrow$ for some t, σ. Thanks to the approximation function, $\mathcal{H}_{\mathcal{B}, \neg\varphi}$ is *finite*. We note $H_0 = H(s_0)$ and $\mathcal{F} = H(\alpha)$. Then, our model-checking algorithm consists in checking whether there is, in $\mathcal{H}_{\mathcal{B}, \neg\varphi}$, a path starting in H_0 and visiting $\mathcal{F}$ infinitely often.

To this end, we let $\mathsf{Post}(W) = \{W \mid W \rightarrow^{\mathcal{H}} W'\}$ for all $W \in H(S)$. We let $\mathsf{Post}^+(W)$ and $\mathsf{Post}^*(W)$ be respectively the transitive, and reflexo-transitive closures of Post. We solve the model-checking problem by means of a fix point computation [13]. Let $E_0 = \mathsf{Post}^*(H_0) \cap \mathcal{F}$, and, for all $i \geq 1$: $E_i = \mathsf{Post}^+(E_i) \cap \mathcal{F}$. One can check that this sequence eventually stabilises to a set that we denote E^*. Then, the answer to the model-checking problem is 'yes' (i.e., there is no accepting path in $\mathcal{H}_{\mathcal{B}, \neg\varphi}$) iff $E^* = \emptyset$. To obtain an algorithm for *satisfiability*, one simply needs to replace $\mathcal{S}_{\mathcal{B}, \neg\varphi}$ by $\mathsf{MHTS}(\mathcal{A}_\varphi)$ in the construction above, and to declare φ satisfiable iff $E^* \neq \emptyset$. In practice, this fix point computation can be implemented *on-the-fly* because the set $\mathsf{Post}(W)$ can be computed directly from all words W by adapting the construction of [16]. To characterise the complexity of this algorithm, we show that the number of states of $\mathcal{H}_{\mathcal{B}, \neg\varphi}$ is at most doubly exponential in the sizes of $\mathcal{B}$ and φ. Thus, our algorithms can be considered as optimal, since MITL model-checking and satisfiability are ExpSpace-c [3]:

Theorem 13. *Let φ be an MITL formula, and $\mathcal{B}$ be a TA with n clocks and m locations. Then $\mathcal{H}_{\mathcal{B}, \neg\varphi}$ has $O(2^m)$ states, with $m \leq 16 \times (m + |\varphi| + 1) \times c_{max} \times \max(M(\neg\varphi), n)^2$.*

Zone-based algorithms. In the case of TAs, zones have been advocated as a data structure which is more efficient in practice than regions [1]. Let us close this section by showing how zones for OCATA [2] can be adapted to represent set of states of $\mathcal{S}_{\mathcal{B}, \neg\varphi}$. Intuitively, a zone is a constraint on the values of the clock copies, with additional information ($loc_\mathcal{A}$ and $loc_\mathcal{B}$) to associate clock copies of $\mathcal{A}_{\neg\varphi}$ and clocks of $\mathcal{B}$ respectively to locations and Miyano-Hayashi markers.

Formally, assume $\mathcal{A}_{\neg\varphi} = (\Sigma, L, \ell_0, F, \delta)$, with clock x, and assume $\mathcal{B} = (\Sigma, B, b_0, X, \delta^\mathcal{B}, F^\mathcal{B})$ is a TA with $X = \{x_1^\mathcal{B}, x_2^\mathcal{B}, \ldots, x_n^\mathcal{B}\}$. An *extended clock constraints* on a set of clocks C, is a constraint of the form the form $c \bowtie k$ or $c_1 - c_2 \bowtie k$ for $c, c_1, c_2 \in C$, $k \in \mathbb{N}$ and $\bowtie \in \{<, \leq, >, \geq\}$. We also use $c_1 = c_2$ as shorthand for $c_1 - c_2 \geq 0 \wedge c_1 - c_2 \leq 0$. For all $m \leq M(\neg\varphi)/2$, we let $\mathcal{X}_m$ be the set of clocks $\{x_1, x_2, \ldots, x_m, y_1, y_2, \ldots, y_m\} \uplus X$ (intuitively, each pair of clock copies (x_i, y_i) will represent an interval). Then, a *zone* $\mathcal{Z}_m$ of dimension m (with $0 \leq m \leq M(\neg\varphi)/2$) is a tuple $\mathcal{Z}_m = (loc_\mathcal{A}, loc_\mathcal{B}, Z)$ where: (i) $loc_\mathcal{A} : \{x_1, x_2, \ldots, x_m\} \rightarrow L \times \{\bot, \top\}$; (ii) $loc_\mathcal{B} \in B \times \{\bot, \top\}$; and (iii) Z is a finite set of extended clock constraints on $\mathcal{X}_m$, interpreted as a conjunction (it is a 'classical zone' on $\mathcal{X}_m$ [1]). A zone $\mathcal{Z}$ is interpreted as the set of states of $\mathcal{S}_{\mathcal{B}, \neg\varphi}$ it represents. Let $s = (\{(\ell_1, [a_1, b_1], k_1), \ldots (\ell_m, [a_m, b_m], k_m)\}, (\ell^\mathcal{B}, v, k))$ be such a state. Then, $s \in \mathcal{Z}$ iff $\mathcal{Z}$ is of dimension m, $loc_\mathcal{B} = (\ell^\mathcal{B}, k)$ and there is a bijection $h : \{1, \ldots, m\} \mapsto \{1, \ldots, m\}$ s.t. (i) for all $1 \leq i \leq m$: $loc_\mathcal{A}(x_i) = (\ell_{h(i)}, k_{h(i)})$; and (ii) the valuation v' satisfies Z, where v' is s.t. for all $x \in X$: $v'(x) = v(x)$, for all $1 \leq i \leq m$, $v'(x_i) = a_{h(i)}$ and $v'(y_i) = b_{h(i)}$. Thanks to these definitions we can define a symbolic version of the Post operator, working directly on zones,

Table 1. Benchmark for satisfiability (top) and model-checking (bottom). Reported values are execution time in ms / number of visited states.

Sat ?	Formula	Size	Regions	Reduced regions	Zones	Reduced zones
Sat	$E(5, [0, +\infty))$	5	74 / 61	16 / 31	58 / 36	39 / 31
Sat	$E(10, [0, +\infty))$	10	3296 / 2045	369 / 1023	1374 / 1033	2515 / 1023
Sat	$E(5, [5, 8))$	5	382 / 228	394 / 228	83 / 33	86 / 33
Sat	$E(10, [5, 8))$	10	70129 / 7172	79889 / 7172	1982 / 1025	2490 / 1025
Sat	$A(10, [0, +\infty))$	10	1 / 1	1 / 1	4 / 1	5 / 1
Sat	$A(10, [5, 8))$	10	1926 / 7	2036 / 5	3036 / 2	3153 / 2
Sat	$U(10, [0, +\infty))$	9	231 / 7	5 / 4	16 / 1	6 / 1
Unsat	$U(2, [5, 8])$	2	13 / 6	15 / 8	4 / 2	4 / 2
Unsat	$U(3, [5, 8])$	3	OOM	OOM	OOM	OOM
Sat	$T(10, [0, +\infty[)$	9	> 5min	3 / 2	33 / 3	7 / 2
Sat	$T(10, [5, 8))$	9	52 / 2	40 / 2	11 / 2	11 / 2
Sat	$R(5, [0, +\infty))$	20	> 5min	301 / 270	4307 / 1321	145 / 81
Sat	$R(10, [0, +\infty))$	40	> 5min	OOM	OOM	> 5min
Sat	$R(5, [5, 8))$	20	OOM	6996 / 117	1299 / 36	1518 / 36
Sat	$R(10, [5, 8))$	40	> 5min	> 5min	> 5min	> 5min
Sat	$Q(5, [0, +\infty))$	10	44 / 39	11 / 20	43 / 29	22 / 20
Sat	$Q(10, [0, +\infty))$	20	1209 / 1041	286 / 521	841 / 540	933 / 521
Sat	$Q(5, [5, 8))$	10	497 / 98	378 / 57	167 / 32	181 / 32
Sat	$Q(10, [5, 8))$	20	35776 / 2646	20324 / 2912	81774 / 782	86228 / 782

Floors	Formula	Form./ TA size	OK ?	Regions	Zones	Red. zones
2	$\Box \bigwedge_{i=1,2} (o_i \Rightarrow \Diamond_{]1,2]} c_i)$	3 / 10	×	166 / 89	57 / 35	56 / 32
2	$\Box \bigwedge_{i=1,2} (b_i \Rightarrow \Diamond_{[0,4]} o_i)$	3 / 10	✓	302 / 225	31 / 31	26 / 25
2	$\Box \bigwedge_{i=1,2} (l_i \Rightarrow \Diamond_{[0,6]} o_i)$	3 / 10	✓	820 / 690	68 / 51	60 / 40
3	$\Box \bigwedge_{i=1,\ldots,3} (o_i \Rightarrow \Diamond_{]1,2]} c_i)$	4 / 37	×	681 / 480	463 / 154	337 / 140
3	$\Box \bigwedge_{i=1,\ldots,3} (b_i \Rightarrow \Diamond_{[0,12]} o_i)$	4 / 37	✓	>5min	1148 / 541	1008 / 376
3	$\Box \bigwedge_{i=1,\ldots,3} (l_i \Rightarrow \Diamond_{[0,14]} o_i)$	4 / 37	✓	>5min	1321 / 774	1387 / 540
4	$\Box \bigwedge_{i=1,\ldots,4} (o_i \Rightarrow \Diamond_{]1,2]} c_i)$	5 / 114	×	5570 / 1638	1381 / 498	1565 / 461
4	$\Box \bigwedge_{i=1,\ldots,4} (b_i \Rightarrow \Diamond_{[0,20]} o_i)$	5 / 114	✓	>5min	26146 / 5757	22776 / 3156
4	$\Box \bigwedge_{i=1,\ldots,4} (l_i \Rightarrow \Diamond_{[0,22]} o_i)$	5 / 114	✓	>5min	52167 / 7577	48754 / 4337
5	$\Box \bigwedge_{i=1,\ldots,5} (o_i \Rightarrow \Diamond_{]1,2]} c_i)$	6 / 311	×	61937 / 4692	3216 / 1402	3838 / 1310
5	$\Box \bigwedge_{i=1,\ldots,5} (b_i \Rightarrow \Diamond_{[0,28]} o_i)$	6 / 311	✓	>5min	>5min	OOM
5	$\Box \bigwedge_{i=1,\ldots,5} (l_i \Rightarrow \Diamond_{[0,30]} o_i)$	6 / 311	✓	OOM	>5min	>5min

and obtain a zone-based version of the fix point algorithm given above. We rely on the $Approx_\beta$ widening operator [4] to ensure convergence of the fix point.

Eliminating useless clock copies. In many practical examples, MITL formulas contain modalities of the form $U_{[0,+\infty)}$ or $\tilde{U}_{[0,+\infty)}$ that do not impose any real-time constraints (in some sense, they are LTL modalities). For instance, consider the $\Box$ modality in $\varphi = \Box(a \Rightarrow \Diamond_{[1,2]}b)$. When this occurs in a formula φ, we can simplify the representation of configurations of $\mathcal{A}_\varphi$, by dropping the values of the clocks associated with those modalities (these clocks can be regarded as *inactive* in the sense of [8]). We call those configurations *reduced configurations*. In the example of Fig. 1, this amounts to skipping the clocks associated to $\ell_\Box$, and the configuration $\{(\ell_\Box, 0.1)(\ell_\Diamond, 0)\}$ of $\mathcal{A}_\varphi$ in Fig. 1 can be represented by a pair $(\{\ell_\Box\}, \{(\ell_\Diamond, 0)\})$. As we will see in the next section, maintaining reduced configurations, when possible, usually improves the performance of the algorithms.

6   Experimental Results

To evaluate the practical feasibility of our approach, we have implemented the region and zone-based algorithms for model-checking and satisfiability in a prototype tool. To the best of our knowledge, this is the first implementation to perform MITL model-checking and satisfiability using an automata-based approach. We first consider a benchmark for the *satisfiability problem*, adapted from the literature on LTL [9] and consisting of six parametric formulas (with $k \in \mathbb{N}$ and $I \in \mathcal{I}(\mathbb{N}^{+\infty})$):

$$E(k, I) = \bigwedge_{i=1,\ldots,k} \Diamond_I p_i \qquad U(k, I) = (\ldots (p_1 U_I p_2) U_I \ldots) U_I p_k$$
$$A(k, I) = \bigwedge_{i=1,\ldots,k} \Box_I p_i \qquad T(k, I) = p_1 \tilde{U}_I (p_2 \tilde{U}_I (p_3 \ldots p_{k-1} \tilde{U}_I p_k) \ldots)$$
$$Q(k, I) = \bigwedge_{i=1,\ldots,k} (\Diamond_I p_i \vee \Box_I p_{i+1}) \quad R(k, I) = \bigwedge_{i=1,\ldots,k} (\Box_I (\Diamond_I p_i) \vee \Diamond_I (\Box_I p_{i+1}))$$

Table 1 (top) reports on the running time, number of visited regions and returned answer (column 'Sat ?') of the prototype on several instances of those formulas, for the different data structures. A time out was set after 5 minutes, and OOM stands for 'out of memory'. Our second benchmark evaluates the performance of our *model-checking tool*. We consider a family of timed automata $\mathcal{B}_k^{lift}$ that model a *lift*, parametrised by the number k of floors (see appendix [6]). The alphabet of each $\mathcal{B}_k^{lift}$ contains, for all $0 \leq i \leq k-1$ letters b_i, l_i, o_i, c_i and p_i meaning respectively that the call button number i in the cabin control station is pressed, that the call button is pressed at floor i, and that the lift opens the doors, closes the doors or passes without stopping, at floor i. The lift takes 1 time unit to perform each action. Table 1 (bottom) reports on the performance of our prototype, for several properties, and values of the parameter. We have skipped the results for the 'reduced regions' because the running times are consistently longer (at most 30%) than with classical regions – the overhead induced by the elimination of useless clocks is a heuristic that does not pay off.

References

1. Alur, R., Dill, D.L.: A theory of timed automata. Theor. Comput. Sci. 126(2), 183–235 (1994)
2. Abdulla, P.A., Deneux, J., Ouaknine, J., Quaas, K., Worrell, J.: Universality Analysis for One-Clock Timed Automata. Fundam. Inform. 89(4), 419–450 (2008)
3. Alur, R., Feder, T., Henzinger, T.A.: The benefits of relaxing punctuality. J. ACM 43(1), 116–146 (1996)
4. Bouyer, P.: Timed Automata may cause some troubles. Research Report LSV-02-9, Lab. Spécification et Vérification, CNRS & ENS de Cachan, France (2002)
5. Brihaye, T., Estiévenart, M., Geeraerts, G.: On MITL and Alternating Timed Automata. In: Braberman, V., Fribourg, L. (eds.) FORMATS 2013. LNCS, vol. 8053, pp. 47–61. Springer, Heidelberg (2013)
6. Brihaye, T., Estiévenart, M., Geeraerts, G.: On MITL and Alternating Timed Automata over infinite words. Technical report arXiv.org., http://arxiv.org/abs/1406.4395
7. Clarke, E.M., Grumberg, O., Peled, D.: Model checking. MIT Press (2001)

8. Daws, C., Yovine, S.: Reducing the number of clock variables of timed automata. Real-Time Systems, 73–81 (1996)
9. Geeraerts, G., Kalyon, G., Le Gall, T., Maquet, N., Raskin, J.-F.: Lattice-Valued Binary Decision Diagrams. In: Bouajjani, A., Chin, W.-N. (eds.) ATVA 2010. LNCS, vol. 6252, pp. 158–172. Springer, Heidelberg (2010)
10. Gastin, P., Oddoux, D.: Fast LTL to Büchi Automata Translation. In: Berry, G., Comon, H., Finkel, A. (eds.) CAV 2001. LNCS, vol. 2102, pp. 53–65. Springer, Heidelberg (2001)
11. Koymans, R.: Specifying real-time properties with metric temporal logic. Real-Time Systems 2(4), 255–299 (1990)
12. Kupferman, O., Vardi, M.Y.: Weak alternating automata are not that weak. ACM Trans. Comput. Log. 2(3), 408–429 (2001)
13. Maquet, N.: New Algorithms and Data Structures for the Emptiness Problem of Alternating Automata. PhD thesis, Université Libre de Bruxelles (2011)
14. Miyano, S., Hayashi, T.: Alternating Finite Automata on omega-Words. Theor. Comput. Sci. 32, 321–330 (1984)
15. Ouaknine, J., Worrell, J.: On the decidability of metric temporal logic. In: LICS 2005, pp. 188–197. IEEE (2005)
16. Ouaknine, J., Worrell, J.: On the decidability and complexity of metric temporal logic over finite words. Logical Methods in Computer Science 3(1) (2007)
17. Parys, P., Walukiewicz, I.: Weak Alternating Timed Automata. Logical Methods in Computer Science 8(3) (2012)

Time Petri Nets with Dynamic Firing Dates: Semantics and Applications[*]

Bernard Berthomieu[1,2], Silvano Dal Zilio[1,2],
Łukasz Fronc[1,2], and François Vernadat[1,3]

[1] CNRS, LAAS, 7 avenue du Colonel Roche, 31400 Toulouse, France
[2] Université de Toulouse, LAAS, 31400 Toulouse, France
[3] Université de Toulouse, INSA, LAAS, 31400 Toulouse, France

Abstract. We define an extension of time Petri nets such that the time at which a transition can fire, also called its *firing date*, may be dynamically updated. Our extension provides two mechanisms for updating the timing constraints of a net. First, we propose to change the static time interval of a transition each time it is newly enabled; in this case the new time interval is given as a function of the current marking. Next, we allow to update the firing date of a transition when it is persistent, that is when a concurrent transition fires. We show how to carry the widely used state class abstraction to this new kind of time Petri nets and define a class of nets for which the abstraction is exact. We show the usefulness of our approach with two applications: first for scheduling preemptive task, as a poor man's substitute for stopwatch, then to model hybrid systems with non trivial continuous behavior.

1 Introduction

A *Time Petri Net* [16,6] (TPN) is a Petri net where every transition is associated to a static time interval that restricts the date at which a transition can fire. In this model, time progresses with a common rate in all the transitions that are enabled; then a transition t can fire if it has been continuously enabled for a time θ_t and if the value of θ_t is in the static time interval, denoted $\mathbf{I}_s(t)$. The term static time interval is appropriate in this context. Indeed, the constraint is immutable and do not change during the evolution of the net. In this paper, we lift this simple restriction and go one step further by also updating the timing constraint of persistent transitions, that is transitions that remain enabled while a concurrent transition fires. In a nutshell, we define an extension of TPN where the time at which a transition can fire, also called its *firing date*, may be dynamically updated. We say that these transitions are fickle and we use the term Dynamic TPN to refer to our extension.

Our extension provides two mechanisms for updating the timing constraints of a net. First, we propose to change the static time interval of a transition each time it is newly enabled. In this case the new time interval $\mathbf{I}_s(t, m)$ is

---

[*] This work has been partially supported by the ITEA2 project OpenETCS.

A. Legay and M. Bozga (Eds.): FORMATS 2014, LNCS 8711, pp. 85–99, 2014.

obtained as a function of the current marking m of the net. Likewise, we allow to update the deadline of persistent transitions using an expression of the form $\mathbf{I}_d(t, m, \varphi_t)$, that is based on the previous firing date of t. The first mechanism is straightforward and quite similar to an intrinsic capability of Timed Automata (TA); namely the possibility to compare a given clock to different constants depending on the current state. Surprisingly, it appears that this extension has never been considered in the context of TPN. The second mechanism is far more original. To the best of our knowledge, it has not been studied before in the context of TPN or TA, but there are some similarities with the updatable timed automata of Bouyer et al. [9].

The particularity of timed models, such as TPN, is that state spaces are typically infinite, with finite representations obtained by some abstractions of time. In the case of TPN, states are frequently represented using composite abstract states, or *state classes*, that capture a discrete information (e.g. the marking) together with a timing information (represented by systems of difference constraints or zones). We show how to carry the state class abstraction to our extended model of TPN. We only obtain an over-approximation of the state space in the most general case, but we define a class of nets for which the abstraction is exact. We conjecture that our approach could be used in other formal models for real-time systems, such as timed automata for instance.

There exist several tools for reachability analysis of TPN based on the notion of state class graph [5,3], like for example Tina [7] or Romeo [15]. Our construction provides a simple method for supporting fickle transitions in these tools. We already provide a prototype implementation of fickle transitions in Tina, see `http://projects.laas.fr/tina/fickle/`. We have used this prototype to test the usefulness of our approach in the context of two possible applications: first for scheduling preemptive task, as a poor man's substitute for stopwatch; next to model dynamical systems with non trivial continuous behavior.

2   Time Petri Nets and Fickle Transitions

A *Time Petri net* is a Petri net where transitions are decorated with static time intervals that constrain the time a transition can fire. We denote $\mathbb{I}$ the set of possible time intervals. We use a dense time model in our definitions, meaning that we choose for $\mathbb{I}$ the set of real intervals with non negative rational endpoints. To simplify the definitions, we only consider the case of closed intervals, $[a, b]$, and infinite intervals of the form $[a, +\infty)$. For any interval i in $\mathbb{I}$, we use the notation $\downarrow i$ for its left end-point and $\uparrow i$ for its right end-point.

We use the expression Dynamic TPN (DTPN) when it is necessary to make the distinction between our model and more traditional definitions of TPN. With our notations, a dynamic TPN is a tuple $\langle P, T, \mathbf{Pre}, \mathbf{Post}, m_0, \mathbf{I}_s, \mathbf{I}_d \rangle$ in which:

- $\langle P, T, \mathbf{Pre}, \mathbf{Post}, m_0 \rangle$ is a Petri net, with P the set of places, T the set of transitions, $m_0 : P \to \mathbb{N}$ the initial marking, and $\mathbf{Pre}, \mathbf{Post} : T \to P \to \mathbb{N}$ the precondition and postcondition functions.

- $\mathbf{I}_s$ is the *static interval function*, that associates a time interval (in $\mathbb{I}$) to every transition (in T).
- $\mathbf{I}_d$ is the *dynamic interval function*. It will be used to update the firing date of persistent transitions.

We slightly extend the "traditional" model of TPN and allow to define the static time interval of a transition as a function of the markings, meaning that $\mathbf{I}_s$ is a function of $T \to (P \to \mathbb{N}) \to \mathbb{I}$. We will sometimes use the curryied function $\mathbf{I}_s(t)$ to denote the mapping from a marking m to the time interval $\mathbf{I}_s(t, m)$.

We also add the notion of *dynamic interval function*, $\mathbf{I}_d$, that is used to update the firing date of persistent transitions. The idea is to update the firing date φ_t of a persistent transition t using a function of φ_t. Hence $\mathbf{I}_d$ is a function of $T \to (P \to \mathbb{N}) \to \mathbb{R}_{\geq 0} \to \mathbb{I}$. For example, a transition t such that $\mathbf{I}_d(t, m, \theta) = [\theta + 1, \theta + 2]$, for all $\theta \geq 0$, models an event that is delayed by between 1 and 2 units of time (u.t.) when a concurrent transition fires.

2.1   A Semantics for Time Petri Nets Based on Firing Functions

As usual, we define a *marking* m of a TPN as a function $m : P \to \mathbb{N}$ from places to naturals. A transition $t \in T$ is *enabled* at m if and only if $m \geq \mathbf{Pre}(t)$ (we use the pointwise comparison between functions). We denote $\mathcal{E}(m)$ the set of transitions enabled at m.

A *state* of a TPN is a pair $s = (m, \varphi)$ in which m is a marking and $\varphi : T \to \mathbb{R}_{\geq 0}$ is a mapping, called the *firing function* of s, that associates a firing date to every transition enabled at m. Intuitively, if t is enabled at m, then φ_t is the date (in the future, from now) at which t should fire. Also, the transitions that may fire from a state (m, φ) are exactly the transitions t in $\mathcal{E}(m)$ such that φ_t is minimal; they are the first scheduled to fire.

For any date θ in $\mathbb{R}_{\geq 0}$, we denote $\varphi \dot{-} \theta$ the partial function that associates the transition t to the value $\varphi_t - \theta$, when $\varphi_t \geq \theta$, and that is undefined elsewhere. This operation is useful to model the effect of time passage on the enabled transitions of a net. We say that the firing function $\varphi \dot{-} \theta$ is well-defined if it is defined on exactly the same transitions as φ.

The following definitions are quite standard. The semantics of a TPN is a Kripke structure $\langle S, S_0, \to \rangle$ with only two possible kind of actions: either $s \xrightarrow{t} s'$ (meaning that the transition $t \in T$ is fired from s); or $s \xrightarrow{\theta} s'$, with $\theta \in \mathbb{R}_{\geq 0}$ (meaning that we let time θ elapse from s). A transition t may fire from the state (m, φ) if t is enabled at m and firable instantly (that is $\varphi_t = 0$). In a state transition $(m, \varphi) \xrightarrow{t} (m', \varphi')$, we say that a transition k is *persistent* (with $k \neq t$) if it is also enabled in the marking $m - \mathbf{Pre}(t)$, that is if $m - \mathbf{Pre}(t) \geq \mathbf{Pre}(k)$. The transitions that are enabled at m' and not at m are called *newly enabled*. We define the predicates prs and nbl that describe the set of persistent and newly enabled transitions after t fires from m:

$$\mathrm{prs}(m, t) = \{\, k \in \mathcal{E}(m) \setminus \{t\} \mid m - \mathbf{Pre}(t) \geq \mathbf{Pre}(k) \,\}$$
$$\mathrm{nbl}(m, t) = \{\, k \in (T \setminus \mathcal{E}(m)) \cup \{t\} \mid m - \mathbf{Pre}(t) + \mathbf{Post}(t) \geq \mathbf{Pre}(k) \,\}$$

We use these two predicates to define the semantics of DTPN.

Definition 1. *The semantics of a DTPN* $\langle P, T, \mathbf{Pre}, \mathbf{Post}, m_0, \mathbf{I}_s, \mathbf{I}_d \rangle$ *is the timed transition system* $SG = \langle S, S_0, \rightarrow \rangle$ *such that:*

- *S is the set of states of the TPN;*
- *S_0, the set of initial states, is the subset of states of the form (m_0, φ), where m_0 is the initial marking and $\varphi_t \in \mathbf{I}_s(t, m_0)$ for every t in $\mathcal{E}(m_0)$;*
- *the state transition relation $\rightarrow \subseteq S \times (T \cup \mathbb{R}_{\geq 0}) \times S$ is the smallest relation such that for all state (m, φ) in S:*
  - *(i) if t is enabled at m and $\varphi_t = 0$ then $(m, \varphi) \xrightarrow{t} (m', \varphi')$ where $m' = m - \mathbf{Pre}(t) + \mathbf{Post}(t)$ and φ' is a firing function such that $\varphi'_k \in \mathbf{I}_d(k, m', \varphi_k)$ for all persistent transition $k \in \mathrm{prs}(m, t)$ and $\varphi'_k \in \mathbf{I}_s(k, m')$ otherwise.*
  - *(ii) if $\varphi \div \theta$ is well-defined then $(m, \varphi) \xrightarrow{\theta} (m, \varphi \div \theta)$.*

The state transitions labelled over T (case (i) above) are the *discrete* transitions, those labelled over $\mathbb{R}_{\geq 0}$ (case (ii)) are the *continuous*, or time elapsing, transitions. It is clear from Definition 1 that, in a discrete transition $(m, \varphi) \xrightarrow{t} (m', \varphi')$, the transitions enabled at m' are exactly $\mathrm{prs}(m, t) \cup \mathrm{nbl}(m, t)$. In the target state (m', φ'), a newly enabled transition k gets assigned a firing date picked "at random" in $\mathbf{I}_s(k, m')$. Similarly, a persistent transition k get assigned a firing date in $\mathbf{I}_d(k, m', \varphi_k)$. Because there may be an infinite number of transitions, the state spaces of TPN are generally infinite, even when the net is bounded. This is why we introduce an abstraction of the semantics in Sect. 3.

2.2   Interesting Classes of DTPN

In the standard semantics of TPN [16], the firing date of a persistent transition is left unchanged. We can obtain a similar behavior by choosing for $\mathbf{I}_d(t, m, \theta)$ the time interval $[\theta, \theta]$. We say in this case that the dynamic interval function is *trivial*. Another difference with respect to the standard definition of TPN is the fact that the (static!) time interval of a transition may change. We say that a dynamic net is a TPN if its static function, $\mathbf{I}_s$, is constant and its dynamic function, $\mathbf{I}_d$, is trivial. We say that a DTPN is *weak* if only the function $\mathbf{I}_d$ is trivial. We show that TPN are as expressive as weak DTPN when the nets are bounded. Weak nets are still interesting though, since the use of non-constant interval functions can lead to more concise models. On the other hand, the results of Sect. 3 show that, even in bounded nets, fickle transitions are more expressive than weak ones. (Proofs can be found in a long version of this paper [19]).

Theorem 1. *For every weak DTPN that has a finite set of reachable markings, there is a TPN that has an equivalent semantics.*

We define a third class of nets, called *translation DTPN*, obtained by restricting the dynamic interval function $\mathbf{I}_d$. This class arises naturally during the definition of the State Class Graph construction in Sect. 3. Intuitively, with this restriction, a persistent transition can only shift its firing date by a "constant time". The constant can be negative and may be a function of the marking.

More precisely, we say that a DTPN is a translation if, for every transitions t, there are two functions κ_1 and κ_2 from $(P \to \mathbb{N}) \to \mathbb{Q}$ such that $\mathbf{I}_d(t, m, \theta)$ is the time interval $[A, B]$ where $A = \max(0, \theta + \kappa_1(m))$ and $B = \max(A, \theta + \kappa_2(m))$. (The use of max in the definition of A, B is necessary to accomodate negative constants $\kappa_i(m)$); weak DTPN are a trivial example of translation DTPN.

2.3   Interpretation of the Quantized State System Model

With the addition of fickle transitions, it is possible to model systems where the timing constraints of an event depend on the current state. This kind of situations arises naturally in practice. For instance, we can use the function $\mathbf{I}_s$ to model the fact that the duration of a communication depends on the length of a message (the marking of a place).

In this section, we consider a simple method for analyzing the behavior of a system with one continuous variable, x, governed by the ordinary differential equation $\dot{x} = f(x)$. The idea is to define a TPN that computes the value $x(\theta)$ of the variable x at the date θ. To this end, we use an extension of TPN with shared variables, $x, y, \ldots$, where every transition may be guarded by a boolean predicate (**on** b) and such that, upon firing, a transition can update the environment (using a sequence of assignments, **do** e). This extension of TPN with shared variables can already be analyzed using the tool Tina.

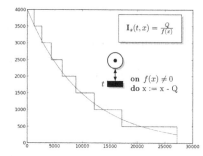
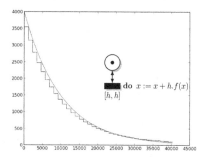

Fig. 1. A simple QSS simulation (left) and the Euler method (right) for $\dot{x} = -x$. ($Q = 500$, $h = 1150$, global error smaller than 500.)

The simplest solution is based on the Euler forward method. This is modeled by the TPN of Fig. 1 (right) that periodically executes the instruction $x :=$ $x + h.f(x)$ every h (the value of the time step, h, is the only parameter of the method). This solution is a typical example of (synchronous) discrete time system, where we sample the evolution of the system using a "quantum of time". A discrete time approach answers the following question: given the value of x at time $k.h$, what is its value at time $(k + 1).h$?

The second solution is based on the Quantized State System (QSS) method [11,12], which can be interpreted as the dual of the Euler method. QSS uses a "quantum of value", Q, meaning that we only consider discrete values for x, of the form $k.Q$ with $k \in \mathbb{N}$. The idea is to compute the time necessary for x to change by an amount of Q. To paraphrase [12], the QSS method answers the following modified question: given that x has value $k.Q$, what is the earliest time at which x has value $(k \pm 1).Q$? This method has a direct implementation using fickle transitions: at first approximation, the time φ_t for x to change by an amount of Q is given by relation $Q = \varphi_t.f(x)$, that is $\varphi_t = Q/|f(x)|$. We have that the *time slope* of x is equal to $1/f(x)$.

We compare the results obtained with these two different solutions in Fig. 1, where we choose $f(x) = -x$ and $x(0) = 4000$. Each plot displays the evolution of the TPN compared to the analytic solution, in this case $x(\theta) = 4000e^{-\theta}$. Numerical methods are of course approximate; in both cases (Euler and QSS) the global error is proportional to the quantum. The plots are obtained with the largest quantum values giving a global error smaller than 500, that is a step h of 1150 and a quantum Q of 500. The dynamic TPN has 10 states while the standard TPN has 38. The ratio improves when we try to decrease the global error. For instance, for an error smaller than 100 (which gives $Q = 100$ and $h = 250$) we have 42 states against 182. We observe that in this case the "asynchronous" solution is more concise than the synchronous one.

The Euler method is the simplest example in a large family of iterative methods for approximating the solutions of differential equations. The QSS method used in this section can be enhanced in just the same way, leading to more precise solutions, with better numerical stability. Some of the improved QSS methods have been implemented in our tool, but we still experiment the effect of numerical instability on some stiff systems. In these cases, the synchronous approach (that is deterministic) may sometimes exhibit better performances.

Although we make no use of the fickle function $\mathbf{I}_d$ here, it arises naturally when the system has multiple variables. Consider a system with two variables, x, y, such that $\dot{x} = f(x, y)$. We can use the same solution than in Fig. 1 to model the evolution of x and y. When the value of x just changes, the next update is scheduled at the date $Q/f(x,y)$ (the time slope is $f_1 = 1/f(x,y)$). If the value of y is incremented before this deadline—say that the remaining time is θ_1—we need to update the time slope and use the new value $f_2 = 1/f(x,y+Q)$.

We illustrate the situation in the two diagrams of Fig. 2, where we assume that f_1 is positive. For instance, if the two slopes have the same sign (diagram to the left), we need to update the firing date to the value θ_2 such that $|f_1|.\theta_1 = |f_2|.\theta_2$. Likewise, when f_2 is negative, we have the relation $|f_1|.\theta_1 + |f_2|.\theta_2 = 2.Q$. Therefore, depending on the sign of $f_1.f_2$ (the sign of $\dot{y}$ tell us whether y is incremented or decremented) we have $\mathbf{I}_d(t, x, y, \theta) = [A(\theta), A(\theta)]$ with:

$$A(\theta) = \frac{|f(x, y \pm Q)|}{|f(x, y)|}.\theta \quad \text{or} \quad \frac{|f(x, y \pm Q)|}{|f(x, y)|}.(2.Q.|f(x, y)| - \theta)$$

This example shows that it is possible to implement the QSS method using only linear fickle functions.

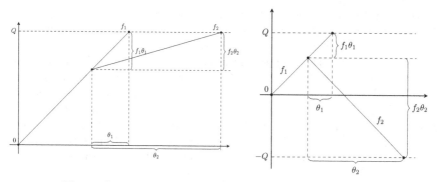

Fig. 2. Computing the updated firing date in the QSS method

3   A State Class Abstraction for Dynamic TPN

In this section, we generalize the state class abstraction method to the case of DTPN. A State Class Graph (SCG) is a finite abstraction of the timed transition system of a net that preserves the markings and traces. The construction is based on the idea that temporal information in states (the firing functions) can be conveniently represented using systems of difference constraints [18]. We show that the SCG faithfully abstracts the semantics of a net when the dynamic interval functions are translations. We only over-approximate the set of reachable markings in the most general case.

A state class C is defined by a pair (m, D), where m is a marking and the firing domain D is described by a (finite) system of difference constraints. In a domain D, we use variables $x_t, y_t, \ldots$ to denote a constraint on the value of φ_t. A domain D is defined by a set of difference constraints, that is a system of inequalities: $\alpha_i \leq x_i \leq \beta_i$ and $x_i - x_j \leq \gamma_{i,j}$, where i, j range over a given subset of "enabled transitions" and the coefficients α, β and γ are rational numbers. We can improve the reduced form of D by choosing the tightest possible bounds that do not change its associated solutions set. In this case we say that D is in closure form. We show in Th. 2 how to compute the coefficients of the closure form incrementally.

In the remainder of this section, we use the notation $A_t^s(m)$ and $B_t^s(m)$ for the left and right endpoints of $\mathbf{I}_s(t, m)$. Likewise, when the marking m is obvious from the context, we use the notations $A_t(\theta)$ and $B_t(\theta)$ for the left and right endpoints of $\mathbf{I}_d(t, m, \theta)$, that is $A_t(\theta) = \downarrow\mathbf{I}_d(t, m, \theta)$ and $B_t(\theta) = \uparrow\mathbf{I}_d(t, m, \theta)$. We call A_t and B_t the fickle functions of t. In the remainder of the text, we assume that $0 \leq A_t(\theta) \leq B_t(\theta)$ for all possible (positive) date θ and that $B(\infty) = \lim_{\theta \to \infty} B(\theta)$. We also require these functions to be monotonically increasing. We impose no other restrictions on the fickle functions.

We define inductively a set of classes C_σ, where $\sigma \in T^*$ is a sequence of discrete transitions firable from the initial state. This is the State Class Graph construction of [5,3]. Intuitively, the class $C_\sigma = (m, D_\sigma)$ "collects" the states reachable from the initial state by firing schedules of support sequence σ. The initial class C_ϵ is (m_0, D_0) where D_0 is the domain defined by the set of inequalities $A_i^s(m_0) \leq x_i \leq B_i^s(m_0)$ for all i in $\mathcal{E}(m_0)$.

Assume $C_\sigma = (m, D)$ is defined and that t is enabled at m. We detail how to compute the domain for the class $C_{\sigma.t}$. First we test whether the system D extended with the constraints $D_t = \{x_k - x_t \geq 0 \mid t \neq k, k \in \mathcal{E}(m)\}$ is consistent. This is in order to check that transition t can be fired before any other enabled transitions k at m. If $D \wedge D_t$ is consistent, we add $C_{\sigma.t} = (m', D')$ to the set of reachable classes, where m' is the result of firing t from m, i.e. $m' = m - \mathbf{Pre}(t) + \mathbf{Post}(t)$. The computation of D' follows the same logic than with standard TPN.

We choose a set of fresh variables, say y_k, for every transition k that is enabled at m'. For every persistent transition, $k \in \mathrm{prs}(m, t)$, we add the constraints $y_k = x_k - x_t$ to the set of inequalities in $D \wedge D_t$. The variable y_k matches the firing date of k at the time t fires, that is, the value of φ_k used in the expression $\mathbf{I}_d(k, m', \varphi_k)$ (see Definition 1, case (i)). For every newly enabled transition, $k \in \mathrm{nbl}(m, t)$, we add the constraints $A_k^s(m') \leq y_k \leq B_k^s(m')$. This constraint matches the fact that φ_k' is in the interval $\mathbf{I}_s(k, m')$ if k is newly enabled at m'. As a result, we obtain a set of inequations where we can eliminate all occurrences of the variables x_k and x_t. After removing redundant inequalities and simplifying the constraints on transitions in conflicts with t—so that the variables only range over transitions enabled at m'—we obtain an "intermediate" domain D_{int} that obeys the constraints: $\kappa_i \leq y_i \leq \lambda_i$ and $y_i - y_j \leq \mu_{i,j}$, where i, j range over $\mathcal{E}(m')$ and the constants κ, λ and μ are defined as follows.

$$
\kappa_i = \begin{cases} A_i^s(m') & \text{if } i \text{ is newly enabled,} \\ \max(0, \{-\gamma_{i,j} \mid j \in \mathcal{E}(M)\}) & \text{otherwise} \end{cases}
$$

$$
\lambda_i = \begin{cases} B_i^s(m') & \text{if } i \text{ is newly enabled,} \\ \gamma_{i,t} & \text{otherwise} \end{cases} \tag{C1}
$$

$$
\mu_{i,j} = \begin{cases} \lambda_i - \kappa_j & \text{if either } i \text{ or } j \text{ newly enabled,} \\ \min(\gamma_{i,j}, \lambda_i - \kappa_j) & \text{otherwise} \end{cases}
$$

Finally, we need to apply the effect of the fickle functions. For this, we rely on the fact that A_i and B_i are monotonically increasing functions. To obtain D', we choose a set of fresh variables, say x_i', for every transition $i \in \mathcal{E}(m')$ and add the following relations to D_{int}. To simplify the notation, we assume that in the case of a newly enabled transition, j, the functions A_j and B_j stand for the identity function (with this shorthand, we avoid to distinguish cases where both or only one of the transitions are persistent):

$$
\begin{aligned} x_i' &= y_i && \text{if } i \text{ newly enabled} \\ A_i(y_i) \leq x_i' &\leq B_i(y_i) \text{ and } x_i' - x_j' \leq B_i(y_i) - A_j(y_j) && \text{if } i \text{ or } j \text{ are persistent} \end{aligned}
$$

The relation for newly enabled transitions simply states that y_i already captures all the constraints on the firing time φ_i'. For persistent transitions, the first relation states that x_i' is in the interval $[A_i(y_i), B_i(y_i)]$, that is in $\mathbf{I}_d(i, m', \varphi(i))$.

We obtain the domain D' by eliminating all the variables of the kind y_i. First, we can observe that, by monotonicity of the functions A_i and B_i, we have $A_i(\kappa_i) \leq A_i(y_i)$ and $B_i(y_i) \leq B_i(\lambda_i)$. This gives directly a value for the coefficients α_i' and β_i'. The computation of the coefficient $\gamma_{i,j}'$ is more complex, since it amounts to computing the maximum of a function over a convex sets of points. Indeed $\gamma_{i,j}'$ is the least upper-bound for the values of $x_i' - x_j'$ over D_{int} or, equivalently:

$$\gamma_{i,j}' = \max \{B_i(y_i) - A_j(y_j) \mid y_i, y_j \in D_{int}\}$$
$$= \max \{B_i(y_i) - A_j(y_j) \mid \kappa_i \leq y_i \leq \lambda_i, \kappa_j \leq y_j \leq \lambda_j, y_i - y_j \leq \mu_{i,j}\}$$

It is possible to simplify the definition of $\gamma_{i,j}'$. Indeed, if we fix the value of y_j then, by monotonicity of B_i, the maximal value of $B_i(y_i) - A_j(y_j)$ is reached when y_i is maximal. Hence we have two possible cases: either (i) it is reached for $y_i = y_j + \mu_{i,j}$ if $\kappa_j \leq y_j \leq \lambda_i + \mu_{i,j}$; or (ii) it is reached for $y_i = \lambda_i$ if $\lambda_i - \mu_{i,j} \leq y_j \leq \lambda_j$. This result is illustrated in the schema of Fig. 3a, where we display an example of domain D_{int}. When y_j is constant (horizontal line), the maximal value is on the "right" border of the convex set (bold line). We also observe that in case (ii), by monotonicity of A_j, the maximal value is equal to $B_i(\lambda_i) - A_j(\lambda_i + \mu_{i,j})$. Therefore the value of $\gamma_{i,j}'$ is obtained by computing the maximal value of the expression $B_i(\theta) - A_j(\theta - \mu_{i,j})$, that is:

$$\gamma_{i,j}' = \max \{B_i(\theta) - A_j(\theta - \mu_{i,j}) \mid \kappa_j + \mu_{i,j} \leq \theta \leq \lambda_i\} \qquad \text{(C2)}$$

As a consequence, the value of $\gamma_{i,j}'$ can be computed by finding the minimum of a numerical function (of one parameter) over a real interval.

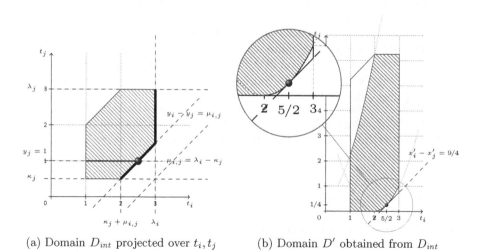

(a) Domain D_{int} projected over t_i, t_j (b) Domain D' obtained from D_{int}

Fig. 3. Computing the coefficient $\gamma_{i,j}'$ in the domain D'

We display in Fig. 3b the domain D' obtained from D_{int} after applying the fickle functions. In this example, t_j is the only fickle transition and we choose $A_j(\theta) = B_j(\theta) = (\theta - 1/2)^2$ when $\theta \geq 1/2$. With our method we have that $\mu_{i,j} = 3/2$ and the value of $\gamma'_{i,j}$ is obtained by computing the maximal value of the expression $(\theta - 1/2)^2 - (\theta - 3/2)$ with $\theta \in [2, 3]$, that is $9/4$.

Theorem 2. *Assume $C = (m, D)$ is a class with D in closure form. Then for every transition t in $\mathcal{E}(m)$ there is a unique class (m', D') obtained from C by firing t. The domain D' is also in closure form and can be computed incrementally as follows (we assume that A_i and B_i stands for the identity functions when i is newly enabled).*

$$
\begin{aligned}
\alpha'_i &= A^s_i(m') && \textit{if } i \textit{ is newly enabled,} \\
&= \max\left(A_i(0), \{A_i(-\gamma_{i,j}) \mid j \in \mathcal{E}(M)\}\right) && \textit{otherwise} \\
\beta'_i &= B^s_i(m') && \textit{if } i \textit{ is newly enabled,} \\
&= B_i(\gamma_{i,t}) && \textit{otherwise} \\
\gamma'_{i,j} &= \min(\gamma_{i,j}, \beta'_i - \alpha'_j) && \textit{if } i, j \textit{ are newly enabled,} \\
&= \max\{B_i(\theta) - A_j(\theta - \mu_{i,j}) \mid \mu_{i,j} + \kappa_j \leq x \leq \lambda_i\} && \textit{otherwise} \\
&&& \textit{(where } \lambda_i, \kappa_j \textit{ and } \mu_{i,j} \textit{ are defined as in (C1))}
\end{aligned}
$$

Moreover, if the state (m, φ) is reachable in the state graph of a net, say N, and $(m, \varphi) \xrightarrow{\theta} \xrightarrow{t} (m', \varphi')$ then there is a class $C_\sigma = (m, D)$ reachable in the SCG computed for N with $\varphi \in D$, $C_{\sigma.t} = (m', D')$ and $\varphi' \in D'$.

The hatched area inside the domain displayed in Fig. 3b is the image of the domain D_{int} after its transformation by the fickle function $A_j(\theta)$. We see that some points of D' have no corresponding states in D_{int}. Hence we only have an over-approximation. (We do not have enough space to give an example of net with a marking that is reachable in the SCG but not reachable in the state space, but such an example is quite easy to build.) If we consider the definition of the coefficients γ' in equation (C2), we observe that the situation is much simpler if the fickle functions are translations. Actually, it is possible to prove that, in this case, the SCG construction is exact.

Theorem 3. *If the DTPN N is a translation then the SCG defined in Th. 2 has the same set of reachable markings and the same set of traces as the timed transition system of N.*

Proof (sketch). If the net is a translation then there are two constants c_i, c_j such that $B_i(\theta) = \theta + c_i$ and $A_j(\theta) = \theta + c_j$. Therefore the expression $B_i(\theta) - A_j(\theta - \mu_{i,j})$, used in equation (C2), is constant and equal to $c_i - c_j - \mu_{i,j}$ (the maximum is reached all over the boundary of the domain). In this case, every state in D' has a corresponding state in D_{int}. □

We can also observe that, if the dynamic interval bounds A_i and B_i are linear functions, then we can follow a similar construct using (general) systems of inequations for the domains instead of difference constraints. This solution gives also an exact abstraction for the state space but is not interesting from a computational point of view (since we loose the ability to compute a canonical form for the domain incrementally). In this case, we are in a situation comparable to the addition of stopwatch to TPN where systems of difference constraints are not enough to precisely capture state classes. With our computation of the coefficient γ', we use instead the "best difference bound matrix" that contains the states reachable from the class C. This approximation is used in some tools that support stopwatches, like Romeo [15] or ORIS [10].

4   Two Application for Dynamic TPN

We study two possible applications for fickle transitions. First to model a system of preemptive, periodic tasks with fixed duration. Next to model hybrid system with non trivial continuous behavior. These experiments have been carried out using a prototype extension of Tina. The tool and all the models are available online at http://projects.laas.fr/tina/fickle/.

4.1   Scheduling Preemptive Tasks

We consider a simple system consisting of two periodic tasks, Task1 and Task2, executing on a single processor. Task2 has a period of 10 unit of time (u.t.) and a duration of 6 u.t. ; Task1 has a period of 5 u.t. and a duration of 1 and can preempt Task2 at any time. We display in Fig. 4 a TPN model for this system. Our model makes use of a *stopwatch arc*, drawn using an "open box" arrow tip (—□), and of an inhibitor arc (—○).

The net is the composition of four components. The roles of Sched1 and Sched2 is to provide a token in place psched at the scheduling date of the tasks. The behavior of the nets corresponding to Task1 and Task2 are similar. Both nets are 1-safe and their (unique) token capture the state of the tasks. When the token is in place e, the task execute; when it is in place w it is waiting for its scheduling event. Hence we have a scheduling error if there is a token in place psched and not in place w.

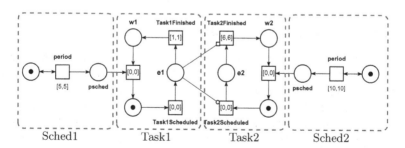

Fig. 4. System with one preemptive and one simple task

We use an inhibitor arc between the place e1 and the transition Task2Scheduled to model the fact that Task2 cannot use the processor if Task1 is already running. We use a stopwatch arc between e1 and the transition Task2Finished to model the fact that Task1 can preempt Task2 at any moment. A stopwatch (inhibitor) arc "freezes" the firing date of its transition. Therefore the completion of Task2 (the firing date of Task2Finished) is postponed as long as Task1 is running. Using the same approach, we can define a TPN modeling a system with one preemptive task and n "simple"tasks.

We can define an equivalent model using fickle transitions instead of stopwatch. The idea is to add the duration of Task1 to the completion date of Task2 each time Task1 starts executing (that is Task1Scheduled fires). This can be obtained by removing stopwatch arcs and using for Task2Finished the fickle functions $A(\theta) = B(\theta) = \theta + 1$ when Task1Scheduled fires and the identity otherwise. The resulting dynamic TPN is a translation and therefore the SCG construction is exact. In this new model, we simulate preemption by adding the duration of the interrupting thread to the completion date of the other running thread. The same idea was used by Bodeveix et al. in [17], where they prove the correctness of this approach using the B method.

The following table gives the results obtained when computing the SCG for different number of tasks. The models with fickle transitions have slightly more classes than their stopwatch counterpart. Indeed, in the fickle case, the firing date of Task2Finished can reach a value of 7, while it is always bounded by 6 with stopwatches. The last row of the Table gives the computation time speedup between our implementation of fickle transitions and the default implementation of stopwatch in Tina. We observe that the computation with fickle transitions is (consistently) two times faster; this is explained by the fact that the algorithmic for stopwatches is more complex. Memory consumption is almost equal between the two versions approaches, with a slight advantage for the fickle model.

# tasks	2	3	5	10	12
# states $\left(\text{fickle}/\text{stopwatch}\right)$	84 83	208 205	1 786 1 771	539 902 539 391	5 447 504 5 445 457
time speedup $\left(\text{fickle}/\text{stopwatch}\right)$	$\times 2.00$ $\left(0.005s/0.010s\right)$	$\times 1.90$ $\left(0.022s/0.042s\right)$	$\times 2.12$ $\left(0.37s/0.784s\right)$	$\times 2.31$ $\left(170s/392s\right)$	$\times 1.95$ $\left(3077s/6024s\right)$

4.2   Verification of Linear Hybrid systems

The semantics of fickle transitions came naturally from our goal of implementing the QSS method using TPN (see Sect. 2.3). We give some experimental results obtained using this approach on two very simple use cases.

Our first example is a model for the behavior of hydraulic cylinders in a landing gear system [8]. The system can switch between two modes, extension and retraction. The only parameter is the position x of the cylinder head. (It is possible to stop and to inverse the motion of a cylinder at any time.) The system is governed by the relation $\dot{x} = 5 - x$ while opening, with $x \in [0, 5]$, and $\dot{x} = -1$ while closing. We can model this system using two fickle transitions.

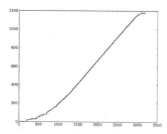 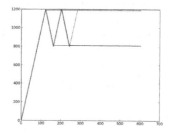

Fig. 5. Evolution of the PI-controller: fickle (left) and discrete (right) versions

The second example is a model for a *double integrator*, an extension of the simple integrator of Fig. 1 to a system with two interdependent variables x_1 and x_2. The system has two components, P_1, P_2, where P_i is in charge of the evolution of x_i, for $i \in \{1, 2\}$, and each x_i is governed by the relation $\dot{x}_i = f_i(x_1, x_2)$. The components P_1 and P_2 are concurrent and interact with each other by sending an event when the value of x_i changes. Therefore the system mixes message passing and hybrid evolution. This system can be used to solve second order linear differential equations of the form $\ddot{y} = k_P \dot{y} + k_I(S - y)$; we simply take $\dot{x}_1 = x_2$ and $\dot{x}_2 = k_P x_2 + k_I(S - x_1)$. This family of equations often appears in control-loop feedback mechanisms, where they model the behavior of proportional-integral (PI) controller. For example, a system with double quantized integrators is studied in [14] in the context of a dynamic cruise controller.

We compare the results obtained with our two versions of the integrator: fickle and discrete (synchronous). Figure. 5 displays the evolution of the variable x_1 in the PI-controller for our two models, with a quantum of $1/10$. We observe that the discrete version does not converge with this time step (we need to choose a value of $1/100$).

System	Landing Gear		Cruise Control (PI-controller)		
(version)	(fickle)	(discrete)	(fickle)	(discrete)	(discrete)
parameters	$Q = 1/10$	$h = 1/10$	$Q = 1/10$	$h = 1/10$	$h = 1/100$
# states	1 906	2 590	259	2 049	20 549
time (s)	0.076	0.125	0.004	0.017	0.185
memory (MB)	1.00	1.56	0.11	0.90	9.02

5 Conclusion and Related Work

We have shown how to extend the *SCG* construction to handle fickle transitions. The *SCG* is certainly the most widely used state space abstraction for Time Petri nets: it is a convenient abstraction for LTL model checking; it is finite when the set of markings is bounded; and it preserves both the markings and traces of the net. The results are slightly different with dynamic TPN, even for the restricted class of translation nets. In particular, we may have an infinite *SCG* even when the net is bounded. This may be the case, for instance, if we have a transition that can stay persistent infinitely and that is associated to the fickle function $\mathbf{I}_d(\theta) = [\theta + 1, \theta + 1]$. This entails that our construction may not terminate, even if the set of markings is bounded. This situation is quite comparable to what occurs with *updatable timed automata* [9] and, like in this model, it is possible to prove that the model-checking problem is undecidable in the general case. This does not mean that our construction is useless in practice, as we show in our examples of Sect. 4.

The notion of fickle transitions came naturally as the simplest extension of TPN able to integrate the Quantized State System (QSS) method inside Tina. Although there are still problems left unanswered, this could provide a solution for supporting hybrid systems inside a real-time model-checker. Section 3 gives clues on how to support fickle transitions in existing tools for standard TPN. Indeed, the incremental computation of the coefficients (α, β and γ) in the *SCG* construction is not very different from what is already implemented in tools like Tina or Romeo.

There are two main differences. First, we need to apply a numerical function over the coefficients of D_{int}; this is easy if the tool already supports associating a function to a transition in a TPN, as it is the case with Tina. Next, we need to compute the maximal value of a numerical function over a given interval; this can be easily added to the tool or delegated to a numerical solver. Actually, for the examples presented in Sect. 4, we only need to use affine functions, for which the maximal value can be defined by a simple analytical expression. As a result, it should be relatively easy to adapt existing tools to support the addition of fickle transitions. This assessment is supported by our experience when extending Tina. ; once the semantics of fickle transitions was stable, it took less than a week to adapt our tools and to obtain the first results.

To our knowledge, updatable TA is the closest model to dynamic TPN. The relation between these two models is not straightforward. We consider very general update functions but do not allow the use of multiple firing dates in an update (that would be the equivalent of using other clocks in TA). Also, the notion of persistent transitions does not exist in TA while it is central in our approach. While the work on updatable TA is geared toward decidability issues, we rather concentrate on the implementation of our extension and its possible applications. Nonetheless, it would be interesting to define a formal, structural translations between the two models, like it was done in [2,6] between TA and TPN. Some of our results also show similarities between fickle transitions and the use of stopwatch [4]. In the general case, it does not seem possible to encode one extension with the other, but it would be interesting to look further into this question. Finally, since the notion of slope is central in our implementation of the QSS method (see Sect. 2.3), it would be interesting to compare our results with an approach based on multirate transitions [13], that is a model where time does not advance at the same rate in all the transitions.

References

1. Berthomieu, B., Vernadat, F.: State class constructions for branching analysis of time petri nets. In: Garavel, H., Hatcliff, J. (eds.) TACAS 2003. LNCS, vol. 2619, pp. 442–457. Springer, Heidelberg (2003)
2. Bérard, B., Cassez, F., Haddad, S., Lime, D., Roux, O.H.: Comparison of the expressiveness of timed automata and time petri nets. In: Pettersson, P., Yi, W. (eds.) FORMATS 2005. LNCS, vol. 3829, pp. 211–225. Springer, Heidelberg (2005)
3. Berthomieu, B., Diaz, M.: Modeling and verification of time dependent systems using time Petri nets. IEEE Trans. on Software Engineering 17(3), 259–273 (1991)
4. Berthomieu, B., Lime, D., Roux, O.H., Vernadat, F.: Reachability problems and abstract state spaces for time Petri nets with stopwatches. Journal of Discrete Event Dynamic Systems 17, 133–158 (2007)
5. Berthomieu, B., Menasche, M.: A state enumeration approach for analyzing time Petri nets. In: Proc. of ATPN, Applications and Theory of Petri Nets (1982)
6. Berthomieu, B., Peres, F., Vernadat, F.: Bridging the gap between timed automata and bounded time petri nets. In: Asarin, E., Bouyer, P. (eds.) FORMATS 2006. LNCS, vol. 4202, pp. 82–97. Springer, Heidelberg (2006)
7. Berthomieu, B., Ribet, P.-O., Vernadat, F.: The tool TINA – construction of abstract state spaces for Petri nets and time Petri nets. International Journal of Production Research 42(14), 2741–2756
8. Boniol, F., Wiels, V.: The landing gear system case study. In: Boniol, F., Wiels, V., Ait Ameur, Y., Schewe, K.-D. (eds.) ABZ 2014. CCIS, vol. 433, pp. 1–18. Springer, Heidelberg (2014)
9. Bouyer, P., Dufourd, C., Fleury, E., Petit, A.: Updatable timed automata. Theoretical Computer Science 321(23), 291–345 (2004)
10. Bucci, G., Fedeli, A., Sassoli, L., Vicario, E.: Timed state space analysis of real-time preemptive systems. IEEE Transactions on Software Engineering 30(2) (2004)
11. Cellier, F.-E., Kofman, E.: Continuous System Simulation. Springer (2006)
12. Cellier, F.-E., Kofman, E., Migoni, G., Bortolotto, M.: Quantized state system simulation. In: Proc. GCMS 2008, Grand Challenges in Modeling and Simulation (2008)
13. Daws, C., Yovine, S.: Two examples of verification of multirate timed automata with kronos. In: Proc. of RTSS, IEEE Real-Time Systems Symposium (1995)
14. Foures, D., Albert, V., Nketsa, A.: Formal compatibility of experimental frame concept and FD-DEVS model. In: Proc. of MOSIM, International Conference on Modeling, Optimization and Simulation (2012)
15. Gardey, G., Lime, D., Magnin, M., Roux, O(H.): Romeo: A tool for analyzing time petri nets. In: Etessami, K., Rajamani, S.K. (eds.) CAV 2005. LNCS, vol. 3576, pp. 418–423. Springer, Heidelberg (2005)
16. Merlin, P.M.: A study of the recoverability of computing systems. PhD thesis, Department of Information and Computer Science, University of California (1974)
17. Nasr, O., Rached, M., Bodeveix, J.-P., Filali, M.: Spécification et vérification d'un ordonnanceur en B via les automates temporisés. L'Objet 14(4) (2008)
18. Ramalingam, G., Song, J., Joscovicz, L., Miller, R.E.: Solving difference constraints incrementally. Algorithmica 23 (1995)
19. Dal Zilio, S., Fronc, L., Berthomieu, B., Vernadat, F.: Time petri nets with dynamic firing dates: Semantics and applications. Technical Report 14148, LAAS-CNRS (2014) arXiv: 1404.7067

Verification and Performance Evaluation of Timed Game Strategies⋆

Alexandre David[1], Huixing Fang[2],
Kim Guldstrand Larsen[1], and Zhengkui Zhang[1]

[1] Department of Computer Science, Aalborg University, Denmark
{adavid,kgl,zhzhang}@cs.aau.dk
[2] Software Engineering Institute, East China Normal University, China
wxfang@sei.ecnu.edu.cn

Abstract. Control synthesis techniques, based on timed games, derive strategies to ensure a given control objective, e.g., time-bounded reachability. Model checking verifies correctness properties of systems. Statistical model checking can be used to analyse performance aspects of systems, e.g., energy consumption. In this work, we propose to combine these three techniques. In particular, given a strategy synthesized for a timed game and a given control objective, we want to make a deeper examination of the consequences of adopting this strategy. Firstly, we want to apply model checking to the timed game under the synthesized strategy in order to verify additional correctness properties. Secondly, we want to apply statistical model checking to evaluate various performance aspects of the synthesized strategy. For this, the underlying timed game is extended with relevant price and stochastic information. We first explain the principle of translating a strategy produced by UPPAAL-TIGA into a timed automaton, thus enabling the deeper examination. However, our main contribution is a new extension of UPPAAL that automatically synthesizes a strategy of a timed game for a given control objective, then verifies and evaluates this strategy with respect to additional properties. We demonstrate the usefulness of this new branch of UPPAAL using two case-studies.

1   Introduction

Model checking (MC) of real-time systems [12] has been researched for over 20 years. Mature tools such as UPPAAL [3] and KRONOS [5] have been applied to numerous industrial case studies. Nowadays, more interesting formal methods for real-time systems are inspired by or derived from model-checking. Two remarkable ones are controller synthesis and statistical model checking. Controller synthesis techniques [6], based on games, derive strategies to ensure some given objective while handling uncertainties of the environment. Statistical model-checking (SMC) [14], based on statistical analysis of simulations, is used to analyse reliability and performance aspects of systems, e.g., energy consumption.

⋆ This work has been supported by Danish National Research Foundation – Center for Foundations of Cyber-Physical Systems, a Sino-Danish research center.

A. Legay and M. Bozga (Eds.): FORMATS 2014, LNCS 8711, pp. 100–114, 2014.

In the UPPAAL toolbox, efficient implementations of these new techniques are found in the branches UPPAAL-TIGA [2] and UPPAAL-SMC [9].

We believe the three techniques can complement each other. Given a timed game and a control objective, controller synthesis will generate a strategy if the game is controllable. The strategy may ensure hard timing guarantees for a controller to win the game. We aim at verifying additional correctness properties by applying MC to the timed game under this strategy. Similarly, SMC should allow to infer more refined performance consequences (cost, energy consumption etc) of the synthesized strategy. For this, we extend the underlying timed game with prices and stochastic semantics.

There have been a few previous attempts to combine modelling, synthesis, verification and performance evaluation in a single paradigm. In [7] Franck et al. presented a tool chain – UPPAAL-TIGA for synthesis, PHAVER for verification, SIMULINK for simulation – to solve the energy consumption and wear control problem of an industrial oil pump case-study. In [10] UPPAAL-TIGA was combined with MATLAB and SIMULINK to achieve synthesis, simulation and executable code generation for the climate controller of a pig stable. These tool chains are not integrated inside one tool and require translations to let the different tools interact.

As the first contribution in this paper, we propose the principle of translating a synthesized strategy, as obtained from UPPAAL-TIGA, into a controller timed automaton. One can build a closed system using the controller and do model-checking in UPPAAL or statistical model-checking in UPPAAL-SMC. The second contribution is an extension of the semantics and algorithms of MC and SMC to use a synthesized strategy when exploring the state space (for MC) or generating random runs (for SMC). The third contribution is an implementation of this extension based on UPPAAL referred here as Control-SMC, which allows users to synthesize a timed game strategy then verify and evaluate this strategy automatically. It is worth noting that UPPAAL-TIGA may not guarantee that the synthesized strategy is time optimal and here we are interested in evaluating a given strategy w.r.t. a number of different cost measures.

The rest of the paper is organized as follows. Section 2 defines timed games and strategies. Section 3 provides the stochastic semantics of SMC. Section 4 describes the translation of a strategy to a timed automaton. Section 5 presents the extended SMC semantics and implementation of Control-SMC. Section 6 gives the experiment results on two case-studies using Control-SMC. The paper concludes with the future work in Section 7.

2   Timed Game

This section recalls the basic theory of timed game and controller synthesis. Controller synthesis aims at solving the following problem: Given a system S and an objective ϕ, synthesize a controller C such that C can supervise S to satisfy ϕ ($C(S) \models \phi$) regardless how the environment behaves. The problem can be formulated as a two-player game between the controller and the environment.

2.1 Timed Game Automata

Let $X = \{x, y, ...\}$ be a finite set of clocks. We define $\mathcal{B}(X)$ as the set of clock constraints over X generated by grammar: $g, g_1, g_2 ::= x \bowtie n \mid x - y \bowtie n \mid g_1 \wedge g_2$, where $x, y \in X$ are clocks, $n \in \mathbb{N}$ and $\bowtie \in \{\leq, <, =, >, \geq\}$.

Definition 1. *A* Timed Automaton (TA) [1] *is a 6-tuple* $\mathcal{A} = (L, \ell_0, X, \Sigma, E, Inv)$ *where: L is a finite set of locations, $\ell_0 \in L$ is the initial location, X is a finite set of non-negative real-valued clocks, Σ is a finite set of actions, $E \subseteq L \times \mathcal{B}(X) \times \Sigma \times 2^X \times L$ is a finite set of edges, $Inv : L \to \mathcal{B}(X)$ sets an invariant for each location.*

Definition 2. *The semantics of a timed automaton $\mathcal{A}$ is a* Timed Transition System (TTS) $S_{\mathcal{A}} = (Q, Q_0, \Sigma, \to)$ *where: $Q = \{(\ell, v) \mid (\ell, v) \in L \times \mathbb{R}_{\geq 0}^X$ and $v \models Inv(\ell)\}$ are states, $Q_0 = (\ell_0, 0)$ is the initial state, Σ is the finite set of actions, $\to \subseteq Q \times (\Sigma \cup \mathbb{R}_{\geq 0}) \times Q$ is the transition relation defined separately for action $a \in \Sigma$ and delay $d \in \mathbb{R}_{\geq 0}$ as:*

(i) $(\ell, v) \xrightarrow{a} (\ell', v')$ *if there is an edge* $(\ell \xrightarrow{g, \alpha, r} \ell') \in E$ *such that $v \models g$, $v' = v[r \mapsto 0]$ and $v' \models Inv(\ell')$,*

(ii) $(\ell, v) \xrightarrow{d} (\ell', v + d)$ *such that $v \models Inv(\ell)$ and $v + d \models Inv(\ell)$.*

A timed game automaton is an extension of a timed automaton whose actions are partitioned into controllable actions for the controller and uncontrollable actions for the environment. Besides discrete actions, each player can decide to wait in the current location. As soon as one player decides to play one of his available actions, time will stop elapsing and the action will be taken.

Definition 3. *A* Timed Game Automaton (TGA) [13] *is a 7-tuple* $\mathcal{G} = (L, \ell_0, X, \Sigma_c, \Sigma_u, E, Inv)$ *where: Σ_c is the finite set of controllable actions, Σ_u is the finite set of uncontrollable actions, Σ_c and Σ_u are disjoint, and $(L, \ell_0, X, \Sigma_c \cup \Sigma_u, E, Inv)$ is a timed automaton.*

Let $S_{\mathcal{G}}$ be the timed transition system of $\mathcal{G}$. A *run* ρ of $\mathcal{G}$ can be expressed in $S_{\mathcal{G}}$ as a sequence of alternative delay and action transitions: $\rho = q_0 \xrightarrow{d_1} q_0' \xrightarrow{a_1} q_1 \xrightarrow{d_2} q_1' \xrightarrow{a_2} \cdots \xrightarrow{d_n} q_{n-1}' \xrightarrow{a_n} q_n \cdots$, where $a_i \in \Sigma_c \cup \Sigma_u$, $d_i \in \mathbb{R}_{\geq 0}$, q_i is state (ℓ_i, v_i), and q_i' is reached from q_i after delay d_{i+1}. $Exec_{\mathcal{G}}$ denotes the set of runs of $\mathcal{G}$ and $Exec_{\mathcal{G}}^f$ denotes the set of its finite runs.

Definition 4. *Given a timed game automaton $\mathcal{G}$ and a set of states $K \subseteq L \times \mathbb{R}_{\geq 0}^X$, the* control objective ϕ *can be: (i) a reachability control problem if we want $\mathcal{G}$ supervised by a strategy to reach K eventually, or (ii) a safety control problem if we want $\mathcal{G}$ supervised by a strategy to avoid K constantly.*

We can define a run $\rho \in Exec_{\mathcal{G}}$ as *winning* in terms of its control objective. For a reachability game, ρ is winning if $\exists k \geq 0, (\ell_k, v_k) \in K$. For a safety game, ρ is winning if $\forall k \geq 0, (\ell_k, v_k) \notin K$.

Definition 5. *A strategy for a controller in the timed game $\mathcal{G}$ is a mapping $s : Exec_{\mathcal{G}}^{f} \rightarrow \Sigma_c \cup \{\lambda\}$ satisfying the following conditions: given a finite run ρ ending in state $q = last(\rho)$, if $s(\rho) = a \in \Sigma_c$, then there must exist a transition $q \xrightarrow{a} q'$ in $S_{\mathcal{G}}$, or if $s(\rho) = \lambda$, λ being the delay action, then there must exist a positive delay $d \in \mathbb{R}_{>0}$ such that $q \xrightarrow{d} q'$ in $S_{\mathcal{G}}$.*

When a strategy only depends on the current state of the game, that is $\forall \rho, \rho' \in Exec_{\mathcal{G}}, last(\rho) = last(\rho')$ implies $s(\rho) = s(\rho')$, it is called a *positional* or *memoryless* strategy. The strategies for reachability and safety games, as the ones handled by UPPAAL-TIGA, are memoryless.

The analysis of TA and TGA is based on the exploration of a finite *symbolic reachability graph*, where the nodes are *symbolic states*. A symbolic state S is a pair (ℓ, Z), where $\ell \in L$, and $Z = \{v \mid v \models g_z, g_z \in \mathcal{B}(X)\}$ is a *zone* [12], which is normally efficiently represented and stored in memory as *difference bound matrices* (DBM) [4]. UPPAAL-TIGA uses efficient on-the-fly algorithms [6] that manipulate zones to solve timed games. The winning strategy $\hat{s}$ produced by UPPAAL-TIGA is also represented using zones. More precisely, for each location ℓ, $\hat{s}$ gives a finite set of pairs as $\hat{s}(\ell) = \{(Z_1, a_1), \ldots, (Z_n, a_n)\}$, where $a_i \in \Sigma_c \cup \{\lambda\}, Z_i \cap Z_j = \emptyset$ if $i \neq j$.

2.2 A Running Example

Fig. 1 [6] shows a timed game automaton named `Main` which has one clock x and two types of edges: controllable (solid) and uncontrollable (dashed). The control objective is to find a strategy that can supervise `Main` to reach `goal`, regardless of the environment's behavior. The object is expressed as `control: A<> Main.goal`. The game is controllable, and UPPAAL-TIGA provides a strategy as shown in Fig. 2 if running the command line version of UPPAAL-TIGA– `verifytga` with the option `-w0`. The strategy is a list of (zone, action) pairs indexed by locations.

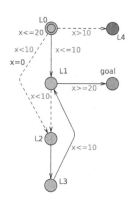

```
State: ( Main.L1 )
While you are in (10<=Main.x && Main.x<20), wait.
When you are in (20<=Main.x), take transition
      Main.L1->Main.goal { x >= 20, tau, 1 }
State: ( Main.L3 )
While you are in (Main.x<10), wait.
When you are in (Main.x==10), take transition
      Main.L3->Main.L1 { x <= 10, tau, 1 }
State: ( Main.L0 )
When you are in (Main.x==10), take transition
      Main.L0->Main.L1 { x <= 10, tau, 1 }
While you are in (Main.x<10), wait.
State: ( Main.L2 )
When you are in (Main.x<=10), take transition
      Main.L2->Main.L3 { 1, tau, 1 }
State: ( Main.goal )
While you are in     true, wait.
```

Fig. 1. TGA `Main`   **Fig. 2.** A Strategy for `Main`

For example when `Main` is at `L1`, the action is to wait if $10 \leq x < 20$, or to take the action to reach `goal` if $x \geq 20$.

3   Stochastic Priced Timed Automata

In this section, we briefly recall the definition of priced timed automata and stochastic semantics of SMC. We borrow the definitions from [8].

3.1   Priced Timed Automata

Priced timed automata are a generalization of timed automata where clocks may have different rates in different locations. We note by $R(\ell) : X \to \mathbb{N}$ the *rate vector* assigning a rate to each clock of X at location ℓ. For $v \in \mathbb{R}_{\geq 0}^{X}$ and $d \in \mathbb{R}_{\geq 0}$, we write $v + R(\ell) \cdot d$ to denote the clock valuation defined by $(v + R(\ell) \cdot d)(x) = v(x) + R(\ell)(x) \cdot d$ for any $x \in X$.

Definition 6. *A Priced Timed Automaton (PTA) is a tuple $\mathcal{P} = (L, \ell_0, X, \Sigma, E, R, I)$ where: (i) L is a finite set of locations, (ii) $\ell_0 \in L$ is the initial location, (iii) X is a finite set of clocks, (iv) $\Sigma = \Sigma_i \uplus \Sigma_o$ is a finite set of actions partitioned into inputs (Σ_i) and outputs (Σ_o), (v) $E \subseteq L \times \mathcal{B}(X) \times \Sigma \times 2^X \times L$ is a finite set of edges, (vi) $R : L \to \mathbb{N}^X$ assigns a rate vector to each location, and (vii) $I : L \to \mathcal{B}(X)$ assigns an invariant to each location.*

3.2   Stochastic Semantics

Consider a closed network of PTAs $\mathbf{A} = (\mathcal{P}_1 | \ldots | \mathcal{P}_n)$ with a state space $St = St_1 \times \cdots \times St_n$. For a concrete global state $q = (q_1, \ldots, q_n) \in St$ and $a_1 a_2 \ldots a_k \in \Sigma^*$ we denote by $\pi(q, a_1 a_2 \ldots a_k)$ the set of all maximal runs from q with a prefix $t_1 a_1 t_2 a_2 \ldots t_k a_k$ for some $t_1, \ldots, t_2 \in \mathbb{R}_{\geq 0}$, that is, runs where the i'th action a_i has been output by the component $\mathcal{P}_{c(a_i)}$. We give the probability for getting such sets of runs as:

$$\mathbb{P}_{\mathbf{A}}(\pi(q, a_1 a_2 \ldots a_k)) = \int_{t \geq 0} \mu_q^c(t) \cdot \Big(\prod_{j \neq c} \int_{\tau > t} \mu_q^j(\tau) d\tau\Big) \cdot \gamma_{q^t}^c(a_1) \cdot \mathbb{P}_{\mathbf{A}}\big(\pi((q^t)^{a_1}, a_2 \ldots a_n)\big) dt$$

where $c = c(a_i)$ is the *index* of component taking a_1, μ_q^c is the *delay density function* for component c to choose a delay t_i at q, and $\gamma_{q^t}^c$ is the *output probability function* for component c to choose an action a_i after q is delayed by t. The above nested integral reflects that the stochastic semantics of the network is defined based on race among components. All components are independent in giving their delays which are decided by the given delay density functions. The player component who offers the minimum delay is the winner of the race, and takes the turn to make a transition and (probabilistically) choosing the action to output.

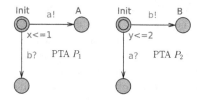

Fig. 3. A Tiny Example

Fig. 3 gives the intuition of the SMC semantics. Two PTAs P_1 and P_2 race to reach locations A or B. If P_1 enters A, it blocks P_2 to enter B, and vice versa. Furthermore, either PTA can delay uniformly within the invariants from its initial state before firing its output transition. We can use the SMC semantics to calculate the probability for P_1 to enter location A within 2 time units as:

$$\mathbb{P}(\pi(q_0, a)) = \int_{x=0}^{1} 1 \cdot \left(\int_{y=x}^{2} \frac{1}{2} dy \right) dx = \frac{1}{2} \int_{x=0}^{1} (2 - x) dx = \frac{3}{4}$$

where q_0 is the initial state of the network of P_1 and P_2, and the delay density functions for P_1 and P_2 at q_0 are 1 and $\frac{1}{2}$ respectively. P_1 can reach A only if it takes its transition before P_2.

4   Translating Strategies to Timed Automata

In this section, we provide a systematic way to translate a synthesized strategy of a timed game $\mathcal{G}$ produced by UPPAAL-TIGA into a controller timed automaton C. Once the controller is built, we can verify additional correctness properties or evaluate performance aspects of the closed system $C(\mathcal{G})$ in UPPAAL.

4.1   The Method

We recall from Section 2.1 that strategies have the form $\hat{s}(\ell) = \{(Z_1, a_1), \ldots, (Z_n, a_n)\}$. Given a concrete state $q = (\ell, v)$, one can lookup which action a_i to take by finding Z_i such that $v \in Z_i$. Fig. 4 illustrates how to translate the strategy from a location ℓ with the schematic zone representation (left) into a basic

$$\hat{s}(\ell) = \{(Z_1, a_1), (Z_2, a_2), (Z_3, \lambda), (Z_4, \lambda)\}, \ell \in L$$

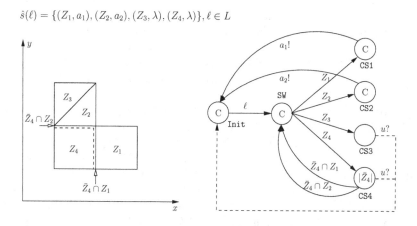

Fig. 4. Translating the Strategy

controller TA (right). The complete controller TA is obtained by repeating the same translation procedure for all locations and connecting all resulting basic controller TAs to the same initial state. The symbol "C" inside states indicates committed states. Time does not elapse in committed states, and the outgoing transitions are taken atomically. We use $\bar{Z}$ to denote the *closure* of the zone Z.

The small controller TA on the right is constructed as follows. For a given discrete state (ℓ) (location only), a transition from Init to a switch state SW is added with a guard encoding ℓ. From there we add transitions guarded by Z_i for each (Z_i, a_i) entry of $\hat{s}(\ell)$ to a choice state CSi. Then, we have tree basic cases: Either (1) a_i is a controllable action, (2) a_i is an unbounded delay, or (3) it is a bounded delay. In case (1), the controller takes a_i immediately with the synchronization $a_i!$ (e.g. from CS1 and CS2 in Fig. 4). In case (2) corresponding to $a_i = \lambda$, the controller stays idle waiting for a move from the environment with the synchronization $u?$. Finally, case (3) is similar to case (2) except for the upper bound on the delay (encoded with an invariant) and additional transitions to go back to SW whenever the upper bound is reached and a controllable action is enabled.

4.2   The Running Example

We translate the strategy in Fig. 2 into a controller TA C. Before translating, we need to synchronize C and $\mathcal{G}$ so that C can observe the state of $\mathcal{G}$ and control it. To observe the locations, we assign unique IDs and use global flags for each component to keep track of the current active location. Then we rename the local clocks to be global to make them visible. To monitor every uncontrollable transition in $\mathcal{G}$, we use a unique channel u and the synchronizations $u!$ in $\mathcal{G}$ and $u?$ in C. Similarly, to control $\mathcal{G}$, controllable actions a_i use the corresponding channel synchronizations $a_i!$ in C and $a_i?$ in $\mathcal{G}$.

In Fig. 5, we define location IDs for Main.L0 – Main.L4 and Main.goal from 0 to 5. Then we use the global location flag loc to keep track of the current location of Main, and the global clock x to replace the local one, then the broadcast channels $u1, u2, a1 - a4$ to synchronize Main and its controller TA MyCon in Fig. 6. In MyCon, by testing loc on the predefined location IDs, transitions from Init lead to the switch states L0 – L3 and L5, which correspond to the strategies at locations Main.L0 – Main.L3 and Main.goal. Choice states M00, M10, M20 and M30 depict case (1) in Fig. 4. Accept corresponds to case (2). M01, M11 and M31 match case (3).

We also add price and a delay distribution to Main for performance evaluation in SMC. This essentially turns Main into a priced timed automaton. We use an integer s to count the number of transitions to reach goal, and a clock e to measure the energy consumption to reach goal. The rate of the clock e is specified at all locations as $e' == n, n \in \mathbb{N}$ except at L4 because L4 is not reachable under the strategy. e' is stopped at goal by setting to 0. Besides, an exponential rate of 3 is defined for the delay density function at L1. Now a closed system can be made from Main and MyCon. We can verify correctness properties and evaluate performance aspects of this strategy as shown in Table 1.

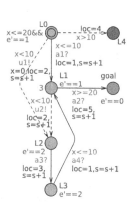

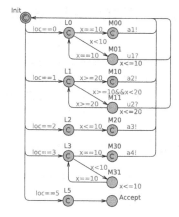

Fig. 5. Decorated TGA `Main`   **Fig. 6.** Controller TA `MyCon`

Table 1. MC & SMC Experiments of the Running Example

	#	Queries	Results
MC	1	`A<> Main.goal`	Yes
	2	`A<> Main.goal and time<=20`	No
SMC	3	`Pr[<=30] (<> Main.goal)`	[0.902606,1]
	4	`E[<=30;200] (max: Main.s)`	3.05
	5	`E[<=30;200] (max: Main.e)`	27.5137

Experiment 1 verifies the original control objective that is satisfied (`Yes`) for sure. Experiment 2 verifies if the strategy ensures `Main` to reach `goal` within 20 time units, where `time` is a global clock. The result is not satisfied (`No`). We evaluate reachability of `goal` within 30 time units under the strategy in experiment 3. The probability is [0.902606,1] with confidence 0.95 if the probability uncertainty factor ϵ is 0.05. Besides, several kinds of statistical

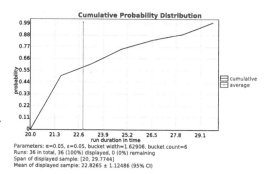

Fig. 7. Distribution on Time to Reach `goal`

plots can be generated by UPPAAL-SMC such as probability distribution, probability density distribution, cumulative probability distribution, and frequency histogram. Fig. 7 shows the cumulative probability distribution of 36 runs. The curve shows that over 55% of runs reach `goal` between 20.0 and 22.6 time units, and almost 90% runs can reach `goal` within 29.1 time units. The last two experiments report the expected number of steps and energy consumption to reach `goal` for 200 simulated runs within 30 time units.

5   MC and SMC under Strategies

Control-SMC is a new extension of UPPAAL. It automatically synthesizes a strategy of a timed game, keeps the strategy in memory, then verifies and evaluates the strategy on a number of SMC properties. We extended the semantics and algorithms of MC and SMC to apply the synthesized strategy when exploring the state space (for MC) and generating random runs (for SMC).

5.1   Extended Stochastic Semantics

Let $\mathbf{A} = (\mathcal{P}_1 | \ldots | \mathcal{P}_n)$ be a network of priced timed automata modelling an environment to be controlled. That is $\mathbf{A}$ may be seen as a timed game with global state space $St = St_1 \times \cdots \times St_n$, and with sets Σ_c and Σ_u of controllable and uncontrollable actions, respectively. Now assume that – using UPPAAL-TIGA– we have synthesized a strategy $s : St \to (\mathbb{R} \times \Sigma_c) \cup \{\lambda\}$ for $\mathbf{A}$ ensuring some desired reachability or safety objective. That is $s(q) = (d, a)$ indicates that the strategy s in state q proposes to perform controllable action a after a delay of d; $s(q) = \lambda$ indicates that the strategy will delay indefinitely until the environment has performed an uncontrollable action. Now we may view the *extended* network:

$$\mathbf{A}^e = (\mathcal{P}_1 | \ldots | \mathcal{P}_n | A_s)$$

as a closed *stochastic* network over $\Sigma_u \cup \Sigma_c$, where the components $\mathcal{P}_1, \ldots, \mathcal{P}_n$ have been given delay density functions $\mu^1, \ldots, \mu^n$ and output probability functions $\gamma^1, \ldots, \gamma^n$. Now A_s is a one-state component implementing the strategy s. That is s has delay density function $\mu_q^s = \delta_d$, when $s(q) = (d, a)$ and δ_d is the Dirac delta function with probability mass concentrated at time-point d[1]. Moreover the output probability function γ_q^s for s is given by:

$$\gamma_q^s(b) = \begin{cases} 1 & ; s(q) = (0, a), a = b \\ 0 & ; s(q) = (0, a), a \neq b \\ \perp & ; s(q) = (d, a), d > 0 \\ \perp & ; s(q) = \lambda \end{cases}$$

In this way $\mathbf{A}^e$ may be subject to statistical model checking provided. We extend the capability of UPPAAL-SMC to generate random runs for networks of environment components extended with control strategies.

5.2   Implementation

Fig. 8 shows the work-flow of Control-SMC. The UPPAAL-TIGA engine receives the timed game model $\mathcal{G}$ and the control objective ϕ. It synthesizes a strategy that is kept in memory if $\mathcal{G}$ is controllable. The strategy can be printed out with the option -w0. If the option -X is used then subsequent MC or SMC queries

---

[1] Which should formally be treated as the limit of a sequence of delay density functions with decreasing, non-zero support around d.

ρ_i are checked under this strategy. For the purpose of evaluating performance, the model $\mathcal{G}$ can be extended with costs to $\mathcal{G}'$. These costs are modeled with clocks that must be declared as *hybrid clock*. They are ignored for the purpose of symbolic model-checking (synthesis or MC) and taken into account for SMC. Furthermore, floating-point variables can be used in the same way. These additional variables may not be *active* for the purpose of controlling the behavior.

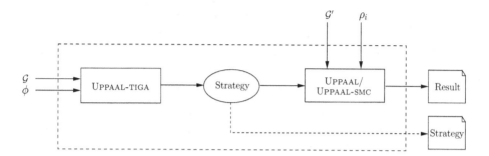

Fig. 8. Workflow of Control-SMC

The exploration under a given strategy is similar to standard MC or SMC when considering uncontrollable transitions since they are played by an opponent. The opponent is stochastic for the purpose of SMC and when doing MC, all possible successors are tried. However, only the controllable transitions allowed by the strategy are allowed. In addition, delay is constrained by the delays of the strategy, e.g., if a controllable transition is to be taken after 5 time units, UPPAAL will not delay more. For SMC, this is resolved naturally through the semantics with a race between components. For the symbolic exploration, the strategy specifies how much delay is allowed and this constrains the standard delay operation. Furthermore, we have to add the upper border of bounded delays to enable following transitions. More precisely UPPAAL-TIGA maintains a partition so we could have the case to wait while in $x \in [0,5[$ and take a transition at $x = 5$, but $x = 5$ is then unreachable. Therefor we have to wait while $x \in [0,5]$. Finally, when an action follows a delay it has an urgent semantics, i.e., the states in which such an action is enabled are not allowed to delay.

5.3 The Running Example

We demonstrates how to use Control-SMC on the running example described in Section 2.2 and 4.2 without the need to translate the strategy. We add prices and stochastic information directly on the TGA `Main` as shown in Fig. 9. The clocks used for cost are declared as `hybrid clock` (e.g. e), while counters for SMC evaluation are declared as `double` (e.g. s).

Fig. 10 shows the query file we use here. A control query that expresses the control objective starts on the first line with a list of MC and SMC queries on

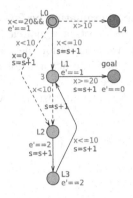

```
control: A<> Main.goal
A<> Main.goal
A<> Main.goal and time<=20
Pr[<=30] (<> Main.goal)
E[<=30;200] (max: Main.s)
E[<=30;200] (max: Main.e)
```

Fig. 9. TGA Main with Prices   **Fig. 10.** Combined Query File

the following lines. For now, Control-SMC is available only from the command line checker `verifytga` and is enabled with the option `-X`. Given the model as in Fig. 9 and the query file as in Fig. 10 as inputs, it first synthesizes a strategy for the control query, then processes the rest MC and SMC queries in a batch fashion, and gives the same results as in Table 1 in Section 4.2.

6   Experiments Results

We show the experiments of two case-studies by first using the Control-SMC method of Section 5, then using the strategy translation method in Section 4 as a cross-check. The two methods gave the same results for MC and SMC queries. We also measured the execution time of the queries for both methods, because we want to know the runtime benefit of applying a strategy in time and memory compared with using a translated controller from a strategy. All models in the experiments are available on our SMC web-page[2].

6.1   Case Study 1: Jobshop

The Jobshop problem is about scheduling a set of machines for a set of jobs, where each job needs to use those machines in a particular order for a particular time limit. This case-study involves two professors Kim and Jan who want to read a single piece of four-section newspaper. Each person has his own preferred order on sections, and can spend different times on different sections. The control objective, which is expressed as `control: A<> Kim.Done and Jan.Done and time<=80`, is to find a scheduling strategy that guarantees both people finish reading within 80 time units. UPPAAL-TIGA finds such a strategy. The full explanation about this model can be found on web-page of examples [11]. The model is down-sized for the purpose of the manual conversion to a controller automaton.

_____

[2] Section Control-SMC at `http://people.cs.aau.dk/~adavid/smc/cases.html`

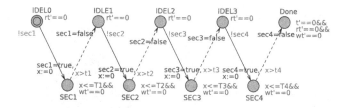

Fig. 11. Job Template with Prices

Table 2. MC & SMC Experiments of Jobshop

	#	Queries	Results	T (CS)	T (M)
MC	1	`A[] Jan.Done imply Kim.Done`	Yes	-	-
	2	`E<> Kim.Done and Jan.Done and time<=45`	Yes	-	-
	3	`E<> Kim.Done and Jan.Done and time<=44`	No	-	-
SMC	4	`Pr[<=80] (<> Kim.Done and Jan.Done)`	1*	76.5s	148.3s
	5	`E[time<=80 ; 2000000] (max: Kim.wt)`	5.40221	62.1s	132.5s
	6	`E[time<=80 ; 2000000] (max: Kim.rt)`	22.7469	61.7s	138.7s
	7	`E[time<=80 ; 2000000] (max: Jan.wt)`	11.5652	60.9s	136.8s
	8	`E[time<=80 ; 2000000] (max: Jan.rt)`	47.3951	62.1s	138.8s

1^* in `[0.999998,1]` with confidence `0.95`.

Fig. 11 shows the TGA template with prices for each person for Control-SMC. The availability of four sections are maintained by four global boolean variables. During the initialization of Kim and Jan, the references to the boolean variables are assigned to `sec1` – `sec4` according to each person's preferred order of reading. The strategy tells a person when to acquire a section (controllable, solid edge), while a person can release a section at any time within a time bound (uncontrollable, dashed edge). We add respectively three stop-watches[3] wt, rt and t to measure the accumulated time on waiting, reading and finishing the newspaper respectively.

We obtain the same results when checking the MC and SMC queries in Control-SMC and UPPAAL. Thus in Table 2 we use the single column Result to show the MC results (Yes for satisfied or No for not satisfied), and SMC results (probabilities or evaluations). The T (CS) column shows the execution time of a query in seconds by Control-SMC, while the T (M) column shows that by using a manually translated controller. We do not compare the runtime of MC queries because the size of this model is not big enough to make the runtime distinguishable. But we compare the runtime of SMC queries, because we can let the SMC engine to generate a large number of runs to make the runtime difference noticeable.

Experiment 1 shows that Kim always finishes reading before Jan. We get the shortest time (= 45 time units) for both to finish from experiments 2 and 3. Experiment 4 measures the probability for Kim and Jan to finish reading within 80 time units if the probability uncertainty $\epsilon = 0.000001$.

---

[3] Stop-watches are clocks whose rates are reset to zero.

In UPPAAL-SMC we can get the plot of probability distribution of this query as shown in Fig. 12. The plot gives the mean value of around 59 time units. The remaining SMC experiments show the expected time for Kim and Jan to wait and read the newspaper individually. The strategy biases Kim because Kim waits less than Jan. The runtime experiments of SMC queries were carried out on a PC with Intel i7-2640M CPU @ 2.80GHz, 8GB main memory and Ubuntu 12.04

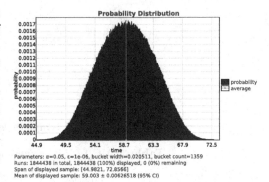

Fig. 12. Distribution on Time to Finish Reading for Both People

x86_64 with the upcoming version 0.18 of UPPAAL-TIGA. Experiment 4 set $\epsilon = 0.000001$ to force the SMC engine to generate a large number of runs (1844438 runs). In experiments 5 – 8, we set the number of runs to 2000000. We can conclude that applying a strategy in memory improves the performance of SMC engine inside Control-SMC by a factor of two. This is due to the strategy look-up in a hash table instead of simulating it within the model.

6.2   Case Study 2: Train-Gate

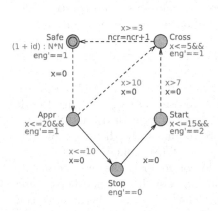

Fig. 13. Train Template with Prices

Train-Gate is a classical case-study for real-time model checking. It is distributed with UPPAAL with an detailed explanation in [3]. Fig. 13 shows the game version of it with prices and stochastic extensions. The control objective, which is expressed as `control: A[] forall (i : id_t) forall (j : id_t) Train(i).Cross and Train(j).Cross imply i == j`, is finding a strategy to guarantee the exclusive access to `Cross` by two trains. If necessary, the strategy should stop a train at `Appr` in time ($x \le 10$) by the controllable solid edge to `Stop`, otherwise the train goes to `Cross` directly by the uncontrollable dashed edge. The train can resume at `Stop` by the other controllable solid edge to `Start`. The exponential rate ((1+id):N*N) appears at `Safe` for specifying the delay density function. A counter ncr records the throughput at `Cross`.

Table 3. MC & SMC Experiments of Train-Gate

	#	Queries	Result		T (CS)	T (M)
			Syn	Que		
MC	1	`E<> Train(0).Cross && Train(1).Start`	Yes	No	-	-
SMC	2	`Pr[<=100] (<> Train(0).Cross)`	1*	1*	45.9s	88.5s
	3	`E[<=100 ; 1000000] (max: ncr)`	8.0665	5.8065	72.3s	173.3s
	4	`E[<=100 ; 1000000] (max: Train(0).eng)`	124.938	88.402	69.3s	169.5s

1* in [0.999998,1] with confidence 0.95.

A hybrid clock e measures the energy consumption of a train. The interesting point of this case-study is that we compare the behavior and performance of the synthesized strategy with the manually programmed queue-based controller available in the train-gate example provided in the distribution of UPPAAL.

Table 3 shows the comparative experiments of the synthesized strategy Syn and the queue-based controller Que. Experiment 1 shows Syn allows Train(1) to approach Cross while Train(0) is still crossing. This is forbidden by Que. Experiment 2 measures the probability for Train(0) to reach Cross within 100 time units with the probability uncertainty $\epsilon = 0.000001$. Experiment 3 shows that Syn gives a bigger throughput from Que, because Syn allows different trains to approach Cross concurrently as witnessed by experiment 1. Experiment 4 gives the expected energy consumption for Train(0). We compare the execution time of SMC queries in seconds by Control-SMC in the T (CS) column with that using a manually translated controller in the T (M) column. In experiment 2, we set $\epsilon = 0.000001$ to force the SMC engine to generate a large number of runs (1844438 runs). In experiments 3 and 4, we set the number of runs to 1000000. We can conclude that applying a strategy in memory improves the performance of SMC engine inside Control-SMC by a factor of two.

7   Future Work

The future work are in three directions. Our first goal is to merge UPPAAL and UPPAAL-TIGA, which will enable Control-SMC from the graphical interface with all its capabilities, in particular the plot composer. Next, we aim to make the clocks for measuring prices in Control-SMC to become real hybrid as in UPPAAL-SMC. The clock rates can be floating-point, negative, or in the form of ordinary differential equations (ODE). The third direction is exploring more potential use of the synthesized strategy in memory. We can try to refine or optimize the strategy using machine learning methods.

References

1. Alur, R., Dill, D.L.: A theory of timed automata. Theor. Comput. Sci. 126(2), 183–235 (1994)
2. Behrmann, G., Cougnard, A., David, A., Fleury, E., Larsen, K.G., Lime, D.: UPPAAL-tiga: Time for playing games! In: Damm, W., Hermanns, H. (eds.) CAV 2007. LNCS, vol. 4590, pp. 121–125. Springer, Heidelberg (2007)
3. Behrmann, G., David, A., Larsen, K.G.: A tutorial on UPPAAL. In: Bernardo, M., Corradini, F. (eds.) SFM-RT 2004. LNCS, vol. 3185, pp. 200–236. Springer, Heidelberg (2004)
4. Bengtsson, J., Yi, W.: Timed automata: Semantics, algorithms and tools. In: Desel, J., Reisig, W., Rozenberg, G. (eds.) Lectures on Concurrency and Petri Nets. LNCS, vol. 3098, pp. 87–124. Springer, Heidelberg (2004)
5. Bozga, M., Daws, C., Maler, O., Olivero, A., Tripakis, S., Yovine, S.: Kronos: A model-checking tool for real-time systems. In: Vardi, M.Y. (ed.) CAV 1998. LNCS, vol. 1427, pp. 546–550. Springer, Heidelberg (1998)
6. Cassez, F., David, A., Fleury, E., Larsen, K.G., Lime, D.: Efficient on-the-fly algorithms for the analysis of timed games. In: Abadi, M., de Alfaro, L. (eds.) CONCUR 2005. LNCS, vol. 3653, pp. 66–80. Springer, Heidelberg (2005)
7. Cassez, F., Jessen, J.J., Larsen, K.G., Raskin, J.-F., Reynier, P.-A.: Automatic synthesis of robust and optimal controllers – an industrial case study. In: Majumdar, R., Tabuada, P. (eds.) HSCC 2009. LNCS, vol. 5469, pp. 90–104. Springer, Heidelberg (2009)
8. David, A., Larsen, K.G., Legay, A., Mikucionis, M., Poulsen, D.B., van Vliet, J., Wang, Z.: Stochastic semantics and statistical model checking for networks of priced timed automata. CoRR abs/1106.3961 (2011)
9. David, A., Larsen, K.G., Legay, A., Mikučionis, M., Wang, Z.: Time for statistical model checking of real-time systems. In: Gopalakrishnan, G., Qadeer, S. (eds.) CAV 2011. LNCS, vol. 6806, pp. 349–355. Springer, Heidelberg (2011)
10. Jessen, J.J., Rasmussen, J.I., Larsen, K.G., David, A.: Guided controller synthesis for climate controller using UPPAAL TIGA. In: Raskin, J.-F., Thiagarajan, P.S. (eds.) FORMATS 2007. LNCS, vol. 4763, pp. 227–240. Springer, Heidelberg (2007)
11. Larsen, K.G.: Quantitative model checking exercise (2010), http://people.cs.aau.dk/~kgl/QMC2010/exercises/; 28. Job Shop Scheduling
12. Larsen, K.G., Pettersson, P., Yi, W.: Model-checking for real-time systems. In: Reichel, H. (ed.) FCT 1995. LNCS, vol. 965, pp. 62–88. Springer, Heidelberg (1995)
13. Maler, O., Pnueli, A., Sifakis, J.: On the synthesis of discrete controllers for timed systems (an extended abstract). In: Mayr, E.W., Puech, C. (eds.) STACS 1995. LNCS, vol. 900, pp. 229–242. Springer, Heidelberg (1995)
14. Younes, H.L.S.: Planning and verification for stochastic processes with asynchronous events. In: McGuinness, D.L., Ferguson, G. (eds.) AAAI, pp. 1001–1002. AAAI Press / The MIT Press (2004)

The Power of Proofs: New Algorithms for Timed Automata Model Checking*

Peter Fontana and Rance Cleaveland

Department of Computer Science,
University of Maryland, College Park, MD 20742, USA

Abstract. This paper presents the first model-checking algorithm for an expressive modal mu-calculus over timed automata, $L_{\nu,\mu}^{rel,af}$, and reports performance results for an implementation. This mu-calculus contains extended time-modality operators and can express all of TCTL. Our algorithmic approach uses an "on-the-fly" strategy based on proof search as a means of ensuring high performance for both positive and negative answers to model-checking questions. In particular, a set of proof rules for solving model-checking problems are given and proved sound and complete; our algorithm then model-checks a property by constructing a proof (or showing none exists) using these rules. One noteworthy aspect of our technique is that we show that verification performance can be improved with *derived rules*, whose correctness can be inferred from the more primitive rules on which they are based. In this paper, we give the basic proof rules underlying our method, describe derived proof rules to improve performance, and we compare our implementation to UPPAAL.

1 Introduction

Timed automata are used to model real-time systems in which time is continuous and timing constraints may refer to elapsed time between system events [4]. The timed automata model provides a balance between expressiveness and tractability: a variety of different real-time systems can be captured in the formalism, and various properties, including safety (reachability) and liveness, can also be decided automatically for a given automaton [1, 2, 3].

To specify these properties, different logics have been devised. One popular logic, Timed Computation Tree Logic (TCTL) [3], extends the untimed Computation Tree Logic (CTL) [9] by adding time constraints to the modal operators. Other researchers explored timed extensions to the modal mu-calculus [12]. One such extension, called T_μ [18] extends the untimed modal mu-calculus with a single-step operator. Another extension, which we refer to as $L_{\nu,\mu}$ [21, 26, 27], extends the modal mu-calculus with separate time and action modal operators. This logic is sufficient for expressing some basic safety and liveness properties. However, it cannot express all of TCTL [14]. To address this, $L_{\nu,\mu}$ was extended with *relativization operators* by [7]; we denote this logic as $L_{\nu,\mu}^{rel}$. These additional

---

* Research supported by NSF grant CCF-0926194. The Appendix to this paper is available as a supplement on arXiv [16].

operators make the logic expressive enough to express all of TCTL [14]. (Bouyer et al. [7] included only greatest fixpoints, yielding L_ν, which they referred to as L_c; the least fixpoints in $L_{\nu,\mu}^{rel}$ not in L_ν^{rel} add expressive power [14].)

Over the model of timed automata, the model checking problem for $L_{\nu,\mu}$ is EXPTIME-complete [1]. Bouyer et al. [7] show that formulas using the relativization operators can be model-checked in EXPTIME. Hence, model checking $L_{\nu,\mu}^{rel}$ over timed automata is EXPTIME-complete. The same model-checking problem for TCTL over timed automata is PSPACE-complete [3].

While timed logics were being studied, tools and implementation algorithms were developed as well. Much of the development focused on handling subsets of properties specified in TCTL. A widely-used tool, UPPAAL [6], supports a fragment of TCTL, which includes many safety and liveness properties; other tools, including KRONOS [25], Synthia [20], and RED/REDLIB [23], have also been developed, some of which are able to model-check all of TCTL. Additionally, some tools were developed for timed modal-mu calculi. Two tools that can model check fragments of a timed mu-calculus include CMC [19], which can handle L_ν, and CWB-RT [13, 26, 27], which can check safety properties written in L_ν.

The contributions of this paper include the first algorithm, and an implementation, to model check $L_{\nu,\mu}^{rel,af}$. By definition, $L_{\nu,\mu}^{rel,af}$ consists of the so-called *alternation-free* formulas of $L_{\nu,\mu}^{rel}$ and is thus a superset of L_ν^{rel}. Assuming non-zeno and timelock-free automata, $L_{\nu,\mu}^{rel,af}$ is strong enough to express all of TCTL [14]. Our implementation extends the tool CWB-RT [13, 26, 27]. Implementation details of the model checker are discussed in Section 5; in Section 6, we give a demonstration of some models and properties that can be model checked by our tool as well as a performance comparison to UPPAAL.

CWB-RT is a proof-search model checker: it verifies properties by constructing a proof using a set of proof rules. These proof rules decompose the given goal (does the automaton satisfy a formula) into (smaller) subgoals. These proof search methods were used for the untimed modal mu-calculus in [10], explored in [21], and extended to the timed setting in [26, 27] in order to produce a fast on-the-fly model checker that can model check timed automata incrementally. The generated proofs not only give additional correctness information but also can be used as a mechanism to improve model-checking performance. We develop the additional proof rules to check the relativized operators, extending the proof rules used in [26, 27]. The additional rules are discussed in Section 3.

Furthermore, through select *derived* proof rules, we can enhance performance. These derived rules, together with a judicious use of *memoization*, yield dramatic performance improvements. We discuss the derived proof rules in Section 4.

2 Background

2.1 Timed Automata

This section defines the syntax of timed automata and sketches their semantics. The interested reader is referred to [2, 15] for a fuller account. To begin with, timed automata rely on *clock constraints*.

Definition 1 (Clock constraint $cc \in \Phi(CX)$). *Given a nonempty finite set of clocks $CX = \{x_1, x_2, \ldots, x_n\}$ and $d \in \mathbb{Z}^{\geq 0}$ (a non-negative integer), a clock constraint cc may be constructed using the following grammar:*

$$cc ::= x_i < d \mid x_i \leq d \mid x_i > d \mid x_i \geq d \mid cc \wedge cc$$

$\Phi(CX)$ is the set of all possible clock constraints over CX. We also use the following abbreviations: true (tt) for $x_1 \geq 0$, false (ff) for $x_1 < 0$, and $x_i = d$ for $x_i \leq d \wedge x_i \geq d$.

Timed automata may now be defined as follows.

Definition 2 (Timed automaton). *A timed automaton is a tuple $(L, l_0, \Sigma, CX, I, E)$, where:*

- *L is the finite set of locations.*
- *$l_0 \in L$ is the initial location.*
- *Σ is the finite set of action symbols.*
- *$CX = \{x_1, x_2, \ldots, x_n\}$ is the nonempty finite set of clocks.*
- *$I : L \longrightarrow \Phi(CX)$ maps each location l to a clock constraint, $I(l)$, referred to as the invariant of l.*
- *$E \subseteq L \times \Sigma \times \Phi(CX) \times 2^{CX} \times L$ is the set of edges. In an edge $e = (l, a, cc, \lambda, l')$ from l to l' with action a, $cc \in \Phi(CX)$ is the guard of e, and λ represents the set of clocks to reset to 0.*

The semantics of timed automata rely on *clock valuations*, which are functions $\nu : CX \longrightarrow \mathbb{R}^{\geq 0}$ ($\mathbb{R}^{\geq 0}$ is the set of non-negative real numbers); intuitively, $\nu(x_i)$ is the current time value of clock x_i. A timed automaton begins execution in its initial location with the initial clock valuation ν_0 assigning 0 to every clock. When the automaton is in a given clock location l with current clock valuation ν, two types of transitions can occur: time advances and action executions. During a time advance, the location stays the same and the clock valuation ν advances $\delta \in \mathbb{R}^{\geq 0}$ units to the valuation $\nu + \delta$, where $\nu + \delta$ is defined as $(\nu + \delta)(x_i) = \nu(x_i) + \delta$. For a time advance to be allowed, for all $0 \leq \delta' \leq \delta$, $\nu + \delta'$ must satisfy the invariant of location l. Due to convexity of clock constraints, it suffices to ensure that both ν and $\nu + \delta$ satisfy $I(l)$. An *action execution* of action a can occur when ν satisfies the guard for an edge leading from l to l', the edge is labeled by action a, and , the invariant of l' is satisfied after the clocks are reset as specified in the edge. In this case the location changes to l' and the clocks in λ are reset to 0. These intuitions can be formalized as a labeled transition system whose states consist of locations paired with clock valuations, each state notated as (l, ν). A *timed run* of the automaton is a sequence of transitions starting from the initial location and ν_0. On occasion, we also augment each timed automaton with a set of atomic propositions AP and a labeling function $M : L \longrightarrow 2^{AP}$ where $M(l)$ is the subset of propositions in AP that location l satisfies.

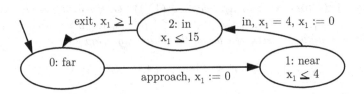

Fig. 1. Timed automaton of a train

Example 1 (Train timed automaton). The timed automaton in Figure 1 models a train component of the GRC (Generalized Railroad Crossing) protocol [17]. There are three locations: 0: far (initial), 1: near, and 2: in; and one clock x_1. Σ has the actions *approach*, *in*, and *exit*. Here, location 1: near has the invariant $x_1 \leq 4$ while 0: far has the vacuous invariant **tt**. The edge (1: near, in, $x_1 = 4, \{x_1\}$, 2: in) has action *in*, guard $x_1 = 4$, and resets x_1 to 0.

A sample timed run of this timed automaton is: (0: far, $x_1 = 0$) $\xrightarrow{5}$ (0: far, $x_1 = 5$) $\xrightarrow{approach}$ (1: near, $x_1 = 0$) $\xrightarrow{4}$ (1: near, $x_1 = 4$) $\xrightarrow{in}$ (2: in, $x_1 = 0$) $\xrightarrow{3}$ (2: in, $x_1 = 3$) $\xrightarrow{2}$ (2: in, $x_1 = 5$) $\xrightarrow{exit}$ (0: far, $x_1 = 5$)...

2.2   Timed Logic $L_{\nu,\mu}^{rel}$ and Modal Equation Systems (MES)

The following definition of $L_{\nu,\mu}^{rel}$ uses the modal-equation system (MES) format used in [11] for untimed systems and in [26, 27] for $L_{\nu,\mu}$.

Definition 3 ($L_{\nu,\mu}$, $L_{\nu,\mu}^{rel}$ **basic formula syntax**). *Let* $CX = \{x_1, x_2, \ldots\}$ *and* $CX_f = \{z, z_1, \ldots\}$ *be disjoint sets of clocks. Then the syntax of a* $L_{\nu,\mu}$ *basic formulas is given by the following grammar:*

$$\psi ::= p \mid \neg p \mid \mathbf{tt} \mid \mathbf{ff} \mid cc \mid Y \mid \psi \wedge \psi \mid \psi \vee \psi \mid \langle a \rangle(\psi)$$
$$\mid [a](\psi) \mid \exists(\psi) \mid \forall(\psi) \mid z.(\psi)$$

Here, $p \in AP$ *is an atomic proposition,* $cc \in \Phi(CX)$ *is a clock constraint over clock set* CX, $Y \in Var$ *is a propositional variable (Var is the set of propositional variables), and* $a \in \Sigma$ *is an action. In formula* $z.\psi$ z *is a clock in* CX_f; *the* z. *operator is often referred to as* freeze *quantification.*

The relativized timed modal-mu calculus $L_{\nu,\mu}^{rel}$ *syntax replaces* $\exists(\psi)$ *and* $\forall(\psi)$ *with* $\exists_{\psi_1}(\psi_2)$ *and* $\forall_{\psi_1}(\psi_2)$, *where each* ψ_1 *and* ψ_2 *are basic formulas in* $L_{\nu,\mu}^{rel}$.

What follows is a sketch of the semantics; [7, 14] contains a formal definition. Formulas are interpreted with respect to states (i.e. (location, clock valuation) pairs) of a timed automaton whose clock set is CX and labeling function is M, and an environment θ associating each propositional variable Y with a set of states. A state (l, ν) satisfies an atomic proposition p if and only if p is in the set $M(l)$. A state satisfies Y if and only if $(l, \nu) \in \theta(Y)$. $\langle a \rangle(\psi)$ holds in a state if, after executing action a, ψ is true of the state after the action transition; $[a](\psi)$

means after all action transitions involving a, ψ holds in the target state; $\exists(\psi)$ holds of a state if after some time advance of $\delta \geq 0$, ψ holds in the new state, while $\forall(\psi)$ is satisfied in a state if for all possible time advances of $\delta \geq 0$, ψ is true in the resulting states. Formula $z.(\psi)$ holds in a state if, after introducing a new clock z (z is not a clock of the timed automaton) and setting it to 0 without altering other clocks, ψ is true. The formula $\exists_{\psi_1}(\psi_2)$ means, "there exists a time advance where ψ_2 is true and ψ_1 is true for all times up to, but not including, that advance", and $\forall_{\psi_1}(\psi_2)$ means, "either ψ_2 is true for all time advances or ψ_1 releases ψ_2 from being true after some time advance."

We also introduce two derived operators: $[-](\psi)$ for $\bigwedge_{a \in \Sigma_{TA}}[a](\psi)$ (for all next actions) and $\langle-\rangle(\psi)$ for $\bigvee_{a \in \Sigma_{TA}}\langle a\rangle(\psi)$ (there exists a next action). It may be seen that $\exists(\psi)$ is equivalent to $\exists_{\tt{tt}}(\psi)$, and $\forall(\psi)$ to $\forall_{\tt{ff}}(\psi)$.

$L_{\nu,\mu}^{rel}$ MESs are mutually recursive systems of equations whose right-hand sides are basic formulas as specified above. The formal definition follows.

Definition 4 ($L_{\nu,\mu}^{rel}$ MES syntax). *Let $X_1, X_2, \ldots, X_v$ be propositional variables, and let $\psi_1, \ldots \psi_v$ all be $L_{\nu,\mu}^{rel}$ basic formulae. Then a $L_{\nu,\mu}^{rel}$ modal equation system (MES) is an ordered system of equations as follows, where each equation is labeled with a parity (μ for least fixpoint, ν for greatest fixpoint):*
$$X_1 \overset{\mu/\nu}{=} \psi_1, X_2 \overset{\mu/\nu}{=} \psi_2, \ldots, X_v \overset{\mu/\nu}{=} \psi_v.$$
In our MES, we will assume that all variables are bound *(every variable in the right of the equation appears as some left-hand variable).*

The formal definition of the semantics of MESs may be found in [26, 27]; we recount the highlights here. Given a timed automaton and atomic-proposition interpretation M, a basic $L_{\nu,\mu}^{rel}$ formula may be seen as a function mapping sets of timed-automaton states (corresponding to the meaning of the propositional variables to the formula) to a single set of states (the states that make the formula true, given the input sets just referred to). The set of subsets of timed-automaton states ordered by set inclusion form a complete lattice; it turns out that the functions over this lattice definable by basic formulae are monotonic over this lattice, meaning they have unique greatest and least fixpoints. This fact is the lynch-pin of the formal semantics of MESs. Specifically, given MES $X_1 \overset{\mu/\nu}{=} \psi_1, \ldots, X_v \overset{\mu/\nu}{=} \psi_v$, we may construct a function that, given a set of states for X_1, returns the set of states satisfying ψ_1, where the values for $X_2, \ldots, X_v$ have been computed recursively. This function is monotonic, and therefore has a unique least and greatest fixpoint. If the parity for X_1 is μ, then the set of states satisfying X_1 is the least fixpoint of this function, while if the parity is ν then the set of states satisfying X_1 is the greatest fixpoint. By convention, the meaning of a MES is the set of states associated with X_1, the first left-hand-side in the sequence of equations. However, in the MES, each variable X_i can be interpreted as its own subformula; this interpretation will prove useful constructing proofs that a state satisfies a MES.

Given timed automaton TA, atomic-proposition interpretation function M, and propositional variable environment θ, we use $[\![\psi]\!]_{TA,M,\theta}$ to denote the set of states satisfying ψ. For an MES $\mathcal{M}$ of form $X_1 \overset{\mu/\nu}{=} \psi_1 \ldots X_v \overset{\mu/\nu}{=} \psi_v$, we write $[\![\mathcal{M}]\!]_{TA,M,\theta}$, or equivalently $[\![X_1]\!]_{TA,M,\theta}$ when there is no confusion, for the set of states satisfying the MES.

To handle the clocks used in freeze quantification $(z.(\psi))$, we extend the timed automaton's states (l, ν) to *extended states* (l, ν, ν_f) using the additional valuation component $\nu_f : CX_f \longrightarrow \mathbb{R}^{\geq 0}$. This formalism comes from [7]. When clear from context, we will refer to an extended state as (l, ν) and omit the explicit notation of ν_f.

In this paper we only consider MESs that are *alternation-free*. Intuitively, an MES is alternation free if there is no mutual recursion involving variables of different parities. For more information on the notion, see [12]. We denote the alternation-free fragment of $L_{\nu,\mu}^{rel}$ as $L_{\nu,\mu}^{rel,af}$. By definition, $L_{\nu,\mu}^{rel,af}$ is a superset of L_ν^{rel} because any formula with an alternation must have at least one greatest fixpoint and at least one least fixpoint. The alternation-free restriction is not prohibitive because for any timelock-free nonzeno timed automaton (see [8]), we can express any TCTL formula into a $L_{\nu,\mu}^{rel,af}$ MES [14].

Example 2 (Specifying properties with MES). Again consider the timed automaton in Figure 1 of Example 1. Two $L_{\nu,\mu}^{rel,af}$ specifications we can ask are:

$$X_1 \overset{\nu}{=} \neg broke \wedge \forall([-](X_1)) \tag{1}$$

$$X_1 \overset{\nu}{=} \neg far \vee \left(\forall([-](X_1)) \wedge \exists(z.(\forall(z < 1))) \right) \tag{2}$$

Equation 1 says "it is always the case the the train is not broken," and equation 2 says "it is inevitable that a train is not far."

3   Checking $L_{\nu,\mu}^{rel,af}$ Properties: A Proof-Based Approach

The $L_{\nu,\mu}^{rel,af}$ model-checking problem for timed automata may be specified as follows: given timed automaton $TA = (L, l_0, \Sigma_{TA}, CX, I, E)$, atomic-proposition interpretation function M, and $L_{\nu,\mu}^{rel,af}$ formula ψ with initial environment θ, determine if the initial state of TA satisfies ψ, i.e.: is $(l, \nu) \in [\![\psi]\!]_{TA,M,\theta}$. This section describes the proof-based approach that we use to solve such problems.

Our model-checking technique relies on the construction of proofs that are intended to establish the truth of judgments, or *sequents*, of the form $(l, cc) \vdash \psi$, where $l \in L$ is a location, $cc \in \Phi(CX \cup CX_f)$ is a clock constraint, and ψ is a $L_{\nu,\mu}^{rel,af}$ formula. Note that cc includes clocks from the timed automaton as well as any clocks used in freeze quantifications. Note that semantically, a clock constraint cc can be viewed as the set of valuations $cc = \{\nu \mid \nu \models cc\}$; likewise, we can encode a valuation ν as the clock constraint $cc_\nu = x_1 = \nu(x_1) \wedge \ldots \wedge x_n = \nu(x_n)$. A *proof rule* contains a finite number of hypothesis sequents and a conclusion sequent and may be written as follows.

$$\frac{\text{Premise 1} \quad \ldots \quad \text{Premise } n}{\text{Conclusion}} \; (\textit{Rule Name})$$

The intended reading of such a rule is that if each premise is valid, then so is the conclusion. Some proof rules, *axioms*, have no premises and thus assert the truth the validity of their conclusion. Given a collection of rules, our verifier builds a *proof* by chaining these proof rules together. A proof is *valid* if the proof rules are applied properly, meaning that the premise of the previous rule is the conclusion of the next rule. The proof rules are designed to be sound and complete, meaning: $(l, \nu) \in [\![\psi]\!]_{TA,M,\theta}$ if and only if there is a valid proof for $(l, cc_\nu) \vdash \psi$. The proof-construction process proceeds in an "on-the-fly" manner: rules whose conclusion matches the sequent to be proved are applied to this goal sequent, yielding new sequents that must be proved. This procedure is applied recursively, and systematically, until either a proof is found, or none can be.

3.1 Proof Rules for $L_{\nu,\mu}^{af}$ Over Timed Automata

The proof-based approach in this paper is inspired by a generic proof framework in [26, 27] based on a general theory called Predicate Equation Systems (PES). PES involved fixpoint equations over first-order predicates and used the proof-search to establish the validity of a PES. For practical reasons, one generally wishes to avoid the construction of the PES explicitly; this paper adopts this point of view, and the proof rules that it presents thus involve explicit mention of timed-automata notions, including location and edge. A selection of proof rules derived from [26, 27] is given in Figure 2. The remaining rules are in Appendix A of the supplement [16]. Several comments are in order.

1. Each rule is intended to relate a conclusion sequent involving a formula with a specific outermost operator to premise sequents involving the maximal subformula(e) of this formula. The name of the rule is based on this operator.
2. The premises also involve the use of functions *succ* and *pred*. Intuitively, $succ((l, cc))$ represents all states that are time successors of any state whose location component is l and whose clock valuation satisfies cc, while $pred((l, cc))$ are the time predecessors of these same states. These operators may be computed symbolically; that is, for any (l, cc) there is a cc' such that (l, cc') is equivalent to $succ((l, cc))$.
3. Some of the rules involve *placeholders*, which are (potentially) unions of clock constraints, given as (subscripted versions of) ϕ. Given a specific placeholder, the premise sequent $(l, cc), \phi$ is semantically equivalent to $(l, cc \wedge \phi)$; however, for notational and implementation ease, the placeholder ϕ is tracked separately from the clock constraint cc.

More discussion of placeholders is in order. Intuitively, placeholders encode a set of clock valuations that will make a sequent valid, and which will be computed once the proof is complete. In practice, we are interested in computing the largest such set. To understand their use in practice, consider the operator $\exists$. To check $\exists$, we need to find some time advance δ such that ψ is satisfied after δ time units. Rather than non-deterministically guessing δ, we use a placeholder ϕ_s in the left premise in rule $\exists_{t1}$ to encode all the time valuations that

$$\frac{(l_1, cc \wedge g_1) \vdash \psi[\lambda_1 := 0] \quad \ldots \quad (l_n, cc \wedge g_n) \vdash \psi[\lambda_n := 0]}{(l, cc) \vdash [a](\psi)} \ ([a]_{Act}), \text{cond}[a]$$

$$\text{cond}[a]: \bigcup_i \{(g_i, \lambda_i, l_i)\} = \{(l', g', \lambda') \mid (l, a, g', \lambda', l') \in E\}$$

$$\frac{(l, cc), \phi_s \vdash \psi_1 \quad (l, cc), \neg\phi_s \vdash \psi_2}{(l, cc) \vdash \psi_1 \vee \psi_2} \ (\vee_c) \qquad \frac{succ((l, cc)) \vdash \psi}{(l, cc) \vdash \forall(\psi)} \ (\forall_{t1})$$

$$\frac{succ((l, cc)), \phi_s \vdash \psi \quad succ((l, cc), \phi_\forall) \vdash succ((l, cc)) \wedge \phi_s}{(l, cc), \phi_\forall \vdash \forall(\psi)} \ (\forall_{t2})$$

$$\frac{succ((l, cc)), \phi_s \vdash \psi \quad (l, cc) \vdash pred(\phi_s)}{(l, cc) \vdash \exists(\psi)} \ (\exists_{t1}) \qquad \frac{succ((l, cc)), \phi_s \vdash \psi \quad \phi_\exists \vdash pred(\phi_s)}{(l, cc), \phi_\exists \vdash \exists(\psi)} \ (\exists_{t2})$$

Fig. 2. Select proof rules from [26, 27] adapted for timed automata and MES

ensure satisfaction of ψ. The right premise then checks that the placeholder ϕ_s is some δ-unit time elapse from (l, cc). The placeholder allows us to delay the non-deterministic guess of the value of ϕ_s until it is no longer required to guess. Additionally, for performance reasons, we use *new placeholders* to handle time advance operators for sequents with placeholders. An example may be found in Rule $\exists_{t2}$, where a new placeholder $\phi_\exists$ is introduced in the right premise. While useful for performance, this choice results in subtle implementation complexities, which we discuss in Section 5.3.

Constructing Proofs. Given sequents and proof rules, proofs now may be constructed in a goal-directed fashion. A sequent is proven by applying a proof rule whose conclusion matches the form of that sequent, yielding as subgoals the corresponding premises of that rule. These subgoals may then recursively be proved. If a sequent may be proved using a rule with no premises, then the proof is complete; similarly, if a sequent is encountered a second time (because of loops in the timed automaton and recursion in an MES), then the second occurrence is also a leaf. Details may be found in [26, 27]. If the recurrent leaf involves an MES variable with parity μ, then the leaf is unsuccessful; if it involves a variable with parity ν, it is successful. A proof is valid if all its leaves are successful.

Example 3. To illustrate the proof rules, consider the timed automaton in Figure 1. Suppose we wish to prove the sequent $(2 : in, x_1 \leq 3) \vdash [exit](0 : far)$. Utilizing the first proof rule in Figure 2, we get the proof:

$$\frac{(0 : far, 1 \leq x_1 \leq 3) \vdash 0 : far}{(2 : in, x_1 \leq 3) \vdash [exit](0 : far)}$$

In this rule, we intersect the clock constraint with the guard $x_1 \geq 1$ (if $x_1 < 1$, then there are no possible actions so the formula is true), make the destination location the new sequent, and ask if the destination satisfies the formula. Since the location is $0 : far$, the proof is complete.

$$\frac{(l,cc),\phi_{s_1} \vdash \psi_1 \qquad (l,cc),\phi_{s_2} \vdash \psi_2 \qquad (l,cc) \vdash \phi_{s_1} \vee \phi_{s_2}}{(l,cc) \vdash \psi_1 \vee \psi_2} \; (\vee_s)$$

$$\frac{(l,cc),\phi_{s_1} \vdash \psi_1 \qquad (l,cc),\phi_{s_2} \vdash \psi_2 \qquad (l,cc),\phi_\vee \vdash \phi_{s_1} \vee \phi_{s_2}}{(l,cc),\phi_\vee \vdash \psi_1 \vee \psi_2} \; (\vee_{s2})$$

$$\frac{succ((l,cc)),\phi_s \vdash \psi_2 \qquad succ((l,cc)),pred_<(\phi_s) \vdash \psi_1 \qquad (l,cc) \vdash pred(\phi_s)}{(l,cc) \vdash \exists_{\psi_1}(\psi_2)} \; (\exists_{r1})$$

$$\frac{succ((l,cc)),\phi_{s'} \vdash \psi_2 \qquad succ((l,cc)),pred_<(\phi_{s'}) \vdash \psi_1 \qquad (l,cc),\phi_s \vdash pred(\phi_{s'})}{(l,cc),\phi_s \vdash \exists_{\psi_1}(\psi_2)} \; (\exists_{r2})$$

Fig. 3. Proof Rules for $\vee$ and $\exists_{\phi_1}(\phi_2)$

3.2   New Proof Rules for the Relativized Operators of $L_{\nu,\mu}^{rel,af}$

We now introduce rules for handling the relativized time-passage modalities in $L_{\nu,\mu}^{rel,af}$. Figure 3 gives the rules for the operator $\exists_{\psi_1}(\psi_2)$. For the $\forall_{\psi_1}(\psi_2)$ operator, we use the derivation given in Lemma 1.

Here is an explanation of the proof rule $\exists_{r1}$; the proof rule $\exists_{r2}$ is similar. The idea is for the placeholder ϕ_s to encode the δ time advance needed for ψ_1 to be true. The proof-rule premises enforce that this placeholder has three properties:

1. *Left premise:* This premise checks that after the time advance taken by ϕ_s, ψ_2 is satisfied.
2. *Middle premise:* This premise checks that until all δ time-units have elapsed, that ψ_1 is indeed true. The $pred_<(\phi_s)$ encodes the times before ϕ_s.
3. *Right premise:* This premise checks that ϕ_s encodes some range of time elapses δ, ensuring that the state can elapse to valuations in ϕ_s.

To implement this rule, we check the premises in left-to-right order. Some subtleties involving the middle premise are discussed in Section 5.3.

Now we give the claims ensuring the correctness of these new proof rules. Their proofs are in Appendix B of the supplement [16]. This first lemma is a corrected version of a similar lemma in [7].

Lemma 1. $\forall_{\phi_1}(\phi_2)$ *is logically equivalent to* $\forall(\phi_2) \vee \exists_{\phi_2}(\phi_1 \wedge \phi_2)$.

Theorem 1 (Soundness and Completeness). *The additional* $L_{\nu,\mu}^{rel,af}$ *proof rules are sound and complete: for any* $L_{\nu,\mu}^{rel,af}$ *formula* ψ *and any state* (l,ν), $(l,\nu) \in [\![\psi]\!]_{M,TA,\theta}$ *if and only if* $(l,cc_\nu) \vdash \psi$.

4   Optimizing Performance via Derived Proof Rules

To simplify reasoning about soundness and completeness, sets of proof rules are often kept small and simple. However, we can improve the performance or proof search by having the computer work with *derived* proof rules. We describe two such situations where we use derived proof rules. We discuss a third situation, invariants, in Appendix C.2 of the supplement [16].

Optimizing $\vee$. For performance reasons we replace a rule for $\vee$ in [26, 27]. Those papers use the proof rule $\vee_c$ given in Figure 2. We instead use the proof rule $\vee_s$, which we give in Figure 3. By pushing fresh placeholders for both branches, we avoid computing the complementation operator, which often results in forming a placeholder involving a union of clock constraints.

Optimizing $\forall_{\psi_1}(\psi_2)$. Recall the derived formula for $\forall_{\psi_1}(\psi_2)$ from Lemma 1: $\forall_{\psi_1}(\psi_2)$ is equivalent to $\forall(\psi_2) \vee \exists_{\psi_2}(\psi_1 \wedge \psi_2)$. This formula requires ψ_2 to be checked three times. However, by modifying the proof rule, we notice that we can perform the checking of ψ_2 *only once*. First, we rewrite $\exists_{\psi_2}(\psi_1 \wedge \psi_2)$ as $\exists_{\leq,\psi_2}(\psi_1)$, pushing the boundary case into the left subformula. Second, the key is to compute the largest placeholder that satisfies ψ_2, to remember those states (memoize), and then to reason with this placeholder (and its time predecessor) to find the placeholders needed to satisfy the two branches of the derived formula. This reasoning allows the tool to reason with the subformula ψ_2 only once, reusing the obtained information. The derived proof rules are in Figure 4. The first two handle the simpler cases when either ψ_2 is always true (or when ψ_1 is always false) or ψ_1 is immediately true (such as when ψ_1 is an atomic proposition); the third rule ($\forall_{ro3}$) is the more complex case. The proof rules involving placeholders are similar. Their derivations as well as their proofs of soundness and completeness are in Appendix C.1 of the supplement [16].

$$\frac{(l, cc) \vdash \forall(\psi_2)}{(l, cc) \vdash \forall_{\psi_1}(\psi_2)} \; (\forall_{ro1}) \qquad \frac{(l, cc) \vdash \psi_1 \wedge \psi_2}{(l, cc) \vdash \forall_{\psi_1}(\psi_2)} \; (\forall_{ro2})$$

$$\frac{\begin{array}{c} succ((l, cc)), \phi_{s_1} \vdash \psi_1 \\ succ((l, cc)), \phi_{s_2} \vdash \psi_2 \\ succ((l, cc)), pred(\phi_{s_1}) \vdash succ((l, cc)), \phi_{s_2} \end{array} \qquad \begin{array}{c} \phi_\exists \vdash pred(\phi_{s_1}) \\ succ((l, cc), \phi_\forall) \vdash succ((l, cc)) \wedge \phi_{s_2} \\ (l, cc) \vdash \phi_\exists \vee \phi_\forall \end{array}}{(l, cc) \vdash \forall_{\psi_1}(\psi_2)} \; (\forall_{ro3})$$

Fig. 4. Derived proof rules for $\forall_{\psi_1}(\psi_2)$

5   Implementation Details

5.1   Addressing Non-convexity: Zone Unions

For a subset of properties including safety properties, *clock zones*, or convex sets of clock valuations, are used to make the model-checking as coarse-grained as possible. However, as shown in [24], certain automata with certain formulas require non-convex sets of clock valuations (unions of clock zones) to be model-checked correctly. For simplicity, we use a list of Difference Bound Matrices

(DBMs) to implement unions of clock zones. Other more complex data structures have been developed which include the Clock Difference Diagram (CDD) [5] and Clock Restriction Diagram (CRD) [22].

5.2   Addressing Performance: Simpler PES Formulas

When writing safety and liveness properties, we can use the formulas from [14]. However, in the common case where there are no nested temporal operators and the formula does not involve clock constraints, we can simplify the formulations considerably. In these cases, the subformula is a conjunction and disjunction of atomic propositions, and is represented by p or q. Here are some simplifications:

$$AG\,[p] \equiv Y \stackrel{\nu}{=} p \wedge \forall([\,-\,](Y)) \tag{3}$$

$$AF\,[p] \equiv Y \stackrel{\mu}{=} p \vee \left(\forall([\,-\,](Y)) \wedge \exists(z.(\forall(z < 1))) \right) \tag{4}$$

$$EF\,[p] \equiv Y \stackrel{\mu}{=} p \vee \exists(\langle-\rangle(Y)) \tag{5}$$

$$EG\,[p] \equiv Y \stackrel{\nu}{=} p \wedge \left(\exists(\langle-\rangle(Y)) \vee \forall(z.(\exists(z \geq 1))) \right) \tag{6}$$

The correctness proofs for these simplified formulations are in Appendix C.3 of the supplement [16].

The TCTL operators here are: $AG\,[p]$ (always p), $AF\,[p]$ (inevitably p), $EG\,[p]$ (there exists a path where always p), and $EF\,[p]$ (possibly p). One noticeable feature is that these simplified liveness properties do not require relativization. Another noticeable feature is that the $\vee$ can be simplified to not use placeholders; consequently, $AG\,[p]$ and $AF\,[p]$ do not require placeholders. Additionally, our tool directly computes $\exists(z.(\forall(z < 1)))$, time can elapse forever without an action transition, and its dual, $\forall(z.(\exists(z \geq 1)))$.

5.3   Placeholder Implementation Complexities

Consider the two placeholder premises in the $\forall(\psi)$ and $\exists_{\psi_1}(\psi_2)$ proof rules in Figures 2 and 3. The placeholder sequents are given here:

$$succ((l, cc), \phi_\forall) \vdash succ((l, cc)) \wedge \phi_s \text{ and } succ((l, cc)), pred_<(\phi_s) \vdash \psi_1 \tag{7}$$

In soundness and completeness proofs, we use soundness to give us a placeholder to show that the formula holds, and with completeness, we argue that some placeholder exists. Given the complexities of the formulas, the tool needs to find the *largest* such placeholder. The rules are designed for the tool to implement them in a left-to-right fashion, where placeholders are tightened by right-hand rules. However, as the placeholders are tightened, we need to make sure that the tightened placeholder still satisfies the left-hand premise. For instance, consider the second of the above placeholders. As we tighten the placeholder to satisfy ψ_1, we need to check that this placeholder is the predecessor$_<$ of the placeholder that satisfies ψ_2. These checks take extra algorithmic work.

6   Performance Evaluation

We present the results of an experimental evaluation of our method that demonstrates the types of timed automata and specifications the system can model check. Furthermore, on the subset of specifications that UPPAAL supports, we compare our tool's time performance to their tools's time performance.

6.1   Methods: Evaluation Design

In our case study, we use four different models: Carrier Sense, Multiple Access with Collision Detection (CSMA); Fischer's Mutual Exclusion (FISCHER); Generalized Railroad Crossing (GRC); and Leader election (LEADER). For more information on these models, see Appendix D.1 of the supplement [16] or [17, 26, 27].

For each model, we start at 4 processes and scale the model up by adding more processes (up to 8 processes). For each model we model-checked one valid safety (always) specification (as), one invalid safety specification (bs), one valid liveness (inevitably) specification (al), and one invalid liveness specification (bl). Each of these cases involves only one temporal operator: ψ_1 involves conjunctions and disjunctions of atomic propositions and clock constraints. In addition we tested 4 additional specifications on each property ($M1$, $M2$, $M3$, and $M4$), some of which are the leads to property $p \rightsquigarrow q$. Out of these specifications, at least one (usually $M4$) is a property with no known equivalent TCTL formula. The specifications checked are listed in Appendix D.2 of the supplement [16]. The experiments were run on an Intel Mac with 8GB ram and a quad-core 2 GHz Intel Core i7 processor running OS 10.7. Times were measured with the UNIX utility `time`.

6.2   Data and Results

The data is provided in Tables 1 and 2. Table 1 contains the remaining specifications that are not supported by UPPAAL. Table 2 contains the examples that

Table 1. Examples that UPPAAL does not support. All times are in seconds (s).

File	PES4	PES5	PES6	PES7	PES8
CSMA-as	0.29	4.62	139.16	6696.08	TO
CSMA-M3	0.01	0.03	0.14	0.80	3.99
CSMA-M4	0.01	0.03	0.14	0.71	3.66
FISCHER-M3	0.14	2.51	79.17	TO	TOsm
FISCHER-M4	0.00	0.00	0.00	2.04	2.42
GRC-M2	0.01	0.01	0.01	0.02	0.03
GRC-M4	0.00	0.00	0.01	0.02	0.01
GRC-M4ap	0.00	0.00	0.01	0.01	0.01
LEADER-M1	0.00	0.00	0.00	0.01	0.01
LEADER-M3	0.01	0.08	2.12	79.05	4242.97
LEADER-M4	0.00	0.00	0.04	0.03	0.01

Table 2. Time performance in seconds (s) on examples comparing PES and UPPAAL

File	PES4	UPP4	PES5	UPP5	PES6	UPP6	PES7	UPP7	PES8	UPP8
CSMA-al	0.01	1.45	0.03	0.24	0.13	0.25	0.72	0.26	3.65	0.26
CSMA-bl	0.01	0.26	0.03	0.27	0.13	0.27	0.73	0.28	3.53	0.33
CSMA-bs	0.01	0.33	0.05	0.27	0.22	0.27	1.14	1.33	5.09	4.66
CSMA-M1	0.01	0.29	0.03	0.27	0.14	0.28	0.73	0.27	3.69	0.27
CSMA-M2	0.33	0.35	5.21	7.00	154.56	1194.74	TO	TO	TOsm	TOsm
FISCHER-al	0.00	0.51	0.00	0.27	0.00	0.28	0.00	0.40	0.00	0.27
FISCHER-as	0.07	0.27	0.51	0.28	13.44	0.67	864.04	0.96	TO	4.26
FISCHER-bl	0.00	0.26	0.00	0.26	0.00	0.28	0.00	0.34	0.00	0.26
FISCHER-bs	0.04	0.28	0.01	0.27	0.02	0.32	0.39	0.47	0.39	0.90
FISCHER-M1	0.00	0.26	0.00	0.26	0.00	0.28	0.00	0.28	0.00	0.25
FISCHER-M2	0.00	0.26	0.00	0.26	0.00	0.27	0.00	0.30	0.03	0.28
GRC-al	0.00	0.27	0.01	0.28	0.47	0.59	0.07	0.44	0.08	5.45
GRC-as	53.09	0.36	TO	7.11	TOsm	940.51	TOsm	3433.14	TOsm	TO
GRC-bl	0.00	0.27	0.00	0.27	0.01	0.27	0.01	0.61	0.01	0.66
GRC-bs	0.11	0.41	1.91	0.41	433.59	1.76	O/M	16.19	O/M	52.03
GRC-M1	0.01	0.27	0.04	0.27	0.01	0.29	0.05	0.35	0.03	0.32
GRC-M3	0.00	0.27	0.00	0.31	0.01	0.56	0.04	1.23	0.01	3.85
LEADER-al	0.00	0.28	0.01	0.33	0.17	4.30	5.80	747.82	573.84	TO
LEADER-as	0.00	0.27	0.01	0.27	0.22	0.33	6.23	0.86	649.52	8.21
LEADER-bl	0.00	0.28	0.00	0.27	0.01	0.28	0.17	0.32	4.25	0.29
LEADER-bs	0.00	0.27	0.00	0.28	0.01	0.28	0.03	4.99	0.40	1.57
LEADER-M2	0.00	0.28	0.02	0.31	0.38	3.05	13.53	504.89	1570.37	TO

are supported both by our tool (PES) and by UPPAAL (UPP), with the number indicating the number of processes used in the model. We use the following abbreviations: TO (timeout: the example took longer than 2 hours), TOsm (the example timed out with fewer process), and O/M (out of memory). Since our tool supports a superset of the specifications that UPPAAL can support, there are specifications that our tool supports that UPPAAL does not. A scatter plot of the data in Table 2 is given in Appendix D.3 of the supplement [16].

6.3 Analysis and Discussion

After analyzing the data, we may draw three conclusions. First, on the examples that both our PES tool and UPPAAL support, we see that UPPAAL's performance is generally faster than ours, although, our tool performs faster on some examples. Additionally, while our tool does time out more often than UPPAAL does, most examples are verified quickly by both tools. Second, our tool can reasonably efficiently verify specifications that UPPAAL cannot. Third, for these examples, the performance bottleneck seems to be safety properties. Even with the additional complexity of supporting the more complicated specifications (in both tables), liveness was often verified more quickly than safety properties. Here is one possible explanation: while the verifier must check the entire state space for a valid safety property, often only a subset of the state space must be checked for a liveness property.

7   Conclusion

We provide the first implementation of a $L_{\nu,\mu}^{rel,af}$ timed automata model checker. Additionally, this model checker is on-the-fly, allowing for verification to explore both the timed automaton and the $L_{\nu,\mu}^{rel,af}$ formula incrementally. To support the full fragment of this logic, we extended the proof-rule framework of [26, 27] to support the relativization operators, and we optimize the tool's performance using derived proof rules. We also provided simpler $L_{\nu,\mu}^{rel,af}$ formulas for common safety and liveness formulas. While these may seem to be straightforward extensions, the rules and the extensions were *designed* to be straightforward, designing the proof rules to be both easy to implement efficiently.

We then compared our tool to UPPAAL. While UPPAAL seems to perform faster more often, our tool is competitive for many of those examples, including liveness formulas. Additionally, our tool was able to quickly verify specifications that UPPAAL does not currently support.

Future work is to both further optimize the performance of our tool and to augment our tool to provide more information than just a yes or no answer. Potential information includes providing answers to these questions: Was the formula true because the premise of an implication was always false? Was the formula true because certain states were never reached?

Acknowledgements. We thank Dezhuang Zhang for providing the code base [26] and for his insights.

References

[1] Aceto, L., Laroussinie, F.: Is your model checker on time? on the complexity of model checking for timed modal logics. Journal of Logic and Algebraic Programming 52-53, 7–51 (2002)

[2] Alur, R.: Timed Automata. In: Halbwachs, N., Peled, D.A. (eds.) CAV 1999. LNCS, vol. 1633, pp. 8–22. Springer, Heidelberg (1999)

[3] Alur, R., Courcoubetis, C., Dill, D.: Model-checking in dense real-time. Information and Computation 104(1), 2–34 (1993)

[4] Alur, R., Dill, D.L.: A theory of timed automata. Theoretical Computer Science 126(2), 183–235 (1994)

[5] Behrmann, G., Larsen, K.G., Pearson, J., Weise, C., Yi, W.: Efficient Timed Reachability Analysis Using Clock Difference Diagrams. In: Halbwachs, N., Peled, D.A. (eds.) CAV 1999. LNCS, vol. 1633, pp. 341–353. Springer, Heidelberg (1999)

[6] Behrmann, G., David, A., Larsen, K.G.: A tutorial on UPPAAL. In: Bernardo, M., Corradini, F. (eds.) SFM-RT 2004. LNCS, vol. 3185, pp. 200–236. Springer, Heidelberg (2004)

[7] Bouyer, P., Cassez, F., Laroussinie, F.: Timed modal logics for real-time systems. Journal of Logic, Language and Information 20(2), 169–203 (2011)

[8] Bowman, H., Gomez, R.: How to stop time stopping. Formal Aspects of Computing 18(4), 459–493 (2006)

[9] Clarke, E.M., Emerson, E.A., Sistla, A.P.: Automatic verification of finite-state concurrent systems using temporal logic specifications. TOPLAS 8(2), 244–263 (1986)

[10] Cleaveland, R.: Tableau-Based Model Checking in the Propositional Mu-Calculus. Acta Informatica 27(9), 725–747 (1990)
[11] Cleaveland, R., Steffen, B.: A Linear-Time Model-Checking Algorithm for the Alternation-Free Modal Mu-Calculus. Formal Methods in System Design 2(2), 121–147 (1993)
[12] Emerson, E.A., Lei, C.L.: Efficient Model Checking in Fragments of the Propositional Mu-Calculus. In: LICS 1986, pp. 267–278. IEEE Computer Society (1986)
[13] Fontana, P., Cleaveland, R.: Data Structure Choices for On-the-Fly Model Checking of Real-Time Systems. In: DIFTS 2011, pp. 13–21 (2011)
[14] Fontana, P., Cleaveland, R.: Expressiveness results for timed modal-mu calculi (2014) (in Preparation Preprint available upon request)
[15] Fontana, P., Cleaveland, R.: A menagerie of timed automata. ACM Computing Surveys 46(3), 40:1–40:56 (2014)
[16] Fontana, P., Cleaveland, R.: The power of proofs: New algorithms for timed automata model checking (appendix). arXiv.org (2014)
[17] Heitmeyer, C., Lynch, N.: The generalized railroad crossing: a case study in formal verification of real-time systems. In: RTSS 1994, pp. 120–131 (December 1994)
[18] Henzinger, T., Nicollin, X., Sifakis, J., Yovine, S.: Symbolic model checking for real-time systems. Information and Computation 111(2), 193–244 (1994)
[19] Laroussinie, F., Larsen, K.G.: CMC: A tool for compositional model-checking of real-time systems. In: Budkowski, S., Cavalli, A., Najm, E. (eds.) Formal Description Techniques and Protocol Specification, Testing and Verification. IFIP, pp. 439–456. Springer, US (1998)
[20] Peter, H.J., Ehlers, R., Mattmüller, R.: Synthia: Verification and synthesis for timed automata. In: Gopalakrishnan, G., Qadeer, S. (eds.) CAV 2011. LNCS, vol. 6806, pp. 649–655. Springer, Heidelberg (2011)
[21] Sokolsky, O.V., Smolka, S.A.: Local model checking for real-time systems. In: Wolper, P. (ed.) CAV 1995. LNCS, vol. 939, pp. 211–224. Springer, Heidelberg (1995)
[22] Wang, F.: Efficient verification of timed automata with BDD-like data structures. STTT 6(1), 77–97 (2004)
[23] Wang, F.: Redlib for the formal verification of embedded systems. In: ISoLA 2006, pp. 341–346. IEEE Computer Society, Piscataway (2006)
[24] Wang, F., Huang, G.D., Yu, F.: TCTL inevitability analysis of dense-time systems: From theory to engineering. IEEE Transactions on Software Engineering 32(7), 510–526 (2006)
[25] Yovine, S.: KRONOS: a verification tool for real-time systems. STTT 1(1), 123–133 (1997)
[26] Zhang, D., Cleaveland, W.R.: Fast generic model-checking for data-based systems. In: Wang, F. (ed.) FORTE 2005. LNCS, vol. 3731, pp. 83–97. Springer, Heidelberg (2005)
[27] Zhang, D., Cleaveland, R.: Fast on-the-fly parametric real-time model checking. In: RTSS 2005, pp. 157–166. IEEE Computer Society, Washington, DC (2005)

Anonymized Reachability of Hybrid Automata Networks

Taylor T. Johnson[1] and Sayan Mitra[2]

[1] University of Texas at Arlington, Arlington, TX 76019, USA
taylor.johnson@uta.edu
[2] University of Illinois at Urbana-Champaign, Urbana, IL 61801, USA
mitras@illinois.edu

Abstract. In this paper, we present a method for computing the set of reachable states for networks consisting of the parallel composition of a finite number of the same hybrid automaton template with rectangular dynamics. The method utilizes a symmetric representation of the set of reachable states (modulo the automata indices) that we call anonymized states, which makes it scalable. Rather than explicitly enumerating each automaton index in formulas representing sets of states, the anonymized representation encodes only: (a) the classes of automata, which are the states of automata represented with formulas over symbolic indices, and (b) the number of automata in each of the classes. We present an algorithm for overapproximating the reachable states by computing state transitions in this anonymized representation. Unlike symmetry reduction techniques used in finite state models, the timed transition of a network composed of hybrid automata causes the continuous variables of all the automata to evolve simultaneously. The anonymized representation is amenable to both reducing the discrete and continuous complexity. We evaluate a prototype implementation of the representation and reachability algorithm in our satisfiability modulo theories (SMT)-based tool, Passel. Our experimental results are promising, and generally allow for scaling to networks composed of tens of automata, and in some instances, hundreds (or more) of automata.

Keywords: hybrid automata network, reachability, verification, symmetry.

1 Introduction

Networks consisting of automata that communicate via shared variables are useful for modeling distributed algorithms such as mutual exclusion algorithms, media access control (MAC) such as time-division multiple access (TDMA) protocols, and distributed cyber-physical systems (CPS) such as air-traffic control systems [17]. However, as the state-space of the network consisting of parallel compositions of these automata grows exponentially in the number of automata N, automated analysis is challenging. It is particularly challenging for timed and hybrid systems, where the number of continuous variables (dimensions) also grows. Such networks are often specified in a symmetric manner—such as being composed of instantiations of an automaton template $\mathcal{A}(N, i)$—and are often amenable to methods that exploit symmetries. Formal analysis and state-space construction methods that exploit symmetries have been thoroughly

A. Legay and M. Bozga (Eds.): FORMATS 2014, LNCS 8711, pp. 130–145, 2014.
© Springer International Publishing Switzerland 2014

investigated for many classes of system models, because such methods ameliorate the state-space explosion problem [1, 2, 5, 6, 9–11, 14, 15, 20–22].

For example, several methods exploiting symmetry have been developed and implemented for the Murφ verification system [8] for discrete systems, such as the *scalarset* data structure [14], and the *repetitive id* data structure [15]. Advances in tools like UP-AAAL [3] and PAT [23] that exploit state-space symmetries have enabled scaling to larger models. For instance, the scalarset data structure from Murφ was extended for timed systems and implemented in UPAAAL [11, 12], and a clock-symmetry reduction method has been implemented in the PAT model checker [21]. Quasi-equal clocks and variables for timed [13] and hybrid (multi-rate) [4] automata networks also allow reductions in state-space explosion, but do not require automata in the network to be identical (modulo identifiers), as we do. We focus on safety properties, and to the best of our knowledge, before this paper, such symmetry techniques have not yet been applied to systems with general continuous dynamics like the rectangular differential inclusions we consider (e.g., [4] analyzes multi-rate automata and does not allow differential inclusions). The method described in this paper and implemented in our *Passel* verification tool [16, 18, 19] uses the SMT solver Z3 [7]. The method is used as a subroutine in methods for performing uniform verification of parameterized networks of hybrid automata (e.g., verification for all network sizes, $\forall \mathsf{N} \in \mathbb{N}$, $\mathcal{A}(\mathsf{N}, 1) \| \ldots \| \mathcal{A}(\mathsf{N}, \mathsf{N}) \models \zeta(\mathsf{N})$), although we highlight that this paper addresses fixed, constant choices of N only.

2 Hybrid Automata Network Syntax and Semantics

We specify the behavior of each participant in the network using a syntactic structure called a hybrid automaton template, denoted by $\mathcal{A}(\mathsf{N}, i)$.[1] The special symbols N and i are natural numbers that respectively refer to the number of automata, and the ith automaton. For a natural number n, the set $[n]$ is $\{1, \ldots, n\}$. For a set S, the set $S_\perp$ is $S \cup \{\perp\}$. Fixing a particular value of N gives concrete instances of $[\mathsf{N}]$ and $[\mathsf{N}]_\perp$.

Terms and Formulas. We use a class of formulas to: (a) specify the syntactic components of a hybrid automaton template $\mathcal{A}(\mathsf{N}, i)$, and (b) represent sets of states symbolically in the reachability computation. Formulas are built-up from constants, variables, and terms of several types. The grammar for formulas is:

$\mathsf{ITerm} ::= \perp \mid 1 \mid \mathsf{N} \mid i \mid p[i]$

$\mathsf{DTerm} ::= l_c \mid q \mid q[\mathsf{ITerm}]$

$\mathsf{RTerm} ::= 0 \mid 1 \mid r_c \mid x \mid x[\mathsf{ITerm}]$

$\mathsf{RPoly} ::= \mathsf{RTerm} \mid \mathsf{RPoly}_1 + \mathsf{RPoly}_2 \mid \mathsf{RPoly}_1 - \mathsf{RPoly}_2 \mid (\mathsf{RPoly}_1 * \mathsf{RPoly}_2)$

$\mathsf{Atom} ::= \mathsf{ITerm}_1 = \mathsf{ITerm}_2 \mid \mathsf{DTerm}_1 = \mathsf{DTerm}_2 \mid \mathsf{RPoly} < 0$

$\mathsf{Formula} ::= \mathsf{Atom} \mid \neg\mathsf{Formula} \mid \mathsf{Formula}_1 \wedge \mathsf{Formula}_2 \mid \exists x\, \mathsf{Formula}$

The grammar is composed of *index terms* (ITerm) with type $[\mathsf{N}]_\perp$, *discrete terms* (DTerm) with type L, and *real terms* (RTerm) with type $\mathbb{R}$. For a discrete term, l_c is constant from L and q is a discrete variable. For a real term, r_c is a real numerical

---

[1] Readers interested in additional technical details are referred to [16, Chapters 2 and 4].

constant and x is a real variable. Index ($p[i]$), discrete (q[ITerm]), and real (x[ITerm])
pointer variables are names for arrays composed of N elements of the corresponding
type, respectively referenced at an index variable i, or an evaluation of an index term
ITerm. Atoms (Atom) are composed of ordered relations between real polynomials
(RPoly), as well as equality relations between index terms and discrete terms. Formulas
are composed of Boolean combinations of atoms and shorter formulas. Comparison operators are expressed using negation ($\neg$) and conjunction ($\wedge$) in formulas. Combining
the Boolean operators $\wedge$ and $\neg$ with the $<$ operator, other comparison operators like
$=$, $\neq$, $\leq$, $>$, and $\geq$, can be expressed. We assume the language contains the standard
quantifiers and Boolean operators, even if not explicitly specified in the grammar (e.g.,
universal quantification $\forall$, implication $\Rightarrow$, disjunction $\vee$, less-than-or-equal $\leq$, etc.).

Variables. A hybrid automaton $\mathcal{A}(N, i)$ has a set of *variables*, each of which is a name
used for referring to state and is a term in the grammar just defined. As specified in the
grammar, each variable v is associated with a *type*—denoted $type(v)$—that defines a
set of values the variable may take. The type of a variable may be: (a) L: a finite set
of locations names, (b) $[N]_\perp$: a set of automaton indices—called pointers—with the
special element $\perp$ that is not equal to any automaton's index, or (c) $\mathbb{R}$: the set of real
numbers. A variable may be a *local* variable with a name of the form $variable\_name[i]$,
or *global*, in which case its name does not have a symbolic index $[i]$. For example, $q[i]$:
L, $p[i]$: $[N]_\perp$, and $x[i]$: $\mathbb{R}$ respectively define location, pointer, and real typed local
variables, while g : $[N]_\perp$ is a global variable of pointer type. The sets of local and global
variables are denoted by $V_L(i)$ and $V_G(i)$, respectively. The *valuation* of a variable v
is a function that associates the variable name v to a value in its type $type(v)$. For a
set of variables V, $val(V)$ is the set of valuations of each $v \in V$. For a set of variables
V, $V' \triangleq \{v'|v \in V\}$ and $\dot{V} \triangleq \{\dot{v}|v \in V \wedge type(v) = \mathbb{R}\}$. V' is used for specifying
resets of discrete transitions and $\dot{V}$ is used for specifying continuous dynamics. For a
formula ϕ, let: (a) $vars(\phi)$ be the set of variables appearing in ϕ, (b) $ivars(\phi)$ be the
set of distinct index variables appearing in ϕ.

Let N be a symbol representing an arbitrary natural number and i be a symbol representing an arbitrary element of [N]. For the remainder of the paper, we fix N and
refer to it implicitly in the remaining definitions. When clear from context, we drop the
parameter N, for instance, a hybrid automaton template $\mathcal{A}(N, i)$ is written $\mathcal{A}(i)$, etc.

Definition 1. *A hybrid automaton template $\mathcal{A}(N, i)$ is specified by the syntactic components: (a)* $V(i)$: *a finite set of variable names with associated types. (b)* L: *a finite set
of location names. (c)* Init(i): *an initial condition formula over* $V(i)$. *(d)* Trans(i): *a fi-
nite set of discrete transition statements, each of which is a tuple* $\langle \mathbf{from}, \mathbf{to}, \mathbf{grd}, \mathbf{rst} \rangle$,
where $\mathbf{from}$, $\mathbf{to}$ $\in$ L, $\mathbf{grd}$ *is a formula over* $V(i)$ *called a* guard *and* $\mathbf{rst}$ *is a formula over* $V(i) \cup V'(i)$ *called a* reset. *The guard is an enabling condition that must
be satisfied so that a transition may be taken, and the reset models the update of
state. (e)* Traj(i): *for each element in* L, *there is a* trajectory *statement, each of which
is a tuple* $\langle \mathbf{loc}, \mathbf{inv}, \mathbf{frate} \rangle$, *where* $\mathbf{loc} \in$ L, $\mathbf{inv}$ *is a formula over the real variables
X(i) called an* invariant, *and* $\mathbf{frate}$ *is a formula over* X(i) $\cup$ $\dot{X}(i)$ *called a* flowrate *that
specifies how the real variables evolve over time. The invariant is an assertion that must
be satisfied while $\mathcal{A}(i)$ is in $\mathbf{loc}$, and the flow rate associates each real-valued variable
of $\mathcal{A}(i)$ with a rectangular differential inclusion.*

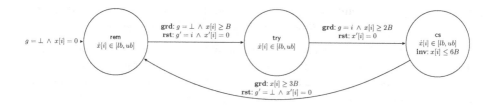

Fig. 1. Hybrid automaton template $\mathcal{A}(i)$ for MUX-INDEX-RECT mutual exclusion algorithm

Let $X(i) \triangleq \{v \in V(N, i) | type(v) = \mathbb{R}\}$ be the set of variables of $\mathcal{A}(i)$ with real type.

MUX-INDEX-RECT (Figure 1) is a timed mutual exclusion algorithm with an imprecise real clock $x[i]$ that evolves between rates $lb \leq ub$. There is a global variable g with type $[N]_\perp$. Each automaton i starts in rem with $x[i] = 0$ and $g = \perp$, then after waiting B time i may enter try which also sets the global variable g to the identifier i. After waiting at least $2B$ time, it may enter the critical section cs and stay there for at least $3B$ and at most $6B$ time before returning to rem and setting $g = \perp$.

2.1 Semantics of Hybrid Automata Networks

For a hybrid automaton template $\mathcal{A}(i)$, we define a transition system to formalize the semantics of the network where N instantiations of $\mathcal{A}(i)$ operate concurrently.

Definition 2. *Let* N *be a symbol representing an arbitrary natural number. A* hybrid automata network *is a tuple* $\mathcal{A}^N \triangleq \langle V^N, Q^N, \Theta^N, T^N \rangle$, *where: (a)* V^N *are the variables of the network,* $V^N \triangleq V_G \cup \bigcup_{i=1}^N V_L(i)$, *(b)* $Q^N \subseteq val(V^N)$ *is the state-space, (c)* $\Theta^N \subseteq Q^N$ *is the set of initial states, and (d)* $T^N \subseteq Q^N \times Q^N$ *is the transition relation, which is partitioned into sets of discrete transitions* $\mathcal{D}^N \subseteq Q^N \times Q^N$ *and continuous trajectories* $\mathcal{T}^N \subseteq Q^N \times Q^N$.

A *state* $\mathbf{x}$ of $\mathcal{A}^N$ is a valuation of *all* the variables in V^N and is denoted by boldface $\mathbf{v}, \mathbf{v}'$, etc. The set of all states is called the state-space and is denoted Q^N. If a state $\mathbf{v} \in Q^N$ satisfies a formula ϕ—that is, the corresponding variable valuations result in ϕ evaluating to *true*—we write $\mathbf{v} \models \phi$. For a formula ϕ with $vars(\phi) \subseteq V(i)$, the corresponding states $\mathbf{x} \in Q^N$ satisfying ϕ are $[\![\phi]\!] \triangleq \{\mathbf{x} \in Q^N | \mathbf{v} \models \phi\}$. For instance, the initial states $\Theta^N \triangleq [\![\mathsf{Init}(i)]\!]$ are the states satisfying $\mathsf{Init}(i)$. For some state $\mathbf{v}$, the valuation of a particular local variable $x[i] \in V_L(i)$ for automaton $\mathcal{A}(i)$ is denoted by $\mathbf{v}.x[i]$, and $\mathbf{v}.g$ for some global variable g in $V_G(i)$. For a set of variables V, the valuations of each $v \in V$ at state $\mathbf{v}$ is denoted by $\mathbf{v}.V$. For a formula ϕ and a set of variables $V \subseteq vars(\phi)$, let $\phi\!\downarrow V$ be the projection of ϕ onto the variables V, such that $vars(\phi\!\downarrow V) = V$ and $[\![\phi]\!] \subseteq [\![\phi\!\downarrow V]\!]$, which can be computed by eliminating the existential quantifiers from the formula $\exists vars(\phi) \setminus V : \phi$. The evolution of the states of $\mathcal{A}^N$ are describing by a transition relation $T^N \subseteq Q^N \times Q^N$. For a pair $(\mathbf{v}, \mathbf{v}') \in T^N$, we use the notation $\mathbf{v} \to \mathbf{v}'$, where $\mathbf{v}$ is called the *pre-state* and $\mathbf{v}'$ is called the *post-state*. There are two ways variables may be updated by T^N. Discrete transitions $\mathcal{D}^N$ model instantaneous changes and continuous trajectories $\mathcal{T}^N$ model evolution over a real time interval.

When necessary to disambiguate state updates owing to either discrete transitions and continuous trajectories, we write $\mathbf{v} \to_{\mathcal{D}^N} \mathbf{v}'$ or $\mathbf{v} \to_{\mathcal{T}^N} \mathbf{v}'$, respectively.

Discrete Transitions. Discrete transitions model atomic, instantaneous updates of state due to *one* automaton in the network $\mathcal{A}^N$. Informally, a discrete transition from pre-state $\mathbf{v}$ to post-state $\mathbf{v}'$ models the discrete transition of one particular hybrid automaton $\mathcal{A}(i)$ by some transition $\mathsf{t} \in \mathsf{Trans}(i)$. There is a discrete transition $\mathbf{v} \to \mathbf{v}' \in \mathcal{D}^N$ iff: $\exists i \in [N] \, \exists \mathsf{t} \in \mathsf{Trans}(i) : \mathbf{v}.\mathsf{V}(i) \models \mathbf{grd}(\mathsf{t}, i) \wedge \mathbf{v}'.\mathsf{V}(i) \models \mathbf{rst}(\mathsf{t}, i) \wedge$ $(\forall j \in [N] : j \neq i \Rightarrow \mathbf{v}'.\mathsf{V}(j) = \mathbf{v}.\mathsf{V}(j))$. From the pre-state $\mathbf{v}$, any automaton $\mathcal{A}(i)$ in the network $\mathcal{A}^N$ that has some transition where $\mathbf{v}$ satisfies its guard *may* update its post-state according to the transition's reset, while the variable valuations of all the other automata in $\mathcal{A}^N$ remain unchanged.[2]

Continuous Trajectories. Continuous trajectories model update of state over intervals of real time. Informally, there is a trajectory $\mathbf{v} \to \mathbf{v}' \in \mathcal{T}^N$ iff some amount of time—t_e—can elapse from $\mathbf{v}$, such that, (a) the states of *all* automata in the network $\mathcal{A}^N$ are updated to $\mathbf{v}'$ according to their individual trajectory statements, and (b) while ensuring the invariants of *all* automata along the entire trajectory. Formally, trajectories are defined as solutions of differential equations or inclusions specified in the trajectory statements of $\mathcal{A}(i)$. For a state $\mathbf{v}$, a location m, a real time t, and a real variable $v \in \mathsf{X}(i)$, let $\mathbf{flow}(\mathbf{v}, \mathsf{m}, v, t) = \mathbf{v}.v + \int_{\tau=0}^{t} \mathbf{frate}(\mathsf{m}, v) d\tau$. Since $\mathbf{frate}$ may specify a differential inclusion, $\mathbf{flow}$ is a set-valued function. There is a trajectory $\mathbf{v} \to \mathbf{v}' \in \mathcal{T}^N$ iff: $\exists t_e \in \mathbb{R}_{\geq 0} \, \forall t_p \in \mathbb{R}_{\geq 0} \, \forall i \in [N] \, \exists \mathsf{m} \in \mathsf{L} : t_p \leq t_e \wedge \mathbf{flow}(\mathbf{v}, \mathsf{m}, \mathsf{X}(i), t_p) \models \mathbf{inv}(\mathsf{m}, i) \wedge \mathbf{v}'.\mathsf{X}(i) \in \mathbf{flow}(\mathbf{v}, \mathsf{m}, \mathsf{X}(i), t_e)$. For each $i \in [N]$ and each real variable $x[i]$, $\mathbf{v}.x[i]$ must evolve to the valuations $\mathbf{v}'.x[i]$, in exactly t_e time in some location $\mathsf{m} \in \mathsf{L}$ according to the flow rates allowed for $x[i]$ in location m. In addition, all intermediate states along the trajectory must satisfy the invariant $\mathbf{inv}(\mathsf{m}, i)$.

Executions and Invariants. An execution of the network $\mathcal{A}^N$ models a particular behavior of all the automata in the network. An *execution* of $\mathcal{A}^N$ is a sequence of states $\alpha = \mathbf{v}_0, \mathbf{v}_1, \ldots$ such that $\mathbf{v}_0 \in \Theta^N$, and for each index k appearing in the sequence, $(\mathbf{v}_k, \mathbf{v}_{k+1}) \in T^N$. A state $\mathbf{x}$ is *reachable* if there is a finite execution ending with $\mathbf{x}$. The set of reachable states for $\mathcal{A}^N$ is $\mathsf{Reach}(\mathcal{A}^N)$. The set of reachable states for $\mathcal{A}^N$ starting from an arbitrary subset $\mathbf{V}_0 \subseteq Q^N$ is $\mathsf{Reach}(\mathcal{A}^N, \mathbf{V}_0)$. An *invariant* for $\mathcal{A}^N$ is any set of states that contains $\mathsf{Reach}(\mathcal{A}^N)$.

3   Anonymized State-Space Representation

For any fixed $N \in \mathbb{N}$, let i be a symbol representing an arbitrary element of $[N]$, and for the hybrid automaton template $\mathcal{A}(N, i)$, the composed automaton modeling a network of size N is $\mathcal{A}^N$ (Definition 2). We present an algorithm for computing $\mathsf{Reach}(\mathcal{A}^N)$ that takes advantage of the symmetries in the template $\mathcal{A}(i)$ instantiated in $\mathcal{A}^N$. The representation of $\mathsf{Reach}(\mathcal{A}^N)$ is *anonymized*, so numerical automaton indices—$1, 2, \ldots$, N—are not explicitly enumerated and are instead modeled using symbolic indices—i_1,

---

[2] The guard may depend on the variables of some automaton $j \neq i$, so automata may communicate via global variables and local variables, for details, see [16, Chapter 2].

$i_2, \ldots, i_N$. Frequently, the number of symbolic indices needed to represent equivalent states is significantly smaller than the number N of numerical indices. For example, in MUX-INDEX-RECT (Figure 1), a single symbolic index is sufficient independent of N. For a given state $\mathbf{x} \in Q^N$, the set of corresponding states $\mathbf{X} \subseteq Q^N$ that are equivalent modulo indices is obtained by substituting any numerical index i of all local variables $v[i] \in V_L(i)$ with a symbolic index j with type $[N]$.

Definition 3. *Two states* $\mathbf{x}, \mathbf{x}' \in Q^N$ *of* $\mathcal{A}^N$, *are* equivalent modulo indices *if there exists a bijection* $\pi : [N] \to [N]$ *such that for each* $v[i] \in V(i)$, $\mathbf{x}.v[i] = \mathbf{x}'.v[\pi(i)]$. *For a state* $\mathbf{x} \in Q^N$ *of* $\mathcal{A}^N$, *the set of states* $\varepsilon(\mathbf{x})$ *that is equivalent modulo indices to* $\mathbf{x}$ *is:*
$$\varepsilon(\mathbf{x}) \triangleq \{\mathbf{x}' \in Q^N \mid \mathbf{x} \text{ and } \mathbf{x}' \text{ are equivalent modulo indices}\}.$$

We note this is the same type of definition as the existence of an automorphism used in [6, 9, 14]. A state is equivalent modulo indices to itself by picking the bijection π to be the identity mapping. For a formula ϕ, we will overload π and write $\pi(\phi)$, which modifies ϕ by applying π to each index variable $i \in ivars(\phi)$. The anonymized representation takes this idea a step further by utilizing symbolic names for process indices along with counters, and a formula representing the valuations of any global variables. We use the (.) notation to refer to particular elements of tuples. For example, C.Count refers to the count of anonymized class C, C.Form refers to C's formula, etc. If C is clear from context, we refer to C.Count as Count, etc.

Definition 4. *An* anonymized state S *of the network* $\mathcal{A}^N$ *is a tuple* $\langle \texttt{Classes}, \texttt{G} \rangle$, *where:*

(a) *Each* anonymized class $\texttt{C} \in \texttt{Classes}$ *is a tuple* $\texttt{C} \triangleq \langle \texttt{Count}, \texttt{I}, \texttt{Form} \rangle$, *where:*
   (i) Form *is a quantifier-free formula over the variables* $V_L(i_1) \cup \ldots \cup V_L(i_I)$, *where* $i_1, \ldots, i_I$ *are* I *distinct symbolic index variables.*
   (ii) $\texttt{I} \geq 1$ *is a natural number called the* class's rank, *which is equal to the number of distinct symbolic index variables appearing in* Form: $\texttt{I} \triangleq |ivars(\texttt{Form})|$.
   (iii) Count *is a natural number called the* class's count, *and satisfies* $\texttt{N} \geq \texttt{Count} \geq |\texttt{I}|$. *The count is the number of automata of class* C. *Additionally, the sum of all the class counts in* S *equals* N: $\texttt{N} = \sum_{\texttt{C} \in \texttt{S.Classes}} \texttt{C.Count}$, *where* C.Count *is the count of class* C.
(b) G *is a quantifier-free formula over the global variables* V_G.

For an anonymized class C, requirement (iii) of Definition 4 that $\texttt{Count} \geq |\texttt{I}|$ means the number of automata satisfying Form is at least the rank (the number of distinct index variables appearing in Form). When the rank I is clear from context, we drop it from the C tuple and write $\langle \texttt{Count}, \texttt{Form} \rangle$. We say two anonymized classes $\texttt{C}_1$ and $\texttt{C}_2$ over the same symbolic indices ($ivars(\texttt{C}_1.\texttt{Form}) = ivars(\texttt{C}_2.\texttt{Form})$) are equivalent and write $\texttt{C}_1 \equiv \texttt{C}_2$ iff they have equivalent class formulas and equal class counts:[3]

---

[3] It is possible for classes with different ranks to represent the same states. For example, consider states arising from MUX-INDEX-RECT, $\texttt{S}_1 = \langle \{\langle 2, 2, q[i_1] = \texttt{rem} \wedge q[i_2] = \texttt{rem} \rangle\}, g = \bot \rangle$ and $\texttt{S}_2 = \langle \{\langle 2, 1, q[i_1] = \texttt{rem} \rangle\}, g = \bot \rangle$, which both represent there are two automata with location rem and g is $\bot$, i.e., $[\![\texttt{S}_1]\!] = [\![\texttt{S}_2]\!]$. However, a class of a particular rank may not be expressible as a different rank. For example, there is no way to express the following using rank 1 classes: $\langle \{\langle 2, 2, q[i_1] = \texttt{rem} \wedge q[i_2] = \texttt{rem} \wedge x[i_1] \geq x[i_2] \rangle\}, g = \bot \rangle$, which expresses that there are two automata in rem with one's clock at least as large as the other's.

Definition 5. *Two classes* C_1 *and* C_2 *are* equivalent, *written* $C_1 \equiv C_2$ *iff* $C_1.\mathsf{Count} = C_2.\mathsf{Count} \wedge C_1.\mathsf{Form} \equiv C_2.\mathsf{Form}$.

Here, equivalence between the class formulas is a semantic and not syntactic notion, and means the formula $C_1.\mathsf{Form} \equiv C_2.\mathsf{Form}$ is valid.We say two anonymized states S_1 and S_2 are equivalent and write $S_1 \equiv S_2$ iff they have the same state counts, the classes in their sets of classes are equivalent, and their global formulas are equivalent. See Footnote 3 for an example from MUX-INDEX-RECT.

Definition 6. *Two anonymized states* S_1 *and* S_2 *are* equivalent, *written* $S_1 \equiv S_2$, *iff* $\forall C_1 \in S_1.\mathsf{Classes} \, \exists \, C_2 \in S_2.\mathsf{Classes} \, C_1 \equiv C_2 \wedge G_1 \equiv G_2$.

We make the following assumption about the format of class formulas.

Assumption 1. *For an anonymized state* S, *for each class* $C \in \mathsf{Classes}$, *the class formula* $C.\mathsf{Form}$ *is in conjunctive normal form (CNF). For each index* $i \in \{i_1, \ldots, i_{C.I}\}$, $C.\mathsf{Form}$ *contains an equality* $q[i] = \mathbf{loc}$ *for some location* $\mathbf{loc} \in L$.

For example, Equation 1 (arsing from MUX-INDEX-RECT) satisfies this assumption. This assumption ensures that each class corresponds to a concrete state, and has a control location specified to determine the transitions and trajectories that may be possible (recall Definition 1). Under Assumption 1, the interpretation of an anonymized state S corresponds to a set of states of Q^N, which we write as $[\![S]\!]$ and define formally next. Since the class formulas of S are over the variables of automata with symbolic indices, the interpretation instantiates the symbolic indices with specific elements of $[N]$, which yields the set of states that are equivalent modulo indices.

Definition 7. *For an anonymized state*

$$S = \langle \{ \underbrace{\langle \mathsf{Count}_1, I_1, \mathsf{Form}_1 \rangle}_{C_1}, \ldots, \underbrace{\langle \mathsf{Count}_k, I_k, \mathsf{Form}_k \rangle}_{C_k} \}, G \rangle,$$

we instantiate the set of symbolic indices $\{i_1, \ldots, i_{I_k}\}$ *with all possible values in* $[N]$ *as follows. A* consistent partition *of* $[N]$,

$$P = \{ \underbrace{\{P_1^1, \ldots, P_1^{I_1}\}}_{P_1}, \ldots, \underbrace{\{P_k^1, \ldots, P_k^{I_k}\}}_{P_k} \},$$

is a partition of $[N]$, *such that, for any* $P_j \in P$, (a) $|P_j| = \mathsf{Count}_j$ *and* (b) P_j *is partitioned into* I_j *sets* $P_j^1, \ldots, P_j^{I_j}$ *(and we recall that* I_j *is the rank of* C_j).

For a consistent partition P, we note that (a) $\sum_{P_j \in P} |P_j| = N$, since P partitions $[N]$, and (b) $\mathsf{Count}_j \geq I_j$ (by Definition 4, (iii)). For example, consider the anonymized state (arsing from MUX-INDEX-RECT, Figure 1) with count three and rank two:

$$\langle \{ \langle 3, 2, q[i_1] = \mathsf{try} \wedge q[i_2] = \mathsf{rem} \wedge x[i_1] \geq x[i_2] + B \rangle \}, g = i_1 \rangle. \tag{1}$$

One consistent partition is: $P = \{P_1, P_2\}$ where $P_1 = \{1\}$ and $P_2 = \{2, 3\}$. The set $\{\{1, 2, 3\}\}$ is *not* a consistent partition since it is partitioned into one set, but the rank $I = 2$, and Definition 7 requires each $P_j \in P$ be partitioned into I_j partitions.

For an anonymized state S, the set of consistent partitions $ConsPart(S)$ are all consistent partitions of $[N]$. Continuing MUX-INDEX-RECT for Equation 1, $ConsPart(S)$ is $\{\{\{1\}, \{2, 3\}\}, \{\{2\}, \{1, 3\}\}, \{\{3\}, \{1, 2\}\}, \{\{1, 2\}, \{3\}\}, \{\{1, 3\}, \{2\}\}, \{\{2, 3\}, \{1\}\}\}$. All these partitions define the set of states $[\![S]\!]$ the anonymized state S represents. This is the same as all the states equivalent modulo indices to the states $[\![S_P]\!]$ for a particular consistent partition P.

Definition 8. *For an anonymized state S and a consistent partition $P \in ConsPart(S)$, the set of states of network $\mathcal{A}^N$ represented by S corresponding to P are:*

$$[\![S_P]\!] \triangleq \{\mathbf{x} \in Q^N \mid \mathbf{x} \models \mathsf{G} \wedge \mathtt{Form}_1(P_1) \wedge \ldots \wedge \mathtt{Form}_k(P_k)\}, \qquad (2)$$

where each $\mathtt{Form}_j(P_j) \triangleq \forall i_j^1 \in P_j^1, \ldots, i_j^{\mathtt{I}_j} \in P_j^{\mathtt{I}_j} : \mathtt{Form}_j(i_j^1, \ldots, i_j^{\mathtt{I}_j})$. *The set of states of network $\mathcal{A}^N$ represented by S with all consistent partitions is:*

$$[\![S]\!] \triangleq \bigcup_{P \in ConsPart(S)} [\![S_P]\!]. \qquad (3)$$

We have written $\mathtt{Form}_j(i_j^1, \ldots, i_j^{\mathtt{I}_j})$ to highlight that $\mathtt{Form}_j$ is over $\mathtt{I}_j$ symbolic index variables. Note that $\mathtt{Form}_j(P_j)$ is equivalent to a finite-length conjunction since each $P_j^{\mathtt{I}_j}$ is a finite set. The next lemma states that this definition of interpretations of anonymized states yields the same set of states as equivalence modulo identifiers.

Lemma 1. *For an anonymized state S, for any* $\mathbf{x} \in [\![S]\!]$, *for any* $\mathbf{x}' \in \varepsilon(\mathbf{x})$, $\mathbf{x}' \in [\![S]\!]$.

Continuing the MUX-INDEX-RECT Equation 1 example with the consistent partition $P = \{\{1\}, \{2, 3\}\}$, the states represented by S_P are:

$$\begin{aligned}
[\![S_P]\!] &= \{\mathbf{x} \in Q^3 \mid \mathbf{x} \models \forall i_1^1 \in P_1^1, i_1^2 \in P_1^2 : q[i_1] = \mathsf{try} \wedge q[i_2] = \mathsf{rem} \wedge \\
&\qquad x[i_1] \geq x[i_2] + B \wedge g = i_1\} \\
&= \{\mathbf{x} \in Q^3 \mid \mathbf{x} \models (q[1] = \mathsf{try} \wedge q[2] = \mathsf{rem} \wedge q[3] = \mathsf{rem} \wedge \\
&\qquad x[1] \geq x[2] + B \wedge x[1] \geq x[3] + B \wedge g = 1)\}.
\end{aligned}$$

Applying Lemma 1, $[\![S]\!] = \varepsilon([\![S_P]\!])$.

4   Anonymized Reachability of Hybrid Automata Networks

Next we describe an on-the-fly algorithm for overapproximating the reachable states of a network $\mathcal{A}^N$ using anonymized states. We note that the CNF requirement (Assumption 1) is not restrictive: if a new class is created during the execution of the algorithm that contains disjunctions, it is split into multiple classes with CNF formulas. Recall from Section 2.1, that $\phi\!\downarrow \mathsf{V}$ is the projection of ϕ onto the variables V.

Pseudocode for the reachability algorithm, areach appears in Figure 2. The algorithm operates on frontiers of reachable states represented by Frontier, which is initialized (line 3) to a singleton set with one class with count N and formula $\mathsf{Init}(i)\!\downarrow \mathsf{V}_L(i)$, which is $\mathsf{Init}(i)$ projected onto the local variables. The global formula is initialized with

```
 1    function areach(A(i), Init(i), N)
          AnonReach ← ∅
 3        Frontier ← {⟨{⟨N, Init(i)↓ V_L(i)⟩}, Init(i)↓ V_G(i)⟩}  // initial anonymized state
          while Frontier ≠ ∅  // repeat until no new states are added to the frontier
 5            Frontier_New ← ∅  // initialize next frontier
              AnonReach ← AnonReach ∪ Frontier  // add frontier to reachable states
 7            // compute successors of each anonymized state in the frontier
              foreach anonymized state S in Frontier
 9                Frontier_New ← Frontier_New ∪ discPost(S)  // Figure 4
                  Frontier_New ← Frontier_New ∪ contPost(S)  // Figure 5
11                Frontier_New ← mergeAndDrop(Frontier_New, AnonReach)  // Figure 3
                  Frontier ← Frontier_New
13        return AnonReach
```

Fig. 2. On-the-fly anonymized reachability algorithm. The inputs are an automaton template $\mathcal{A}(i)$, an initial condition $\mathsf{Init}(i)$, and a constant natural number N. The anonymized reachable states AnonReach are computed as a fixed-point starting from the anonymized initial states.

$\mathsf{Init}(i)\downarrow V_G(i)$, which is $\mathsf{Init}(i)$ projected onto the global variables. The set of reachable anonymized states computed so far is the set AnonReach. Next (line 4), we remove an anonymized state S from Frontier, compute anonymized post-states from S, and continue until no new anonymized states are added to Frontier. Anonymized post-states are added to the frontier using the set $\mathsf{Frontier}_{New}$ (line 5). Computing successors (post-states)—the states reachable from S in one step—is composed of two parts: (a) computing the discrete successors corresponding to transitions (line 9), and (b) computing the continuous successors corresponding to trajectories (line 10).

Equivalent Class Merging Subroutine. We first describe the mergeAndDrop subroutine (Figure 3). It takes a set of anonymized states $\mathsf{Frontier}_{New}$ and returns a set of anonymized states guaranteed to (a) not have any equivalent classes (lines 7 through 8) and (b) be new (not already represented in AnonReach) (line 3). Invariant 1 states no two class formulas in any reachable anonymized state are equivalent, and Invariant 2 states no two anonymized states in AnonReach are equivalent (Definition 6).

Invariant 1. *For any* $S \in \mathsf{AnonReach}, C_1, C_2 \in S.\mathsf{Classes}, C_1.\mathsf{Form} \not\equiv C_2.\mathsf{Form}$.

Invariant 2. *For any distinct* $S_1, S_2 \in \mathsf{AnonReach}, S_1 \not\equiv S_2$.

Discrete Successors. The function discPost (Figure 4) computes the discrete successors from an anonymized state S in the frontier (Figure 2, line 9). The post-states States_{New} are added to the frontier $\mathsf{Frontier}_{New}$. First, we iterate over each class C in $S.\mathsf{Classes}$ (line 3), and then we iterate over each index variable i in the set of index variables in the class formula, $\{i_1, \ldots, i_{C.I}\}$ (line 5). Next, we iterate over the (syntactic) transitions $\mathsf{Trans}(i)$ of $\mathcal{A}(i)$ (line 6). For a transition $t \in \mathsf{Trans}(i)$ and an anonymized class C, line 7

```
 1    function mergeAndDrop(Frontier_New, AnonReach)
          foreach S in Frontier_New
 3            if S ∈ AnonReach then Frontier_New = Frontier_New \ {S}
              else
 5                foreach distinct pair of anonymized classes ⟨C_1, C_2⟩ in S.Classes
                      if ¬(C_1.Form ≡ C_2.Form) is UNSAT then
 7                        C_1.Count ← C_1.Count + C_2.Count  // if equivalent, sum counts
                          S.Classes ← S.Classes \ {C_2}  // if equivalent, drop equivalent class
 9        return Frontier_New
```

Fig. 3. mergeAndDrop combines classes with equivalent class formulas and sums their counts

```
1    function discPost(S)
         States_New ← ∅
3        foreach anonymized class C in S.Classes
             Vs ← V'(i_1) ∪ ... ∪ V'(i_C.I)
5            foreach symbolic index i in ivars(Vs)
                 foreach transition t in Trans(i)
7                    C_New.Form ← (C.Form ∧ S.G ∧ grd(t, i) ∧ rst(t, i))↓ V'(i)  // make post-state class
                     // substitute primed variables with unprimed variables
9                    C_New.Form ← Substitute(C_New.Form, V'(i), V(i))
                     // project onto global variables for global constraint
11                   S_New.G ← C_New.Form↓ V_G(i)
                     // project onto local variables for local constraint
13                   ⟨C_New.Count, C_New.I, C_New.Form⟩ ← ⟨1, 1, C_New.Form↓ V_L(i)⟩
                     S_New.Classes ← S.Classes \ {C}  // remove pre-state from post-state classes
15                   // add pre-state class to post-state classes if count at least rank
                     if C.Count > C.I then S_New.Classes ← S.Classes ∪ {(C.Count - 1, CI, C.Form)}
17                   // otherwise, pre-state class no longer exists (count less than rank)
                     else S_New.Classes ← S.Classes ∪ {(C.Count - 1, C.I - 1, C.Form↓ Vs \ V(i))}
19                   S_New.Classes ← S_New.Classes ∪ {C_New}  // add class to post-state
                 States_New ← States_New ∪ {S_New}
21   return States_New
```

Fig. 4. discPost computes the post-states of an anonymized state S due to discrete transitions for an automaton with index i and states satisfying C's formulas.

computes the subsequent class from C by transition t, made by the automaton with index i. This computation can be carried out using quantifier elimination procedures over the types of the variables appearing in the guard and reset of the transition t, and then syntactically unpriming all primed variables (representing successors) following quantifier elimination using Substitute (line 9). This step is an overapproximation, since it computes the successors of each class regardless of the number of automata with states satisfying the anonymized class formula Form, and just presumes *there is some* automaton with variable valuations satisfying Form.

The anonymized post-state S_{New} is constructed using the classes of the anonymized pre-state S along with the new anonymized class, C_{New} (lines 14 through 19). First, the classes for S_{New} are set to be the anonymized classes of S, without the anonymized class of the current iteration, C (line 14). Next, if the class count of C is larger than its rank, then it is added to the classes of the post-state, with its count reduced by one to indicate some automaton has left the set of states satisfying the corresponding class formula (line 16). On the other hand, if the class count is equal or less than its rank, then the pre-state's anonymized class C would no longer satisfy the requirements of Definition 4, (iii), so its class formula is projected onto the variables of all automata except those of automaton i, the one making a transition (line 18). If a class has count or rank equal to 0, then it is removed. This process may result in two classes with equivalent formulas, since the algorithm has not yet detected if any other classes had the same formula and presumed the post-state class C_{New} had a count of one, which is why we use mergeAndDrop (Figure 2, line 11).

Lemma 2. *(Discrete Successor Soundness) For an anonymized state S, for any corresponding concretized state* $\mathbf{x} \in [\![S]\!]$, *if* $\mathbf{x} \rightarrow_{\mathcal{D}N} \mathbf{x}'$, *then* $\mathbf{x}' \in [\![discPost(S)]\!]$.

Continuous Successors. An overapproximation of continuous successors are computed using contPost—shown in Figure 5—called from symreach (Figure 2, line 10). For an anonymized state S in the frontier, contPost computes an overapproximation of the post-states from S owing to the individual trajectories of all automata in the network for up to the most amount of time that can elapse before any invariant is

```
1   function contPost(S)
        Vs ← V'_G
3       // formula to encode trajectories for all automata in the network
        pf ← (t_e > 0 ∧ S.G)
5       foreach anonymized class C in S.Classes // iterate over each class in pre-state
            Vs ← Vs ∪ V'(i_1) ∪ ... ∪ V'(i_{C.I})
7           pf ← pf ∧ C.Form // encode pre-state class formula
            // determine locations any automaton may be in (recall Assumption 1)
9           foreach location loc in L
                foreach i in {i_1, ..., i_{C.I}} // iterate over all indices (ranks)
11                  if C.Form ⊬ (q[i] = loc) is UNSAT then // use loc if automaton i is in loc
                        // add the trajectory semantics overapproximating the post-states
13                      pf ← pf ∧ inv(loc, i) ∧ X(i) ∈ flow(pf, loc, X(i), t_e)
            pf ← pf↓ Vs
15          pf ← Substitute(pf, V'(i), V(i))
            S_New ← RemapClasses(S, pf) // Figure 6
17      return S_New
```

Fig. 5. contPost function that computes the continuous successors from an anonymized state S

```
1   function RemapClasses(S, pf)
        S_New.Classes = ∅
3       foreach anonymized class C in S.Classes
            // project pf onto variables of indices in each pre-state class
5           Vs ← V(i_1) ∪ ... ∪ V(i_{C.I})
            // create new class with post-state formula and copy pre-state count
7           ⟨C_New.Count, C_New.I, C_New.Form⟩ ← ⟨C.Count, C_New.I, pf↓ Vs⟩
            S_New.Classes ← S_New.Classes ∪ C_New // add post-state class to classes
9       S_New.N ← S.N
        return S_New
```

Fig. 6. RemapClasses uses pf and the pre-state indices, class counts, and ranks to create the anonymized post-state S_{New}. It first projects onto variables with indices of each class in the pre-state and then uses the pre-state to ensure class counts and ranks remain constant over trajectories.

violated. The anonymized state specifies a location $loc \in L$ for each automaton in the network (recall Assumption 1). Each location loc specifies a trajectory statement, so trajectories are defined for each automaton in the network. Each new anonymized state $S_{New} \in States_{New}$ computed corresponds to the trajectory semantics updating the real variables of *all* automata in the network $\mathcal{A}^N$. The variable pf encodes the trajectory semantics of all automata in the network $\mathcal{A}^N$ (line 4), which is initially the constraint $t_e > 0$, indicating that some positive real amount of time t_e will elapse. However, for an anonymized state S, for distinct anonymized classes C_1, C_2 in S.Classes, the symbolic indices appearing in the formulas may be equal, i.e., $\exists i \in ivars(C_1)$ and $\exists j \in ivars(C_2)$ such that $i = j$. Since pf encodes the states of all automata in the network, the symbolic index variables appearing in any class formula of any anonymized class must be distinct. Rather than performing these tedious syntactic manipulations, we assume that for an anonymized state S, for distinct classes C_1, C_2 in S.Classes, $\forall i \in ivars(C_1)$, $\forall j \in ivars(C_2)$, we have $i \neq j$.[4]

Each anonymized class formula C.Form of an anonymized state S specifies the location(s) of the automata, so the first step is to determine the dynamics that will modify each class formula. This is accomplished by first determining the appropriate flow-rate conditions to use for each class in S.Classes, which can be detected by finding which

---

[4] This is a tedious, but trivial invariant that we maintain in our implementation in *Passel*, so we make this assumption for clarity of presentation only.

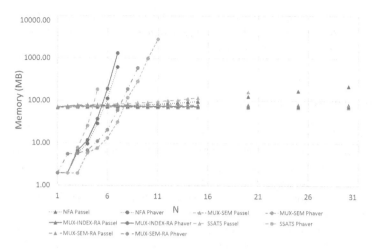

Fig. 7. Memory usage comparison of PHAVer and *Passel*'s anonymized reachability. Vertical axis scale is logarithmic and has units of megabytes, and horizontal axis is number of automata, N.

Form implies the location variable $q[i]$ is in some location $\mathbf{loc} \in \mathsf{L}$. If the control location of automaton i is found to be equal to location $\mathbf{loc}$, then the trajectory statement of location $\mathbf{loc}$ is used to define the semantics of the time-evolution of i's real variables (line 13). The semantics of trajectories result in *all* the automata's real variables evolving over time t_e, so the formula encoding the trajectory statements of all automata is conjuncted (line 13). The post-states are computed by projecting onto the primed variables of all classes, and then renaming primed variables with their unprimed counterparts (line 15).[5] We call RemapClasses with the pre-state S and pf, which encodes the post-state constraints, to recreate classes from sub-formulas of pf (Figure 6 called at line 16). This is done to ensure the class counts are constant when computing post-states due to trajectories.

Lemma 3. *(Continuous Successor Soundness) For an anonymized state* S, *for any corresponding concretized state* $\mathbf{x} \in [\![\mathsf{S}]\!]$, *if* $\mathbf{x} \rightarrow_{\mathcal{T}^N} \mathbf{x}'$, *then* $\mathbf{x}' \in [\![\mathsf{contPost}(\mathsf{S})]\!]$.

The next invariant states the sum of all class counts equals N. It follows from the definitions of discPost and contPost, since discPost always decreases class counts by the same amount it increases them—so the sum remains invariant—and contPost does not change class counts (only formulas). Additionally, mergeAndDrop changes class counts, but their sum remains the same since it removes any duplicate classes after adding their counts (Figure 3, lines 7 through 8).

Invariant 3. *For any* $\mathsf{S} \in \mathsf{AnonReach}$, $\mathsf{N} = \sum_{C \in \mathsf{S.Classes}} \mathsf{C.Count}$.

Theorem 1 states soundness of the algorithm: the concretization of the anonymized reachable states AnonReach contains the reachable states for network $\mathcal{A}^N$. It follows from Lemmas 2 and 3. The approximation comes from: (a) transitions are allowed as long as *some* automaton satisfies a guard, (b) index-typed variables are abstracted to be equal or not equal only, and (c) rectangular dynamics are overapproximated.

---

[5] This may result in a DNF formula, and if so, each conjunctive clause is added as a new anonymized state by iterating over the conjunctive clauses so all class formulas are CNF.

Theorem 1. *(Soundness) For a fixed* $N \in \mathbb{N}$, *for the network* $\mathcal{A}^N$ *composed of* N *instantiations of the template* $\mathcal{A}(N, i)$, *the anonymized reachable states* AnonReach *computed by* areach *overapproximate the reachable states of* $\mathcal{A}^N$: $\mathsf{Reach}(\mathcal{A}^N) \subseteq [\![\mathsf{AnonReach}]\!]$.

5 Experimental Results

The anonymized reachability algorithm is implemented in *Passel* [16, 18, 19]. The current implementation of *Passel* uses the SMT solver Z3 [7] for proving validity, checking satisfiability, and performing quantifier elimination. *Passel* is written in C# and uses the managed .NET API to Z3, with experimental results reported using version 4.1. *Passel* proves validity of a formula ϕ by checking unsatisfiability of $\neg\phi$. The variables $V(i)$ used in defining $\mathcal{A}(i)$ are specified to the SMT solver. Each local variable $v[i] \in V_L(i)$ is modeled as an uninterpreted function $v : [N] \to type(v)$. *Passel* automatically generates and asserts trivial data-type lemmas that the SMT solver requires. The experiments were conducted in an Ubuntu 12.04 VMWare virtual machine with 4 GB RAM allocated running *Passel* through Mono, executed on a modern laptop with a quad-core Intel i7 processor running Windows 8 with 16 GB RAM physically available. For comparison purposes, we evaluated *Passel*, PHAVer (version 0.38), and SpaceEx (version 0.9.8b). We do not present results for SpaceEx, as the only scenario—out of the PHAVer, LeGuernic-Girard (LGG), and STC scenarios—that can compute the reachable states of systems with rectangular differential inclusion dynamics ($\dot{x} \in [a, b]$ for real constants $a \leq b$) adequately is the PHAVer scenario, so the results are equivalent.

Figures 7 and 8 show, respectively, a runtime and memory usage comparison between PHAVer and *Passel* for several examples as a function of N, the number of

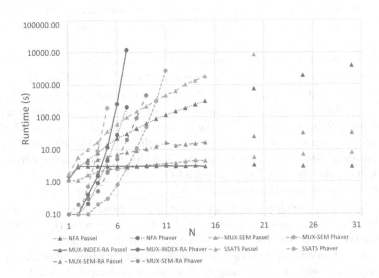

Fig. 8. Runtime comparison of PHAVer and *Passel*'s anonymized reachability. Vertical axis is logarithmic and has units of seconds, and horizontal axis is number of automata, N.

automata.[6] The examples include several timed mutual exclusion algorithms (such as MUX-INDEX-RECT from Figure 1), a simplified SATS model [16, 18, 19], and several purely discrete examples. All properties were safety properties (invariants), such as mutual exclusion, separation (collision avoidance) in SATS, etc. Comparing all the examples, the anonymized reachability method implemented in *Passel* allows us to compute the reachable states of networks composed of many more automata than PHAVer, which runs out of memory on all examples for $N \geq 11$. The experimental results indicate the primary advantage is reduced memory growth. Even for networks of tens of automata, in all examples, *Passel* never uses more than a few hundred megabytes of memory as shown in Figure 7.[7] For protocols that are highly asymmetric, the worst-case asymptotic memory growth may be exponential. The runtime required by *Passel* could be reduced by performing some operations more efficiently in the implementation—particularly the checks to determine if a new anonymized state representation is actually new or not—which we plan to implement for future work.

For MUX-INDEX-RECT, PHAVer runs out of memory for $N \geq 8$. As shown in Figures 7 and 8, for $N = 7$, PHAVer uses over 1.3 GB memory and completes in over 3 hours, while *Passel* uses over an order of magnitude less memory at about 70 MB and nearly four orders of magnitude less runtime at about three seconds. Because of the anonymized representation, *Passel* is able to compute the reachable states of $N = 30$ in a few seconds using about 70 MB memory, and we have experimented successfully up to hundreds and even thousands of automata for this example.

6 Summary

In this paper, we present an on-the-fly forward reachability algorithm that computes an anonymized representation of the reachable states for hybrid automata networks consisting of N instantiations of a template $\mathcal{A}(N, i)$. The anonymized representation uses symbolic automato indices instead of explicit ones to avoid generating all permutations of automata indices and states. We showed it to be effective at computing the reachable states of networks with tens of automata for several examples, with significantly lower memory usage than PHAVer. The restriction to rectangular inclusion dynamics is due in part to *Passel*'s implementation, but a future direction is to evaluate the anonymized reachability method on examples with linear and nonlinear dynamics.

Acknowledgments. The authors are grateful for the anonymous reviewers' feedback. This material is based upon work supported by the National Science Foundation under Grant No. NSF CNS 10-54247 CAR. This work was supported by the Air Force Office of Scientific Research Young Investigator Program Award FA9550-12-1-0336.

---

[6] *Passel* and the examples may be downloaded from:
  https://publish.illinois.edu/passel-tool/.
[7] For small N, PHAVer uses less memory than *Passel* because *Passel* must load runtime components (e.g., the .NET framework via Mono) and libraries (e.g., Z3).

References

1. Basler, G., Mazzucchi, M., Wahl, T., Kroening, D.: Symbolic counter abstraction for concurrent software. In: Bouajjani, A., Maler, O. (eds.) CAV 2009. LNCS, vol. 5643, pp. 64–78. Springer, Heidelberg (2009)
2. Behrmann, G., Bouyer, P., Fleury, E., Larsen, K.G.: Static guard analysis in timed automata verification. In: Garavel, H., Hatcliff, J. (eds.) TACAS 2003. LNCS, vol. 2619, pp. 254–270. Springer, Heidelberg (2003)
3. Bengtsson, J., Larsen, K., Larsson, F., Pettersson, P., Yi, W.: UPPAAL: A tool suite for automatic verification of real-time systems. In: Alur, R., Sontag, E.D., Henzinger, T.A. (eds.) HS 1995. LNCS, vol. 1066, pp. 232–243. Springer, Heidelberg (1996)
4. Bogomolov, S., Herrera, C., Muñiz, M., Westphal, B., Podelski, A.: Quasi-dependent variables in hybrid automata. In: 17th International Conference on Hybrid Systems: Computation and Control (2014)
5. Braberman, V., Garbervetsky, D., Olivero, A.: Improving the verification of timed systems using influence information. In: Katoen, J.-P., Stevens, P. (eds.) TACAS 2002. LNCS, vol. 2280, pp. 21–36. Springer, Heidelberg (2002)
6. Clarke, E.M., Enders, R., Filkorn, T., Jha, S.: Exploiting symmetry in temporal logic model checking. Formal Methods in System Design 9, 77–104 (1996)
7. de Moura, L., Bjørner, N.S.: Z3: An efficient SMT solver. In: Ramakrishnan, C.R., Rehof, J. (eds.) TACAS 2008. LNCS, vol. 4963, pp. 337–340. Springer, Heidelberg (2008)
8. Dill, D.L.: The murφ verification system. In: Alur, R., Henzinger, T.A. (eds.) CAV 1996. LNCS, vol. 1102, pp. 390–393. Springer, Heidelberg (1996)
9. Emerson, E.A., Sistla, A.P.: Symmetry and model checking. Formal Methods in System Design 9(1-2), 105–131 (1996)
10. Emerson, E., Wahl, T.: Dynamic symmetry reduction. In: Halbwachs, N., Zuck, L.D. (eds.) TACAS 2005. LNCS, vol. 3440, pp. 382–396. Springer, Heidelberg (2005)
11. Hendriks, M., Behrmann, G., Larsen, K.G., Niebert, P., Vaandrager, F.W.: Adding symmetry reduction to UPPAAL. In: Larsen, K.G., Niebert, P. (eds.) FORMATS 2003. LNCS, vol. 2791, pp. 46–59. Springer, Heidelberg (2004)
12. Hendriks, M.: Model checking timed automata: Techniques and applications. Ph.D. thesis, University of Nijmegen, The Netherlands (2006)
13. Herrera, C., Westphal, B., Feo-Arenis, S., Muñiz, M., Podelski, A.: Reducing Quasi-Equal Clocks in Networks of Timed Automata. In: Jurdziński, M., Ničković, D. (eds.) FORMATS 2012. LNCS, vol. 7595, pp. 155–170. Springer, Heidelberg (2012)
14. Ip, C.N., Dill, D.L.: Better verification through symmetry. Formal Methods in System Design 9, 41–75 (1996)
15. Ip, C.N., Dill, D.L.: Verifying systems with replicated components in Murφ. Formal Methods in System Design 14(3) (1999)
16. Johnson, T.T.: Uniform Verification of Safety for Parameterized Networks of Hybrid Automata. Ph.D. thesis, University of Illinois at Urbana-Champaign, Urbana, IL 61801 (2013)
17. Johnson, T.T., Mitra, S.: Parameterized verification of distributed cyber-physical systems: An aircraft landing protocol case study. In: ACM/IEEE 3rd International Conference on Cyber-Physical Systems (April 2012)
18. Johnson, T.T., Mitra, S.: A small model theorem for rectangular hybrid automata networks. In: Giese, H., Rosu, G. (eds.) FORTE 2012 and FMOODS 2012. LNCS, vol. 7273, pp. 18–34. Springer, Heidelberg (2012)
19. Johnson, T.T., Mitra, S.: Invariant synthesis for verification of parameterized cyber-physical systems with applications to aerospace systems. In: Proceedings of the AIAA Infotech at Aerospace Conference (AIAA Infotech 2013), Boston, MA (August 2013)

20. Obal, W.D., McQuinn, M., Sanders, W.: Detecting and exploiting symmetry in discrete-state Markov models. IEEE Transactions on Reliability 56(4), 643–654 (2007)

21. Si, Y., Sun, J., Liu, Y., Wang, T.: Improving model checking stateful timed csp with non-zenoness through clock-symmetry reduction. In: Groves, L., Sun, J. (eds.) ICFEM 2013. LNCS, vol. 8144, pp. 182–198. Springer, Heidelberg (2013)

22. Sun, J., Liu, Y., Dong, J.S., Liu, Y., Shi, L., André, E.: Modeling and verifying hierarchical real-time systems using stateful timed csp. ACM Trans. Softw. Eng. Methodol. 22(1), 1–29 (2013)

23. Sun, J., Liu, Y., Dong, J.S., Pang, J.: PAT: Towards flexible verification under fairness. In: Bouajjani, A., Maler, O. (eds.) CAV 2009. LNCS, vol. 5643, pp. 709–714. Springer, Heidelberg (2009)

Combined Global and Local Search
for the Falsification of Hybrid Systems[*]

Jan Kuřátko[1,2] and Stefan Ratschan[1,**]

[1] Institute of Computer Science, Academy of Sciences of the Czech Republic
[2] Faculty of Mathematics and Physics, Charles University in Prague, Czech Republic

Abstract. In this paper we solve the problem of finding a trajectory that shows that a given hybrid dynamical system with deterministic evolution leaves a given set of states considered to be safe. The algorithm combines local with global search for achieving both efficiency and global convergence. In local search, it exploits derivatives for efficient computation. Unlike other methods for falsification of hybrid systems with deterministic evolution, we do not restrict our search to trajectories of a certain bounded length but search for error trajectories of arbitrary length.

1 Introduction

In this paper we provide an algorithm that solves the problem of unbounded safety falsification of hybrid systems with deterministic evolution. This means that, given a hybrid system with deterministic evolution, and a set of initial and a set of unsafe states, we search for a trajectory of arbitrary length starting in an initial state and ending in an unsafe state.

Existing methods for falsification of hybrid systems with deterministic evolution roughly fall into the following two categories:

- Local search [1,26]: Such methods use local optimization to incrementally bring a starting trajectory closer to an error trajectory, ideally based on information on the derivative of the objective function. The advantage of local search is its relative efficiency. The disadvantage is that for convergence it needs to be started close enough to an error trajectory. At the very least it needs to start from a sequence of modes that contains an error trajectory. However, the number of sequences of modes grows exponentially with the length of the sequence which makes the search for starting trajectories for local search a difficult problem.
- Black-box global search [19,2]: Such methods search for error trajectories globally, but use black-box optimization techniques [13,24] that do not explicitly exploit the structure specific to hybrid systems (partially continuous

---

[*] This work was supported by the Czech Science Foundation (GAČR) grant number P202/12/J060 with institutional support RVO:67985807.
[**] ORCID: 0000-0003-1710-1513.

A. Legay and M. Bozga (Eds.): FORMATS 2014, LNCS 8711, pp. 146–160, 2014.
© Springer International Publishing Switzerland 2014

behavior, unbounded time variable). This extends their applicability (e.g., to Simulink models), but this may also result in loss of efficiency and restrict search to trajectories up to a given user-provided length. Of course it is possible to repeatedly restart such methods with higher upper bounds on the trajectory length, but every restart loses the information computed before.

The contribution of this paper is an algorithm that combines the scalability of local search with global convergence for error trajectories of *unbounded* length. Moreover, the resulting algorithm is reasonably simple and easy to analyze and implement. Note however, that efficiency is not primary goal of this paper— since the generic structure of the resulting algorithm allows the simple incorporation more sophisticated global search techniques [13,17]. Of course, one can use local search from any result of an algorithm based on black-box global search, but this has the following drawbacks:

- It is not clear how to handle the unbounded time variable.
- Black-box global search does not explicitly exploit the structure of hybrid systems.
- Black-box global search does not exploit the fact that it is combined with a local search method and hence may both duplicate some of the efforts of local search and fail to steer its search to good starting points for local search.

Our approach is based on a standard technique in global optimization for combining local with global search, so called two-phase methods [25]. But we adapt those methods to the situation that we have here: A direct application of two-phase methods would use a search space that is spanned by variables of two kinds: the initial point of trajectories, and the trajectory length (wrt. time). However, trajectory length is special, since it is unbounded, and since computing a trajectory of the given length from a given initial point also computes all trajectories from that initial point with shorter length. Moreover, hybrid systems combine continuous with discrete behavior and local search can exploit derivatives for searching the continuous part of the states space, but no such derivatives are available for discrete search which is another obstacle to the direct application of two-phase methods.

Hence, our approach modifies two-phase methods in such a way that—instead of treating trajectory length as a problem variable—they build trajectories incrementally from trajectory segments, and use derivative based continuous local search to glue together those segments based on continuous search (the literature on numerical algorithms for solving boundary value problems calls such an approach "multiple shooting" [3,26]).

The structure of the paper is as follows: In the next section we precisely define the problem and introduce some basic definitions. In Section 3 we introduce the main algorithm. In Section 4 we present an improved, more incremental version of the algorithm. In Section 5 we describe how to do local search for error trajectories. In Section 6 we provide some termination proofs for the algorithm. In Section 7 we present computational experiments. In Section 8 we describe related work, and in Section 9 we conclude the paper.

We thank Aditya Zutshi and Sriram Sankaranarayanan for interesting discussions on the subject of this papers.

2   Problem Formulation

In this section we introduce notation and key concepts which we use, and present the problem we try to solve.

Definition 1. *A hybrid dynamical system is a quintuple $H = (Q, \Omega, F, G, R)$, where*

- *Q is a finite set whose elements we call modes;*
- *$\Omega \subseteq Q \times \mathbb{R}^n$ (the state space of the hybrid system);*
- *F assigns to each mode $q \in Q$ a system of differential equations $F_q(t, x, \dot{x}) = 0$, where $(q, x) \in \Omega$ and $t \in \mathbb{R}^{\geq 0}$ is time;*
- *$G \subseteq \Omega$ (the set of guards);*
- *$R : \Omega \mapsto \Omega$ (the reset function).*

For a given $q \in Q$, we will sometimes denote by X_q the set $\{x \mid (q, x) \in \Omega\}$.

Definition 2. *A trajectory of a hybrid dynamical system H is a sequence of the form $((q_1, x_1), (q_2, x_2), \ldots, (q_k, x_k))$, where $q_i \in Q$ and $x_i : [0, t_i] \mapsto X_q$ is a continuous trajectory of the system of differential equations given by F_{q_i}, $i = 1, \ldots, k$. For all $i \in \{1, \ldots, k-1\}$, for all $t \in [0, t_i)$, not $G(q_i, x_i(t))$, but for the trajectory endpoints $G(q_i, x_i(t_i))$. Moreover, the starting points of subsequent trajectories are determined by the reset function, that is, $R((q_i, x_i(t_i))) = (q_{i+1}, x_{i+1}(0))$.*

We call $t_i \in \mathbb{R}^{\geq 0}$ the length of x_i. Moreover, we denote by $(q_i, x_i^s) \in \Omega$ the starting point of a trajectory (q_i, x_i) and $(q_i, x_i^e) \in \Omega$ its endpoint.

Now we are ready to formulate the problem of *falsification of hybrid dynamical systems*.

Problem 1. Let H be a hybrid dynamical system and Init $\subset \Omega$, Unsafe $\subset \Omega$ be two sets. The set Init is called the set of initial states and the set Unsafe is called the set of unsafe states. The problem of falsification of H is to find any trajectory $((q_1, x_1), (q_2, x_2), \ldots, (q_k, x_k))$ of H such that $(q_1, x_1^s) \in$ Init and $(q_k, x_k^e) \in$ Unsafe. Such a trajectory is called an error trajectory of H.

3   Algorithm

We now present the main algorithm. Throughout this section we will assume a given hybrid system H with set of initial states Init and set of unsafe states Unsafe.

Informally, we intend to transform Problem 1 into the minimization of a cost function. A value of this cost function will measure how far or close a sequence of points in Ω is to an error trajectory. We will minimize this cost function until we find an error trajectory.

The algorithm will maintain a finite set of points $P \subseteq \Omega$ on which it will analyze the behavior of the given hybrid system H. We call sequences of elements from P *paths*. The algorithm will do this analysis by starting numerical simulations from points in P. Such a simulation will conclude that there is a trajectory from the starting point p of a simulation to the endpoint p'. This will be stored in a relation $\rightarrow$ on P that will relate all those points p, p' in P for which simulation showed that there is a trajectory from p to p' according to H. If there is a path from an initial point to an unsafe point according to the relation $\rightarrow$, we are done. However, since this is difficult to achieve, we allow paths of points in P for which subsequent points are not in $\rightarrow$. In order to measure how far such a path is from being a trajectory we will now introduce a distance measure for points in P:

Definition 3. *Given a finite set of states $P \subseteq \Omega$ and a relation $\rightarrow \subseteq P \times P$, the distance $d((q, x), (q', x'))$, of states (q, x) and (q', x') in P, is*

- *0, if $(q, x) \rightarrow (q', x')$, otherwise*
- *$\|x - x'\|$, if $q = q'$, and*
- *∞, otherwise.*

Here, the symbol $\| \cdot \|$ denotes the Euclidean norm. Note that our distance function is not symmetrical because of the relation $\rightarrow$ that, in general, is not symmetrical which corresponds to the intuition that the existence of a trajectory from p to p' does not imply the existence of a trajectory from p' to p.

We measure the difficulty of getting from an initial state of H to a given state (q, x), and from a given state (q, x) to an unsafe state as follows:

Definition 4. *For a state $(q, x) \in P$ we put $d_I((q, x)) \equiv \inf_{u \in \text{Init}} d(u, (q, x))$ and $d_U((q, x)) \equiv \inf_{u \in \text{Unsafe}} d((q, x), u)$.*

Now we model how close a path is to yielding an error trajectory, as follows:

Definition 5. *The cost of a path $(p_1, \ldots, p_n)$ is given by $c(p_1, \ldots, p_n) = d_I(p_1) + \sum_{i=1}^{n-1} d(p_i, p_{i+1}) + d_U(p_n)$.*

Notice that we have an error trajectory of H if the cost $c(p_1, \ldots, p_n)$ is equal to zero. In practice, we are satisfied if the distances $d_I(p_1)$ and $d_U(p_n)$ are zero and $\sum_{i=1}^{n-1} d(p_i, p_{i+1}) < \varepsilon$ for some small threshold ε.

Now we can formulate our method for falsification of hybrid dynamical systems. In a similar way as two-phase methods [25] the algorithm iterates between two phases for exploring the state space of a given hybrid dynamical system.

The first phase is local optimization. For a given path of finite cost from P we compute another path with lower cost. In this phase we employ standard techniques for continuous optimization and use gradient information based on sensitivity analysis of hybrid dynamical systems [14]. If we find a local minimum which yields an error trajectory, we are finished. However, if the minimal cost is greater than a given threshold ε, we need to proceed to phase two and explore the state space further. The reader can find more details on the first phase in Section 5.

The second phase is called global exploration. If local optimization in the first phase does not produce an error trajectory, we add additional states to the set P. There are many options for adding new states such as a random sampling, states resulting from forward and backward simulation from existing states, states suggested by more sophisticated global search techniques [13,17], and even states given by a designer of the system. The complete Algorithm 1 follows:

Input: a set of states $P \subseteq \Omega$ and a relation $\rightarrow \subseteq P \times P$ s.t.
 - $p \rightarrow p'$ implies that there is a trajectory from p to p' in H
 - there is a path of points in P that has finite cost with respect to $\rightarrow$

Output: an error trajectory

while *local optimization of the path with minimal cost does not yield an error trajectory* **do**
    add a new state $r \in \Omega$ to the set P
    for *some $p \in P$* **do**
        simulate forward from p for some time to a new state p'
        $\rightarrow := \rightarrow \cup \{(p, p')\}$
    end
    for *some $p \in P$* **do**
        simulate backward from p for some time to a new state p'
        $\rightarrow := \rightarrow \cup \{(p', p)\}$
    end
end

Algorithm 1: Combined Global and Local Search for the Falsification

The second requirement on the input (existence of a path of finite cost) allows us to use derivative based continuous local optimization from the beginning. For fulfilling this requirement, we observe that paths can only have infinite cost due to sub-sequent states in different modes that are not connected by the relation $\rightarrow$. We can make this more precise by the following property:

Property 1. Assume a set $P \subseteq \Omega$ and $\rightarrow \subseteq P \times P$. Let $\rightarrow_Q \subseteq P \times P$ be such that $(q, x) \rightarrow_Q (q', x')$ iff $q = q'$ or $(q, x) \rightarrow (q', x')$, and let $\rightarrow_Q^*$ be the transitive closure of $\rightarrow_Q$. If P contains at least one initial state p and one unsafe state p' such that $p \rightarrow_Q^* p'$, then there is a path of points in P that has finite cost with respect to $\rightarrow$.

The necessary elements of $\rightarrow$ can be easily formed by pairs (p, p') such that $G(p)$ and $p' = R(p)$. For example, for each pair of modes (q, q') for which there are x and x' s.t. $G(q, x)$ and $(q', x') = R(q, x)$ we could add such (q, x) and

(q', x'). If H has an error trajectory then this fulfills the assumptions of the above property resulting in a path of finite cost.

The algorithm stops when we find a path whose cost is lower than some threshold ε. A concrete implementation might add another stopping criterion, for example stating a maximum number of states in P in order to ensure termination for inputs that do not feature any error trajectory.

4   Algorithmic Details

4.1   Computation of the Path of Minimal Cost

We make the following observation: In Algorithm 1, one can view the problem of computation of a path of minimal cost as a problem on weighted directed graphs: The vertices of the graph are formed by the elements of the set P and there is an edge from $p \in P$ to $p' \in P$ iff the distance $d(p, p')$ is finite. The weight of this edge is given by this value $d(p, p')$. Now the path of minimal cost is the shortest path in this graph from an initial to an unsafe state. This is a classical problem in algorithm theory with solutions such as the Floyd-Warshall algorithm.

Examining the situation more closely, we observe that our problem is neither of the all-pair shortest path, nor of the single-source shortest path kind. Instead, the paths have to start in a certain given set (call it S for source) and end in another given set (call it G for goal). This can be reduced to a problem with single vertices instead of sets by introducing two new, auxiliary vertices s and g such that s has an edge of zero cost to each element of S and such that there is an edge of zero cost from each element of G to g.

Now we are left with a single-source single-goal shortest path problem (also called point-to-point shortest path). Of course, such problems can be solved by algorithms solving the single-source shortest path problem, for example, by Dijkstra's algorithm [9]. But there are also specialized algorithms, for example, algorithm based on a bi-directional [22,4] application of Dijkstra's algorithm.

4.2   Heuristics

The algorithm can be instantiated with many heuristics resulting in special versions of Algorithm 1, for example:

- Forward version: only add initial points and only do forward simulation
- Backward version: only add unsafe points and only do backward simulation
- Complete random search version: never prolong existing simulations, only simulation from newly added points.

The algorithm also leaves open the length of the employed simulations. A simple possibility is to fix a certain length at the beginning and stick to it throughout computation.

Note that simulation might run into problems, for example due to Zeno behavior, or due to the fact that it leaves the state space of the given hybrid system. In this case we simply ignore the result of simulation and continue with the algorithm. See also more on this at the end of Section 5.

It is also possible to use information from verification tools here. Especially, one can restrict the choice of points to an abstraction computed by a verification tool [10,23].

4.3   Paths of Minimal Cost

We will now investigate the form of paths of minimal cost. For a given hybrid system H we assume the following.

1. The sets $\{x \mid (q, x) \in \text{Init}\}$ and $\{x \mid (q, x) \in \text{Unsafe}\}$ are closed and convex.
2. For all $q \in Q$ the set $\{x \mid (q, x) \in \Omega\}$ is convex.
3. For $p, p' \in P$, $p \to p'$ implies there is a trajectory from p to p' in H.
4. There is at least one path of finite cost in P with respect to $\to$.

Lemma 1. *Let H be a given hybrid system and P be a set of states such that assumptions 1.–4 hold. Let $(p_1, \ldots, p_n)$ be the path of minimal cost. Let r be a state such that $r \neq p_i$, $i = 1, \ldots, n$, and neither $r \to p_i$ nor $p_i \to r$ for any $i \in \{1, \ldots, n\}$. Then the cost of a path which is formed by either including state r in $(p_1, \ldots, p_n)$ or substituting r for any p_i's, $i \in \{1, \ldots, n\}$, in $(p_1, \ldots, p_n)$ is greater or equal to $c(p_1, \ldots, p_n)$.*

The reader can find the proof of Lemma 1 in the extended version of the paper. The consequence of this lemma can be stated like this: Assuming 1.–4. the value of $c(p_1, \ldots, p_n)$, where $(p_1, \ldots, p_n)$ is the path of minimal cost, does not depend on states $p \in P$ which are in no relation to other states in the path wrt. $\to$. In other words, for a state p_i, $i = 1, \ldots, n$, which is in no relation with other states in a path, we have $c(p_1, \ldots, p_i, \ldots, p_n) = c(p_1, \ldots, p_{i-1}, p_{i+1}, \ldots, p_n)$.

This is important for finding paths of lower cost. Whenever we add a new state r in Algorithm 1 we should simulate either forward in time or backward in time to create a pair of states in a relation $\to$. Solitary states do not affect the resulting value of the cost function.

Lemma 2. *Let H be a given hybrid system and P be a set of states such that assumptions 1.–4 hold. Let $(p_1, \ldots, p_n)$, $p_i \in P$, be the path of minimal cost. Let p_j, $j = 2, \ldots, n - 1$, be a state such that $p_{j-1} \to p_j$ and $p_j \to p_{j+1}$. Then $d(p_{j-1}, p_{j+1}) = 0$.* □

Proof. Due to transitivity of the relation $\to$, we have $p_{j-1} \to p_{j+1}$ which gives us $d(p_{j-1}, p_{j+1}) = 0$.

Lemma 2 presents us with a choice for the application of local optimization. If a path contains such a triplet (p_{j-1}, p_j, p_{j+1}), we may either work with them as two separate hybrid trajectories or we may consider a hybrid trajectory which is formed by their connection, thus removing the intermediate state from a path. On the other hand, we also have the option to split a hybrid trajectory into shorter hybrid trajectories before passing it to the local optimizer.

In the first approach we work with shorter trajectories however the resulting optimization problem has higher dimension. The latter case may, on the other hand, cause problems because it is less numerical stable [3]. The choice depends on the system of differential equations that governs the evolution of hybrid system H.

5 Local Optimization

In Algorithm 1, after we form a path $(p_1, \ldots, p_n)$ of finite cost we try to find another path of smaller cost using local search. Therefore, we solve the minimization problem in which we seek new states $\hat{p}_1, \ldots, \hat{p}_n$ which yield a path of lower cost than $(p_1, \ldots, p_n)$. Eventually, such a path of minimal cost may correspond to an error trajectory of a hybrid system.

The efficiency of such local search can be improved by exploiting the gradient of the cost $c(p_1, \ldots, p_n)$. In this section we will develop explicit formulae for the gradient of the cost function which will allow us to use efficient off-the-shelf tools for gradient-based numerical optimization to minimize the cost function.

Without loss of generality, we will assume that for all $i \in \{1, \ldots, n\}$, $p_i \to p_{i+1}$ iff i is odd. This can be easily achieved, since, due to Lemma 1 if there are solitary states that we can remove them from $(p_1, \ldots, p_n)$ without changing the value of the cost function.

Note that in contrast to early work [26], in cases where $p_i \to p_{i+1}$, p_i and p_{i+1} are *not* restricted to be in the same mode. Moreover, points are not restricted to reside in guards of the hybrid system.

We now give explicit formulae for computation of the gradient of the cost function $c(p_1, \ldots, p_n)$. Let us start with the definition of the length of a trajectory $((q_1, x_1), \ldots, (q_k, x_k))$ and its sensitivity to the change of its initial state (q_1, x_1^s) which is essential for evaluation of the gradient of the cost $c(p_1, \ldots, p_n)$.

Definition 6. *The length of a trajectory $((q_1, x_1), \ldots, (q_k, x_k))$ is defined to be the sum $t_f = \sum_{i=1}^{k} t_i$, where t_i is the length of x_i for $i = 1, \ldots, k$.*

Definition 7. *We define a function $M : \mathbb{R} \times \Omega \mapsto \Omega$ such that for a state $(q, x) \in \Omega$ and $t \in [0, t_f]$ we have $M(t, (q, x)) = (q', x')$, where (q', x') is the end-state of the trajectory of length t whose initial state is (q, x). In cases where a reset happens at time t (which results in the trajectory of length t being non-unique), we choose the unique point before the reset.*

Definition 8. *The sensitivity of a trajectory $((q_1, x_1), \ldots, (q_k, x_k))$ of H to the initial state (q_1, x_1^s) is a function $S : \mathbb{R}^{\geq 0} \mapsto \mathbb{R}^{n \times n}$ such that*

$$S(t) \equiv \frac{\partial M(t, (q, x_1^s))}{\partial x_1^s}, \quad t \in [0, t_f].$$

With this sensitivity function we can measure how the states on a hybrid trajectory are affected when we change its initial state. An important observation is that $S(0)$ is the *identity* matrix. However, for hybrid systems, the function M need not be differentiable everywhere, and so the sensitivity is not defined everywhere. Computation of the sensitivity function is subtle [14]. In the sequel let us use the following notation: For any state $(q, x) \in \Omega$, we denote by $\overline{(q, x)}$ its continuous part x.

For our path $(p_1, \ldots, p_n)$, for certain t_i, $i = 1, 3, \ldots, n-1$, we have $M(t_1, p_1) = p_2$, $M(t_3, p_3) = p_4$, $\ldots$, $M(t_{n-1}, p_{n-1}) = p_n$. Local search adjusts the position of the initial state of each trajectory together with its length such that the cost is minimized. It uses the gradient of the cost with respect to $\overline{p_i}$ and lengths t_i for $i < n$ odd. Therefore the gradient is given by the partial derivatives $\frac{\partial c}{\partial \overline{p_i}}(p_1, \ldots, p_n)$ and $\frac{\partial c}{\partial t_i}(p_1, \ldots, p_n)$, $i < n$ odd.

We will illustrate the whole process of computing the gradient of the cost function for one particular definition of distances $d_I, d(\cdot, \cdot)$ and d_U that avoids solving another minimization problem stemming from Definition 4. Hence, we put $d_I(p_1)$ and $d_U(p_n)$ to be weighted norms to some fixed states in Init, and Unsafe respectively. This amounts to the sets Init and Unsafe being ellipsoids. We denote by $u \in \Omega$ and $v \in \Omega$ the centres of these ellipsoids and by E_I, E_U symmetric positive definite matrices which characterize the size and shape of sets Init and Unsafe.

Then we consider the cost of the following special form: $c(p_1, \ldots, p_n) = d_I(p_1) + \sum_{i=1}^{n-2} d(p_i, p_{i+1}) + d_U(p_n) = \|\overline{p_1} - \overline{u}\|_{E_I}^2 + \sum_{i \text{ even}}^{n-2} \|\overline{p_i} - \overline{p_{i+1}}\|^2 + \|\overline{p_n} - \overline{v}\|_{E_U}^2$. When we use the function $M : \mathbb{R} \times \Omega \mapsto \Omega$ from Definition 7, then the cost becomes dependent on p_i and t_i, $i = 1, 3, 5, \ldots, n - 1$, and $c(p_1, p_3, \ldots, p_{n-1}, t_1, t_3, \ldots, t_{n-1}) = \|\overline{p_1} - \overline{u}\|_{E_I}^2 + \sum_{i \text{ even}}^{n-2} \|\overline{M(t_{i-1}, p_{i-1})} - \overline{p_{i+1}}\|^2 + \|\overline{M(t_{n-1}, p_{n-1})} - \overline{v}\|_{E_U}^2$.

We can compute the gradient of the cost $c(p_1, p_3, \ldots, p_{n-1}, t_1, t_3, \ldots, t_{n-1})$ which consists of the following partial derivatives

$$\frac{\partial c}{\partial \overline{p_1}} = 2[\overline{p_1} - \overline{u}]^T E_I + 2\left[\overline{M(t_1, p_1)} - \overline{p_3}\right]^T \frac{\partial M}{\partial \overline{p_1}}(t_1, p_1)$$

and for odd i with $1 < i < n - 1$ we have

$$\frac{\partial c}{\partial \overline{p_i}} = -2\left[\overline{M(t_{i-2}, p_{i-2})} - \overline{p_i}\right]^T + 2\left[\overline{M(t_i, p_i)} - \overline{p_{i+2}}\right]^T \frac{\partial M}{\partial \overline{p_i}}(t_i, p_i)$$

with the last term

$$\frac{\partial c}{\partial \overline{p_{n-1}}} = 2\left[\overline{M(t_{n-1}, p_{n-1})} - \overline{v}\right]^T E_U \frac{\partial M}{\partial \overline{p}_{n-1}}(t_{n-1}, p_{n-1})$$
$$- 2\left[\overline{M(t_{n-2}, p_{n-2})} - \overline{p_{n-1}}\right]^T .$$

For odd $i < n - 1$ we put

$$\frac{\partial c}{\partial t_i} = 2[\overline{M(t_i, p_i)} - \overline{p_{i+1}}]^T \frac{\partial M}{\partial t_i}(t_i, p_i)$$

and the last term is

$$\frac{\partial c}{\partial t_{n-1}} = 2 \left[\overline{M(t_{n-1}, p_{n-1})} - \overline{v} \right]^T E_U \frac{\partial M}{\partial t_{n-1}} (t_{n-1}, p_{n-1}) .$$

In addition we may introduce weights into the cost function to scale the problem.

Now we can use numerical optimization algorithms with the cost function c and its gradient to do local search for paths of minimal cost. If started close enough to an error trajectory, and if the hybrid system is sufficiently well-behaved around the error trajectory, such local search will converge (usually quickly). However, if this is not the case, local search may fail, due to various reasons:

- It may run in a local minimum that is not an error trajectory.
- There may be problems due to the fact that the sensitivity is not everywhere continuously differentiable. This corresponds to the situation where a trajectory is tangential to the boundary of a guard [14].
- Well-known problems with simulation [18] of hybrid systems might arise. For example, the simulation might run into Zeno behavior, or the ODE solver is unable to start close to the boundary of a guard.
- Optimization may result in trajectories that leave the state space of the hybrid system.

In all such cases, we simply terminate local optimization and continue with the global phase of the main algorithm.

6   Termination Proof

We assume a hybrid system H with the following properties:

- The state space of H is compact.
- There exists an error trajectory E with final point in the interior of the set of unsafe points, and an $\varepsilon > 0$ such that starting local search from any sequence of hybrid trajectories with cost not bigger than ε converges to an error trajectory.
- There exists a tube around E such that trajectories starting in this tube depend continuously on their initial value (note that for ODEs this can be ensured by Lipschitz continuous right-hand sides).

Moreover, we will study a variant of the algorithm with the following properties:

- The algorithm does at least one forward simulation in each cycle, always of length (in time) T.
- The algorithm chooses the starting point for its simulations randomly using a distribution that is non-zero on the whole state space.
- If a simulation hits an unsafe state, it finishes (so, in such cases, the length of the simulation may be shorter than T).

– The simulations are exact, that is, we ignore rounding and discretization errors of ODE solvers.

Note that the assumptions are asymmetrical wrt. time and set of initial vs. unsafe states. This is necessary since simulations have to be done in a certain direction, and since convergence requires simulations to be stopped if reaching an unsafe state.

While it is obvious that such an algorithm will densely fill the state space of the hybrid system with initial values of simulation, it is not obvious that this will eventually result in a path of small enough cost, since—from a given initial value—the trajectories follow the dynamics of the hybrid system H. Still, we have:

Theorem 1. *Under the assumption above, the algorithm finds an error trajectory with probability 1.*

The reader can find proofs of Theorems 1 and 2 in the extended version of the paper. Clearly one can easily get a dual version of the theorem and proof by turning around the time axis, switching initial and unsafe states etc.

Only slightly changing the proof, one can prove the following non-probabilistic version of the theorem:

Theorem 2. *Take the same assumptions as the previous theorem with the exception of choice of starting points of simulations. Instead of a choice according to some probability distribution, assume a choice of those starting points that fulfills the following property: For each $\varepsilon > 0$, there is an integer k such that for every ε-ball with center in the state space contains a simulation starting point that the algorithm has chosen in the first k iterations. Then algorithm always finds an error trajectory.*

7   Computational Experiments

Recall that one of the main goals of our method was to handle the absence of an a-priori upper bound on the length of error trajectories. In order to study the cost of having to work without this information we compare our approach (that we will call "unbounded method") with another approach that also combines global with local search, but that does simulations of fixed length (we will call it "bounded method"). The bounded method will also use derivative-based local optimization, but for initializing local optimization it randomly generates initial states in the mode containing I and simulates for the time interval $[0, T]$. Whenever the resulting trajectory reaches the mode containing the set of unsafe states U, we take it as a starting trajectory for local search for an error trajectory. If we obtain an error trajectory then we stop. Otherwise we proceed until we generate a certain number of trajectories (we will denote this number by M).

Note that any method that inspects the given hybrid system only up to a fixed time bound T, if T is too small, it will not find any error trajectory at all. The bounded method that we use here, for T too small, may never reach a mode containing U, preventing it from finding any error trajectory. Moreover, examples for which trajectories leading to the mode containing U lead over a very small guard, become arbitrarily difficult for the bounded method. So we can already conclude now—without running any experiments—that the unbounded method is superior in certain cases.

Still we do some experiments with a widely known benchmark, the Navigation benchmark with 16 modes [12]. We consider the linear dynamics $\dot{x} = Ax - Bu(i,j)$, with A and B as usual for the navigation benchmark, and

$$u(i,j) = \begin{bmatrix} \sin\left(\frac{\pi\, C(i,j)}{4}\right) \\ \cos\left(\frac{\pi\, C(i,j)}{4}\right) \end{bmatrix}, \qquad C = \begin{bmatrix} 4\,3\,3\,4 \\ 4\,4\,4\,4 \\ 4\,6\,6\,4 \\ 1\,0\,7\,6 \end{bmatrix}.$$

Assume the sets of initial and unsafe states to be *ellipsoids* such that their principal axes have length $0.2, 0.2, 2$ and 2, however, I is centred at $[0.5\ 3.5\ 0\ 0]^T$ and U is centred at $[3.5\ 1.5\ 0\ 0]^T$. Our objective is to find any trajectory which starts in set I and reaches set U.

For our experiments we use an instantiation of the unbounded method that fulfills the requirement of starting with a set P that has a path of finite cost as follows: We initialize the set P by putting a point on each boundary of two neighboring modes, simulating forward and backward from each such point (0.05 time units in each direction), and adding the endpoints to the set P.

In the main algorithm, we add a random state to each mode (with velocities x_3 and x_4 ranging from -1 to 1) and then we simulate forward and backward in time from such a state (0.5 time units in each direction). The extremities of the resulting error trajectory (its initial and end states) are stored in P and used for obtaining a path of the minimal cost for local search. If local search returns an error trajectory, then we stop. As in the bounded method we restrict computation, but this time, to add up to M states to the set P.

In all our experiments we do local search using the Scilab function for gradient-based numerical optimization, computing the gradient as described in Section 5. We weighted each distance between two consecutive segments by the weight $\omega = 500$ in order to prefer the continuity of resulting trajectories. We use the Scilab function *rand* for generating random states. For reducing dependence of the result on the random number generator, we always carry out 100 experiments, initializing the random number generator with a different seed (concretely, *rand("seed", i)*, where $i = 1, \ldots 100$). In all our experiments we use the value 500 for the constant M. The results are listed in Tab. 1. The column "successful falsification" lists the number of experiments (from 100) for which the method found an error trajectory. The column "average total simulation time" is the average of the length of all simulation done during a given experiment, but *only* for those experiments that succeeded in finding an error trajectory.

The choices $T = 10$ and $T = 20$ that we used are big enough, so the bounded method does find error trajectories, but still the success rate is lower than with

Table 1. Computation Results

	successful falsification	average total simulation time
unbounded method	99	1937
bounded method, $T = 10$	85	1260
bounded method, $T = 20$	89	2935

the unbounded method, that does not need any bound T at all. In those cases where the bounded method actually finds an error trajectory, if the choice of T is small but large enough to reach a mode containing U, it needs less simulation than the unbounded method. But very quickly, when not choosing T small enough, also the cost of simulations increases beyond the unbounded method.

To sum up, the unbounded method significantly increases the chance of finding an error trajectory, and moreover, it also decreases the amount of simulation needed for that, except for cases where a very good bound on the error trajectory length is available.

8   Related Work

Our algorithm can be viewed as an adaptation of the Best Start two-phase method for global optimization [25] to our context.

The falsification problem can also be viewed as a boundary value problem which is a classical topic in numerical mathematics [3]. However, classical numerical methods assume a fixed final time, whereas we search for error trajectories of arbitrary length. Moreover, classical methods for boundary values problems are restricted to purely continuous systems and the formulation of boundary conditions as equalities.

Zuthsi and co-authors [26] present a method for falsification of hybrid systems that also uses multiple shooting based local search. However, the method assumes a given upper bound on the length of the error trajectory the method searches for. Moreover, their local search method always follows a given sequence of modes and transitions. They propose to search for such a sequence using tools that compute abstractions of hybrid systems, or by random search. The form of the used trajectory segments is more restricted than in our method since trajectory segments always stay in one mode, and end in the guard leading to another mode.

Abbas and co-authors [1] show how to use local search for falsification of hybrid systems with affine dynamics. They propose to start the method from the result of global search algorithms [19].

The usage of abstractions for guiding local search for error trajectories has been proposed earlier [23], in combination with the usage of derivative-free algorithms for local search.

There is more related work for systems that—different from our case—allow input or have non-deterministic dynamics. In the completely discrete case this amounts to finding shortest paths in graphs [4]. We use shortest path algorithms as a sub-algorithm to find starting points for local search. Similar problems are studied in more structured domains by the field of planning [16], and in formal verification by directed model checking [11].

In the continuous case, the classical field studying algorithm for finding paths of dynamical systems that are in some sense optimal (e.g., as short as possible), is optimal control [5,6]. In recent years, also the field of planning has started to study continuous dynamical systems [16, Chapter IV: Planning Under Differential Constraints] from a different perspective. More recently, such techniques have also been applied to hybrid systems [7,8,20,21]. Planning-based techniques search globally, and do not require an upper bound on trajectory length, but they do not incorporate derivative-based local search. The only exception that we are aware of [15] uses optimal control to the result of planning in a purely sequential way, without any iteration between the two phases.

9 Conclusion

We presented an algorithm for the falsification of hybrid system that combines scalability due to local search with convergence due to global search. In future work, we will improve the algorithm in analogy to advanced two-phase methods [25], such as clustering methods that exploit the regions of attraction to local optima of the used local search technique.

References

1. Abbas, H., Fainekos, G.: Linear hybrid system falsification with descent. Technical Report arXiv:1105.1733 (2011)
2. Annpureddy, Y., Liu, C., Fainekos, G., Sankaranarayanan, S.: S-TALiRo: A tool for temporal logic falsification for hybrid systems. In: Abdulla, P.A., Leino, K.R.M. (eds.) TACAS 2011. LNCS, vol. 6605, pp. 254–257. Springer, Heidelberg (2011)
3. Ascher, U.M., Mattheij, R.M.M., Russell, R.D.: Numerical Solution of Boundary Value Problems for Ordinary Differential Equations. SIAM (1995)
4. Bertsekas, D.P.: Network optimization: continuous and discrete models. Athena Scientific Belmont (1998)
5. Betts, J.T.: Survey of numerical methods for trajectory optimization. Journal of Guidance, Control, and Dynamics 21(2) (1998)
6. Branicky, M.S., Borkar, V.S., Mitter, S.K.: A unified framework for hybrid control: Model and optimal control theory. IEEE Transactions on Automatic Control 43(1), 31–45 (1998)
7. Branicky, M.S., Curtiss, M.M., Levine, J., Morgan, S.: Sampling-based planning, control and verification of hybrid systems. IEE Proceedings-Control Theory and Applications 153(5), 575–590 (2006)
8. Dang, T., Nahhal, T.: Coverage-guided test generation for continuous and hybrid systems. Formal Methods in System Design 34(2), 183–213 (2009)
9. Dijkstra, E.: A note on two problems in connexion with graphs. Numerische Mathematik 1(1), 269–271 (1959)
10. Dzetkulič, T., Ratschan, S.: Incremental Computation of Succinct Abstractions for Hybrid Systems. In: Fahrenberg, U., Tripakis, S. (eds.) FORMATS 2011. LNCS, vol. 6919, pp. 271–285. Springer, Heidelberg (2011)

11. Edelkamp, S., Schuppan, V., Bošnački, D., Wijs, A., Fehnker, A., Aljazzar, H.: Survey on Directed Model Checking. In: Peled, D.A., Wooldridge, M.J. (eds.) MoChArt 2008. LNCS, vol. 5348, pp. 65–89. Springer, Heidelberg (2009)
12. Fehnker, A., Ivančić, F.: Benchmarks for Hybrid Systems Verification. In: Alur, R., Pappas, G.J. (eds.) HSCC 2004. LNCS, vol. 2993, pp. 326–341. Springer, Heidelberg (2004)
13. Gendreau, M., Potvin, J.-Y. (eds.): Handbook of Metaheuristics, 2nd edn. Springer, Heidelberg (2010)
14. Hiskens, I., Pai, M.: Trajectory sensitivity analysis of hybrid systems. IEEE Transactions on Circuits and Systems I: Fundamental Theory and Applications 47(2), 204–220 (2000)
15. Lamiraux, F., Ferré, E., Vallée, E.: Kinodynamic motion planning: connecting exploration trees using trajectory optimization methods. In: 2004 IEEE International Conference on Robotics and Automation, Proceedings. ICRA 2004, vol. 4, pp. 3987–3992. IEEE (2004)
16. LaValle, S.M.: Planning Algorithms. Cambridge University Press (2006)
17. Locatelli, M., Schoen, F.: Global Optimization–Theory, Algorithms, and Applications. SIAM (2013)
18. Mosterman, P.J.: An overview of hybrid simulation phenomena and their support by simulation packages. In: Vaandrager, F.W., van Schuppen, J.H. (eds.) HSCC 1999. LNCS, vol. 1569, p. 165. Springer, Heidelberg (1999)
19. Nghiem, T., Sankaranarayanan, S., Fainekos, G., Ivančić, F., Gupta, A., Pappas, G.J.: Monte-carlo techniques for falsification of temporal properties of non-linear hybrid systems. In: Proceedings of the 13th ACM International Conference on Hybrid Systems: Computation and Control, HSCC 2010, pp. 211–220. ACM, New York (2010)
20. Plaku, E., Kavraki, L.E., Vardi, M.Y.: Falsification of LTL safety properties in hybrid systems. In: Kowalewski, S., Philippou, A. (eds.) TACAS 2009. LNCS, vol. 5505, pp. 368–382. Springer, Heidelberg (2009)
21. Plaku, E., Kavraki, L.E., Vardi, M.Y.: Hybrid systems: from verification to falsification by combining motion planning and discrete search. Formal Methods in System Design 34(2), 157–182 (2009)
22. Pohl, I.: Bi-directional search. Machine Intelligence 6, 124–140 (1971)
23. Ratschan, S., Smaus, J.-G.: Finding errors of hybrid systems by optimising an abstraction-based quality estimate. In: Dubois, C. (ed.) TAP 2009. LNCS, vol. 5668, pp. 153–168. Springer, Heidelberg (2009)
24. Rios, L.M., Sahinidis, N.V.: Derivative-free optimization: A review of algorithms and comparison of software implementations. Journal of Global Optimization, 1–47 (2012)
25. Schoen, F.: Two-phase methods for global optimization. In: Pardalos, P., Romeijn, H. (eds.) Handbook of Global Optimization. Nonconvex Optimization and Its Applications, vol. 62, pp. 151–177. Springer, US (2002)
26. Zutshi, A., Sankaranarayanan, S., Deshmukh, J.V., Kapinski, J.: A trajectory splicing approach to concretizing counterexamples for hybrid systems. In: CDC 2013 (2013)

Weak Singular Hybrid Automata[*]

Shankara Narayanan Krishna, Umang Mathur, and Ashutosh Trivedi

Department of Computer Science and Engineering
Indian Institute of Technology - Bombay
Mumbai 400076, India

Abstract. The framework of Hybrid automata—introduced by Alur, Courcourbetis, Henzinger, and Ho—provides a formal modeling and analysis environment to analyze the interaction between the discrete and the continuous parts of hybrid systems. Hybrid automata can be considered as generalizations of finite state automata augmented with a finite set of real-valued variables whose dynamics in each state is governed by a system of ordinary differential equations. Moreover, the discrete transitions of hybrid automata are guarded by constraints over the values of these real-valued variables, and enable discontinuous jumps in the evolution of these variables. Singular hybrid automata are a subclass of hybrid automata where dynamics is specified by state-dependent constant vectors. Henzinger, Kopke, Puri, and Varaiya showed that for even very restricted subclasses of singular hybrid automata, the fundamental verification questions, like reachability and schedulability, are undecidable. Recently, Alur, Wojtczak, and Trivedi studied an interesting class of hybrid systems, called constant-rate multi-mode systems, where schedulability and reachability analysis can be performed in polynomial time. Inspired by the definition of constant-rate multi-mode systems, in this paper we introduce *weak singular hybrid automata* (WSHA), a previously unexplored subclass of singular hybrid automata, and show the decidability (and the exact complexity) of various verification questions for this class including reachability (NP-COMPLETE) and LTL model-checking (PSPACE-COMPLETE). We further show that extending WSHA with a single unrestricted clock or with unrestricted variable updates lead to undecidability of reachability problem.

1 Introduction

Hybrid automata, introduced by Alur et al. [1], provide an intuitive and semantically unambiguous way to model hybrid systems. Various verification questions for such systems can then be naturally reduced to corresponding questions for hybrid automata. Hybrid automata can be considered as finite state-transition graphs with a finite set of real-valued variables with state-dependent dynamics specified using a set of first-order ordinary differential equations. The variables of hybrid automata can be used to constrain the evolution of the system by means of *guards* of the transitions and *local invariants* of the states of the state-transition

---

[*] This work was partly supported by the DST-CNRS project AVeRTS.

A. Legay and M. Bozga (Eds.): FORMATS 2014, LNCS 8711, pp. 161–175, 2014.
© Springer International Publishing Switzerland 2014

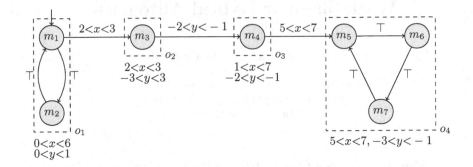

Fig. 1. A weak singular hybrid automaton

graph. The variables can also be reset at the time of taking a transition and thus allowing discrete jumps in the evolution of the system. Considering the richness of the dynamics of hybrid automata, it should come as no surprise that key verification questions, like state reachability, are undecidable for hybrid automata limiting the applicability of hybrid automata for automatic verification of hybrid systems. Henzinger et al. [12,11] observed that this negative result stays even for a severely restricted subclass of hybrid automata, called the *singular hybrid automata* (SHA), where the variables dynamics is specified as state-dependent constant-rate vectors and showed that the reachability problem stays undecidable for singular hybrid automata with three clocks (unit-rate variables) and one non-clock variable. In this paper we introduce a weak version of singular hybrid automata, and show the decidability (and the exact complexity) of reachability, schedulability, and LTL model-checking problems for this class.

Our definition of weak singular hybrid automata is inspired by the definition of constant-rate multi-mode systems (CMS) [5], that are hybrid systems that can switch freely between a finite set of modes (or states) and whose dynamics are specified by a finite set of variables with mode-dependent constant rates. The schedulability problem for CMS is to decide—for a given initial state and convex and bounded safety set—whether there exists a non-Zeno mode-switching schedule such that the system stays within the safety set. On the other hand, the reachability problem is to decide whether there is a schedule that steers the system from a given initial configuration to the target configuration while staying within a specified bounded and convex safety set. Since the system is allowed to switch freely between the enabled modes, the reachability and schedulability problems can be solved in polynomial time [5] by reducing them to a linear program. We say that a singular hybrid automaton is *weak* if there exists an ordering among the states such that the transition to a lower order state is disallowed, and the states with the same ordering form a CMS, i.e. such states have a common invariant and vacuous guards on transitions among themselves.

WSHAs are a natural generalization of CMS with structure, and can be used to model CMS with non-convex safety set. As an example of a WSHA, consider

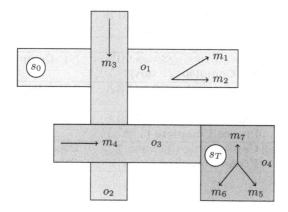

Fig. 2. Multi-mode system corresponding to a robotic motion planning problem

the two dimensional robotic motion planning problem shown in the Figure 2, where the arena is a nonconvex region given as union of four convex polytopes o_1, o_2, o_3 and o_4. The possible motion primitives, or modes, in each region are shown as vectors showing the direction the robot will move given the corresponding mode is chosen. Consider the following reachability and schedulability problems for this example: given an initial valuation s_0 decide if it is possible to compose the motion primitives available in a given valuation so as to reach the final state s_T, while the schedulability problem is to decide if there is a non-Zeno composition of motion specifications such that the robot stays in the safety set forever. This problem can not be solved using the results for constant-rate multi-mode systems sue to non-convexity of the safety set. On the other hand, it is easy to see that the reachability and the schedulability problems for this system can be reduced to corresponding problems on the weak singular hybrid automaton shown in Figure 1, where modes with the same order are shown inside a dashed box with global invariant is specified just below the box.

We extend the results of [5] by recovering decidability for WSHA by showing that the reachability problem and schedulability problems are NP-COMPLETE for this model. We also define LTL and CTL model-checking problems for weak singular hybrid automata, and show that while the complexity of LTL model-checking stays the same as LTL model checking for finite state-transition graphs (PSPACE-COMPLETE), the CTL model-checking is already PSPACE-hard. Inspired by an unpublished result from Bouyer and Markey [16], we show (Section 4) that extending WSHA with single unrestricted clock variable make the reachability problem undecidable for WSHA with three variables. In the same section, we also show that extending WSHA with unrestricted variable updates also make the reachability problem undecidable for WSHA with three variables. Table 1 shows a summary of results on singular hybrid automata, and the contributions of this paper are highlighted with boldface.

Table 1. Summary of decidability results related to (weak) singular hybrid automata

Problem	SHA	WSHA
Reachability	UNDECIDABLE (≥ 3 vars.) [12] NL-Complete (1 var.)	NP-Complete
Schedulability	UNDECIDABLE (≥ 3 vars.) [12] NL-Complete (1 var.)	NP-Complete
LTL model-checking	UNDECIDABLE (≥ 3 vars.) [12] Pspace-Complete (1 var.)	Pspace-Complete
CTL model-checking	Undecidable (≥ 2 vars.) Ptime-Complete (1 var.)	Pspace-Hard (≥ 2 vars.) Ptime-Complete (1 var.)

Related Work. Timed automata are subclasses of SHA with the restriction that all variables are clocks, while stopwatch automata are subclasses of hybrid automata with the restriction that all variables are stopwatches (clocks that can be paused). Using the region construction [2] Alur and Dill showed that the reachability and the schedulability problems for timed automata are decidable and are in fact complete for PSPACE. Čerāns [9] showed that the undecidability result for singular hybrid automata holds even for stopwatch automata. Initialized singular hybrid automata are subclasses of singular hybrid automata with the restriction that if there is a transition between two modes that have different rate for some variable then that transition must reset that variable. Henzinger at al. [12] showed the decidability of reachability problem by reducing the problem to the corresponding problem on timed automata—by appropriate adjustment of the guards of the transitions. Unlike timed automata and initialized SHA, our results for WSHA do not rely on the existence of finitary bisimulation.

Asarin, Maler, and Pnueli [7] studied a subclass of singular hybrid automata, called the piecewise-constant derivative (PCD) systems, that are defined by a partition of the Euclidean space into a finite set of polyhedral regions, where the dynamics in each region is defined by a constant rate vector. PCD systems, unlike our model, are defined as completely deterministic systems where discrete transitions occurs at region boundaries and runs change their directions according to the rate vector available in the new region. They showed that even under such simple dynamics the reachability problem for PCD systems with three or more variables is undecidable [7]. On the positive side, Asarin, Maler, and Pnueli [7] gave an algorithm to solve the reachability problem for two-dimensional PCD systems. The work that is closest to ours is on constant-rate multi-mode systems by Alur et al. [5,3]. However, our model strictly generalizes this model and permits analysis of multi-mode systems with non-convex safety set.

The paper is organized in the following manner. In the next section we introduce technical notations and background required for the paper. In Section 3 we present weak singular hybrid automata and show the decidability and complexity results for the reachability, schedulability, and LTL model-checking problems. In Section 4 we present the two undecidability results related to WSHA. Due to lack of space, detailed proofs of the results are given in [14].

2 Preliminaries

Let $\mathbb{R}$ be the set of real numbers. Let X be a finite set of real-valued variables. A *valuation* on X is a function $\nu : X \to \mathbb{R}$. We assume an arbitrary but fixed ordering on the variables and write x_i for the variable with order i. This allows us to treat a valuation ν as a point $(\nu(x_1), \nu(x_2), \ldots, \nu(x_n)) \in \mathbb{R}^{|X|}$. Abusing notations slightly, we use a valuation on X and a point in $\mathbb{R}^{|X|}$ interchangeably. We denote points in this state space by $\overline{x}, \overline{y}$, vectors by $\boldsymbol{r}, \boldsymbol{v}$, and the i-th coordinate of point $\overline{x}$ and vector $\boldsymbol{r}$ by $\overline{x}(i)$ and $\boldsymbol{r}(i)$, respectively. We write $\boldsymbol{0}$ for a vector with all its coordinates equal to 0. We say that a set $S \subseteq \mathbb{R}^n$ is *bounded* if there exists $d \in \mathbb{R}_{\geq 0}$ such that for all $\overline{x}, \overline{y} \in S$ we have $\|\overline{x} - \overline{y}\| \leq d$.

We define a constraint over a set X as a subset of $\mathbb{R}^{|X|}$. We say that a constraint is *polyhedral* if it is defined as the conjunction of a finite set of linear constraints of the form $a_1 x_1 + \cdots + a_n x_n \bowtie k$, where $k \in \mathbb{Z}$, for all $1 \leq i \leq n$ we have that $a_i \in \mathbb{Z}, x_i \in X$, and $\bowtie \in \{<, \leq, =, >, \geq\}$. Every polyhedral constraints can be written in the standard form $A\overline{x} \leq \boldsymbol{b}$ for some matrix A of size $k \times n$ and a vector $\boldsymbol{b} \in \mathbb{Z}^k$. We call a bounded polyhedral constraint a *convex polytope*. For a constraint G, we write $[\![G]\!]$ for the set of valuations in $\mathbb{R}^{|X|}$ satisfying the constraint G. We write $\top$ (resp., $\bot$) for the special constraint that is true (resp., false) in all the valuations, i.e. $[\![\top]\!] = \mathbb{R}^{|X|}$ (resp., $[\![\bot]\!] = \emptyset$). We write $\mathrm{poly}(X)$ for the set of polyhedral constraints over X including $\top$ and $\bot$.

2.1 Singular Hybrid Automata

Singular hybrid automata extend finite state-transition graphs with a finite set of real-valued variables that grow with state-dependent constant-rates. The transitions of the automata are guarded by predicates on the valuations of the variables, and the syntax allows discrete update of the value of the variables.

Definition 1 (Singular Hybrid Automata). *A singular hybrid automaton is a tuple* $(M, M_0, \Sigma, X, \Delta, I, F)$ *where:*

- *M is a finite set of control* modes *including a distinguished initial set of control modes $M_0 \subseteq M$,*
- *Σ is a finite set of* actions,
- *X is an (ordered) set of* variables,
- *$\Delta \subseteq M \times \mathrm{poly}(X) \times \Sigma \times 2^X \times M$ is the* transition relation,
- *$I : M \to \mathrm{poly}(X)$ is the mode-invariant function, and*
- *$F : M \to \mathbb{Q}^{|X|}$ is the mode-dependent* flow function *characterizing the rate of each variable in each mode.*

For computation purposes, we assume that all real numbers are rational and represented by writing down the numerator and denominator in binary.

For all $\delta = (m, G, a, R, m') \in \Delta$ we say that δ is a *transition* between the modes m and m' with *guard* $G \in \mathrm{poly}(X)$ and *reset set* $R \in 2^X$. For the sake of notational convenience and w.l.o.g., we assume that an action $a \in \Sigma$ uniquely determines a transition (m, G, a, R, m'), and we write $G(a)$ and $R(a)$ for the guard and the reset set corresponding to the action $a \in \Sigma$. This can be assumed without loss of generality, since, in this paper, we do not study language-theoretic properties of a singular hybrid automaton, and assume that the non-determinism is resolved by the controller.

A *configuration* of a SHA $\mathcal{H}$ is a pair $(m, \nu) \in M \times \mathbb{R}^{|X|}$ consisting of a control mode m and a variable valuation $\nu \in \mathbb{R}^{|X|}$ such that that ν satisfies the invariant $I(m)$ of the mode m, i.e. $\nu \in \llbracket I(m) \rrbracket$. We say that the transition $\delta = (m, G, a, R, m')$ is *enabled* in a configuration (m, ν) when guard $G \in \text{poly}(X)$ is satisfied by the valuation, i.e. $\nu \in \llbracket G \rrbracket$. Moreover, the transition δ resets the variables in $R \in 2^X$ to 0. We write $\nu[R:=0]$ to denote the valuation resulting from substituting in valuation ν the value for the variables in the set R to 0, formally $\nu[R:=0](x) = 0$ if $x \in R$ and $\nu[R:=0](x) = \nu(x)$ otherwise. A *timed action* of a SHA is the tuple $(t, a) \in \mathbb{R}_{\geq 0} \times \Sigma$ consisting of a time delay and discrete action. While the system dwells in a mode $m \in M$ the valuation of the system flows linearly according to the rate function $F(m)$. This means that starting from a valuation ν in mode m, the valuation of the variables, after spending t time units, will be $\nu + t \cdot F(m)$.

We say that $((m, \nu), (t, a), (m', \nu'))$ is a transition of a SHA $\mathcal{H}$ and we write $(m, \nu) \xrightarrow{t}_a (m', \nu')$ if (m, ν) and (m', ν') are valid configurations of the SHA $\mathcal{H}$, and there is a transition $\delta = (m, G, a, R, m') \in \Delta$ such that:

- all the valuations resulting from dwelling in mode m for time t from the valuation ν satisfy the invariant of the mode m, i.e. $(\nu + F(m) \cdot \tau) \in \llbracket I(m) \rrbracket$ for all $\tau \in [0, t]$ (observe that due to convexity of the invariant set we only need to check that $(\nu + F(m) \cdot t) \in \llbracket I(m) \rrbracket$);
- The valuation reached after waiting for t time-units satisfy the constraint G (called the guard of the transition δ), i.e. $(\nu + F(m) \cdot t) \in \llbracket G \rrbracket$, and
- $\nu' = (\nu + F(m) \cdot t)[R := 0]$.

A *finite run* of a singular hybrid automaton $\mathcal{H}$ is a finite sequence $r = \langle (m_0, \nu_0), (t_1, a_1), (m_1, \nu_1), (t_2, a_2), \dots, (m_k, \nu_k) \rangle$ such that $m_0 \in M_0$ and for all $0 \leq i < k$ we have that $((m_i, \nu_i), (t_{i+1}, a_{i+1}), (m_{i+1}, \nu_{i+1}))$ is a transition of $\mathcal{H}$. For such a run r we say that ν_0 is the *starting valuation*, while ν_k is the *terminal valuation*. An *infinite run* of an SHA $\mathcal{H}$ is similarly defined to be an infinite sequence $r = \langle (m_0, \nu_0), (t_1, a_1), (m_1, \nu_1), (t_2, a_2), \dots \rangle$ such that $((m_i, \nu_i), (t_{i+1}, a_{i+1}), (m_{i+1}, \nu_{i+1}))$ is a transition of the SHA $\mathcal{H}$ for all $i \geq 0$. We say that ν_0 is the starting configuration of the run. We say that such an infinite run is Zeno if $\sum_{i=1}^{\infty} t_i < \infty$. Zeno runs are physically unrealizable since they require infinitely many mode-switches within a finite amount of time.

2.2   Reachability, Schedulability, and Model-Checking

Given a finite set of atomic propositions $\mathcal{P}$ and a labeling function $L : M \rightarrow 2^{\mathcal{P}}$, a trace of a SHA $\mathcal{H}$ corresponding to an infinite run $r = \langle (m_0, \nu_0), (t_1, a_1), \dots \rangle$ is the sequence $\langle L(m_0), L(m_1), L(m_2), \dots L(m_n), \dots \rangle$ of labels corresponding to the mode sequence of r. We use the standard syntax and semantics of LTL and CTL [8] with the exception that we consider traces corresponding to non-Zeno runs. Given a SHA $\mathcal{H} = (M, M_0, \Sigma, X, \Delta, I, F)$ and a starting valuation $\nu \in \mathbb{R}^{|X|}$, we are interested in the following problems over SHA.

- **Reachability problem.** Given a target polytope $\mathcal{T} \subseteq \mathbb{R}^X$, decide whether there exists a finite run from ν_0 to some valuation $\nu' \in \mathcal{T}$.
- **Schedulability.** Decide whether there exists an infinite non-Zeno run starting from ν.
- **LTL model checking.** Given a set of propositions $\mathcal{P}$, labeling function L, and an LTL formula ϕ decide whether all non-Zeno traces of $\mathcal{H}$ satisfy ϕ.
- **CTL model checking.** Given a set of propositions $\mathcal{P}$, labeling function L, and a CTL formula ϕ decide whether all initial modes of $\mathcal{H}$ satisfy ϕ.

The termination [17] and the recurrent computation [4] problems for two-counter Minsky machines are known to be undecidable. By encoding the two counters as two vairables, and using another variable to do additional book-keeping, the termination and the recurrence problem for Minsky machines can be reduced to reachability and schedulability problems for SHA.

Theorem 1 (Undecidability [12,7,6]). *The reachability, schedulability, LTL and CTL model-checking problems are undecidable for SHA with three variables.*

Improved Complexity Results. Using just two variables x, y (of which y is only a clock variable), with the encoding $x = 2 - \frac{1}{2^{c_1} 3^{c_2}}$ for counters c_1, c_2, we improve the undecidability result for CTL model checking of SHAs:

Theorem 2. *CTL Model-checking problem for singular hybrid automata with two variables is* UNDECIDABLE.

We adapt the construction of Laroussinie et al. [15] for the case of one clock timed automata to show the following results for SHA with one variable.

Theorem 3. *For SHA with one variable we have the following results.*

(a) The reachability and the schedulability problems are NL-COMPLETE.
(b) LTL Model-checking problem is PSPACE-COMPLETE.

Proof. (Sketch.) The NLOGSPACE-hardness of the reachability problem for SHA follows from the complexity of reachability problem for finite graphs [13]. On the other hand, the NLOGSPACE-hardness of the schedulability problem for SHA follows from the complexity of nonemptiness problem for Büchi automata (Proposition 10.12 of [18]). For NLOGSPACE-membership of these problems we adapt the region construction (LMS regions) for one-clock timed automata proposed by Laroussinie, Markey, and Schnoebelen [15].

For LTL model checking the PSPACE-hardness follows from the PSPACE-completeness [19] for LTL model checking on finite automata, while the PSPACE membership follows from the region construction introduced in the proof of (a). However, we need to be extra careful as our semantics are defined with respect to non-Zeno runs. To overcome this complication, we characterize non-Zenoness property of the region graphs as LTL formulas using the following Lemma.

Lemma 1. *Let c_x and C_x denote the smallest and largest constants used in guards of $\mathcal{H}$ and let $\mathcal{RG}_\mathcal{H}$ be the LMS region graph of $\mathcal{H}$. An infinite run in the region graph $\mathcal{RG}_\mathcal{H}$ of the form $((m_0, r_0), a_0, (m_1, r_1), a_1, \ldots)$ is called progressive iff it has a non-Zeno instantiation. Here, r_j and m_j are respectively the regions and modes. An infinite run $((m_0, r_0), a_0, (m_1, r_1), a_1, \ldots)$ in the region graph $\mathcal{RG}_\mathcal{H}$ of a one-variable SHA $\mathcal{H}$ is progressive iff one of the following hold:*

1. *For all $j \geq 0$ there exists $k > j$ such that $F(m_k) = 0$;*
2. *There exists $n \geq 0$ such that for all $j \geq n$ we have that $[\![r_j]\!] = [\![x > C_x]\!]$ and there exists $k > j$ such that $F(m_k) > 0$;*
3. *There exists $n \geq 0$ such that for all $j \geq n$ we have that $[\![r_j]\!] = [\![x < c_x]\!]$ and there exists a $k > j$ such that $F(m_k) < 0$;*
4. *For all $j \geq 0$ there exists $k > j$ s.t. $r_j \neq r_k$; or*
5. *There exists $n \geq 0$ and a thick region r such that for all $j \geq n$ we have that $r_j = r$ and there exists $k > j$ such that $F(m_j).F(m_k) < 0$.*

Given an LTL formula ϕ, and a one variable SHA $\mathcal{H}$, we can express in LTL the conditions characterizing non-zeno runs of $\mathcal{H}$ as given by Lemma 1. Let ϕ_C be this LTL formula. Model checking of ϕ over all non-Zeno runs then reduces to standard model checking against formula $\phi \wedge \phi_C$.   □

3   Weak Singular Hybrid Automata

We begin this section by formally introducing constant-rate multi-mode systems and review the decidability of reachability and schedulability problems for this class. We later present the weak singular hybrid automata model and show the decidability of various verification problems.

3.1   Constant-Rate Multi-mode Systems

Definition 2 (Constant-Rate Multi-mode Systems). *We say that a singular hybrid automaton $\mathcal{H} = (M, M_0, \Sigma, X, \Delta, I, F)$ is a constant-rate multi-mode system if*

- *there is a bounded and open polytope S, called the safety set, such that for all modes $m \in M$ we have that $I(m) = S$, and*
- *all the modes in M form a strongly-connected-component, and for every mode $m, m' \in M$ if there is a transition $(m, G, a, R, m') \in \Delta$ then $G = \top$, and $R = \emptyset$.*

We have slightly modified the definition of CMS from [5] to adapt it to the presentation used in this paper. Moreover, we have restricted the safety set to be an open set to avoid problems in reaching a valuation using infinitely many transitions. Notice that there is no structure in a CMS in the sense that all of the modes can be chosen in arbitrary order as long as the safety set is not violated. Alur et al. [5] showed that due to lack of structure, the schedulability and the reachability problems for CMS can be reduced to LP feasibility problem, and hence can be solved in polynomial time.

Theorem 4 (Reachability and Schedulability for CMS [5]). *The schedulability and the reachability problems for CMS can be solved in polynomial time.*

Proof. **Reachability.** Let $\mathcal{H} = (M, M_0, X, \Delta, I, F)$ be a CMS with the safety set S and the target polytope $\mathcal{T}$ be given as a system of linear inequalities $AX \leq b$. Moreover assume that ν and $\mathcal{T}$ are in the safety set S. Alur et al. showed that the target set $\mathcal{T}$ is reachable from ν iff the following linear program is feasible:

$$\nu + \sum_{m \in M} F(m) \cdot t_m \; = \; \nu',$$

$$A\nu' \; = \; b, \text{ and} \tag{1}$$

$$t_m \; >= 0, \text{ for all } m \in M.$$

If this linear program is not feasible, then it is immediate that it is not possible to reach any valuation in $\mathcal{T}$ from ν using modes in any sequence from $\mathcal{H}$. On the other hand, if the program is feasible, and as long as both the starting valuation and the target set are strictly inside the safety set, a satisfying assignment $\langle t_m \rangle_{m \in M}$ can be used to make progress towards $\mathcal{T}$ by scaling t_m's appropriately without leaving the safety set. Since the feasibility of the linear program can be decided in polynomial time, it follows that reachability for the CMS can be decided in polynomial time.

Schedulability. Let $\mathcal{H} = (M, M_0, X, \Delta, I, F)$ be a CMS with the safety set S, and initial valuation ν. In this case, Alur et al. showed that there exists a non-Zeno run from arbitrary valuation in the safety set if and only if the following linear program is feasible:

$$\sum_{m \in M} F(m) \cdot t_m \; = \; 0,$$

$$\sum_{m \in M} t_m \; = \; 1 \text{ and} \tag{2}$$

$$t_m \; >= 0, \text{ for all } m \in M.$$

If this linear program is not feasible, then by Farkas's lemma it follows that there is a vector v such that taking any mode for nonnegative time makes some progress in the direction of v. Hence any non-Zeno run will eventually leave the safety set. On the other hand, if the program is feasible, then a satisfying assignment $\langle t_m \rangle_{m \in M}$ can be scaled down to stay in a ball of arbitrary size around the initial valuation. Hence, if the starting valuation is strictly in the interior of the safety set, the feasibility of the linear program (2) imply the existence of a non-Zeno run. $\quad\square$

3.2   Syntax and Semantics

Weak singular hybrid automata (WSHA) can be considered as generalized constant-rate multi-mode systems with structure. The restriction on WSHA ensures that the strongly connected components of WSHA form CMS, and thus recovering the decidability for the reachability and the schedulability problem. Formally we define WSHA in the following manner.

Definition 3 (Weak Singular Hybrid Automata). *A weak singular hybrid automaton* $\mathcal{H} = (M, M_0, \Sigma, X, \Delta, I, F)$ *is a SHA with the restriction that there is a partition on the set of modes M characterized by a function $\varrho : M \to \mathbb{N}$ assigning ranks to the modes such that*

- *for every transition* $(m, G, a, R, m') \in \Delta$ *we have that* $\varrho(m) \leq \varrho(m')$, *and*
- *for every rank i the set of modes $M_i = \{m : \varrho(m) = i\}$ is such that*
    - *there is a bounded and open polytope S_i, called the safety set of M_i, such that for all modes $m \in M_i$ we have that $I(m) = S_i$; and*
    - *all the modes in M_i form a strongly-connected-component, and for every mode $m, m' \in M_i$ if there is a transition $(m, G, a, R, m') \in \Delta$ then $G = \top$, and $R = \emptyset$.*

Observe that every CMS is a weak singular hybrid automaton (WSHA), and every strongly connected component of a WSHA is a CMS. Also notice that for every (finite or infinite) run $r = \langle (m_0, \nu_0), (t_1, a_1), (m_1, \nu_1), \ldots \rangle$ of a WSHA we have that $\varrho(m_i) \leq \varrho(m_j)$ for every $i \leq j$. We define the type $\Gamma(r)$ of a finite run $r = \langle (m_0, \nu_0), (t_1, a_1), (m_1, \nu_1), \ldots, (m_k, \nu_k) \rangle$ as a finite sequence of ranks (natural numbers) and actions $\langle n_0, b_1, n_1, \ldots, b_p, n_p \rangle$ defined inductively in the following manner:

$$\Gamma(r) = \begin{cases} \langle \varrho(m_0) \rangle & \text{if } r = \langle (m_0, \nu_0) \rangle \\ \Gamma(r') \oplus (a, \varrho(m)) & \text{if } r = r' :: \langle (t, a), (m, \nu) \rangle, \end{cases}$$

where :: is the cons operator that appends two sequences, while for a sequence $\sigma = \langle n_0, b_1, n_1, \ldots, b_p, n_p \rangle$, $a \in \Sigma$, and $n \in \mathbb{N}$ we define $\sigma \oplus (a, n)$ to be equal to σ if $n_p = n$ and $\langle n_0, b_1, n_1, \ldots, n_p, a, n \rangle$ otherwise. Intuitively, the type of a finite run gives the (non-duplicate) sequence of ranks of modes and actions appearing in the run, where action is stored only when a transition to a mode of higher rank happens. We need to remember only these actions since transitions that stay in the modes of same rank do not reset the variables. It is an easy observation that, since there are only finitely many ranks for a given WSHA, we have that for every infinite run $r = \langle (m_0, \nu_0), (t_1, a_1), (m_1, \nu_1), \ldots \rangle$ there exists an index i such that for all $j \geq i$ we have that $\varrho(m_i) = \varrho(m_j)$. With this intuition we define the type of an infinite run r as the type of the finite prefix of r till index i. We write $\Gamma_{\mathcal{H}}$ for the set of run types of a WSHA $\mathcal{H}$.

Theorem 5. *The reachability and the schedulability problems for weak singular hybrid automata is NP-complete.*

Proof. (Sketch) To show NP-membership we show that to decide the reachability problem, it is sufficient to guess a finite run type, and check whether there is a run with that type that reaches the target polytope. Since the size of every run type is polynomial in the size of the WSHA, and there are only exponentially many run-types, if for a run we can check whether there exists a run of this type reaching target polytope is polynomial time, the NP-membership claim follows. Given a run type $\sigma = \langle n_0, b_1, n_1, \ldots, b_p, n_p \rangle$ an initial valuation ν_0 and a bounded and convex target polytope $\mathcal{T}$ given as $AX \leq b$, there exists a run with type σ that reaches a valuation in $\mathcal{T}$ if and only if the following linear program is feasible: for every $0 \leq i \leq p$ and $m \in M_{n_i}$ there are $\nu_{n_i}, \nu'_{n_i} \in \mathbb{R}^{|X|}$ and $t_i^m \in \mathbb{R}_{\geq 0}$ such that:

$$\nu_0 = \nu_{n_0}, \nu'_{n_p} \in \mathcal{T}$$
$$\nu_{n_i}, \nu'_{n_i} \in S_{M_{n_i}} \text{ for all } 0 \leq i \leq p$$
$$\nu_{n_i} \in G(b_i) \text{ for all } 0 < i \leq p$$
$$\nu_{n_{i+1}}(j) = 0 \text{ for all } x_j \in R(b_{i+1}) \text{ and } 0 < i \leq p$$
$$\nu_{n_{i+1}}(j) = \nu'_{n_i}(j) \text{ for all } x_j \notin R(b_{i+1}) \text{ and } 0 < i \leq p$$
$$\nu'_{n_i} = \nu_{n_i} + \sum_{m \in M_{n_i}} F(m) \cdot t_i^m \text{ for all } 0 \leq i \leq p$$
$$t_i^m \geq 0 \text{ for all } 0 \leq i \leq p \text{ and } m \in M_{n_i}$$

These constraints check whether it is possible to reach some valuation in the target polytope while satisfying the guard and constraints of the WSHA, while exploiting the fact that modes of same rank can be applied an arbitrary number of time in an arbitrary order. The proof for this claim is similar to the proof for the CMS, and hence omitted.

To show NP-hardness we reduce the *subset-sum problem* to solving the reachability problem in a WSHA. Formally, given A, a non-empty set of n integers and another integer k, the *subset-sum problem* is to determine if there is a non-empty subset $T \subseteq A$ that sums to k. Given the set A and the integer k, we construct a WSHA $\mathcal{H}$ with $n + 3$ variables $x_0, x_1, \ldots, x_{n+2}$, $2n + 1$ modes $m_0, \ldots, m_{2n}$ and $2n$ transitions, such that starting from a given valuation, a particular target polytope $\mathcal{T}$ is reachable in the WSHA iff there is a non-empty subset $T \subseteq A$ that sums up to k. Intuitively, the variable x_0 ensures that the variables $x_1, x_2 \ldots x_n$ are initialized with values $a_1, a_2, \ldots a_n$ (the elements of A). The variable x_{n+1} sums up the values of the elements in the chosen subset T, and can be later compared with k. The variable x_{n+2} ensures that the set T is non-empty (specifically when $k = 0$). The rates in the modes $m_i (0 \leq i \leq 2n)$ are given as follows (r_i represents $(F(m_i))$:

- $r_0(x_0) = 1, r_0(x_{n+1}) = r_0(x_{n+2}) = 0$, and $r_0(x_i) = a_i$, where $1 \leq i \leq n$
- $r_{2j-1}(x_j) = -a_j, r_{2j-1}(x_{n+1}) = a_j, r_{2j-1}(x_{n+2}) = 1$, and $r_{2j-1}(x_0) = r_{2j-1}(x_i) = 0$, where $1 \leq i \neq j \leq n$
- $r_{2j}(x_j) = -a_j$, and $r_{2j}(x_0) = r_{2j}(x_i) = r_{2j}(x_{n+1}) = r_{2j}(x_{n+2}) = 0$, where $1 \leq i \neq j \leq n$

The transitions are as follows: (i) There are edges from m_0 to m_1 and to m_2, and (ii) There are edges from m_{2j-1} and from m_{2j} to m_{2j+1} and to m_{2j+2}, $1 \leq j \leq n - 1$. We claim that the polytope $\mathcal{T}$, given by the set of points $\bar{x}$ such that $\bar{x}(0) = 1, \bar{x}(i) = 0, 1 \leq i \leq n, \bar{x}(n+1) = k$ and $\bar{x}(n+2) \in [1, n]$, is reachable

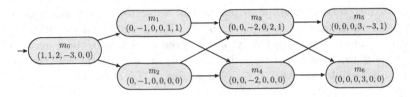

Fig. 3. Constructed WSHA for a set $\{1, 2, -3\}$

from the point **0** iff there is a non-empty subset T of A that sums up to k. Figure 3 gives an illustration of the WSHA construction for a set $\{1, 2, -3\}$.

The proof for schedulability is similar, and hence, omitted.   □

Corollary 1. *The LTL model-checking problem for WSHA is PSPACE-complete.*

We also observe that CTL model checking for weak singular hybrid automata is already hard for PSPACE by using a reduction from subset sum games [10].

Theorem 6. *CTL model checking of weak SHAs with two clock variables is* PSPACE-*hard.*

Proof (Sketch). We give a polynomial reduction from subset-sum games. A subsetsum game is played between an existential player and a universal player. The game is specified by a pair (ψ, T) where $T \in \mathbb{N}$ and ψ is a list:

$$\forall\{A_1, B_1\}\exists\{E_1, F_1\}\dots\forall\{A_n, B_n\}\exists\{E_n, F_n\}$$

where A_i, B_i, E_i, F_i are all natural numbers. The game is played in rounds. In the first round, the universal player chooses an element from $\{A_1, B_1\}$, and the existential player responds by choosing a number from $\{E_1, F_1\}$. In the next round, the universal player chooses an element from $\{A_2, B_2\}$, and the existential player responds by choosing a number from $\{E_2, F_2\}$. This pattern repeats for n rounds, and two players this construct a sequence of number, and the existential player wins iff the sum of those numbers equals T.

For each set $\{A_i, B_i\}$, we construct a widget $W_{\forall_i}$ shown in the left side of Figure 4. Similarly, for each set $\{E_i, F_i\}$, we construct a widget $W_{\exists_i}$ shown in the right side of Figure 4.

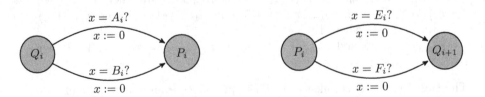

Fig. 4. Widgets $W_{\forall_i}$ (left) and $W_{\exists_i}$ (*right*)

The WSHA $\mathcal{A}$ constructed has 2 clocks x, y and is obtained by connecting the last node of widget $W_{\forall_i}$ with the starting node of widget $W_{\exists_i}$ for $1 \leq i \leq n$, and by connecting the last node of $W_{\exists_i}$ with the initial node of $W_{\forall_{i+1}}$, $1 \leq i \leq n-1$. The last node of $W_{\exists_n}$ (labeled P_n) is connected to a node END with a guard $y = T$. The clock y is never reset in any of the widgets and accumulates the computed sum. Notice that the resulting timed automaton is a WSHA since it is acyclic. Let i_0 be the initial mode of this WSHA. The unique initial mode of the WSHA is labeled with Q_1. It is easy to see that the above WSHA can be constructed in polynomial time; moreover, the constructed WSHA has $3n + 2$ modes, $4n + 1$ edges and 2 clocks. We now give a CTL formula φ of size $\mathcal{O}(n)$ given by $[Q_1 \wedge \mathbf{A} \bigcirc (P_1 \wedge \mathbf{E} \bigcirc (Q_2 \wedge \ldots \mathbf{A} \bigcirc (P_n \wedge \mathbf{E} \bigcirc \text{END})))]$ It can be seen that the existential player wins the subsetsum game iff $\mathcal{A}, i_0 \models \varphi$. $\square$

We conjecture that the problem can be solved in PSPACE, however decidability of the problem is currently open.

4 Undecidable Variants of WSHA

In this section, we present two variants of WSHA and show that both lead to undecidability of the reachability problem.

Theorem 7. *The reachability problem is undecidable for three variable WSHAs with discrete updates.*

Proof (Sketch). We show a reduction from the halting problem for two-counter Minsky machines $\mathcal{M}$. The variables x, y, z of the SHA have global invariants $0 \leq x \leq 1$, $0 \leq y, z \leq 5$ respectively. The counters c_1, c_2 of two-counter machine are encoded in variables y and z as $y = 5 - \frac{1}{2^{c_1}}$ and $z = 5 - \frac{1}{2^{c_2}}$. To begin, we have $c_1 = c_2 = 0$, hence $y = z = 4$, and $x=0$. The rates of x, y, z are indicated by 3-tuples inside the modes of the SHA. The discrete updates on x, y, z are indicated on the transitions. We construct widgets for each of the increment/decrement and zero check instructions. Each widget begins with $x=0, y = 5 - \frac{1}{2^{c_1}}$ and $z = 5 - \frac{1}{2^{c_2}}$, where c_1, c_2 are the counter values.

- **(Increment and Decrement Instructions).** Let us first consider increment instruction $l : c_1 := c_1 + 1$ goto l'. The Figure 5 depicts the increment widget. This widget starts with a mode labeled l, and ends in a mode labeled l'. This widget can be modified to simulate the instructions increment counter c_2, decrement counters c_1 and decrement counter c_2, respectively, by changing the cost rate of z at B to -3, the cost rate of y at B to -12, and the cost rate of z at B to -12, respectively.
- **(Zero Check Instruction).** We next consider the zero check instruction: $l :$ if $c_1 = 0$ goto l' else goto l''. The widget of Figure 6 depicts the zero check widget. The zero check widget starts in a mode l and reaches either the mode l' or mode l''.

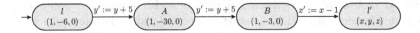

Fig. 5. Increment c_1 widget

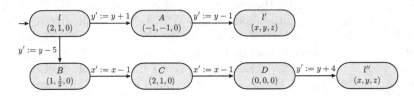

Fig. 6. Zero Check widget

It is straightforward to see that the modules for increment, decrement, and zero check simulate the two counter machine. There is a mode HALT corresponding to the HALT instruction. The halting problem for two counter machines is thus reduced to the reachability of the mode HALT.   □

The next variant that we consider is weak singular hybrid automata extended with discrete updates on the variables even inside the strongly connected components. We prove this result by showing that even CMS with one unrestricted clock variable lead to undecidability.

Theorem 8. *The reachability problem is undecidable for CMS with three variables and one unrestricted clock.*

Proof (Sketch). We simulate a two counter machine using a CMS with 3 variables and one clock. The three variables x_1, x_2, y have global invariants $0 \le x_1, x_2 \le 5$ and $0 \le y \le 1$ respectively. The clock variable is x. The counters c_1, c_2 are encoded as $x_1 = 5 - \frac{1}{2^{c_1}}$, $x_2 = 5 - \frac{1}{2^{c_2}}$. At the beginning of each widget, we have $x_1 = 5 - \frac{1}{2^{c_1}}$, $x_2 = 5 - \frac{1}{2^{c_2}}$ and $y = 1$, where c_1, c_2 are the current counter values. The gadget simulating an increment instruction is shown below.

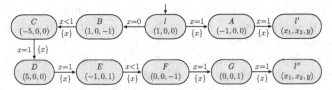

The decrement gadget is similar to the increment gadget. The gadget for a zero check is given in the figure below. Observe that starting at mode l with $y = 1$ and $x_1 = 5 - \frac{1}{2^{c_1}}$, the gadget in this gadget ensures that we reach l' iff $c_1 = 0$, and otherwise reaches l''.

The proof sketch is now complete.   □

5 Conclusion

We introduced weak singular hybrid automata and showed that verification problems like reachability and schedulability are NP-COMPLETE, while LTL property checking is PSPACE-COMPLETE. Extending the model with either unrestricted variable updates or with a single unrestricted clock variable render the reachablity problem undecidable. We showed PSPACE-hardness of the CTL model checking problem, but the exact complexity of the problem remains open.

References

1. Alur, R., Courcoubetis, C., Henzinger, T.A., Ho, P.-S.: Hybrid automata: An algorithmic approach to the specification and verification of hybrid systems. In: Hybrid Systems, pp. 209–229 (1992)
2. Alur, R., Dill, D.: A theory of timed automata. TCS 126(2), 183–235 (1994)
3. Alur, R., Forejt, V., Moarref, S., Trivedi, A.: Safe schedulability of bounded-rate multi-mode systems. In: HSCC, pp. 243–252 (2013)
4. Alur, R., Henzinger, T.A.: A really temporal logic. J. ACM 41(1), 181–203 (1994)
5. Alur, R., Trivedi, A., Wojtczak, D.: Optimal scheduling for constant-rate multi-mode systems. In: HSCC, pp. 75–84 (2012)
6. Asarin, E., Maler, O.: Achilles and the tortoise climbing up the arithmetical hierarchy. Journal of Computer and System Sciences 57(3), 389–398 (1998)
7. Asarin, E., Maler, O., Pnueli, A.: Reachability analysis of dynamical systems having piecewise-constant derivatives. TCS 138, 35–66 (1995)
8. Baier, C., Katoen, J.P.: Principles of model checking. MIT Press (2008)
9. Čerāns, K.: Algorithmic problems in analysis of real time system specifications. PhD thesis (1992)
10. Fearnley, J., Jurdziński, M.: Reachability in two-clock timed automata is PSPACE-complete. In: Fomin, F.V., Freivalds, R., Kwiatkowska, M., Peleg, D. (eds.) ICALP 2013, Part II. LNCS, vol. 7966, pp. 212–223. Springer, Heidelberg (2013)
11. Henzinger, T.A., Kopke, P.W.: Discrete-time control for rectangular hybrid automata. TCS 221(1-2), 369–392 (1999)
12. Henzinger, T.A., Kopke, P.W., Puri, A., Varaiya, P.: What's decidable about hybrid automata? Journal of Comp. and Sys. Sciences 57, 94–124 (1998)
13. Jones, N.D., Lien, Y.E., Laaser, W.T.: New problems complete for nondeterministic log space. Mathematical Systems Theory 10(1), 1–17 (1976)
14. Krishna, S.N., Mathur, U., Trivedi, A.: Weak singular hybrid automata (2014), http://arxiv.org/abs/1311.3826
15. Laroussinie, F., Markey, N., Schnoebelen, P.: Model checking timed automata with one or two clocks. In: Gardner, P., Yoshida, N. (eds.) CONCUR 2004. LNCS, vol. 3170, pp. 387–401. Springer, Heidelberg (2004)
16. Markey, N.: Verification of Embedded Systems – Algorithms and Complexity. Mémoire d'habilitation, ENS Cachan, France (April 2011)
17. Minsky, M.L.: Computation: finite and infinite machines. Prentice-Hall (1967)
18. Perrin, D., Pin, J.E.: Infinite Words—Automata, Semigroups, Logic and Games. Pure and Applied Mathematics, vol. 141. Elsevier (2004)
19. Sistla, A.P., Clarke, E.M.: The complexity of propositional linear temporal logics. J. ACM 32(3), 733–749 (1985)

Non-convex Invariants and Urgency Conditions on Linear Hybrid Automata

Stefano Minopoli and Goran Frehse

VERIMAG, Centre Équation - 2, avenue de Vignate, 38610 GIÉRES, France
{stefano.minopoli,goran.frehse}@imag.fr

Abstract. Linear hybrid automata (LHAs) are of particular interest to formal verification because sets of successor states can be computed exactly, which is not the case in general for more complex dynamics. Enhanced with urgency, LHA can be used to model complex systems from a variety of application domains in a modular fashion. Existing algorithms are limited to convex invariants and urgency conditions that consist of a single constraint. Such restrictions can be a major limitation when the LHA is intended to serve as an abstraction of a model with urgent transitions. This includes deterministic modeling languages such as Matlab-Simulink, Modelica, and Ptolemy, since all their transitions are urgent. The goal of this paper is to remove these limitations, making LHA more directly and easily applicable in practice. We propose an algorithm for successor computation with non-convex invariants and closed, linear urgency conditions. The algorithm is implemented in the open-source tool PHAVer, and illustrated with an example.

1 Introduction

Linear Hybrid Automata (LHA) are discrete automata enhanced with real-valued variables and linear constraints [12]. Despite their syntactical simplicity, they admit a rich variety of behaviors. In LHA, the evolution of the variables over time is governed by differential inclusions, called *flows*, which can be simple intervals such as $\dot{x} \in [1, 2]$, or more complex linear constraints over the derivatives such as the conservation law $\dot{x} + \dot{y} = 0$. Changes of the discrete state admit arbitrary linear updates of the variables. For example, LHA can model discrete-time affine systems, a widely used class of control systems, by using discrete updates of the form $x^+ = Ax + b$.

Linear Hybrid Automata belong to the very few classes of hybrid systems for which set-based successor computations can be carried out exactly [1]. This makes them prime candidates for formal verification. LHA can serve as abstractions of systems that require not only timed behavior but quantitative information, e.g., to capture accumulation effects. The LHA abstraction can then be verified using model checkers such as HyTech [11] or PHAVer [9]. If the abstraction is conservative, verifying it implies that the real system satisfies the

A. Legay and M. Bozga (Eds.): FORMATS 2014, LNCS 8711, pp. 176–190, 2014.
© Springer International Publishing Switzerland 2014

specification; if the abstraction is an approximation that is not entirely conservative, its verification helps to find bugs and identify pertinent test cases.

In model-based design, the basis for building LHA abstractions is often an existing model, given in formats like Matlab-Simulink [14] or Modelica [15], which are the de-facto standard in many industries. Like the academic formalism Ptolemy [7], the semantics of these models are deterministic. In particular, a discrete transition is taken as soon as it is enabled, which is also referred to as urgent or as-soon-as-possible (ASAP) semantics. This can pose a problem when trying to build a corresponding LHA model, since LHA transitions do not force the system to change state when they are enabled. In particular, if the derivatives of the system happen to be zero when the guard is enabled, the system may remain forever at that state. One way to circumvent this problem is to add a clock to the controller model and periodically test (with a self-loop transition) whether the constraint is satisfied or not. This is a formally correct and conservative way to model such a system, and it even corresponds quite closely to actual behavior of process controllers, which periodically sample the sensors and set actuators. But it can tremendously increase the computational complexity of the verification task: the clock ticks introduce discrete state changes at a rate much higher than the time constants of the system, multiplying the number of sets of states that need to be computed. Another way is to build a LHA with extra locations whose invariants depend on the geometry of the urgency and flow conditions. But this requires several operations on polyhedra and one needs to disregard the reachable states in the extra locations. Our approach is to add *urgency* conditions to the LHA formalism and use a corresponding post-operator. Declaring certain states of the controller as urgent prevents time from elapsing, and one can now construct an LHA abstraction (or approximation) of deterministic transitions.

Existing algorithms for set-based successor computations of LHA require urgency conditions to either be independent of the continuous variables [11] or consist of a single constraint [9], which can be quite restrictive in practice. In this paper, we propose an algorithm to compute successor states for arbitrary, non-convex, closed urgency conditions. To be able to do so, we also propose an algorithm for computing successor states for general non-convex invariants, for which so far no algorithm is available. Related work is discussed in more detail for non-convex invariants in Sect. 2.3 and for urgency in Sect. 3.4.

The proposed algorithms are implemented in the open-source tool PHAVer on the SpaceEx tool platform [8]. The tool as well as all examples from this paper are available for download at `spaceex.imag.fr`. Detailed proofs are available in a technical report [16].

In the next section, we recall the basics on LHA and then propose our post operator for non-convex invariants. In Sect. 3, we propose our post operator for urgency conditions and make the connection to urgent transitions. The computation of reachable states with these operators is illustrated by an example in Sect. 4.

2   Linear Hybrid Automata with Non-convex Invariants

In this section, we give the syntax and the semantics description of a particular case of *Linear Hybrid Automata (LHA)*, where it is possible to define, for each location, a non-convex invariant.

2.1   Definition and Semantics

We first need to define some notation. A *convex polyhedron* is a subset of $\mathbb{R}^n$ that is the intersection of a finite number of strict and non-strict affine half-spaces. A *polyhedron* is a subset of $\mathbb{R}^n$ that is the union of a finite number of convex polyhedra. For clarity, we write $\widehat{P}$ if P is convex. The topological closure of P is denoted by $cl(P)$. Given an ordered set $X = \{x_1, \ldots, x_n\}$ of variables, a *valuation* is a function $v : X \to \mathbb{R}$. Let $Val(X)$ denote the set of valuations over X. There is an obvious bijection between $Val(X)$ and $\mathbb{R}^n$, allowing us to extend the notion of (convex) polyhedron to sets of valuations. We denote by $CPoly(X)$ (resp., $Poly(X)$) the set of convex polyhedra (resp., polyhedra) on X. We use $\dot{X}$ to denote the set $\{\dot{x}_1, \ldots, \dot{x}_n\}$ of dotted variables, used to represent the first derivatives, and X' to denote the set $\{x'_1, \ldots, x'_n\}$ of primed variables, used to represent the new values of variables after a discrete transition. Arithmetic operations on valuations are defined in the straightforward way. An *activity* over X is a function $f : \mathbb{R}^{\geq 0} \to Val(X)$ that is continuous on its domain and differentiable except for a finite set of points. Let $Acts(X)$ denote the set of activities over X. The *derivative* $\dot{f}$ of an activity f is defined in the standard way and it is a partial function $\dot{f} : \mathbb{R}^{\geq 0} \to Val(\dot{X})$.

A *Linear Hybrid Automaton* is a tuple $H = (Loc, X, Lab, Edg, Flow, Inv, Init)$ with

- a finite set Loc of *locations*; a finite set $X = \{x_1, \ldots, x_n\}$ of real-valued *variables*; a *state* is a pair $\langle l, v \rangle$ of a location l and a valuation $v \in Val(X)$; a finite set of labels Lab;
- a finite set Edg of *discrete transitions* that describes instantaneous changes of locations, in the course of which variables may change their value. Each transition $(l, \alpha, \eta, l') \in Edg$ consists of a *source location* l, a *target location* l', a label $\alpha \in Lab$, and a *jump relation* $\eta \in Poly(X \cup X')$, that specifies how the variables may change their value during the transition. The *guard* is the projection of η on X;
- a mapping $Flow : Loc \to CPoly(\dot{X})$ attributes to each location a set of valuations over the first derivatives of the variables, which determines how variables can change over time;
- a mapping $Inv : Loc \to Poly(X)$, called the *invariant*;
- a mapping $Init : Loc \to Poly(X)$, contained in the invariant, defining the *initial states* of the automaton.

The set of states of H is $S = Loc \times Val(X)$. Moreover, we use the shorthand notations $InvS = \bigcup_{l \in Loc}\{l\} \times Inv(l)$ and $InitS = \bigcup_{l \in Loc}\{l\} \times Init(l)$. Given a set of states A and a location ℓ, we denote by $A \!\downarrow_\ell$ the projection of A on ℓ, i.e. $A \!\downarrow_\ell = \{v \in Val(X) \mid \langle \ell, v \rangle \in A\}$.

Semantics. The behavior of a LHA is based on two types of steps: *discrete* steps correspond to the Edg component, and produce an instantaneous change in both the location and the variable valuation; *timed* steps describe the change of the variables over time in accordance with the $Flow$ component.

Given a state $s = \langle l, v \rangle$, we set $loc(s) = l$ and $val(s) = v$. An activity $f \in Acts(X)$ is called *admissible from* s if (i) $f(0) = v$ and (ii) for all $\delta \geq 0$, if $\dot{f}(\delta)$ is defined then $\dot{f}(\delta) \in Flow(l)$. An activity is *linear* if there exists a constant slope $c \in Flow(l)$ such that, for all $\delta \geq 0$, $\dot{f}(\delta) = c$. We denote by $Adm(s)$ the set of activities that are admissible from s.

Runs. Given two states s, s', and a transition $e \in Edg$, there is a *discrete step* $s \xrightarrow{e} s'$ with *source* s and *target* s' iff (i) $s, s' \in InvS$, (ii) $e = (loc(s), \alpha, \eta, loc(s'))$, and (iii) $(val(s), val(s')[X'/X]) \in \eta$, where $val(s')[X'/X]$ is the valuation in $Val(X')$ obtained from s' by renaming each variable in X with the corresponding primed variable in X'. Whenever condition (iii) holds, we say that e is *enabled* in s. There is a *timed step* $s \xrightarrow{\delta, f} s'$ with *duration* $\delta \in \mathbb{R}^{\geq 0}$ and activity $f \in Adm(s)$ iff (i) $s \in InvS$, (ii) for all $0 < \delta' \leq \delta$, $(\langle l, f(\delta') \rangle) \in InvS$, and (iii) $s' = \langle loc(s), f(\delta) \rangle$. Given a state $s \in S$ and a hybrid automaton H with initial set of states $Init$, s is said to be *reachable* in H if there exists a finite *run* $r = s_0 \xrightarrow{\delta_0, f_0} s'_0 \xrightarrow{e_0} s_1 \xrightarrow{\delta_1, f_1} s'_1 \xrightarrow{e_1} s_2 \cdots s_n$, such that $s_0 \in Init$ and $s_n = s$. We denote the set of reachable states by $Reach(H)$.

Classically, the algorithm that computes the set $Reach(H)$ is a fixed-point procedure, over all the locations $l \in Loc$, based on the *continuous post operator* and on the *discrete post operator*: given a set of states $S' \subseteq S$, the first one operator is used to compute the set of states reachable from S' by following an admissible trajectory, while the second one operator is used to compute the set of states reachable from S' via discrete transitions. Notice that the computation of the discrete post operator is not affected by the nature of the invariants, so we focus on the continuous post operator. The formal definitions are as follows:

Definition 1 (Post operators). *Given an hybrid automaton H, a location $\ell \in Loc$, a set of valuations $P, I \subseteq Inv(\ell)$, the continuous post operator $Post_\ell(P, I)$ contains the set of all valuations $v \in Val(X)$ reachable from some $u \in P$ without leaving I:*

$$Post_\ell(P, I) = \{v \in val(X) \mid \exists u \in P, f \in Adm(\langle l, u \rangle) \text{ and } \delta \geq 0 :$$
$$\forall 0 < \delta' \leq \delta, f(\delta') \in I \quad and \ f(\delta) = v\}. \quad (1)$$

The discrete post operator $Post_\varepsilon(P)$ contains the set of all valuations $v \in Val(X)$ reachable from some $u \in P$ by taking the discrete transition $\varepsilon = (\ell, \eta, \ell')$:

$$Post_\varepsilon(P) = \{v \in val(X) \mid \exists u \in P, (u, v[X'/X]) \in \eta \text{ and } v \in Inv(\ell')\}.$$

*From these operators on valuations we obtain the continuous and discrete post
operators for a set of states S by iterating over all locations and transitions:*

$$Post_c(S) = \bigcup_{\ell \in Loc} \{\ell\} \times Post_\ell(S\!\restriction_\ell, Inv(\ell)), \quad Post_d(S) = \bigcup_{(\ell, \alpha, \eta, \ell') \in Edg} \{\ell'\} \times Post_\varepsilon(S\!\restriction_\ell).$$

Note that definition (1) is valid regardless whether I is convex or not. It differs
slightly from the classic definition in that we do not require that $P \subseteq I$. This
trick is used in the next section to apply the operator iteratively to convex
partitions of a non-convex invariant. In this case, I is a convex subset of the
invariant but P is not necessarily a subset of I. For the sake of clarity, we will
denote by $Post_\ell(P, I)$ the continuous post operator when I is convex and by
$ncPost_\ell(P, I)$ when I is non-convex.

The reachable states $Reach(H)$ are computed as the smallest fixed point of
the sequence $S_0 = Post_c(InitS)$, and $S_{k+1} = S_k \cup Post_c(Post_d(S_k))$.

2.2 Computing the Continuous Post Operator with Nonconvex Invariants

In this section, after recalling how the continuous post operator is computed
when the invariant is a convex polyhedron, we give a sound and complete procedure that, given a non-convex invariant I and an initial set of valuations $P \subseteq I$,
computes the continuous post operator $ncPost_\ell(P, I)$. Given a linear hybrid automaton H, it is well known that the continuous post operator, on a location
$l \in Loc$, a convex invariant $I = Inv(\ell)$, a flow $F = Flow(\ell)$ and a set of initial
valuations $P \subseteq Inv(\ell)$, is given by:

$$Post_\ell(P, I) = (P \nearrow_F) \cap I, \tag{2}$$

where $P \nearrow_F$ are valuations on straight line trajectories starting in P with constant derivative $\dot{x} = c$ for any $c \in F$:

$$P \nearrow_F = \{x' \mid x \in P, c \in F, t \in \mathbb{R}^{\geq 0}, x' = x + ct\}. \tag{3}$$

The operator (3) is straightforward to compute for polyhedral sets, and is available in computational geometry libraries such as the Parma Polyhedra Library
(PPL) [2].

Before giving the fixed point characterization of $ncPost_\ell$, we need to introduce
some extra notation (some of them similar to operators defined in [6]). Given
polyhedra A and B, their *boundary* is

$$bndry(A, B) = \big(cl(A) \cap B\big) \cup \big(A \cap cl(B)\big). \tag{4}$$

Clearly, $bndry(A, B)$ is nonempty only if A and B are adjacent to one another
or they overlap; otherwise, it is empty.

Definition 2 (Potential entry). *Given a location ℓ and convex polyhedra A
and B, the potential entry region from A to B denotes the set of points on the*

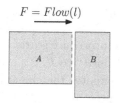
$F = Flow(l)$

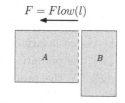
$F = Flow(l)$

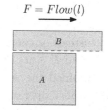
$F = Flow(l)$

(a) Case 1: the flow allows to reach B from $bndry(A, B)$.

(b) Case 2: the flow does not allow to reach B from $bndry(A, B)$.

(c) Case 3: the flow does not allow to reach B from $bndry(A, B)$.

Fig. 1. The computation of potential entry from A to B involves computing the boundary of A and B, and identifying states reachable on that boundary

boundary between A and B that may reach B by following some linear activity in location ℓ, while always remaining in $A \cup B$:

$$pentry_\ell(A, B) = \{p \in bndry(A, B) \mid \exists q \in A, \delta \geq 0 \text{ and } c \in Flow(\ell) :$$
$$p = q + \delta \cdot c \text{ and for all } 0 \leq \delta' < \delta, \ q + \delta' \cdot c \in A\}. \quad (5)$$

We call the above set the "potential" entry because it may happen that, even though $pentry_\ell(A, B)$ is not empty, the system is not able to reach valuations in B starting from a valuation in A (see Example 1, Fig. 1(c)). The following Lemma gives us a way to effectively compute the potential entry region.

Lemma 1. Given a location ℓ and convex polyhedra A and B, let $F = Flow(\ell)$, the potential entry region from A to B can be computed by:

$$pentry_\ell(A, B) = bndry(A, B) \cap A \nearrow_F .$$

From Lemma 1 follows the following Corollary:

Corollary 1. If $A \subseteq B$, then $A \subseteq pentry_\ell(A, B) \subseteq cl(A)$.

Example 1. Figure 1 shows two convex polyhedra A and B whose boundary is non empty (A and B are adjacent), where flow is represented by an arrow. Considering Figure 1(a), it is easy to check that the flow allows to reach valuations on the boundary between A and B starting from a valuation belongs to A, and then $pentry_\ell(A, B) \neq \emptyset$. Considering instead the case depicted in Figure 1(b) (same as the previous one except for the flow), there is no way to reach valuations belong to $bndry(A, B)$ starting from a valuation $u \in A$, and then $pentry_\ell(A, B) = \emptyset$. Figure 1(c) shows a case where the polyhedron B is not closed and then by following the flow, the system can never reach B, even if the starting valuation is on the top border of A. Notice that, even if B is not reachable from A, we have that $pentry_\ell(A, B) \neq \emptyset$: this clearifies why we denote this set as "potential".

Now we are ready to give a way to correctly compute the continuous post operator when the invariants could be non-convex. Given a LHA H and let $l \in$

Loc, $I = Inv(\ell)$, $F = Flow(\ell)$ and $P \subseteq I$. The idea is to build incrementally the sets of reachable valuations by considering each time a single convex component $\widehat{I'} \in [\![I]\!]$ instead of considering the entire invariant I. The procedure starts by finding, for all $\widehat{I'} \in [\![I]\!]$ and $\widehat{P'} \in [\![P]\!]$, the potential entry from $\widehat{P'}$ to $\widehat{I'}$.

Once obtained the set $pentry_\ell(\widehat{P'}, \widehat{I'})$, the procedure computes the classical continuous post operator on $pentry_\ell(\widehat{P'}, \widehat{I'})$ and $\widehat{I'}$. The procedure is applied recursively by building the sequence $W_0 \subseteq W_1 \subseteq \ldots W_{i-1} = W_i$ of the sets of the reachable valuations, with $W_0 = P$, and ends when no new valuation can be added to a set. When this happens, we have that $ncPost_\ell(P, I) = W_i$.

The formal relationship between the fixed-point procedure described above and the computation of the continuous post operator, when the invariant is non-convex, is given by the following theorem:

Theorem 1. *Given a location $\ell \in Loc$ and sets $P \subseteq Inv(\ell)$, $I = Inv(\ell)$, $ncPost_\ell(P, I)$ is the smallest fixed point of the sequence $W_0 = P$,*

$$W_k = \bigcup_{\widehat{W'} \in [\![W_{k-1}]\!]} \bigcup_{\widehat{I'} \in [\![I]\!]} Post_\ell(pentry_\ell(\widehat{W'}, \widehat{I'}), \widehat{I'}).$$

Moreover, the above sequence reaches the fixed point in at most $n = |[\![I]\!]|$ steps, that is $W_{n+1} = W_n$.

Notice that the role of $pentry_\ell(\widehat{W'}, \widehat{I'})$ is crucial in order to compute all and only those valuations that can be reached in $\widehat{I'}$ by always remaining in the global invariant I. This condition can not be ensured by applying the post operator directly on $\widehat{W'}$ instead of $pentry_\ell(\widehat{W'}, \widehat{I'})$ (see Section 2.3 in [16] for more details).

We prove Theorem 1 by induction on the number of the convex components of the invariant in which the system remains during a run. We define this number as follows. Given a polyhedron I and two valuations u and v, assuming that v is reachable from u via an admissible activity that always remains in I (i.e. always avoids $\overline{I}$), we denote by $d(u, v, I)$ the minimum number of convex polyhedra in $[\![I]\!]$ in which the system must remain in order to reach v from u via any admissible activity f:

$$d(u, v, I) = \min\{n > 0 \mid \exists f \in Adm(\langle \ell, u \rangle), \delta \geq 0, \widehat{I_1}, \ldots \widehat{I_n} \in [\![I]\!] :$$
$$f(\delta) = v \text{ and } \forall 0 \leq \delta' \leq \delta \; \exists j \in \{1, \ldots, n\} : f(\delta') \in \widehat{I_j}\}.$$

When there is no activity that can reach v from u avoiding $\overline{I}$, we write $d(u, v, I) = \infty$. Hence either $d(u, v, I) \leq |[\![I]\!]|$ or $d(u, v, I) = \infty$. For the induction proof, we define a version of $ncPost_\ell$ that takes into account only valuations v such that the system, in order to reach v, always remains in a fixed number of convex polyhedra in the invariant. Given a location ℓ and sets $P, I \subseteq Inv(\ell)$ and $i \leq |[\![I]\!]|$,

$$ncPost_\ell(P, I, i) = \{v \in ncPost_\ell(P, I) | \exists u \in P : d(u, v, I) \leq i\}.$$

Note that for all $i \leq j$, $ncPost_\ell(P, I, i) \subseteq ncPost_\ell(P, I, j)$.

We exploit the following, fundamental property of LHA: if there is an activity that goes from u to v inside the invariant, there is also a sequence of linear activities that does the same. Moreover, each linear activity is contained within one convex polyhedron of $[\![I]\!]$ and hence the connecting points between any two consecutive linear activities lie on the boundary between two polyhedra in $[\![I]\!]$. The following formalization is a reformulation of Lemma 2.2 in [18] given as Lemma 5 in [6]:

Lemma 2. *[6] Let u and v be valuations, and I a polyhedron. If $d(u, v, I) = i <$ ∞, then there is a sequence of linear activities $f_1, \ldots, f_i$, delays $\delta_0, \ldots, \delta_i$, and convex polyhedra $\widehat{I}_1, \ldots, \widehat{I}_i \in [\![I]\!]$ such that (i) $f_1 \in Adm(\langle l, u\rangle)$, (ii) $f_{i-1}(\delta_{i-1}) =$ v, (iii) for all $j < i$ it holds $f_j(\delta_j) \in bndry(\widehat{I}_j, \widehat{I}_{j+1})$ and $f_{j+1} \in Adm(\langle l, f_j(\delta_j)\rangle)$, and (iv) for all $j \leq i$ and $0 < \delta' < \delta_j$ it holds $f_j(\delta') \in \widehat{I}_j$.*

For lack of space, we only give a proof sketch of Theorem 1. The complete proof can be found in the appendix and in [16].

PROOF OF THEOREM 1. (Sketch) Let $n = |[\![I]\!]|$, first notice that for two valuation u and v, where $u, v \in ncPost_\ell(P, I)$, by definition of post operator $d(u, v, I) \leq |[\![I]\!]|$. Then trivially holds that $ncPost_\ell(P, I) = ncPost_\ell(P, I, n)$.

We show by induction that for all locations ℓ, polyhedra $P, I \subseteq Inv(\ell)$, and $i \geq 1$, $ncPost_\ell(P, I, i) = W_i$. The base case is straightforward, since it corresponds to a convex invariant.

We first discuss $ncPost_\ell(P, I, i) \subseteq W_i$. Consider a run that goes from some $u \in W_1$ through some $u' \in W_{i-1}$ to some $v \in ncPost_\ell(P, I, i)$. We need to show that $v \in W_i$. Let $\widehat{I}_{i-1}$ be the $i-1$th invariant visited on the run. If $u' \in \widehat{I}_{i-1}$, the proof is straightforward, since all reachable states in $\widehat{I}_{i-1}$ are in W_{i-1}. Otherwise, $u' \in \widehat{I}_i$. With Lemma 2, there is some $u^* \in \widehat{I}_{i-1}$ such that a straight line activity can be extended from u^* to u'. These states are contained in the potential entry set, and by definition also in W_i.

To show $W_i \subseteq ncPost_\ell(P, I, i)$, we need to show that W_i does not contain more states than $ncPost_\ell(P, I, i)$. Using case distinctions similar to the previous paragraph, we can show that W_i consists of states reachable using the convex post operator inside a convex invariant, plus the boundary states reachable by straight line trajectories. From Lemma 2, it follows that these boundary states are also in $ncPost_\ell(P, I, i)$, which concludes the proof.   □

2.3   Related Work

In [13], the author shows a different approach in order to tackle non-convex invariants. The proposed algorithm to compute the reachable set is built only for closed convex invariants, but this is not a restriction because (closed) non-convex invariants can be modeled by splitting locations. This means that starting from an automaton A with non-convex invariants, it is necessary to build an equivalent automaton B whose locations have only convex invariants: this is done by taking, for each location of A, the exact convex covering Q of the corresponding invariant and then, for each convex component $\widehat{Q} \in Q$, by adding a location to B whose associated (convex and closed) invariant is $\widehat{Q}$. Therefore, this approach does not work with non-closed invariants and needs a postprocessing phase in order to build the automaton B. Our approach tries to overcome these limitations: the reachability analysis is directly done by using the $ncPost_\ell$ operator, allowing the usage of non-closed invariants and avoiding the hidden process of building a new automaton.

3   Linear Hybrid Automata with Urgency

In this section, we extend LHA by allowing the possibility to attach to each location a so-called *urgency condition*. The urgency condition impedes time elapse, i.e., no continuous activities continue from a valuation that satisfies the condition. As we will see later, there is a connection between urgency conditions on locations and urgent semantics on transitions.

3.1   Definition and Semantics

We denote by $SPoly(X)$ the subset of $\mathbb{R}^X$ that can be obtained by finite disjunction of closed convex polyhedra. A *Linear Hybrid Automaton with Urgency (LHAU)* $H = (Loc, X, Lab, Edg, Flow, Inv, Urg, Init)$ consists of a LHA defined in Sect. 2 and a mapping $Urg : Loc \to SPoly(X)$, called *urgency condition*. To designate the urgent states, we use the shorthand $UrgS = \bigcup_{l \in Loc} \{\ell\} \times Urg(\ell)$.

Urgent transitions. In our definition, the urgency condition is defined for each location. An alternative approach, popular mainly because of its syntactical simplicity, is to designate each discrete transition as urgent or not. This is also referred to as *as-soon-as-possible (ASAP) transitions*. Urgent transitions can easily be translated to an urgency condition: Let $Edg_U \subseteq Edg$ be the set of urgent transitions. Then the equivalent urgency condition is the union of the outgoing guards, $Urg(\ell) = \{u \mid \exists (\ell, \eta, \ell') \in Edg_U : (u, v) \in \eta\}$.

Semantics. The urgency conditions affect only the timed steps, while the definition of discrete step remains the same as for LHA. Given a state $s = \langle l, v \rangle$, we define $loc(s) = l$ and $val(s) = v$. In order to give the semantics of timed-steps for $LHAU$ we define, for an activity $f \in Adm(s)$, the *Switching Time* of f in l, denoted by $SwitchT(f, U)$, as the value $\delta \geq 0$ such that, for all $0 \leq \delta' < \delta$, $f(\delta') \notin U$ and $f(\delta) \in U$. When for all $\delta \geq 0$ it holds that $f(\delta) \notin U$, we write $SwitchT(f, U) = \infty$. Informally, the switching time of an activity f in the location l specifies the maximum amount of time δ such that the system, by following the activity f, is allowed to remain in the location l.

Given two states s, s', there is a *timed step* $s \xrightarrow{\delta, f} s'$ with *duration* $\delta \in \mathbb{R}^{\geq 0}$ and activity $f \in Adm(s)$ iff *(i)* there exists the timed step $s \xrightarrow{\delta, f} s'$ in the LHA without urgency conditions, and *(ii)* $\delta \leq SwitchT(f, Urg(loc(s)))$.

Parallel Composition. We give a brief formal definition of parallel composition with urgency for the case where both automata range over the same variables. The key here is that the urgency condition of the composition is the union of the urgency conditions of the operands.

Definition 3 (Parallel composition). *Given linear hybrid automata with urgency H_1, H_2 with $H_i = (Loc_i, X, Lab_i, Edg_i, Flow_i, Inv_i, Urg_i, Init_i)$, their parallel composition is the LHAU $H = (Loc_1 \times Loc_2, X, Lab_1 \cup Lab_2, Edg, Flow, Inv, Urg, Init)$, written as $H = H_1 \| H_2$, where*

- $((l_1, l_2), \alpha, \eta, (l_2', l_2')) \in Edg$ *iff*
  - $\alpha \in Lab_1 \cap Lab_2$, *for* $i = 1, 2$, $(l_i, \alpha, \eta_i, l_i') \in Edg_i$, *with* $\eta = \eta_1 \cap \eta_2$, *or*
  - $\alpha \notin Lab_1$, $l_2' = l_2$, *and* $(l_1, \alpha, \eta, l_1') \in Edg_1$, *or*
  - $\alpha \notin Lab_2$, $l_1' = l_1$, *and* $(l_2, \alpha, \eta, l_2') \in Edg_2$ *;*
- $Flow(l_1, l_2) = Flow_1(l_1) \cap Flow_2(l_2)$; $Inv(l_1, l_2) = Inv_1(l_1) \cap Inv_2(l_2)$;
- $Urg(l_1, l_2) = Urg_1(l_1) \cup Urg_2(l_2)$; $Init(l_1, l_2) = Init_1(l_1) \cap Init_2(l_2)$.

3.2   Reachability

The discrete post operator for the class of $LHAU$ is trivially the same of the classical one, while the continuous one, that we call *Urgent Continuous Post Operator*, changes due to the extra condition induced by the operator *SwitchT*:

Definition 4 (Urgent continous post). *Given a linear hybrid automaton with urgency H, a location $\ell \in Loc$, and a set of valuations $P \subseteq Inv(\ell)$, let $I = Inv(\ell)$, and $U = Urg(\ell)$. The urgent continuous post operator $UPost(P, I, U)$ is defined as:*

$$UPost(P, I, U) = \Big\{ v \in val(X) \Big| \exists u \in P, f \in Adm(\langle \ell, u \rangle), \delta \geq 0 :$$

$$f(\delta) = v, \text{ for all } 0 < \delta' \leq \delta, f(\delta') \in I, \text{ and } \delta \leq SwitchT(f, U) \Big\}.$$

3.3   Computing the Urgent Continuous Post Operator

We now derive a construction of the urgent post operator, starting with the post operator for non-convex invariants and adding the states that are missing.

   The urgent post operator has to compute the valuations that are reachable from some set P without passing through states in the urgent set U. This includes the states that are reachable within the complement of U, so $ncPost_\ell(P \cap \overline{U}, I \cap \overline{U})$ is an underapproximation of $UPost_\ell(P, I, U)$. In the following, let $\mathbb{V}_{nc} = ncPost_\ell(P \cap \overline{U}, \overline{U})$ and $\mathbb{V}_U = UPost_\ell(P, I, U)$. The set $\mathbb{V}_{nc}$ trivially does not contain valuations that belong to U (since $\bar{U}$ is used in the invariant), while $\mathbb{V}_U$ also contains those valuations that touch U for the first time on a run. As shown in the examples of Figure 2, the system is allowed to remain on the boundary of an invariant for any time as the invariant is satisfied, while the system can not remain on the boundary of an urgency condition. In the instant the urgency

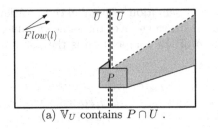 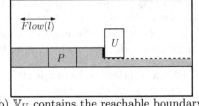

(a) $\mathbb{V}_U$ contains $P \cap U$.   (b) $\mathbb{V}_U$ contains the reachable boundary

Fig. 2. The urgent post states $\mathbb{V}_U = UPost_\ell(P, I, U)$ can be obtained from $\mathbb{V}_{nc} = ncPost_\ell(P \cap \overline{U}, I \cap \overline{U})$ plus the part (identified by the thick lines) of the boundary between $\mathbb{V}_{nc}$ and U that can be reached from $\mathbb{V}_{nc}$. The dashed lines identify the non-closed borders.

condition is met, the system can not evolve any more, i.e., it is forced either to stop the evolution of the continuous variables or to jump in another location. The thick lines in Figure 2(a) and Figure 2(b) identify the valuations on the boundary between $\mathbb{V}_{nc}$ and U that can be reached from $\mathbb{V}_{nc}$, and therefore they belong to $\mathbb{V}_U$.

In summary, we can compute $\mathbb{V}_U$ as the union of P, $\mathbb{V}_{nc}$ and the set of the valuations that belong to the boundary between $\mathbb{V}_{nc}$ and U from where it is possible to reach U by following some admissible activity. The latter set is obtained by using the potential entry operator. This is formalized as follows:

Theorem 2. *Given a location $\ell \in Loc$ and a set $P \subseteq Inv(\ell)$, let $I = Inv(\ell)$, $U = Urg(\ell)$, $\mathbb{V}_{nc} = ncPost_\ell(P \cap \overline{U}, I \cap \overline{U})$, and $B = \bigcup_{\widehat{A}' \in [\![\mathbb{V}_{nc}]\!]} \bigcup_{\widehat{U}' \in [\![U]\!]} pentry_\ell(\widehat{A}', \widehat{U}' \cap I)$. Then $UPost_\ell(P, I, U) = P \cup \mathbb{V}_{nc} \cup B$.*

3.4 Related Work

A general class of hybrid automata with urgency conditions is described in [17], but without giving the computation of the continuous post operator for urgency. In that work, the *Time Can Progress (tcp)* predicate specifies, for each location the maximum sojourn time, which may depend on the values of the variables when entering the location. This corresponds to the complement of our urgency condition. Notice that the semantics in [17] require the *tcp* to be satisfied when the location is entered. In our framework we relax this constraint by allowing to enter a location even if its urgency condition is already satisfied: in this case, the system must exit the location instantaneously. A similar urgency condition is described in the *Computational Interchange Format for Hybrid Systems (CIF)* (see [4]). For a more detailed and formal discussion of urgency, see [10] and references therein.

Urgent locations. In the classic LHA model checker HyTech, a transition can be designated as urgent by adding the keyword ASAP [13]. But this is restricted to transitions without guard constraints [11,13], which is equivalent to having *urgent locations*, i.e., locations in which time progress is not allowed. The real-time verification tool UPPAAL [5] similarly features urgent locations and urgent channels (synchronization labels) that can be used only on transitions without guard constraints. Urgent locations are semantically equivalent to adding an extra variable t, with dynamics $\dot{t} = 1$, that is set to zero when the location is entered and by attaching the invariant $t = 0$ to the location. In previous versions of our model checker PHAVER, transitions could be designated as urgent, but only if the guard consists of a single constraint, locally as well as in the composed model [9]. This restriction was imposed because it suffices to be able to compute the urgent post using the standard post operator for convex invariants.

Almost ASAP. In [19] the authors propose a relaxed semantics on asap transition in the context of the timed automaton, for the so called *almost asap* by delay δ. In practice, they define the *guard enlargement*, that means that transitions can be taken also with δ time delay. The rationale behind this approach is that no hardware can guarantee that a transition will always be taken in the exact moment as defined in theory. We could define a similar approach, not only on clock variables, in a simple but opposite way: it is enough to define the urgency condition by narrowing all the constraints by a quantity that is equal to the maximum variation of the variable in the time δ.

4   Example: Batch Reactor

To showcase the algorithm an its implementation, we present a modular model of a batch-reactor system, which is a variation of the case study in [3]. It shall illustrate that non-urgent transitions as well as urgent transitions with more than one guard constraint arise naturally.

The batch reactor is comprised of a reactor R1 and two buffer tanks B2,B3 connected by pipes. The reactor is used to create a product that is then made available to a consumer in the two buffer tanks, see the schematic in Fig. 3(a). A controller measures the fill levels in the reactor and the buffers, and opens and closes valves connecting the reactor to the buffers in order to produce and deliver the product to the consumer. The specification is to verify that neither buffer ever becomes empty, and that none of the tanks overflows.

We now present the LHA models. The controller automaton is shown in Fig. 3(d). The opening and closing of valves is modeled by synchronization labels. In the production step, the reactor is filled with educts (raw materials) coming from the outside. Details on the filling and reaction process itself are omitted since they are irrelevant to this example, but it does take a certain amount of time and produces an uncertain amount of product. This is modeled by the fact that the controller ends the filling process when the reactor level $x_1 \in [x_{1,full}, x_{1,max}]$, which is accomplished with the invariant $x_1 \leq x_{1,max}$ and a non-urgent transition with label *close_in* and guard condition $x_1 \geq x_{1,full}$. When the product is ready, the controller decides whether to fill buffer B2, buffer B3, or wait. The controller decides which buffer to fill using the following simple criteria:

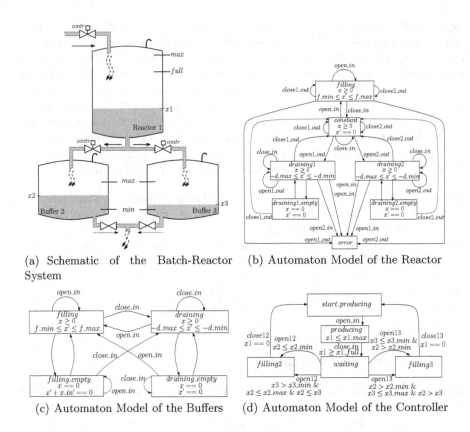

(a) Schematic of the Batch-Reactor System   (b) Automaton Model of the Reactor

(c) Automaton Model of the Buffers   (d) Automaton Model of the Controller

Fig. 3. Batch Reactor System: Schematic and Automata Models

– To avoid overflow, never start filling a buffer above a given maximum level.
– To avoid empty buffers, fill a buffer below a given minimum level.
– If the above is met, fill the buffer with the lower level.
– To be deterministic, prioritize B2.

All transitions for filling buffers B2 and B3 are urgent. The if-then-else structure of the criteria leads to guards with more than one constraint, some of which are strict inequalities. Thanks to the urgency, the controller model requires no clocks or while-loops.

The reactor automaton is shown in Fig. 3(b). The locations of the reactor correspond to the different combinations of open and closed valves. The model is simplified using the assumptions that the reactor must not be filled and drained at the same time (a common requirement in chemical engineering), and that only one of the buffers is filled at any given time. An error location is included so that violations of these assumptions can be detected. The transitions are not set as urgent in this automaton; the urgency in the composed system results from the controller.

The buffers are modeled each as an instantiation of the automaton shown in Fig 3(c). The outflow of the buffers is determined by the consumer, and therefore only known within the bounds (there is no valve to control outflow). The inflow

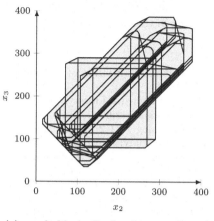 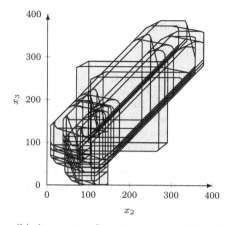

(a) reachable buffer levels x_2 and x_3 for safe parameter values

(b) decreasing the min. reactor outflow by 5% eventually leads to an empty buffer B3

Fig. 4. The evolution of the continuous variables of the batch reactor example, starting from location *start_producing* with initial values $x_1 = 0$, $x_2 = 100$ and $x_2 = 100$

is determined is equal to the outflow of the reactor. This leads to the dynamics $\dot{x}_i = [-d_{i,max}, -d_{i,min}] - \dot{x}_1$. Note that $\dot{x}_1$ is negative when the buffer is filling, so $\dot{x}_i$ is augmented by $-\dot{x}_1$ in this dynamics. Again, the transitions are not set as urgent; the urgency in the composed system results from the controller.

The specification was verified using SpaceEx/PHAVer (an implementation of the PHAVer reachability algorithm built on the SpaceEx platform). The inflow and outflow rates were set nondeterministically to be within intervals; the models incl. parameter values are available at `spaceex.imag.fr`. The computation of the complete reachable states shown in Fig. 4(a) takes 3.0 s and 24 MB of memory on a standard laptop. Finding the fixed point takes a total of 178 continuous post operations. Buffer 3 goes empty if the lower bound on the reactor outflow is reduced by 5%. The fixed point is found in 1153 post operations, which takes 18.7 s and consumes 24 MB of memory.

5 Conclusions

Linear Hybrid Automata stand out in the hybrid systems domain because sets of successor states can be carried out exactly. Available algorithms require convex invariants and single-constraint urgency conditions. In this paper, we propose algorithms that can handle non-convex invariants and (closed) non-convex urgency conditions. The practical impact is that this extension can be used in order to model systems in which transitions have to be taken as soon as possible. This is a common feature in several commercial tools used as de-facto standard in industry (for example in the automotive context) such as Matlab/Simulink or Modelica. We formally proved the correctness and the termination of the proposed procedures, which are based on two operators: the first one is the classical continuous post operator for convex sets $Post_\ell$ and the other one (defined here) is the so-called potential entry operator $pentry_\ell$. To the best of our knowledge, the proposed solutions represent the first sound and complete procedures for the task in the literature.

References

1. Alur, R., Henzinger, T., Ho, P.H.: Automatic symbolic verification of embedded systems. IEEE Trans. Softw. Eng. 22, 181–201 (1996)
2. Bagnara, R., Hill, P.M., Zaffanella, E.: The Parma Polyhedra Library: Toward a complete set of numerical abstractions for the analysis and verification of hardware and software systems. Science of Computer Programming 72(1-2), 3–21 (2008)
3. Bauer, N., Kowalewski, S., Sand, G., Löhl, T.: A case study: Multi product batch plant for the demonstration of control and scheduling problems. In: Engell, S., Kowalewski, S., Zaytoon, J. (eds.) ADPM 2000, pp. 383–388. Shaker (2000)
4. van Beek, D.A., Reniers, M.A., Schiffelers, R.R.H., Rooda, J.E.: Foundations of a compositional interchange format for hybrid systems. In: Bemporad, A., Bicchi, A., Buttazzo, G. (eds.) HSCC 2007. LNCS, vol. 4416, pp. 587–600. Springer, Heidelberg (2007)
5. Behrmann, G., David, A., Larsen, K.G.: A tutorial on UPPAAL. In: Bernardo, M., Corradini, F. (eds.) SFM-RT 2004. LNCS, vol. 3185, pp. 200–236. Springer, Heidelberg (2004)
6. Benerecetti, M., Faella, M., Minopoli, S.: Automatic synthesis of switching controllers for linear hybrid systems: Safety control. TCS 493, 116–138 (2012)
7. Buck, J.T., Ha, S., Lee, E.A., Messerschmitt, D.G.: Ptolemy: A framework for simulating and prototyping heterogeneous systems. Ablex Publishing Corp. (1994)
8. Frehse, G., Le Guernic, C., Donzé, A., Cotton, S., Ray, R., Lebeltel, O., Ripado, R., Girard, A., Dang, T., Maler, O.: SpaceEx: Scalable verification of hybrid systems. In: Gopalakrishnan, G., Qadeer, S. (eds.) CAV 2011. LNCS, vol. 6806, pp. 379–395. Springer, Heidelberg (2011)
9. Frehse, G.: PHAVer: algorithmic verification of hybrid systems past HyTech. STTT 10(3), 263–279 (2008)
10. Gebremichael, B., Vaandrager, F.: Specifying urgency in timed i/o automata. In: SEFM 2005, pp. 64–74. IEEE Computer Society (2005)
11. Henzinger, T.A., Ho, P.H., Wong-Toi, H.: Hytech: the next generation. In: Proc. IEEE Real-Time Systems Symposium, p. 56. IEEE Computer Society (1995)
12. Henzinger, T.: The theory of hybrid automata. In: 11th IEEE Symp. Logic in Comp. Sci., pp. 278–292 (1996)
13. Ho, P.H.: Automatic Analysis of Hybrid Systems. Ph.D. thesis, Cornell University, technical Report CSD-TR95-1536 (August 1995)
14. MathWorks: Mathworks simulink: Simulation et model-based design (Mar 2014), http://www.mathworks.fr/products/simulink
15. Mattsson, S.E., Elmqvist, H., Otter, M.: Physical system modeling with Modelica. Control Engineering Practice 6(4), 501–510 (1998)
16. Minopoli, S., Frehse, G.: Non-convex invariants and urgency conditions on linear hybrid automata. Tech. Rep. TR-2014-4, Verimag (April 2014)
17. Nicollin, X., Olivero, A., Sifakis, J., Yovine, S.: An approach to the description and analysis of hybrid systems. In: Grossman, R.L., Ravn, A.P., Rischel, H., Nerode, A. (eds.) HS 1991 and HS 1992. LNCS, vol. 736, pp. 149–178. Springer, Heidelberg (1993)
18. Wong-Toi, H.: The synthesis of controllers for linear hybrid automata. In: IEEE Conf. Decision and Control, pp. 4607–4612. IEEE (1997)
19. De Wulf, M., Doyen, L., Raskin, J.-F.: Almost ASAP semantics: From timed models to timed implementations. In: Alur, R., Pappas, G.J. (eds.) HSCC 2004. LNCS, vol. 2993, pp. 296–310. Springer, Heidelberg (2004)

Time-Bounded Reachability for Initialized Hybrid Automata with Linear Differential Inclusions and Rectangular Constraints

Nima Roohi and Mahesh Viswanathan

Department of Computer Science, University of Illinois at Urbana-Champaign, USA

Abstract. Initialized hybrid automata with linear differential inclusions and rectangular constraints are hybrid automata where the invariants, guards, resets, and initial values are given by rectangular constraints, the flows are described by linear differential inclusions of the form $ax + b \lhd_1 \dot{x} \lhd_2 cx + d$ (with $\lhd_1, \lhd_2 \in \{<, \leq\}$), and a variable x is reset on mode change whenever the differential inclusion describing the dynamics for x changes. Such automata strictly subsume initialized rectangular automata. Our main result is that while the control state reachability problem for such automata is undecidable, the time-bounded reachability problem is decidable.

1 Introduction

The reachability problem for hybrid automata [17] is very important from the standpoint of safety verification of cyberphysical systems. This problem has been carefully studied in the past couple of decades and boundaries of decidability have been extensively explored. The problem is stubbornly undecidable as evidenced by the many undecidability results in the area [2, 5, 19, 25, 31]. Results identifying decidable subclasses are few and rare. Apart from some low dimensional hybrid systems [5–7,23,28], the main classes of decidable hybrid systems are timed automata [3], initialized rectangular hybrid automata [19], semi-algebraic o-minimal systems [22], and semi-algebraic STORMED systems [31].

Given the computational difficulty of analyzing hybrid systems, time-bounded versions of classical decision problems have received much attention. It has been shown that time-bounded problems in many cases are computationally easier than the corresponding problems without time bounds [21, 26]. One particular problem that has been investigated recently is the time-bounded reachability problem, which asks if a certain control state of a hybrid automaton can be reached within a given time bound T. The time-bounded reachability problem has been shown to be NEXPTIME-complete for monotonic, rectangular hybrid automata, eventhough the same problem for non-monotonic rectangular hybrid automata is undecidable [10, 11].

In this paper we introduce a new class of hybrid automata called initialized hybrid automata with linear differential inclusions and rectangular constraints. Like initialized rectangular automata, the invariants, guards, resets, and initial

A. Legay and M. Bozga (Eds.): FORMATS 2014, LNCS 8711, pp. 191–205, 2014.

values in such automata are described by rectangular constraints, and variables are *initialized, i.e.*, whenever the continuous dynamics of a variable changes due to a mode switch, its value is required to be reset to value in an interval range. However, unlike rectangular automata, the continuous dynamics is given by *linear differential inclusions* of the form $ax + b \lhd_1 \dot{x} \lhd_2 cx + d$ (where $\lhd_1, \lhd_2 \in \{<, \leq\}$) [1]. In other words, the evolution of a continuous variable x is any trajectory $x : \mathbb{R}_{\geq 0} \to \mathbb{R}$ such that at any time t, $ax(t) + b \lhd_1 \dot{x}(t) \lhd_2 cx(t) + d$. Thus, such automata (henceforth called initialized linear inclusion automata for short) strictly subsume the class of initialized rectangular automata. We anticipate such automata to be useful in abstracting hybrid automata more precisely than initialized rectangular automata. Evidence of such an application can be seen in the use of eigenforms for abstracting linear systems [14].

We show that the reachability problem for initialized linear inclusion automata is undecidable by reducing the halting problem of 2-counter machines. In addition, the time bounded reachability for (uninitialized) linear inclusion automata is undecidable. This follows from the undecidability of the time bounded reachability problem for (non-monotonic) rectangular hybrid automata [10, 11]. In contrast, we show that the time-bounded reachability problem is decidable. Our decidability result is proved based on the following observations. Similar to the translation of initialized rectangular automata to timed automata [18, 19], we first reduce the reachability problem of initialized linear inclusion automata to the reachability of problem in an automaton all of whose continuous variables are clocks. Thus, we generalize an observation about rectangular flows to linear inclusion flows. The resulting automaton though is not a timed automaton because the constants used in the constraints could be of the form $r \ln r'$, where r, r' are rationals. We call such automata logarithmic timed automata. This difference is significant because reachability for such automata is undecidable; this is a consequence of our undecidability result for initialized linear inclusion automata. However, we show that the time-bounded reachability for such automata is decidable. Note, that our decidability result does not follow from the result in [11] — while clocks are special monotonic rectangular variables, the presence of irrational constants in our automata complicates matters. Our decidability proof relies on observing that if a control state q is reachable within time T, it is reachable by an execution with at most exponentially many discrete transitions. The algorithm deciding time-bounded reachability then guesses such an execution, and checks if the execution is valid. To check validity of an execution, we reduce the problem of checking negative cost cycles in an exponentially sized graph. The presence of irrational constants in logarithmic timed automata ensures that checking for negative cost cycles involves comparing linear combinations of natural logarithms of rational numbers with integers. All steps of our algorithm, except the step of comparing logs with integers, can be bounded by PSPACE. Even though natural logs can be approximated very efficiently (both in terms of space and running time) with arbitrary precison [9, 20, 29], we are unaware of any complexity bounds for computing a particular bit (say k) of

---

[1] Linear inclusions for each variable are scalar.

the natural logarithm of a rational number. This prevents us from proving hard upper bounds. We conjecture that the problem is in fact PSPACE-complete.

Due to space constraints many detailed proofs have been omitted, but can be found in [30].

Related Work. The decidability/undecidability boundary for the reachability problem in hybrid automata has been delineated through a collection of results; the main results are included in the following references [2,3,5–7,12,19,22,23,25, 28,31]. Given that the reachability problem is in general undecidable, approximations to the reachability problem (and the reachable set of states) have been introduced [1,8,15]. The time bounded reachability problem has been shown to be decidable for monotonic, rectangular hybrid automata in [10,11] and for o-minimal systems [16]. However, these classes of automata are incomparable to the class considered in this paper. O-minimal hybrid systems [16] require the continuous variables to be reset on every discrete transitions (or on every "cycle" of transitions), thus decoupling the discrete and continuous dynamics. Such a requirement is not imposed on our automata. Detailed comparison between monotonic, rectangular hybrid automata, and the automata considered here, is presented in the introduction, and the decidability proof.

2   Preliminaries

2.1   Sets and Functions Notations

$\mathbb{N}$, $\mathbb{Z}$, $\mathbb{Q}$, and $\mathbb{R}$ are respectively the set of *natural, integer, rational,* and *real* numbers. $\mathbb{Q}_+$ and $\mathbb{R}_+$ are respectively the set of *positive* rational, and real numbers, and $\mathbb{R}_{\geq 0}$ is the set of non-negative real numbers. $\leq$, $\geq$, $>$ and $<$ are the *ordering relations* on real numbers with their usual meaning. We assume ∞ is strictly larger and $-\infty$ is strictly smaller than all real numbers. For all $a, b \in \mathbb{R} \cup \{-\infty, \infty\}$, $[a, b]$ is defined to be the set $\{x \in \mathbb{R} | a \leq x \leq b\}$. $(a, b]$, $[a, b)$, and (a, b) are defined in a similar way. For any set A, $\mathcal{P}(A)$ denotes the power set of A and $|A|$ denotes its cardinality. For sets A and B, $A \cup B$, $A \cap B$, and $A - B$ denote respectively union, intersection, and difference of A and B. $A \to B$ is a (total) function from A to B, and $[A \to B]$ is the set of all (total) functions from A to B. For $r \in \mathbb{R}_+$, $\ln(r)$ and $\lg(r)$ are respectively the natural logarithm of r and $\frac{\ln(r)}{\ln(2)}$. For $f \in [A \to B]$ and set $C \subseteq A$, $f(C) = \{b \in B | (\exists a \in C) b = f(a)\}$. For any $f \in [A \to \mathbb{R}]$ and $t \in \mathbb{R}$, we define function $(f + t) \in [A \to \mathbb{R}]$ by $(f + t)(x) = f(x) + t$. We may sometimes omit parenthesis when it causes no confusion and use fa to denote $f(a)$. The set $\{0, \ldots, n - 1\}$ will be denoted by $[n]$.

A *rectangular* region is any subset of real numbers of the form $[a, b]$, $(a, b]$, $[a, b)$, or (a, b). We denote the set of all rectangular regions by $\mathcal{K}$. For $k \in \mathcal{K}$, l_k denotes the lower bound of k, and u_k denotes the upper bound of k. In addition, $\lhd_{l_k} \in \{<, \leq\}$ indicates if k is left closed and $\lhd_{u_k} \in \{<, \leq\}$ indicates if k is right closed. For example, if $k = (a, b]$ then $l_k = a$, $\lhd_{l_k} = <$, $u_k = b$, and

$\lhd_{u_k}$ $=\leq$. For $a \in \mathbb{R}$, we will use a to denote the rectangular region $[a, a]$ when it causes no confusion. Rectangular regions are closed under finite intersection. For $a_l, a_u \in \mathbb{R}$, $b_l, b_u \in \mathbb{R} \cup \{-\infty, \infty\}$, and $\lhd_l, \lhd_u \in \{<, \leq\}$, a *band* is defined to be $\{(y, x) \in \mathbb{R}^2 | a_l x + b_l \lhd_l y \lhd_u a_u x + b_u\}$ [2]. The set of all bands is denoted by $\mathcal{B}$. For each $p \in \mathcal{B}$ we denote elements of p by a_{lp}, a_{up}, b_{lp}, b_{up}, $\lhd_{lp}$, and $\lhd_{up}$. Furthermore, we denote $a_{lp}x + b_{lp}$ and $a_{up}x + b_{up}$ by $l_p(x)$, $u_p(x)$, respectively. We may also write p by $[a_{lp}x + b_{lp}, a_{up}x + b_{up}]$ if $\lhd_{lp} = \lhd_{up} =\leq$. For all $a, b \in \mathbb{R}$ we use $ax + b$ to denote $[ax + b, ax + b]$.

For every function $x \in [\mathbb{R}_{\geq 0} \to \mathbb{R}]$ that maps an input t to $x(t)$, the first derivative with respect to t will be denoted by either $\frac{dx}{dt}$ or $\dot{x}$. If $\dot{x} = ax + b$ for some $a, b \in \mathbb{R}$, then the solution is given by:

$$x(t) = \begin{cases} x(0)e^{at} + \dfrac{be^{at} - b}{a} & \text{if } a \neq 0 \\ x(0) + bt & \text{otherwise} \end{cases} \qquad (1)$$

2.2 Transition Systems and Hybrid Automata

Definition 1. *A transition system T is a tuple $(\mathsf{S}, \Sigma, \to, \mathsf{S}^{\mathsf{init}})$ in which S is a (possibly infinite) set of states, Σ is a (possibly infinite) set of labels, $\to \subseteq \mathsf{S} \times \Sigma \times \mathsf{S}$ is a transition relation, and $\mathsf{S}^{\mathsf{init}} \subseteq \mathsf{S}$ is the set of initial states.*

We write $s \xrightarrow{\alpha} s'$ instead of $(s, \alpha, s') \in \to$. We write $s \to s'$ as a shorthand for $\exists \alpha \in \Sigma \cdot s \xrightarrow{\alpha} s'$ and $\to^*$ denotes the reflexive transitive closure of $\to$. Finally for all $s \in \mathsf{S}$ we define $\mathsf{reach}_T(s)$ to be the set $\{s' \in \mathsf{S} | s \to^* s'\}$, and $\mathsf{reach}(T)$ to be $\bigcup_{s \in \mathsf{S}^{\mathsf{init}}} \mathsf{reach}_T(s)$.

For all transition systems T, we denote the elements of T by S_T, Σ_T, $\to_T$, and $\mathsf{S}_T^{\mathsf{init}}$. In addition, whenever it is clear we drop the subscript T to make the notation simpler.

Hybrid automata are used to model the interaction of a digital controller with physical processes. A hybrid automaton has a set of real-valued continuous variables that evolve with time, in addition to a set of discrete control locations. For an introduction to such automata see [17]. In this paper we consider a special class of hybrid automata that we define formally below.

Definition 2. *A hybrid automaton with linear differential inclusions and rectangular constraints A is a tuple $(\mathsf{Q}, \mathsf{X}, \mathsf{I}, \mathsf{F}, \mathsf{E}, \mathsf{Q}^{\mathsf{init}}, \mathsf{X}^{\mathsf{init}})$, where*

- *Q is a finite non-empty set of (discrete) locations.*
- *X is a finite set of variables.*
- *$\mathsf{I} \in [\mathsf{Q} \times \mathsf{X} \to \mathcal{K}]$ maps each location q and variable x to a rectangular region as the invariant of x in q.*
- *$\mathsf{F} \in [\mathsf{Q} \times \mathsf{X} \to \mathcal{B}]$ maps each location q and variable x to a band as the possible flows of x in q. For $p = \mathsf{F}(q, x)$ and $r \in \mathbb{R}$, we define $\mathsf{F}(q, x)(r)$ to be the rectangular region $\{z \in \mathbb{R} | l_p(r) \lhd_{lp} z \lhd_{up} u_p(r)\}$.*

---

[2] We assume $b_l \in \{-\infty, \infty\} \Rightarrow a_l = 0$ and $b_u \in \{-\infty, \infty\} \Rightarrow a_u = 0$. We also extend the $+$ operator to satisfy $(\forall r \in \mathbb{R}) r + \infty = \infty \wedge r + (-\infty) = -\infty$.

- E *is a finite set of* edges. *Each edge* $e \in \mathsf{E}$ *itself is a tuple of* (s, d, g, j, r) *in which*
  - $s, d \in \mathsf{Q}$ *are* source *and* destination *locations, respectively.*
  - $g \in [\mathsf{X} \to \mathcal{K}]$ *maps each variable* x *to a rectangular region as the* guard *condition of* e *for* x.
  - $j \in \mathcal{P}(\mathsf{X})$ *is the set of variables that their values will have* jump *after traversing* e.
  - $r \in [j \to \mathcal{K}]$ *maps each variable* x *to a rectangular region as the possible* reset *values of* x *after traversing* e.

  We write Se, De, Ge, Je, *and* Re *to denote different elements of an edge* e, *respectively. Also we denote* $(\mathsf{G}e)(x)$ *and* $(\mathsf{R}e)(x)$ *respectively by* $\mathsf{G}(e, x)$ *and* $\mathsf{R}(e, x)$.
- $\mathsf{Q}^{\mathrm{init}} \subseteq \mathsf{Q}$ *is the set of initial locations.*
- $\mathsf{X}^{\mathrm{init}} \in [\mathsf{Q}^{\mathrm{init}} \times \mathsf{X} \to \mathcal{K}]$ *maps each location* q *and variable* x *to the set of initial values for* x *in* q.

We only consider this class of hybrid automata in this paper, therefore whenever we write linear inclusion automaton we mean hybrid automaton with linear differential inclusions and rectangular constraints. Also a linear inclusion automaton is said to be initialized *iff for every edge* $e \in \mathsf{E}$ *and variable* $x \in \mathsf{X}$, *if* $\mathsf{F}(\mathsf{S}e, x) \neq \mathsf{F}(\mathsf{D}e, x)$ *then* $x \in \mathsf{J}e$, *i.e.* x*'s value is reset on taking edge* c. *Linear inclusion automaton that is initialized will be called initialized linear inclusion automaton. For all linear inclusion automata* A, *we display elements of* A *by* Q_A, X_A, I_A, F_A, E_A, S_A, D_A, G_A, J_A, R_A, $\mathsf{Q}_A^{\mathrm{init}}$, *and* $\mathsf{X}_A^{\mathrm{init}}$. *A valuation function* $\nu_A \in [\mathsf{X}_A \to \mathbb{R}]$ *assigns a value to each variable of* A *and we denote the set of all valuations by* Val_A. *We may omit the subscript when it is clear from the context.*

Semantics of Hybrid Automata. We define the semantics of hybrid automata as transition systems they represent [27]. The semantics of a hybrid automaton A is defined by the transition system $[\![A]\!] = (\mathsf{S}, \Sigma, \to, \mathsf{S}^{\mathrm{init}})$ in which

- $\mathsf{S} = \mathsf{Q} \times \mathsf{Val}$,
- $\Sigma = \mathsf{E} \cup \mathbb{R}_{\geq 0}$,
- $\mathsf{S}^{\mathrm{init}} = \{(q, \nu) \in \mathsf{S}_{[\![A]\!]} \mid q \in \mathsf{Q}^{\mathrm{init}} \wedge \nu \in \mathsf{X}^{\mathrm{init}}(q) \cap \mathsf{I}(q)\}$, and
- $\to = \to_1 \cup \to_2$ where
  - $\to_1$ is the set of time transitions and for all $t \in \mathbb{R}_{\geq 0}$ $(q, \nu) \overset{t}{\to}_1 (q', \nu')$ iff $q = q'$ and for all $x \in \mathsf{X}$ there exists a function $f_x \in [[0, t] \to \mathbb{R}]$ with a free variable x such that $f_x(0) = \nu(x)$, $f_x(t) = \nu'(x)$, $\forall u \in [0, t] \bullet f_x(u) \in \mathsf{I}(q, x)$, and $\frac{df_x}{dx}(u) \in \mathsf{F}(q, x)(f_x(u))$.
  - $\to_2$ is the set of jump transitions and for all $e \in \mathsf{E}$, $(q, \nu) \overset{e}{\to}_2 (q', \nu')$ iff $q = \mathsf{S}e$, $q' = \mathsf{D}e$, $\nu \in \mathsf{I}(q) \cap \mathsf{G}(e)$, $\nu' \in \mathsf{I}(q')$, and $\forall x \in \mathsf{X} \bullet x \in \mathsf{J}_A e \Rightarrow \nu'(x) \in \mathsf{R}(e, x)$ and $x \notin \mathsf{J}_A e \Rightarrow \nu(x) = \nu'(x)$.

  For all transition systems T, we display elements of T by S_T, Σ_T, $\to_T$, and $\mathsf{S}_T^{\mathrm{init}}$. We may omit the subscript when it is clear from the context.

For an initialized linear inclusion automaton A, any variable $x \in \mathsf{X}_A$, and any location $q \in \mathsf{Q}_A$, we define $\mathsf{cnst}_A(q, x)$ to be the set of constants appearing in invariants, guards, resets, and initialization involving variable x and location q (we may omit the subscript A when it is clear from the context). Formally $\mathsf{cnst}_A(q, x) = C_{A,\mathrm{I}}(q, x) \cup C_{A,\mathrm{G}}(q, x) \cup C_{A,\mathrm{R}}(q, x) \cup C_{A,\mathsf{X}^{\mathrm{init}}}(q, x)$ in which

- $C_{A,\mathrm{I}}(q, x) = \{r \in \mathbb{R} | r \in \{l_{\mathrm{I}(q,x)}, u_{\mathrm{I}(q,x)}\}\}$
- $C_{A,\mathrm{G}}(q, x) = \{r \in \mathbb{R} | \exists e \in \mathsf{E} \cdot q = \mathrm{S}e \land r \in \{l_{\mathrm{G}(e,x)}, u_{\mathrm{G}(e,x)}\}\}$
- $C_{A,\mathrm{R}}(q, x) = \{r \in \mathbb{R} | \exists e \in \mathsf{E} \cdot q = \mathrm{S}e \land r \in \{l_{\mathrm{R}(e,x)}, u_{\mathrm{R}(e,x)}\} \land x \in \mathrm{J}e\}$
- $C_{A,\mathsf{X}^{\mathrm{init}}}(q, x) = \{r \in \mathbb{R} | q \in \mathsf{Q}^{\mathrm{init}} \land r \in \{l_{\mathsf{X}^{\mathrm{init}}(q,x)}, u_{\mathsf{X}^{\mathrm{init}}(q,x)}\}\}$

We also define $\mathsf{cnst}_A(x)$ to be $\bigcup_{q \in \mathsf{Q}} \mathsf{cnst}_A(q, x)$, $\mathsf{cnst}^+{}_A(x)$ to be $\mathsf{cnst}_A(x) - \{0\}$, and $\mathsf{cnst}_A^{\max}(x)$ to be $\max(\mathsf{cnst}_A(x))$.

Observe that rectangular automata, stopwatch automata, and timed automata are all special kinds of linear inclusion automata obtained by restricting its elements. In a rectangular automaton all flows are given by rectangular regions (instead of bands), in a stopwatch automaton the flows are either 0 or 1 and initial values as well as reset values are always singleton, and in a timed automaton the flows are always 1 and initial values as well as reset values are always 0. In this paper we introduce a slight generalization of timed automata that we call logarithmic timed automata that have constraints that involve some irrational numbers. The formal definition of this class is presented next.

Definition 3. *Timed automata with logarithmic constants (logarithmic timed automata for short) is a class of timed automata in which constants could be in the form of r or $r \ln r'$ for some $r \in \mathbb{Q}$ and $r \in \mathbb{Q}_+$. In addition, we need the following conditions to be satisfied:*

1. *For any $x \in \mathsf{X}$ and $q \in \mathsf{Q}$ (at least) one of the following conditions must hold:*
   - *$\mathsf{cnst}(q, x) \subset \mathbb{Q}$. It means all constants in $\mathsf{cnst}(q, x)$ are rational.*
   - *$\exists c' \in \mathbb{Q} \cdot \forall c \in \mathsf{cnst}(q, x) \cdot \exists c'' \in \mathbb{Q}_+ \cdot c = c' \ln c''$. It means all constants in $\mathsf{cnst}(q, x)$ are in the form of $c' \ln c''$ for some fixed c'.*
2. *For any variable $x \in \mathsf{X}$ and edge $e \in \mathsf{E}$, if the following condition is satisfied then x must be reset by e (i.e. $x \in \mathrm{J}e$):*
   - *$\exists c_1 \in \mathsf{cnst}(\mathrm{S}e, x), c_2 \in \mathsf{cnst}(\mathrm{D}e, x) \cdot (c_1 \in \mathbb{Q} \Leftrightarrow c_2 \notin \mathbb{Q}) \lor (\nexists c, c_1', c_2' \cdot c_1 = c \ln c_1' \land c_2 = c \ln c_2')$. It means there are two constants c_1 and c_2 in the source and destination locations of e such that c_1 and c_2 are of different types.*

We call a timed automaton in which all constants are rational a rational timed automaton.

For a linear inclusion automaton A, a *path* is defined to be a finite sequence e_1, $e_2, \ldots, e_n$ of edges in E such that $\mathrm{D}e_i = \mathrm{S}e_{i+1}$ for all $1 \leq i \leq n-1$. A *timed path* π is a finite sequence of the form $(t_1, e_1), (t_2, e_2), \ldots, (t_n, e_n)$ such that $e_1, \ldots, e_n$ is a path in A and $t_i \in \mathbb{R}_{\geq 0}$ for all $1 \leq i \leq n$. A *run* ρ from s_0 to s_n is a finite sequence $s_0, (t_1, e_1), s_1, (t_2, e_2), \ldots, (t_n, e_n), s_n$ such that (a) $(t_1, e_1), \ldots, (t_n, e_n)$ is a timed path in A, (b) for all $0 \leq i \leq n$ we have $s_i \in \mathsf{S}_{[\![A]\!]}$, and (c) for all $0 \leq i < n$ there exists a state $s_i' \in \mathsf{S}_{[\![A]\!]}$ for which $s_i \xrightarrow{t_{i+1}} s_i' \xrightarrow{e_{i+1}} s_{i+1}$. We define duration$(\rho) = \sum\limits_{1 \leq i \leq n} t_i$. For any $T \in \mathbb{N}$, we say that ρ is T-*time-bounded* iff duration$(\rho) \leq T$.

The Reachability and Time-Bounded Reachability Problems. Given an initialized linear inclusion automaton A and $R \in [\mathbb{Q} \times \mathbb{X} \to \mathcal{K}]$ the (unbounded-time) *reachability* problem is to decide if for some $(q_0, \nu_0) \in \mathsf{S}^{\text{init}}_{[\![A]\!]}$ and $(q, \nu) \in$ flat(R), there is a run ρ from (q_0, ν_0) to (q, ν), where flat$(R) = \{(q, \nu) \in \mathsf{S}_{[\![A]\!]} | \forall x \in \mathbb{X} \bullet \nu(x) \in R(q, x)\}$. The *time-bounded reachability* problem asks if, given an initialized linear inclusion automaton A, $R \in [\mathbb{Q} \times \mathbb{X} \to \mathcal{K}]$, and $T \in \mathbb{R}_{\geq 0}$, there is some $(q_0, \nu_0) \in \mathsf{S}^{\text{init}}_{[\![A]\!]}$, $(q, \nu) \in$ flat(R), and run ρ such that ρ is a run from (q_0, ν_0) to (q, ν) and duration$(\rho) \leq T$.

3   Time-Bounded Reachability

In this section we consider the problems of reachability and time-bounded reachability in initialized linear inclusion automata. We begin by observing that the (unbounded time) reachability problem is undecidable.

Theorem 1. *Unbounded time reachability for initialized linear inclusion automata is undecidable.*

Proof (Sketch). The result is proved by reducing the halting problem for 2-counter machines. It is an adaptation of Miller's proof [24] showing that the reachability problem for timed automata with irrational constants is undecidable. The reason why the construction needs to be modified is because Miller's automata compares variables with both rational and irrational constants without resetting them between the two comparisons. However the initialization requirement of initialized linear inclusion automaton forces one to reset variables when it is compared to different constants.

Though the reachability problem is undecidable for initialized linear inclusion automata (Theorem 1), we will show that time-bounded reachability is decidable. We begin by observing that the reachability problem (bounded and unbounded) for initialized linear inclusion automata can be reduced to the reachability problem (bounded and unbounded) for logarithmic timed automata. Thus, our algorithm for time-bounded reachability will be presented for logarithmic timed automata.

Proposition 1. *For any initialized linear inclusion automaton A with size n, there is a logarithmic timed automaton D with size at most $2^{O(n \lg n)}$ such that D has the same (bounded as well as unbounded time) reachability information.*

Proof (Sketch). The construction of the logarithmic timed automaton D is similar to the construction of rational timed automaton for an initialized rectangular automaton [19]. Thus, we first construct an automaton that tracks the extremal flows in each control state, then replace each variable by a clock that tracks the time since the last reset, and finally tranform this stopwatch automaton to a logarithmic timed automaton. The correctness relies on observing that even though the set of reachable states for a single control mode is not convex under linear inclusion flows (unlike rectangular dynamics), the set of values reached for any variable at a given time is an interval.

The constants in the logarithmic timed automaton D constructed by Proposition 1 are not rational. Thus, we cannot use the well known techniques for analyzing rational timed automata [3]. Our proof relies on first observing that if a configuration (q, ν) is reachable in D within bounded time T, it is reachable by an execution of bounded length. Our algorithm therefore guesses an execution of this length and checks if it is a valid execution by solving some constraints (Section 3.2). Finally, we show that the problem is PSPACE-hard in Section 4.

3.1 Bounding the Execution Length in Logarithmic Timed Automata

Our algorithm guesses a path of a bounded length and decides whether it is a valid path that starts from some initial state and ends in some unsafe state. In this section we bound the length of this path that we need to guess. Our proof closely follows the proof outlined in [11] for monotonic hybrid automata. Notice that a logarithmic timed automaton is a special monotonic hybrid automaton with the difference that it may have irrational constants in its constraints. The presence of irrational constants introduces challenges that we address in this proof. We begin by giving a short outline of the proof in [11] to highlight the key challenges that will need to be addressed when considering logarithmic timed automata. We then present our proof.

Brihaye et al.'s Algorithm for Monotonic Hybrid Automata. The main observation in [11] is that if there is a run ρ of monotonic hybrid automaton D from state (q_1, ν_1) to (q_2, ν_2) such that duration$(\rho) \leq T$ then there is a shorter run ρ' from (q_1, ν_1) to (q_2, ν_2) of the same duration, whose length is exponential in the size of D and linear in T. The construction of ρ' from ρ relies on a *contraction operator*. The contraction operator identifies positions $i < j$ in ρ that have the same location such that all the locations between i and j are also visited before i in ρ. The operator then deletes all the locations $i+1, \ldots, j$ and adds their time to the other occurrences before i. Brihaye *et al.* apply this operator as many times as required until a fixpoint is reached. They show that resulting run (after contraction) has at most $|Q_D|^2 + 1$ edges. The problem of course is that the run after contraction may no longer be a valid run. The contracted run would be valid only if the run to which we apply contraction has some special properties. Brihaye *et al.*, therefore, first partition the run ρ carefully into exponentially many fragments such that the contraction operator can be reliable applied to these fragments, and the resulting run is a genuine run.

We now describe how they partition the run into fragments to which the contraction operator can be applied. Observe that since the contraction operator removes certain locations from the run by adding the time spent in these locations to the time spent in the same locations earlier in the run, such an operation can be sound only if the valuations in the merged locations satisfy the same constraints. If valuations in the merged location don't satisfy the same constraints then invariants and guards of transitions maybe violated by the merging process. Thus, Brihaye *et al.* first transform the automaton D into an automaton E that keeps track of the "region" of the valuation in its control state. Let D be an automaton with positive rates such that all constants appearing in the constraints are natural numbers (any automaton with rational constants can be transformed into such a machine) and cmax is the maximum constant in D. A region r (according to [11]) is a set of valuations that satisfy the same set of constraints of the form $x \lhd c$, where x is a variable of D, $\lhd \in \{<, \leq\}$ and c is a natural number $\leq$ cmax; thus a region r is similar to region of a timed automaton, except that the order of the fractional values is not maintained. The automaton E has locations of the form (q, r) where q is a location of D and r is a region, such that all its runs are *region consistent*. A run $\rho = ((q_0, r_0), \nu_0)$, $(t_1, e_1), ((q_1, r_1), \nu_1), \ldots, (t_n, e_n), ((q_n, r_n), \nu_n)$ is region consistent if $\nu_i \in r_i$ for all i. In addition, for variables x that enter a location with value 0, E keeps track of whether the value of x never changes from 0 before the next transition, or x becomes > 0 before the next transition. This is required to bound the number of sub-runs that are constructed later, and prevents the contraction operator from merging states where x stays 0 with those where x becomes > 0. The construction ensures that D admits a run between two states of duration T iff E admits a run between the same states and for the same duration T and length.

Let us consider an arbitrary T-bounded run ρ of E. Assuming that each location in E has a self loop that can be taken at anytime, one can construct an "equivalent" run ρ_0 that is the concatenation of at most $T \times$ rmax $+ 1$ shorter runs, each of duration at most $\frac{1}{\text{rmax}}$; these shorter runs are called type-1 runs. If rmax is taken to be the maximum rate of flow of any variable in E, then a type-1 run has the property that any variable changes its non-zero region at most 3 times within that run, because within $\frac{1}{\text{rmax}}$ time, no variable can change its value by more than 1. Splitting each type-1 run at the points when a variable changes its non-zero region, results in $3 \times |\mathsf{X}_E|$ type-2 runs, where variables with value ≥ 1 never change their region. The only change in regions involves variables whose value changes from 0 to a value in $(0, 1)$, and there could be unbounded number of region changes of this form. The contraction operator when applied to a type-2 results in a valid run, but the problem is that the valuation in the end state can be different after contraction. Changing the end state of run does not allow one to concatenate all the contracted type-2 runs to get a valid run of E. To address this problem each type-2 run is subdivided into type-3 runs based on when a variable was first and last reset within a type-2 run. Applying the contraction operator to type-3 runs, and then concatenating them back, results in a valid contracted type-2 run of the same duration, and same starting and ending states. These contracted type-2 runs are then concatenated back to get a run ρ_1 that is bounded length, has the same duration as ρ_0, and has the same start and end states. Having established that E has T-bounded runs iff E has T-bounded runs of length at most $F(D,T) = 24 \times (T \times \mathsf{rmax} + 1) \times |\mathsf{X}_D|^2 \times |\mathsf{Q}_D|^2 \times (2 \times \mathsf{cmax} + 3)^{2|\mathsf{X}_D|}$, the NEXPTIME algorithm to solve time-bounded reachability nondeterministically guesses a run of length at most $F(D,T)$ and solves a linear program to check if there are time values and valuations for each step that make the run feasible.

Time-Bounded Reachability for Logarithmic Timed Automata. The algorithm described in [11] (and outlined in above) cannot be directly applied to logarithmic timed automata due to the presence of irrational constants. There are 2 main challenges we need to address.

1. For the contraction operator to be correctly applied, we need a way to partition valuations into finitely many regions that ensures that all valuations in a region satisfy the same constraints. When irrational constants appear in constraints, we can no longer define regions based on how the values of variables compare to a finite set of natural numbers. Instead we need a new definition of regions.
2. Type-1 runs are runs of short duration, where there are only a bounded number of certain types of region changes. The duration for such a type-1 has to be such that any run can be divided into at most exponentially many type-1 runs. We will need to identify what the right duration of a type-1 run should be given the changed definition of regions.

We solve each of these challenges in order. We begin by describing a new definition of regions.

Definition 4. *Given a logarithmic timed automaton D, for each variable $x \in \mathsf{X}$ we define $\mathsf{reg}(x)$ as the set of intervals created by the constants used in constraints of x.*

$$\mathsf{reg}(x) = \{0^=, 0^+, (\mathsf{cnst}^{\max}(x), \infty)\} \qquad\qquad \cup$$
$$\{[c,c] | c \in \mathsf{cnst}^+(x)\} \qquad\qquad\qquad \cup$$
$$\{(a,b) | a, b \in \mathsf{cnst}(x) \wedge \forall c \in \mathsf{cnst}(x) \centerdot c \notin (a,b)\}$$

$\mathsf{Region}(D)$ *is the set of all functions that map each variable $x \in \mathsf{X}$ to an element of $\mathsf{reg}(x)$.*

A region $r \in \mathsf{Region}(D)$ can be thought of as the set of valuations ν such that for every variable x, $\nu(x) \in r(x)$ (where $\nu(x) \in 0^=$ and $\nu(x) \in 0^+$ iff $\nu(x) = 0$). We will interchangeably think of regions in this way.

Just like [11], in the definition of regions, we distinguish between the case when a variable is 0 and no time will be spent before the next transition ($0^=$), and when a variable is 0 but some non-zero time is promised to be spent before the next transition (0^+). The region definition above is different from [11] in that we only compare the value of variable to the constants that appear in the constraints, as opposed to all numbers upto some maximum bound. Using this new definition of regions, given a logarithmic timed automaton D, we construct automaton E that remembers the region of the valuation when a run enters a location.

The second challenge pertains to determining the duration of type-1 runs (and hence type-2 runs). In [11] the duration is picked to ensure two properties: (a) any run can be divided into an exponential number of type-2 runs, where the regions of variables don't change; (b) in a type-2 run, since the region of a variable does not change, all valuations in a type-2 run satisfy the same set of constraints, and so contracting the run results in valid run of E [3]. Now, we could pick the duration of a type-1 run to such that in any such run there are at most 3 changes to the region of any variable, by estimating the distance between any two constants that define regions. However, any estimation of the closest distance between two constants (of the form $r_1 \ln r_2$ and $r_3 \ln r_4$) appearing in a logarithmic timed automaton yields a doubly-exponential bound. This prevents us from exponentially bounding the number of type-2 runs.

Instead, we relax condition (b) when picking our duration to ensure that there are only exponentially many type-2 runs. Observe that in logarithmic timed automata, by definition, a variable cannot be compared with constants of different types (q_1 and $q_2 \ln q_3$, or $q_1 \ln q_2$ and $q_3 \ln q_4$ for $q_1 \neq q_3$) without being reset in between. Therefore, instead of requiring that type-2 runs consist of valuations belonging to the same region, we will instead define type-2 runs to be ones where the flows of the variables (in the original initialized linear inclusion automaton A) remain the same, and all valuations satisfy the same set of *relevant* constraints. Thus, even though two valuations in a type-2 run may satisfy different constraints (and don't belong to the same region, since they satisfy the same constraints that would pertain to them (without a reset), applying the contraction operation will yield a valid run. We, therefore, pick the duration of a type-1 run to be determined by the minimum distance between constants of the form r_1 and r_2, where r_1 and r_2 are rationals, or between constants of the form $r \ln r_1$ and $r \ln r_2$, where r, r_1, and r_2 are rational numbers. We have three cases:

- Both constants are rationals. In this case, the difference between two distinct constants cannot be smaller than $\frac{1}{2^{10n+2}}$.
- Both constants are logarithmic. In this case, if constants are in the form of $r \ln r_1$ and $r \ln r_2$ then $\ln \frac{r_1}{r_2}$ cannot be smaller than $\frac{1}{2^{20n+7}}$. When this number is multiplied by r it cannot be smaller than $\frac{1}{2^{21n+7}}$. Note that as a special case, $r \ln r_2 = 0$, the distant between $r \ln r_1$ and 0 cannot be smaller than $\frac{1}{2^{11n+4}}$.
- One constant is rational and the other one is logarithmic. We only need to consider the case when the rational number is 0, which is special case of the previous bullet.

If we take the duration of a type-1 run to be at most $\frac{1}{2^{21n+7}} = \min\{\frac{1}{2^{10n+2}}, \frac{1}{2^{21n+7}}\}$, the set of relevant and satisfied constraints is changed at most 3 times for any variable x. Now, any T-bounded run can be divided into at most $T \times 2^{21n+7} + 1$ type-1 runs. This concludes that $F''(D, T)$ the bound on length of the run that

---

[3] In addition we would like the contracted run to start and end in the same state. But this is easily accomplished by splitting type-2 runs into type-3 runs, and applying the contraction to type-3 runs.

is needed to be guessed is $24 \times (T \times 2^{21n+7} + 1) \times |\mathsf{X}_D|^2 \times |\mathsf{Q}_D|^2 \times (2\mathsf{K}_D + 3)^{2|\mathsf{X}_D|}$. Therefore $F''(D,T) \leq 24 \times (T \times 2^{21n+7} + 1) \times (2n+3)^2 \times 2^{10n+6} \times n^{12n+20} \times (n^3+1)^{4n+6} \times (2n^5+3)^{2n+6} \in 2^{O(n \ln n)}$.

3.2   Algorithm for Time-Bounded Reachability

Since a reachable configuration is reachable by bounded length execution, the algorithm for time-bounded reachability will guess an execution of appropriate length (using polynomial space), and check if the guessed execution is valid. Note that checking the validity of a guessed execution involves contraints with transcendental numbers, and hence cannot be solved using linear programming. We outline how this can be carried out.

Our path validity constraints are difference constraints of a special form. As has been observed in Theorem 3 in [4], checking feasibility of these constraints can be reduced to checking for the existence of negative cost cycles in a weighted directed graph; this graph has as many vertices as the length of run whose feasibility we are checking, and the weights are the constants appearing in the timed automaton. Alur *et al.* present a modified shortest path algorithm that checks the feasibility of these constraints and runs in time $O(|\mathsf{X}|^2 |\pi|)$, where π is the guessed run, and uses space only $O(|\mathsf{X}|)$. Thus, the space requirements are only polynomial in the size of the automaton and is independent of the length of the execution π. However, since this algorithm computes costs of paths, it involves adding weights and comparing them. To complete the description, we need to show how one can compare the costs arising during such a computation. The challenge involves comparing numbers involving natural logarithms. The algorithm in [4] only looks for simple cycles, and thus never adds the weight of an edge more than once in any of the values it computes. Thus, in the worst case, the algorithm requires comparing 0 with the sum of exponentially many constants. Observe that we have at most $O(n)$ distinct constants (n is bound on the size of the input automaton). Thus, the comparisons the algorithm needs to perform will be of the form $\sum_{0 \leq i < n} a_i \ln \frac{b_i}{c_i} < \sum_{0 \leq i < n} d_i$ where a_i, b_i, c_i, d_i are integers of $O(n)$ bits. There are many algorithms that efficiently compute natural logarithms with arbitrary precision; one can compute k bits of a number that approximates $\ln \frac{b}{c}$ (where b and c are n-bit integers) with error at most 2^{-k} using space that is polynomial in n and logarithmic in k by combining ideas in [13,20,29]. However, we are unaware of any complexity bounds on computing the kth bit of $\ln bc$, except in special cases like $\ln 2$ [32]. If the kth bit of a linear combination logarithms of n-bit rationals can be computed in PSPACE, then we can bound the complexity of our algorithm to PSPACE, because we only need to compute $O(n)$ bits of the left-hand side, since the right hand side is an integer with $O(n)$ bits.

In the absence of an algorithm to compute bits of natural log, we observe that the left hand side can never be equal to the right hand side, since the left hand side is an irrational number while the right hand side is an integer. Thus, our algorithm will compute the left hand side with increasing precision using either ideas from [13,20,29] or [9]. If the precision of our approximation is 2^{-k} and the difference between our approximation of the LHS and RHS is $> 2^{-k}$, then we can be sure of whether the inequality holds or not. Since the LHS is not equal to the RHS, we are guaranteed that eventually this will happen, giving us our decidability result.

We can prove the time-bounded reachability problem is PSPACE-hard (see Section 4). The NEXPTIME-hardness lower bound from [10, 11] does not seem to extend to this case. Intuitively, the main reason that in the simulation of a 2-counter machine, monotonic rectangular hybrid automata can multiply a counter by a constant in a constant amount of time. On the other hand, because our machines are initialized, this does not seem possible for initialized linear inclusion automata. Though we cannot give complexity bounds on our algorithm because of difficulties in bounding the complexity of computing natural logs, we conjecture that this problem is PSPACE-complete.

4   Time-Bounded Reachability is PSPACE-hard in Initialized Linear Inclusion Automata

Recall that the reachability problem (without time bound) is PSPACE-hard [3] for rational timed automata. The reduction described in [3] reduces the halting problem of a linear bounded automaton to the reachability problem of timed automata, where each step of the linear bounded automaton is simulated in fixed time τ by the timed automaton. Now, recall that a linear bounded automaton halts iff it halts in $N = |Q| \times (n+1) \times |L|^n$ steps, where $|Q|$ is the number of states of the linear bounded automaton, $|L|$ is the size of its tape alphabet, and n is the size of the input to the linear bounded automaton. Thus, the linear bounded automaton halts iff the constructed timed automaton reaches the desired control location within $T = N \times \tau$ time. Since $N \times \tau = O(2^n)$, we can write T in polynomial time.

5   Conclusion

In this paper, we considered initialized hybrid automata whose flows are described by linear differential inclusions, and whose invariants, guards, and resets are rectangular constraints. Such automata generalize both initialized rectangular automata and timed automata. We proved that the reachability problem (when time is not bounded) is undecidable, while the time-bounded reachability problem is decidable. The only reason why we cannot obtain a complexity bound on our algorithm is because we are unaware of any complexity bounds on computing the ith bit a natural logarithm of a rational number (except in special cases).

There are few open problems left by our investigations. The most interesting is obtaining complexity bounds on computing natural logarithms of rational numbers. Another question is whether the results in [11] can be extended to monotonic linear inclusion automata.

References

1. Agrawal, M., Thiagarajan, P.S.: The discrete time behavior of lazy linear hybrid automata. In: Morari, M., Thiele, L. (eds.) HSCC 2005. LNCS, vol. 3414, pp. 55–69. Springer, Heidelberg (2005)
2. Alur, R., Courcoubetis, C., Halbwachs, N., Henzinger, T.A., Ho, P.H., Nicollin, X., Olivero, A., Sifakis, J., Yovine, S.: The algorithmic analysis of hybrid systems. TCS 138(1), 3–34 (1995)
3. Alur, R., Dill, D.L.: A theory of timed automata. TCS 126, 183–235 (1994)
4. Alur, R., Kurshan, R.P., Viswanathan, M.: Membership questions for timed and hybrid automata. In: RTSS 1998, pp. 254–263. Press (1998)
5. Asarin, E., Maler, O., Pnueli, A.: Reachability analysis of dynamical systems having piecewise-constant derivatives. TCS 138(1), 35–65 (1995)
6. Asarin, E., Schneider, G., Yovine, S.: On the decidability of the reachability problem for planar differential inclusions. In: Di Benedetto, M.D., Sangiovanni-Vincentelli, A.L. (eds.) HSCC 2001. LNCS, vol. 2034, pp. 89–104. Springer, Heidelberg (2001)
7. Asarin, E., Schneider, G., Yovine, S.: Algorithmic analysis of polygonal hybrid systems, Part I: Reachability. TCS 379(1-2), 231–265 (2007)
8. Botchkarev, O., Tripakis, S.: Verification of hybrid systems with linear differential inclusions using ellipsoidal approximations. In: Lynch, N.A., Krogh, B.H. (eds.) HSCC 2000. LNCS, vol. 1790, pp. 73–88. Springer, Heidelberg (2000)
9. Brent, R.P.: Fast algorithms for high-precision computation of elementary functions (invited talk). In: Seventh Conference on Real Numbers and Computers (RNC7), vol. (7-8), July 10-12 (2006)
10. Brihaye, T., Doyen, L., Geeraerts, G., Ouaknine, J., Raskin, J.-F., Worrell, J.: On reachability for hybrid automata over bounded time. In: Aceto, L., Henzinger, M., Sgall, J. (eds.) ICALP 2011, Part II. LNCS, vol. 6756, pp. 416–427. Springer, Heidelberg (2011)
11. Brihaye, T., Doyen, L., Geeraerts, G., Ouaknine, J., Raskin, J.-F., Worrell, J.: Time-bounded reachability for monotonic hybrid automata: Complexity and fixed points. In: Van Hung, D., Ogawa, M. (eds.) ATVA 2013. LNCS, vol. 8172, pp. 55–70. Springer, Heidelberg (2013)
12. Casagrande, A., Piazza, C., Policriti, A., Mishra, B.: Inclusion dynamics hybrid automata. Inf. Comput. 206(12), 1394–1424 (2008)
13. Chadha, R., Kini, D., Viswanathan, M.: Quantitative information flow in boolean programs. In: Abadi, M., Kremer, S. (eds.) POST 2014 (ETAPS 2014). LNCS, vol. 8414, pp. 103–119. Springer, Heidelberg (2014)
14. Duggirala, P.S., Tiwari, A.: Safety verification for linear systems. In: Proceedings of EMSOFT (2013)
15. Fränzle, M.: Analysis of hybrid systems: An ounce of realism can save an infinity of states. In: Flum, J., Rodríguez-Artalejo, M. (eds.) CSL 1999. LNCS, vol. 1683, pp. 126–140. Springer, Heidelberg (1999)
16. Gentilini, R.: Reachability problems on extended O-minimal hybrid automata. In: Pettersson, P., Yi, W. (eds.) FORMATS 2005. LNCS, vol. 3829, pp. 162–176. Springer, Heidelberg (2005)
17. Henzinger, T.A.: The theory of hybrid automata. In: Proceeding of IEEE Symposium on Logic in Computer Science, pp. 278–292 (1996)
18. Henzinger, T.A., Ho, P.H., Wong-Toi, H.: Algorithmic analysis of nonlinear hybrid systems. IEEE Transactions on Automatic Control 43(4), 540–554 (1998)

19. Henzinger, T.A., Kopke, P.W., Puri, A., Varaiya, P.: What's decidable about hybrid automata? Journal of Computer and System Sciences, 373–382 (1995)
20. Hesse, W., Allender, E., Barrington, D.A.M.: Uniform constant-depth threshold circuits for division and iteratd multiplication. Journal of Computer and System Sciences 65(4), 695–716 (2002)
21. Jenkins, M., Ouaknine, J., Rabinovich, A., Worrell, J.: Alternating timed automata over bounded time, pp. 60–69. IEEE Computer Society, Los Alamitos (2010)
22. Lafferriere, G., Pappas, G., Sastry, S.: o-minimal hybrid systems. MCSS 13, 1–21 (2000)
23. Maler, O., Pnueli, A.: Reachability analysis of planar multi-linear systems. In: Probst, D.K., von Bochmann, G. (eds.) CAV 1992. LNCS, vol. 663, pp. 194–209. Springer, Heidelberg (1993)
24. Miller, J.S.: Decidability and complexity results for timed automata and semi-linear hybrid automata. In: Lynch, N.A., Krogh, B.H. (eds.) HSCC 2000. LNCS, vol. 1790, pp. 296–309. Springer, Heidelberg (2000)
25. Mysore, V., Pnueli, A.: Refining the undecidability frontier of hybrid automata. In: Sarukkai, S., Sen, S. (eds.) FSTTCS 2005. LNCS, vol. 3821, pp. 261–272. Springer, Heidelberg (2005)
26. Ouaknine, J., Rabinovich, A., Worrell, J.: Time-bounded verification. In: Bravetti, M., Zavattaro, G. (eds.) CONCUR 2009. LNCS, vol. 5710, pp. 496–510. Springer, Heidelberg (2009)
27. Prabhakar, P., Duggirala, P.S., Mitra, S., Viswanathan, M.: Hybrid automata-based CEGAR for rectangular hybrid systems. In: Giacobazzi, R., Berdine, J., Mastroeni, I. (eds.) VMCAI 2013. LNCS, vol. 7737, pp. 48–67. Springer, Heidelberg (2013)
28. Prabhakar, P., Vladimerou, V., Viswanathan, M., Dullerud, G.E.: A decidable class of planar linear hybrid systems. In: Egerstedt, M., Mishra, B. (eds.) HSCC 2008. LNCS, vol. 4981, pp. 401–414. Springer, Heidelberg (2008)
29. Reif, J.H., Tate, S.R.: On threshold circuits and polynomial computation. SIAM Journal on Computing 21(5), 896–908 (1992)
30. Roohi, N., Viswanathan, M.: Time-bounded reachability for initialized hybrid automata with linear differential inclusions and rectangular constraints. Technical report, University of Illinois at Urbana-Champaign (2014), http://hdl.handle.net/2142/49952
31. Vladimerou, V., Prabhakar, P., Viswanathan, M., Dullerud, G.E.: STORMED hybrid systems. In: Aceto, L., Damgård, I., Goldberg, L.A., Halldórsson, M.M., Ingólfsdóttir, A., Walukiewicz, I. (eds.) ICALP 2008, Part II. LNCS, vol. 5126, pp. 136–147. Springer, Heidelberg (2008)
32. Yap, C.: Pi is in log space, http://www.cs.nyu.edu/exact/doc/pi-log.pdf

Virtual Integration of Real-Time Systems Based on Resource Segregation Abstraction*

Ingo Stierand[1], Philipp Reinkemeier[2], and Purandar Bhaduri[3]

[1] University of Oldenburg, Germany
stierand@informatik.uni-oldenburg.de
[2] OFFIS, Germany
reinkemeier@offis.de
[3] IIT Guwahati, India
pbhaduri@iitg.ernet.in

Abstract. Embedded safety-critical systems must not only be functionally correct but must also provide timely service. It is thus important to have rigorous analysis techniques for determining timing properties of such systems. We consider a layered design process, where timing analysis applies when the system is integrated on a target platform. More precisely, we focus on contract-based design, and ask whether a set of real-time components continues to comply to a given system specification when it is integrated on a common hardware.

We present an approach for compositional timing analysis, and define conditions under which the system integration will preserve all the timing properties given by the system specification. Therefore, engineers can negotiate specifications of the individual components a priori, knowing that no integration issues will occur due to shared resource usage. The approach exploits ω-languages, which enables analysis techniques based on model-checking. Such an analysis is shown by a case study.

1 Introduction and Related Work

Developing safety-critical real-time systems is becoming increasingly complex due to the growing number of functions realized by these systems. Moreover, an increasing number of functions are realized in software, which are then integrated on a common target platform in order to save costs. The integration on a common platform causes interferences between the different software functions due to their shared resource usage. It is desirable to bound these interferences in a way to make guarantees about the timing behavior of the individual software-functions. A schedulability analysis delivers such bounds for interferences between software-tasks sharing a CPU by means of a scheduling strategy.

---

* This work was partly supported by the Federal Ministry for Education and Research (BMBF) under support code 01IS11035M, *Automotive, Railway and Avionics Multicore Systems* (ARAMiS), and by the German Research Council (DFG) as part of the Transregional Collaborative Research Center *Automatic Verification and Analysis of Complex Systems* (SFB/TR 14 AVACS).

A. Legay and M. Bozga (Eds.): FORMATS 2014, LNCS 8711, pp. 206–221, 2014.

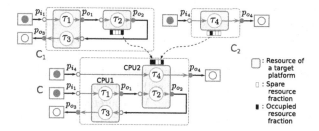

Fig. 1. Exemplary Integration Scenario using Resource Segregation

The platform integration is typically part of a larger design process with different phases. For safety-critical system design it is crucial that, starting with the initial design, all steps ensure that the final implementation indeed satisfies all given requirements. Contract-based design [2] provides a formal foundation allowing us to reason about the validity of a design in all phases. Based on well-defined semantics and operations, all design steps can be checked to verify the result still satisfies the overall system requirements.

Formal verification, such as with contracts, is however not an easy task, and requires carefully selected approaches in order to tackle computational complexity. We focus on the integration phase, where real-time components are allocated to the hardware platform. We present a compositional analysis framework using real-time interfaces based on ω-regular languages. Following the idea of interface-based design, components are described by interfaces and can be composed if their corresponding interfaces are compatible. The contribution of this work allows us to formally capture the resource demand of an interface, which we call *segregation property*. Compatibility of interfaces then can be reduced to compatibility of their segregation properties. Additionally, we put this into the context of contract-based design, enabling us to reason about the overall specification satisfied by the integrated implementation in a compositional way.

More specifically, we consider the following scenario. The bottom part of Figure 1 shows a target platform that is envisioned by say an Original Equipment Manufacturer (OEM). It consists of two processing nodes (CPU_1 and CPU_2). Suppose the OEM wants to implement two applications, components C_1 and C_2, on this architecture and delegates their actual implementation to two different suppliers. Both applications share a subset of the resources of the target platform, e.g. tasks τ_2 and τ_4 are executed on CPU_2 after integration. Furthermore, we assume the system specification C shown in Figure 1 to be given from previous design phases. While some components together with their (local) specifications may also be known (e.g. in case of reuse), the OEM generally has to negotiate proper specifications with the suppliers, in our case C_1 and C_2.

Now two tasks have to be accomplished: It must be ensured that (1) the composition of C_1 and C_2 conforms to the specification C, and (2) the composed implementation satisfies C as well. It is highly desirable that both tasks are performed before the suppliers start to implement the respective components. Later integration issues would require to repeat this step, causing increased development time and costs. To this end, the negotiation between the OEM and the suppliers must include the resource consumption needed by the implementations. Otherwise, the contract theory will fail to detect integration issues that may occur due to shared resource usage. We therefore assign a resource reservation to each component, guaranteeing a certain amount of resource supply. Then the timing behavior of both components can be analyzed independently from each other based on their resource demands and the guaranteed resource supply. Verification of the successful integration of C_1 and C_2 then amounts to checking whether the reserved resource supplies can be composed. We further define conditions under which the integrated application will satisfy its system specification. These conditions allow us to derive proper (real-time) specifications for the negotiation with the suppliers, and hence to tackle the first task.

There has been a considerable amount of study on compositional real-time scheduling frameworks [11,12,9,6,4]. These studies define interface theories for components abstracting the resource requirement of a component by means of demand functions [11,12], bounded-delay resource models [6], or periodic resource models [9,4]. Based on these theories the required resources of a component, captured by its interface, can, for example, be abstracted into a single task. This approach gives rise to hierarchical scheduling frameworks where interfaces propagate resource demands between different layers of the hierarchy. Our proposed resource segregation abstraction is an extension of the real-time interfaces presented in [3]. Contrary to the aforementioned approaches, our real-time interfaces and resource segregation are based on ω-regular languages. This means the approach can for example be employed in automata-based model-checking frameworks. In addition the results we present are not bound to specific task and resource models, like periodic or bounded delay.

Analytical methods provide efficient analysis by abstracting from concrete behavior. This, however, typically leads to over-approximations of the analysis results. Computational methods on the other hand, such as model-checking for automata ([1,7,5]), typically provide the expressive power to model and analyze real-time systems without the need for approximate analysis methods. This flexibility comes with costs. Model-checking is computationally expensive, which often prevents analysis of larger systems. The contribution of this paper will help to reduce verification complexity for the application of computational methods.

The paper is structured as follows: We start with an introduction of real-time interfaces as presented in [10], which characterize components including their resource demands. Section 3 recapitulates the basic notions of contract-based design that are consistent with our interfaces. Sections 4 and 5 provide the notions and results to reason about the integration of interfaces in a compositional way in the context of contract-based design. Section 6 shows the application of the approach by an example, and Section 7 concludes the paper.

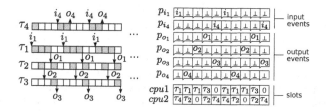

Fig. 2. Scheduling scenario (left) and exemplary trace-extract (right)

2   Real-Time Interfaces

A real-time interface characterizes a component when it is executed on a set of resources such as processing nodes and buses. Each interface represents a set of real-time tasks, and specifies a set of legal schedules when it is executed on the resources in discrete slots of some fixed duration. For example, consider a component with two tasks, τ_1 and τ_3, which are scheduled on a single resource. A schedule for this component can be described by an infinite word over the alphabet $\{0, \tau_1, \tau_3\}$, where 0 means the resource is idle during the slot, and τ_1 and τ_3 means the corresponding task is running.

Example 1. Suppose that task τ_1 is a periodic task with period $p = 5$ and execution time $c = 3$. The slot language of its interface can be described by the regular expression $0^{<5}[\tau_1^3 \, ||| \, 0^2]^\omega$, where $u \, ||| \, v$ denotes all possible interleavings of the finite words u and v. That means, a schedule is legal for the interface, as long as it provides 3 slots during a time interval of length 5. Observe that the slot language captures an assumption about the activation pattern of task τ_1. The part $0^{<5}$ of the regular expression represents all possible phasings of the initial task activation. This correlates to the formalism of event streams, which is a well-known representation of task activation patterns in real-time systems by lower and upper arrival curves $\eta^-(\Delta t)$ and $\eta^+(\Delta t)$ [8].

As interfaces also capture task activations and completions, we consider languages over tuples of symbols. A component has a set $P = P_{in} \uplus P_{out}$ of input and output ports. Symbols occurring at a port represent activation and completion events for the tasks that are connected to this port. The events observed at port $p \in P$ are characterized by the alphabet Σ_p, and we define $\Sigma_P = \Sigma_{p_1} \times \ldots \times \Sigma_{p_n}$. As task activations and completions need not occur at each time step, we define a special symbol $\bot$ denoting that no event occurs. Interfaces talk about sets R of resources that are running in parallel. To each resource $r \in R$ a set of tasks is allocated, which is represented by the alphabet Σ_r, as shown above.

Definition 1. *An interface is a tuple $I_K = (K, \Sigma_K, L_K)$ where $K = P \cup R$ is a set of ports P and resources R, $\Sigma_K = \prod_{k \in K} \Sigma_k$, $L_K \subseteq \Sigma_K^\omega$, and:*

- *For $k \in P$, Σ_k is the set of events, $\bot \in \Sigma_k$, that may occur at port k.*
- *For $k \in R$, Σ_k is the set of tasks, $0 \in \Sigma_k$, that run on resource k.*   ◇

Example 2. Suppose task τ_1 on the system depicted at the bottom of Figure 1 is as in Example 1. Task τ_2 depends on τ_1, i.e., is activated by τ_1, and has an execution time $c_2 = 2$. Task τ_3 depends on τ_2 and has an execution time $c_3 = 1$. Task τ_4 is also a periodic task with period $p_4 = 5$ and $c_4 = 2$. Suppose both CPUs are scheduled using a fixed priority preemptive policy, where tasks τ_1 and τ_4 have high priority on their CPU. The delay of the task-chain $\tau_1 \to \tau_2 \to \tau_3$ depends on the activation-pattern of τ_4 and its execution time. This is illustrated on the left of Figure 2. Once τ_1 completes execution it activates (via port p_{o_1}) τ_2, which in turn might be preempted by τ_4. Finally, τ_3, activated by τ_2, could be preempted by a subsequent instance of τ_1 resulting from another event i_1 of the periodic event stream. The interface of this system is $I_K = (K, \Sigma_K, L_K)$, $K = P \cup R$, $P = \{p_{i_1}, p_{i_4}, p_{o_1}, \ldots, p_{o_4}\}$ and $R = \{cpu1, cpu2\}$, $\Sigma_{p_{i_j}} = \{i_j, \bot\}$, $\Sigma_{p_{o_j}} = \{o_j, \bot\}$, $\Sigma_{cpu1} = \{\tau_1, \tau_3, 0\}$ and $\Sigma_{cpu2} = \{\tau_2, \tau_4, 0\}$. An excerpt of a possible trace in L_K is shown in Figure 2, which corresponds to the discussed scheduling scenario. Observe that every port has its own event tape in the interface, just as each resource has its own tape of time slots. Note that we omitted input ports connected to some output port: we define a connection between tasks by a unification of their ports to characterize a synchronization of the behavior.

The key to dealing with interfaces having different alphabets is a *projection* operation. For alphabet Σ, language $L \subseteq \Sigma^\omega$, and $\Sigma' \subseteq \Sigma$, we consider the projection $proj(\Sigma, \Sigma')(L)$ to Σ', which is the unique extension of the function $\Sigma \to \Sigma'$ that is identity on the elements of Σ' and maps every element of $\Sigma \setminus \Sigma'$ to 0. We will also need the *inverse projection* $proj^{-1}(\Sigma'', \Sigma)(L)$, for $\Sigma'' \supseteq \Sigma$, which is the largest language over Σ'' whose words projected to Σ belong to L. We further define $proj(\Sigma, \emptyset)(L) := \emptyset$, and $proj^{-1}(\Sigma'', \emptyset)(\emptyset) := \Sigma''^\omega$.

For alphabets of the form $\Sigma_K = \Sigma_{k_1} \times \ldots \times \Sigma_{k_n}$, the projection operation is performed component-wise, i.e., for each k_i individually. Furthermore, we want to consider interfaces over different index sets. To this end, we define *normalization* operations. Let K and $K' \subseteq K$ be index sets. For an alphabet $\Sigma_{K'}$ we define $\Sigma_{K' \to K} = \prod_{k \in K} \Sigma'_k$ where $\Sigma'_k = \Sigma_k$ if $k \in K'$, and $\{0\}$ otherwise. For an alphabet Δ_K we define $\Delta_K|_{K'} = \prod_{k \in K'} \Delta_k$. We extend these operations to words and languages, i.e., we define $\omega_{K' \to K}$, $L_{K' \to K}$, $\omega_K|_{K'}$ and $L_K|_{K'}$, respectively.

Definition 2. *Let $N = \{1, \ldots, n\}$, and let $\Sigma = \Sigma_1 \times \ldots \times \Sigma_n$ and $\Delta = \Delta_1 \times \ldots \times \Delta_n$ be alphabets with $\Sigma_i \subseteq \Delta_i$ for $i \in N$. Define projection function $proj(\Delta, \Sigma)$: $\Delta^\omega \to \Sigma^\omega$ by the unique extension of the function $proj(\Delta, \Sigma)$: $\Delta \to \Sigma$ where $proj(\Delta, \Sigma)(\delta_1, \ldots, \delta_n) = (\sigma_1, \ldots, \sigma_n)$ such that $\sigma_i = \delta_i$ if $\delta_i \in \Sigma_i$, and 0 otherwise. For $M = \{i_1, \ldots, i_m\} \subseteq N$ and $\Sigma' = \Sigma_{i_1} \times \ldots \times \Sigma_{i_m}$ we define $proj(\Delta, \Sigma')(L) := proj(\Delta|_M, \Sigma')(L|_M)$.* ◇

In other words, if $\Sigma_i \subseteq \Delta_i$ then projecting a word over the larger alphabet Δ_i into a word over the smaller alphabet Σ_i will map any symbol from Δ_i not belonging to Σ_i to 0; symbols that belong to Σ_i will be mapped to themselves. The projection of a word over Σ then projects all elements i simultaneously. The inverse projection of a word over Σ_i results in a set of words where every 0 in the word is replaced by all the letters in Δ_i which are not in Σ_i. The inverse projection of a word over Σ results in a set of words with all combinations of replacements for the individual elements.

This notion of interfaces exhibits several interesting operations and properties [10]. In the considered context the composition operation is of importance, which obtains the set of schedules when two components are executed together:

Definition 3. *Let* $I_1 = (K_1, \Sigma_{K_1}, L_{K_1})$ *and* $I_2 = (K_2, \Sigma_{K_2}, L_{K_2})$ *be interfaces. The* parallel composition $I_1 \parallel I_2$ *is the interface* (K, Σ_K, L_K), *where*

- $K = K_1 \cup K_2$,
- $\Sigma_K = \prod_{k \in K}(\Sigma_{K_1 \to K}|_k \cup \Sigma_{K_2 \to K}|_k)$,
- $L_K = proj^{-1}(\Sigma_K, \Sigma_{K_1})(L_{K_1}) \cap proj^{-1}(\Sigma_K, \Sigma_{K_2})(L_{K_2})$ ◇

The intuition of this definition is that a schedule is legal for $I_1 \parallel I_2$ if its restriction to resources R_1 and the port set P_1 of interface I_1 is legal in I_1, and similarly for interface I_2. That means the tasks of an interface are allowed to run in a slot of resource $r \in R$ when r is idle in the other interface, i.e., the slot is not used in that other interface.

Note that the projection operation also captures the synchronization of the connected ports of I_1 and I_2, i.e., which events are synchronized in the composition. This is illustrated in Figure 2. Ports connected in the system are unified in the corresponding interface (e.g. port p_{o_1}), which means the same behavior can be observed at connected ports. In the following, we will write $L_1 \widehat{\cap} L_2$ for inverse projection followed by intersection when the common target alphabet is known from the context. So we could write $L_K = L_{K_1} \widehat{\cap} L_{K_2}$ in Definition 3.

3   Contracts and Virtual Integration

While our interfaces are suitable for expressing concurrent resource usage of an implementation, contracts are a suitable notion for specifications in upstream design phases. A main advantage of contract-based design is to distinguish explicitly responsibilities of the individual parts of a design. A contract is a pair (A, G) of assertions where A is an *assumption* about the environment of a component, and G is the *guarantee* the component offers to its environment [2]. Logically, this is equivalent to $A \Rightarrow G$. In the context of this paper, both assumptions and guarantees will talk about bounds on the frequency of task arrivals and time to completions. In addition, they capture dependencies between tasks, for example, by stating that "task 2 is triggered whenever task 1 completes".

Both the assumptions A and the guarantees G consist of task release (or arrival) times as well as task finishing (or completion) times. Again, these are modeled using ω-regular languages. The semantics of a contract is about the behavior observed at the *ports* P of a component. An ω-language of a contract is defined over the set Σ_P of *events*, and corresponds to time instants when either nothing happens (modeled by $\perp$), a task arrives (modeled by an event at the input port of the task) or finishes execution (modeled by an event at an output port). The contract (A, G), where $A \subseteq \Sigma_P^\omega$ and $G \subseteq \Sigma_P^\omega$, specifies promises on the arrival and finishing times of a set of tasks, given the assumptions on the arrival times of the same set of tasks. A dependency between tasks, such as task τ_i triggers task τ_j, is captured by the occurrence of an event at the port that connects the two tasks. When we compose components it becomes important to care about which ports contracts talk about. Hence we define a contract over a set of ports as a tuple $C = (P, \Sigma_P, A, G)$ where $A, G \subseteq \Sigma_P^\omega$.

An important objective of any design process is successive refinement. The contract theory provides the corresponding relation that states whether a specification C' refines another specification C. Indeed this is the case if C' can be used in any context as C, and if C' has a restricted behavior:

Definition 4. *[2] A contract C' refines another contract C, written $C' \preceq C$ if and only if $A \subseteq A'$ and $G' \subseteq G$.*   ◇

As the ultimate goal of the design process is to obtain an implementation, we also need to define under which conditions an implementation behaves as specified:

Definition 5. *[2] Let $C = (P, \Sigma_P, A, G)$ be a contract. An implementation M of the contract satisfies C, written $M \models C$, if and only if $M \cap A \subseteq G$.*   ◇

Note that contract refinement and satisfaction are consistent. When an implementation M satisfies a contract C', and C' refines C, then M also satisfies C. In our scenario, we indeed consider interfaces as implementations.

The last important operation in the present setting is contract composition. Systems are build from individual parts that are put together in order to provide the intended functionality. In a bottom-up design, the composed contract C is obtained from the contracts of the composed components. The operation is based on the observation that the assumption of a composed contract shall be the maximal behavior that does not cause integration errors. For contracts $C_1 = (A_1, G_1)$ and $C_2 = (A_2, G_2)$, the contract $C = C_1 \parallel C_2$ is given by:

$$A = \max\{A \mid A \cap G_1 \subseteq A_2 \wedge A \cap G_2 \subseteq A_1\} \tag{1}$$
$$G = G_1 \cap G_2 \tag{2}$$

For ω-languages the equations above result in the following definition. Note that, in order to reason about contracts over different port sets, the alphabets of the involved assertions must be made equal. This is done exactly as for interfaces:

Definition 6. *Let $C_1 = (P_1, \Sigma_{P_1}, A_1, G_1)$ and $C_2 = (P_2, \Sigma_{P_2}, A_2, G_2)$ be contracts. The composition $C_1 \parallel C_2$ is the contract $C = (P, \Sigma_P, A, G)$ where $P = P_1 \cup P_2$, $\Sigma_P = \prod_{p \in P}(\Sigma_{P_1 \to P}|_p \cup \Sigma_{P_2 \to P}|_p)$, and*

$$A = (A_1' \cap A_2') \cup (A_1' \cap \overline{G_1'}) \cup (A_2' \cap \overline{G_2'}), \qquad G = G_1' \cap G_2',$$

where $A_i' = proj^{-1}(\Sigma_P, \Sigma_{P_i})(A_i)$, $G_i' = proj^{-1}(\Sigma_P, \Sigma_{P_i})(G_i)$.   ◇

In a top-down design process we assume the system specification to be given. Though some components might be known (e.g. from previous versions of the design), the designers have a good understanding of what the system shall do. In this case, one can derive from Eq. (1) and (2) the conditions under which a system composed of individual parts conforms to a given specification. We call them *virtual integration conditions*:

Lemma 1. *For contracts* $C = (A, G)$, $C_1 = (A_1, G_1)$ *and* $C_2 = (A_2, G_2)$ *the following holds:* $C_1 \parallel C_2 \preceq C$ *if and only if* $A \cap G_1 \subseteq A_2$ *and* $A \cap G_2 \subseteq A_1$ *and* $G_1 \cap G_2 \subseteq G$. □

4 Compositional Virtual Integration

One important property of contract based design is that contracts can be *independently implemented*. In [2] this is formalized as follows: For all contracts C_1, C_2, C_1' and C_2', if $C_1' \preceq C_1$ and $C_2' \preceq C_2$ hold, then $C_1' \parallel C_2' \preceq C_1 \parallel C_2$. Thus, contracts can be *independently* refined towards a final implementation and composing these implementations always results in an implementation of the composed contracts. So considering real-time interfaces as implementations, one might expect: Given a system specification C, it can be decomposed into contracts C_i negotiated with suppliers. If $C_1 \parallel ... \parallel C_n \preceq C$ holds, as well as $I_i \models C_i$, then $I_1 \parallel ... \parallel I_n \models C$. However, it can happen that reasoning about integration based on the introduced contract formalism fails to detect integration issues when composing interfaces. To give an example, consider contracts C_1 and C_2, each specifying an assumption about events occurring with a period interval $[5, 6]$ at an input port, and as guarantee a deadline of 6 between events occurring at that input port until an event is sent at an output port. Now assume interfaces $I_1 \models C_1$ and $I_2 \models C_2$, each of which exactly mirrors the input and output behavior of C_1, C_2 respectively. Each interface has a single task with an execution time of 3 and both tasks share the same resource. Observe that all the formulas from above hold. However, $I_1 \parallel I_2$ only accepts input behavior for both input ports with a strict period of 6. This is due to the incompatible resource usages, i.e. the tasks are not schedulable under the assumed activation rates. Of course this is not what we want, since the assumption of $C_1 \parallel C_2$ tells us that a valid environment may send events with a period interval of $[5, 6]$. Hence, relying on the assumption and using $I_1 \parallel I_2$ in a context, where the environment sends events with a period of 5 would cause deadlines of C_1 and C_2 to be missed.

The cause of this problem is twofold: First, our specification in terms of contracts is incomplete. Since the contracts do not talk about resource usage, there is simply no way to detect integration errors due to resource sharing solely based on them. Second, satisfaction as per Definition 5 does not force the implementation to accept every behavior expressed by the assumption.

Our solution to these problems is, first, to define a notion of *characteristic contract* of an interface. This allows us to use the stricter contract refinement relation instead of satisfaction. Second, we define a *composability* criterion for interfaces, which avoids integration errors when composing them. As we consider real-time interfaces as implementations, we develop sufficient conditions for interface composability, which can be checked based on contracts and an abstraction of the resource usage of the interfaces. The latter allows us to check for proper integration in design phases before the actual implementation exists.

For the characteristic contract of an interface, we focus on the case where the assumptions define activations patterns for each input port, and the guarantees define execution deadlines [10]. As an interface includes the behavior observed at the component ports, it can serve as a specification. Expressing such a combined specification of assumption and guarantee as a contract is in general not easy. However, if one is interested in assumptions that talk only about the behavior of the input ports, as in our case, it becomes straightforward:

Definition 7. *Let I be an interface, and P be the set of ports in the index set $K = P \cup R$ of I. We define the characteristic contract $C_I = (A_I, G_I)$ of I, where $A_I = L_I|_{P_{in}}$ and $G_I = L_I|_P$.* ◇

As we have observed, composition of interfaces may restrict their accepted input behavior. The goal is to define *composability* of interfaces, such that this restriction does not occur. More formally, for composable interfaces the following should hold: $C_{I_1\|...\|I_n} \preceq C_{I_1} \| ... \| C_{I_n}$. For the definition of composability, we need a notion of "maximal resource usage" that allows us to reason about the maximum resource demand of an interface:

Definition 8. *Let $\omega = \sigma_0\sigma_1 ...$ and $\omega' = \sigma_0'\sigma_1' ... \in \Sigma^\omega$ where $0 \in \Sigma$. We say $\omega' \leq \omega$ if and only if $\forall i \in \mathbb{N} : \sigma_i = \sigma \implies \sigma_i' \in \{0, \sigma\}$. We extend this to words over tuple of symbols: Let be $\omega_K, \omega_K' \in \Sigma_K^\omega$. We say $\omega_K' \leq \omega_K$ if and only if $\forall k \in K : \omega_K'|_k \leq \omega_K|_k$.* ◇

A word ω' precedes ω if either both words agree on the usage of each slot σ_i, or that slot is not used in ω' (i.e. $\sigma_i' = 0$). In other words, a slot used in ω' ($\sigma_i' \neq 0$) is also used in ω. We extend this order on slot words to languages over Σ_K^ω:

Definition 9. *Let be $L_K, L_K' \subseteq \Sigma_K^\omega$. We define $L_K' \sqsubseteq L_K$ if and only if $\forall \omega_K' \in L_K' : \exists \omega_K \in L_K : \omega_K' \leq \omega_K$.* ◇

Intuitively, $L_K' \sqsubseteq L_K$ means that the slot usage of *all* words $\omega_K' \in L_K'$ is "dominated" by *at least one* word $\omega_K \in L_K$. Note that $(\mathcal{P}(\Sigma_K^\omega), \sqsubseteq)$ is a pre-order, as $L_K \sqsubseteq L_K'$ and $L_K' \sqsubseteq L_K$ does not necessarily imply $L_K = L_K'$. We are interested in a particular subset of a slot language $L_K \subseteq \Sigma_K^\omega$, containing only those words from L_K with maximal execution demands:

Definition 10. *Given a slot language $L_K \subseteq \Sigma_K^\omega$, we define $\widehat{L_K} = \{\omega_K \in L_K \mid \forall \omega_K' \in L_K : \omega_K \leq \omega_K' \Rightarrow \omega_K = \omega_K'\}$* ◇

Intuitively, $\widehat{L_K}$ removes all words from L_K, whose slot usage is "dominated" by another word in L_K. $\widehat{L_K}$ is unique and maximal with respect to the order $\sqsubseteq$:

Lemma 2. *For every $L_K \subseteq \Sigma_K^\omega$ the subset $\widehat{L_K} \subseteq L_K$ is unique and maximal, i.e. $\forall L_K' \subseteq L_K : L_K' \sqsubseteq \widehat{L_K}$.* □

Now we can define the conditions for composability of interfaces, based on Definition 10 and Lemma 1:

Definition 11 (Composability of Interfaces). *Let I_1 and I_2 be two inter-faces. We say I_1 and I_2 are composable if:*

1. $L_1|_{P_{1in}} = \prod_{p \in P_{1in}} L_1|_p$ and $L_2|_{P_{2in}} = \prod_{p \in P_{2in}} L_2|_p$
2. $L_1|_{P_{2in}} \subseteq A_{I_2}$ and $L_2|_{P_{1in}} \subseteq A_{I_1}$
3. $\forall a \in L_1|_{P_{1in}} \overset{\curvearrowright}{\cap} L_2|_{P_{2in}} : \widehat{L_1(a)}|_{R_1} \overset{\curvearrowright}{\cap} \widehat{L_2(a)}|_{R_2} \neq \emptyset,$
   where $L_j(a) = \{\omega \in L_j \mid \omega|_{P_{jin}} = a|_{P_{jin}}\}.$ ◇

The first condition requires the behavior specified for the individual input ports of every component to be independent. The second one provides the virtual integration condition as in Lemma 1 (note that $L_i = A_{I_i} \cap G_{I_i}$). And the third condition requires that all components can be executed even if they expose maximal execution usage, considered separately for every possible activation.

The following result states that under these conditions the involved interfaces can indeed be composed without restricting their original input specification:

Theorem 1. *Let I_1 and I_2 be composable interfaces, and let $I = I_1 \parallel I_2$. Then $A_I = (A_{I_1} \overset{\curvearrowright}{\cap} A_{I_2})|_{P_{in}}$.* □

This result establishes the requested properties: Considering interfaces as implementations of their characteristic contracts, we can check whether their composition restricts input behavior:

Corollary 1. *Let I_1 and I_2 be composable interfaces. Then the following holds: $C_{I_1 \parallel I_2} \preceq C_{I_1} \parallel C_{I_2}$.* □

We use the above results to solve our initial integration problem as follows. Given the system specification $C = (A, G)$, the OEM can decompose it into sub-contracts $C_1 ... C_n$ during the negotiation phase with the suppliers. The property $C_1 \parallel ... \parallel C_n \preceq C$ establishes Condition 2) of Definition 11, provided the characteristic contracts of the interfaces implemented by suppliers refine their local sub-contract, i.e. $C_{I_i} \preceq C_i$. This is the responsibility of the suppliers. Further the assumption of each C_{I_i} must be such that Condition 1) of Definition 11 is satisfied. Condition 3) requires the interfaces to be known, which still remains an obstacle in the design flow. In the remaining part we introduce *segregation properties*, providing sufficient conditions to establish the third condition of Definition 11, which can be negotiated without knowing the final implementation.

5   Resource Segregation

A *segregation property* B_I for an interface I abstracts from the slot allocations of the legal schedules of I, by means of a set of *input-independent* slot reservations for which the interface is schedulable. Note that B_I indeed may reserve more slots than are used by the interface I. The basic idea is that composition of segregation properties B_{I_1} and B_{I_2} of interfaces I_1 and I_2 then combines non-conflicting slot reservations of B_{I_1} and B_{I_2}. If at least one such combination exists, then the third condition for composability of I_1 and I_2 holds.

Definition 12. *Let I_K be an interface, and let $B \subseteq \Sigma_R^\omega$ be a slot reservation language over R, the set of resources in K. B is a segregation property for I_K if and only if*

$$\forall b \in B, \forall a \in L_K|_{P_{in}} : \exists \omega \in \widehat{L_K(a)}|_R : \omega \leq b$$

where $L(a) = \{\omega \in L \mid \omega|_{P_{in}} = a|_{P_{in}}\}$ ◇

Hence B is a segregation property for I_K, if for *all* its possible activation patterns *each* word in B "dominates" at least one of the maximal execution demands resulting from the activation pattern.

The composition of slot reservation languages B_1 and B_2 is defined by $B_1 \widehat{\cap} B_2$. The condition for composability of slot reservation languages is rather simple:

Definition 13. *Two slot reservation languages $B_1, B_2 \subseteq \Sigma_R^\omega$ are composable if and only if $B_1 \widehat{\cap} B_2 \neq \emptyset$.* ◇

The following proposition states the desired sufficient condition for the third condition of interface composability based on their segregation properties.

Theorem 2. *Let I_1 and I_2 be interfaces with disjoint input port sets $P_{1_{in}}, P_{2_{in}}$ and disjoint output port sets $P_{1_{out}}$ and $P_{2_{out}}$. Let $B_i \subseteq \Sigma_R^\omega$ be segregation property for I_i. Then the following holds:*

$$B_1 \widehat{\cap} B_2 \neq \emptyset \implies \forall a \in L_1|_{P_{1in}} \widehat{\cap} L_2|_{P_{2in}} : \widehat{L_1(a)}|_{R_1} \widehat{\cap} \widehat{L_2(a)}|_{R_2} \neq \emptyset$$

where $L_j(a) = \{\omega \in L_j \mid \omega|_{P_{jin}} = a|_{P_{jin}}\}$. □

From Definition 12 follows that, given a segregation property B_I, *any* non-empty subset $B'_I \subseteq B_I$ is also a segregation property for interface I. In particular every $b \in B_I$ is a segregation property for I. Further, if I is schedulable under b, then it is schedulable under any slot reservation b' with $b \leq b'$. In other words, we can always reserve more slots for I without affecting its schedulability. This leads us to the following definition for refinement of slot reservation languages:

Definition 14. *Given slot reservation languages $B, B' \subseteq \Sigma_R^\omega$, we say B' refines B (B abstracts B'), denoted $B' \preceq B$, if and only if $\forall b \in B : \exists b' \in B' : b' \leq b$.* ◇

Similar to the order on slot languages, refinement for slot reservations is a pre-order $(\mathcal{P}(\Sigma_R^\omega), \preceq)$. Given a segregation property B_I, every B'_I with $B_I \preceq B'_I$ is also a segregation property for I. Hence, composability of segregation properties can be checked based on their abstractions, as stated by the following Lemma, which follows directly from Definition 14:

Lemma 3. *Let $B_1, B_2, B'_1, B'_2, \subseteq \Sigma_R^\omega$ be slot reservation languages such that $B'_1 \widehat{\cap} B'_2 \neq \emptyset$, then $B_1 \preceq B'_1$ and $B_2 \preceq B'_2$ implies $B_1 \widehat{\cap} B_2 \neq \emptyset$.* □

This allows us to augment contract-based design with resource reservations by associating with contract C a slot reservation B. In this combined specification (C, B), contracts are refined together with their slot reservation. Composition of (C_1, B_1) and (C_2, B_2) amounts to composing the contracts as well as their slot reservations, i.e. $(C_1, B_1) \parallel (C_2, B_2) = (C_1 \parallel C_2, B_1 \parallel B_2)$. An implementation I satisfies (C, B) if $C_I \preceq C$ and B is a segregation property for I.

6   Case Study

We apply the approach to a case study from the automotive domain as depicted in Figure 3. The system under investigation has two components that control

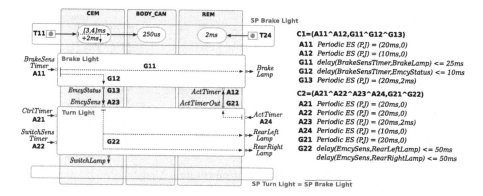

Fig. 3. Case Study: Components, Contracts and Segregation Properties

the signal lights of a car according to the drivers actions. The **Brake Light** component controls the rear brake lights according to the drivers brake pedal position. The pedal position is periodically sensed, which is characterized by the input port *BrakeSensTimer*. The activity of the brake lights is controlled by the output port *BrakeLamp*. The **Turn Light** component controls the turn lights according to the position of the turn switch and the warning light switch at the driver console. To this end, the component senses periodically the position of the switches (input port *SwitchSensTimer*), and actuates the turn indicator lights accordingly. In our case, these are the lights connected to the output ports *RearLeftLamp* and *RearRightLamp*, respectively (the front lights are omitted).

The system also implements an emergency brake signaling feature. Whenever the driver performs an emergency brake (which is indicated by a brute force brake action), then the car should activate both rear turn lights in order to signal following drivers about the emergency brake situation. The emergency brake detection takes place in the **Brake Light** component. It informs the **Turn Light** component via the *EmcyStatus/EmcySens* port connection about the current emergency brake status, which actuates the turn lights accordingly.

The OEM defines two timing requirements for the system. The first one states that the delay between the brake sensing and the activation of the brake light must be no greater than $25ms$. The second requirement states that the end-to-end latency between the brake sensing and the activation of the warning turn lights in case of an emergency brake situation must not exceed $60ms$.

Negotiation Phase: The OEM mandates different suppliers for the two component implementations. According to our approach, the OEM specifies contracts for the individual components, which are shown at the right part of Figure 3. The assumptions **A11** and **A12** define the activation patterns for the component **Brake Light** in terms of periodic event streams as discussed in Section 2. Assumption **A11** defines a periodic event stream with a period of $20ms$ for the sensing part, and **A12** defines a periodic activation with $10ms$ period for the

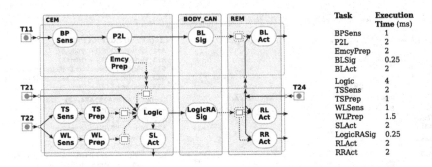

Fig. 4. Case Study: Implementation Model

actuator part. A similar situation holds for the assumptions **A21** and **A22** (20*ms*), and **A24** (10*ms*) for the component **Turn Light**. Note that these assumptions anticipate an implementation detail, as the OEM defined asynchronous activations for the individual parts of the components (sensing (**A11**, **A22**), control (**A21**) and actuator (**A12**, **A24**)). The deadline requirements are expressed by contract guarantees. The first one is local to **Brake Light**, and expressed by the guarantee **G11**. The second requirement expresses an end-to-end deadline across the two components. Here, the OEM has to split the deadline into two parts. In our case, the OEM selects 10*ms* for component **Brake Light**, expressed by the guarantee **G12**, and 50*ms* for component **Turn Light** (**G22**).

The applications shall be deployed on a hardware architecture with two ECUs. The sensing and control part shall be implemented on the ECU **CEM**, and the actuator part on the ECU **REM**. The ECUs are connected to the body CAN bus for exchanging data between the parts. The OEM provides for each part a time budget. The slot reservation for the **Brake Light** component is indicated by a set of real-time tasks (upper part of Figure 3). For example, the OEM ensures that the ECU provides $3 - 4ms$ execution time for sensing and control of the brake light part, and additional 2*ms* for the calculation of the emergency brake situation. This is expressed by the task at the top level corner of Figure 3. For the analysis, the slot reservation is represented by a finite state machine (FSM) that is generated in a separate analysis step. As **Brake Light** shall have higher priority, the slot reservation for the **Turn Light** component is simply the inverted FSM where non-occupied slots can be used, and vice versa.

Implementation: The suppliers eventually generate the implementation depicted in Figure 4. The **Turn Light** component implements sensing and pre-processing tasks for the turn switch (**TSSens**, **TSPrep**) and the warning lights (**WLSens**, **WLPrep**). The pre-processed data is read by the central **Logic** task, which generates control values for the individual actuator tasks. The data is sent via the CAN bus to the actuator tasks **RLAct** and **RRAct**, which are hosted at the ECU **REM**. The task also generates control data for the switch lights that reside in the driver console (**SLAct**). The brake pedal is sensed and preprocessed by the tasks **BPSens** and **P2L**, respectively. The latter sends the generated control

Table 1. Guarantee Verification Results

Guarantee	Brake Light	Turn Light	integrated
G11	$[5.25, 16.25]$	-	$[5.25, 15.25]$
G12	$[5, 6]$	-	-
G22	-	$[10.25, 46.25]$	-
G12+G22	-	-	$[15.25, 45.25]$
FSM states	28.021	225.945.919	41.806.561
explored states	109.262	932.377.509	265.473.150

values via the bus to the actuator task **BLAct**. The task **EmcyPrep** calculates whether an emergency brake took place. The dotted elements with a rectangle symbol indicate shared variables that store control values. The variables at the ECU **CEM** store the data from the pre-processing tasks. Whenever the **Logic** task is activated, it reads the stored values to generate the actuator control values. The shared variables at the ECU **REM** store these values for the actuator tasks. As the analysis has no functional (i.e. data dependency) aspect, we omit the variables in the analysis model in order to reduce computational complexity.

The trigger elements in the model (rectangles with a filled circle symbol) characterize the event streams conforming to the respective assumptions. Trigger **T11** for example implements an event stream that activates task **BPSens** every $20ms$ according to assumption **A11**.

Analysis: We first check the proof obligations imposed by the conditions of Definition 11. The independence of the individual input ports is trivially satisfied due to the definition of independent event streams for all inports. The second condition concerns the ports that connect the involved components. In our case, the required language inclusion is given by definition, which can be checked by comparing the definitions of **A23** and **G13**, and **A12** and **G21**, respectively. In general, however, a formal language inclusion check must be performed. For the third condition, requiring the composability of the component interface, we exploit Theorem 2. Hence, it must be ensured that the composition of the individual slot reservation languages does not impose an empty language. Also this is given by definition in our case, as the slot reservation of the one component is the inverted slot reservation of the other one.

The remaining proof obligation is to check whether the implementations of the individual components satisfy the given requirements, while using only slots that are given by the respective slot reservation language. The analysis employs an evolved version of the tool RTANA$_2$ for computational real-time scheduling analysis [10]. Three analysis runs have been performed. The first analysis checks whether the **Brake Light** implementation satisfies the guarantees **G11** and **G12**. To this end, the analysis model contains both the application tasks and the slot reservation FSM. The tool performs a scheduling analysis where the application tasks can only use time slots that are available according to the slot reservation scheme. The second run does the same with the **Turn Light** implementation and guarantee **G22**, using however the inverted slot reservation of the first run. The third analysis checked the integrated model for comparison, and also performed an end-to-end analysis of the guarantees **G12+G22**. The results are shown in Table 1. Note that the number of states are consistently larger for the analysis of the separate **Turn Light** component compared to the integrated analysis. This is due to the fact that the slot reservation scheme introduces an additional non-determinism for the analysis of the component.

Verification for the guarantees **G13** and **G21** is not shown. The latter is trivially given as the events of trigger **T24** are directly put through to component **Brake Light**. **G13** can be derived from **A11** and **G12**. A formal verification would require a language inclusion check, which is however not yet available in the tool. Finally, the (over-approximated) end-to-end latency **G12+G22** can be easily derived by adding the results from the separated analysis runs.

7   Conclusion

In this paper we have proposed a compositional method to verify proper component integration at an early design stage, while taking into account resource usage of implementations of respective components. The method combines contract-based reasoning for verifying refinement of a system specification by a set of component specifications, with resource segregation properties. We provided a set of conditions for the composability of resource segregation that guarantees preservation of the validity of the contract-based refinement check, when resource usage of implementations of the contracts are considered in a later design step.

We showed the application of the approach by a case-study from the automotive domain, containing all steps of the proposed design process. The verification steps employed an extended version of the prototype analysis tool for interfaces discussed in [10] with preliminary support of segregation properties.

References

1. Basu, A., Bozga, M., Sifakis, J.: Modeling Heterogeneous Real-time Components in BIP. In: Proc. Software Engineering and Formal Methods, SEFM (2006)
2. Benveniste, A., Caillaud, B., Nickovic, D., Passerone, R., Raclet, J.B., Reinkemeier, P., Sangiovanni-Vincentelli, A., Damm, W., Henzinger, T., Larsen, K.: Contracts for Systems Design (2013), INRIA Research Report No. 8147 (November 2012)
3. Bhaduri, P., Stierand, I.: A Proposal for Real-Time Interfaces in SPEEDS. In: Proc. Design, Automation Test in Europe, DATE (2010)
4. Easwaran, A., Anand, M., Lee, I.: Compositional Analysis Framework using EDP Resource Models. In: Proc. Real-Time Systems Symposium, RTSS 2007 (2007)
5. Guan, N., Ekberg, P., Stigge, M., Yi, W.: Effective and Efficient Scheduling of Certifiable Mixed-Criticality Sporadic Task Systems. In: Proc. Real-Time Systems Symposium, RTSS (2011)
6. Henzinger, T., Matic, S.: An Interface Algebra for Real-Time Components. In: Proc. of the 12th IEEE Real-Time and Embedded Technology and Applications Symposium (RTAS), pp. 253–266 (2006)

7. Perathoner, S., Lampka, K., Thiele, L.: Composing Heterogeneous Components for System-wide Performance Analysis. In: Design, Automation Test in Europe Conference Exhibition, DATE (2011)
8. Richter, K.: Compositional Scheduling Analysis Using Standard Event Models. Ph.D. thesis, TU Braunschweig, Germany (2005)
9. Shin, I., Lee, I.: Periodic Resource Model for Compositional Real-Time Guarantees. In: Proc. International Real-Time Systems Symposium (RTSS), pp. 2–13 (2003)
10. Stierand, I., Reinkemeier, P., Gezgin, T., Bhaduri, P.: Real-Time Scheduling Interfaces and Contracts for the Design of Distributed Embedded Systems. In: Proc. Symposium on Industrial Embedded Systems, SIES (2013)
11. Thiele, L., Wandeler, E., Stoimenov, N.: Real-Time Interfaces for Composing Real-Time Systems. In: Proc. International Conference on Embedded Software (EM-SOFT), pp. 34–43 (2006)
12. Wandeler, E., Thiele, L.: Interface-Based Design of Real-Time Systems with Hierarchical Scheduling. In: Proc. Real-Time and Embedded Technology and Applications Symposium (RTAS), pp. 243–252 (2006)

Timed Pattern Matching

Dogan Ulus[1], Thomas Ferrère[1], Eugene Asarin[2], and Oded Maler[1]

[1] VERIMAG, CNRS and the University of Grenoble-Alpes, France
[2] LIAFA, Université Paris Diderot / CNRS, Paris, France

Abstract. Given a timed regular expression and a dense-time Boolean signal we compute the set of all matches of the expression in the signal, that is, the set of all segments of the signal that satisfy the regular expression. The set of matches is viewed as a set of points in a two-dimensional space with each point indicating the beginning and end of a matching segment on the real time axis. Our procedure, which works by induction on the structure of the expression, is based on the following result that we prove in this paper: the set of all matches of a timed regular expression by a signal of finite variability and duration can be written as a finite union of zones.

1 Introduction

Pattern matching, the determination of all sub-sequences of a string of symbols that match some pre-specified pattern, is a fundamental operation in searching over texts and elsewhere. Pattern matching has been studied extensively for textual data starting from the 60s. The basic string matching algorithms for single words [KMP77, BM77] as well as specialized data structures such as suffix trees [Wei73] and later advancements can be found in [Ste94, CR02]. For more complex patterns, the classical regular expressions of [Kle56] is an adequate pattern description language supporting a minimal set of features (concatenation, alternation and repetition). It has been enhanced over the years by various features such as anchors, character sets and any-character [Fri06]. Pattern matching based on variants of regular expressions is implemented in many software tools ranging from the *grep* [Tho68] family to regular expression modules of modern programming languages, notably Perl and Python. Besides texts, pattern matching has important applications in Biology (DNA and protein searches) [AGM+90] and in database querying (especially temporal databases [FRM94]).

In this work we introduce a quantitative-time variant of the pattern matching problem where discrete sequences are replaced by dense-time, discrete-valued signals. As a pattern specification formalism we use a variant of the *timed regular expressions* of [ACM02] which are expressively related, in terms of timed languages, to the *timed automata* of [AD94]. We provide a complete solution to the timed pattern matching problem defined as: find *all* sub-segments of the signal that match the expression. Note that a straightforward application of the classical translations of regular expressions to automata can be used to detect whether the *prefix* of a string matches the pattern. The classical algorithm of Thompson [Tho68] adapted the automaton construction for the matching context but still, the discrete case, finding *all* matches of an expression in a

A. Legay and M. Bozga (Eds.): FORMATS 2014, LNCS 8711, pp. 222–236, 2014.
© Springer International Publishing Switzerland 2014

string is considered a very difficult problem and is not part of the mainstream (some exceptions are [Pik87] and [Lau00]). One reason might be that without a symbolic representation, which is necessary for the timed case, the set of matches may be prohibitively large to represent.

In addition to the theoretical interest, we believe that the problem of finding patterns in real-time data has numerous applications in many domains. This particular work was triggered by assertion-based circuit (dynamic) verification which is the hardware equivalent of what is called runtime verification in software. This form of lightweight verification consists in monitoring simulation traces against temporal specifications. Monitoring procedures for *temporal logic* formulas are well-studied and have been extended successfully to real-time and analog signals [MN04, MNP08]. However, standard assertion languages used in the semi-conductor industry such as PSL [EF06, CVK04] and SVA [VR06, Spe06] combine temporal logic with regular expressions in a non trivial way. The results of this paper can be used to extend monitoring procedures toward such specification languages and their timed extensions such as the one proposed in [HL11].

To give an intuition of what we do, consider the expression $\varphi := \langle (p \wedge q) \cdot \bar{q} \cdot q \rangle_{[4,5]} \cdot \bar{p}$ whose verbal description is as follows. Inside a time window of a duration between 4 and 5 there exists an interval where both p and q are high, followed by q going down and up again; after that time window there is an interval where p is low. If we look at signals p and q plotted in Fig. 1-(a), we can see φ is matched by any time intervals $[t, t']$ such that $t \in [1, 2]$ and $t' \in [6, 7]$. Clearly, the number of such segments of the signal (the *matches*) is infinite and two of them, $[1.3, 6.8]$ and $[1.5, 7.0]$ are shown in Fig. 1-(b).

Technically, our contribution is based on the following result. Let w be a Boolean signal defined over an interval $[0, d]$, let its restriction to the temporal interval $[t, t']$ be

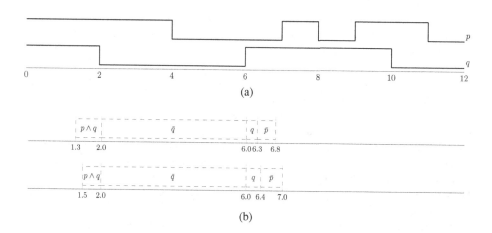

Fig. 1. (a) Boolean signals p and q; (b) Intervals $[1.3, 6.8]$ and $[1.5, 7.0]$ are two possible matches that satisfy φ over p and q

denoted by $w[t, t']$ and let φ be a timed regular expression. Then, the set of matches for φ in w,

$$\mathcal{M}(\varphi, w) = \{(t, t') : w[t, t'] \in [\![\varphi]\!]\}$$

is a finite union of zones. Zones are a special class of convex polytopes definable by intersections of inequalities of the form $c_1 \leq x_i \leq c_2$ and $c_1 \leq x_i - x_j \leq c_2$. They are used extensively in the verification of timed automata and admit a data-structure (difference-bound matrices, DBM) on which various operations, including all those required by the recursive computation of $\mathcal{M}(\varphi, w)$, can be carried out efficiently.

The rest of the paper is organized as follows. Section 2 defines the syntax and semantics of timed regular expressions. Section 3 illustrates the zone-based decomposition of match-sets, states the main result that is the finiteness of such a decomposition, and proves it by showing the following lemma: for every signal w of finite variability and expression φ there exist some k such that $\mathcal{M}(\varphi^*, w) = \mathcal{M}(\varphi^{\leq k}, w)$. Section 4 gives more details about the implementation of our algorithm with a practical bound on the convergence to a fixed point for φ^*. Section 5 reports the performance of the algorithm on several families of examples and is followed by a discussion of future work.

2   Timed Regular Expressions over Signals

Signals are the dense-time analogues of sequences, functions from a time domain into a value domain. We will work with Boolean signals but the results can be easily extended to any discrete value domain.

Definition 1 (Boolean Signals). *Let $\mathbb{T} = [0, d]$ be a bounded interval of $\mathbb{R}_+$ and let m be a positive integer. A* Boolean signal *is a function $w : \mathbb{T} \to \mathbb{B}^m$.*

We use $w[t]$ to denote the value of the signal at time t. An interval $I \subseteq [0, d]$ is *uniform* with respect to w if $w[t] = w[t']$ for every $t, t' \in I$. A maximally uniform interval is a uniform interval such that any interval strictly containing it is not uniform. We focus on non-Zeno signals of bounded duration which thus have a finite number of maximally-uniform intervals. We use $w[t, t']$ to denote the segment of w on the interval $[t, t']$.

Remark: To keep the fluidity of the presentation we do not give too much attention to the issue of open/closed intervals in the definitions of signals and expressions. In fact, the semantics of timed regular expressions in [ACM02] is not based on total functions from $\mathbb{T}$ to the alphabet. An element from the underlying signal monoid is written as $w = p^5 \cdot \bar{p}^3$ which means 5 time of p followed by 3 time of $\bar{p}$. As a function, it is clear that $w[t] = 1$ when $t \in (0, 5)$ and $w[t] = 0$ when $t \in (5, 8)$. However concerning its value at points 0, 5 and 8 there are different schools of thought. One possibility is to let $w = 1$ at $[0, 5)$, $w = 0$ at $[5, 8)$ and undefined elsewhere. Another possibility is to consider the value of the signal be non-deterministic or undefined at boundary points. In this paper our regular expressions semantics simply ignore the value of signal w at boundary points.

As a pattern specification language we use a variant of the timed regular expression of [ACM02]. Such expressions admit, in addition to the standard *concatenation*, *union* and *star*, also *intersection*, *time restriction* and *renaming* (we do not use the latter operator which was introduced to match the full expressive power of timed automata).

Definition 2 (Timed Regular Expressions). *The syntax of timed regular expressions is given by the grammar*

$$\varphi := \epsilon \mid p \mid \overline{p} \mid \varphi \cdot \varphi \mid \varphi \vee \varphi \mid \varphi \wedge \varphi \mid \varphi^* \mid \langle \varphi \rangle_I$$

where $p \in \{p_1, \ldots, p_m\}$ is a propositional variable and I is an interval of $\mathbb{R}_+$ with integer endpoints.

We use an exponent notation with $\varphi^0 = \epsilon$, $\varphi^{k+1} = \varphi^k \cdot \varphi$, $\varphi^{<1} = \epsilon$ and $\varphi^{<k+1} = \varphi^{<k} \vee \varphi^k$. Note that the expressions used in the paper are more "symbolic" than in the standard "flat" theory of regular expression and closer in spirit to temporal logic where an atomic expression like p_i denotes (or can be viewed as a syntactic sugar for) the set of all tuples in $\mathbb{B}^m$ whose i^{th} coordinate is 1. The identity of signal w should always be clear from context, so that we use $p_i[t]$ as a shorthand for the value at time t of the projection of w on propositional variable p_i.

Typically, the semantics of real-time temporal logics such as MTL [Koy90] and MITL [AFH96] is expressed in terms of a satisfaction relation of the form $(w, t) \models \varphi$, indicating that the signal w satisfies φ *from* position t. For the past fragment of a temporal logic this is a statement about $w[0, t]$ while for the future fragment it is a statement about $w[t, d]$, see [MNP05]. For regular expressions we found necessary to parameterize the satisfaction relation by two time points $t \leq t'$, as concatenation requires equality between the *end* time of its left argument with the *begin* time of its right argument. In this setting we note $(w, t, t') \models \varphi$ the fact that $w[t, t']$ is part of the semantics of expression φ. Such a satisfaction relation also appears in extensions to real-time temporal logics such as freeze quantification which has been shown in [DBS12] to be monitorable by working directly in $\mathbb{R}^2$.

Definition 3 (Semantics). *The satisfaction relation $\models$ of a timed regular expression φ by a signal w, relative to start time t and end time $t' \geq t$ is defined as follows:*

$$
\begin{aligned}
(w, t, t') &\models \epsilon & &\leftrightarrow t = t' \\
(w, t, t') &\models p & &\leftrightarrow t < t' \text{ and } \forall t''.\, t < t'' < t' \rightarrow p[t''] = 1 \\
(w, t, t') &\models \overline{p} & &\leftrightarrow t < t' \text{ and } \forall t''.\, t < t'' < t' \rightarrow p[t''] = 0 \\
(w, t, t') &\models \varphi \cdot \psi & &\leftrightarrow \exists t''.\, (w, t, t'') \models \varphi \text{ and } (w, t'', t') \models \psi \\
(w, t, t') &\models \varphi \vee \psi & &\leftrightarrow (w, t, t') \models \varphi \text{ or } (w, t, t') \models \psi \\
(w, t, t') &\models \varphi \wedge \psi & &\leftrightarrow (w, t, t') \models \varphi \text{ and } (w, t, t') \models \psi \\
(w, t, t') &\models \varphi^* & &\leftrightarrow \exists k \geq 0.\, (w, t, t') \models \varphi^k \\
(w, t, t') &\models \langle \varphi \rangle_I & &\leftrightarrow t' - t \in I \text{ and } (w, t, t') \models \varphi
\end{aligned}
$$

The set of segments of w that match an expression φ is captured by the match-set.

Definition 4 (Match-Set). *For any signal w and expression φ, we let*

$$\mathcal{M}(\varphi, w) := \{(t, t') \in \mathbb{T} \times \mathbb{T} : (w, t, t') \models \varphi\}$$

Geometrically speaking, match-sets are subsets of $[0, d] \times [0, d]$ confined to the upper triangle defined by $t \leq t'$. In the sequel we show constructively that for every timed regular expression φ and a finite-variability signal w, the match-set can be written as a finite union of zones.

3   Match-Sets and Zones

Zones constitute a restricted class of convex polyhedra defined by orthogonal constraints $c \prec t_i$ and difference constraints $c \prec t_i - t_j$ with $\prec \in \{<, \leq, \geq, >\}$. They are used extensively to represent clock values in the analysis of timed automata. In this paper we use them to represent absolute time values in a match-set. While the constants for the diagonal constraints may be taken as integers, those of the orthogonal constraints have fractional parts inherited from the time stamps of events in w. Such a zone z also lies in the upper quadrant of $\mathbb{R}^2$ and not below the diagonal. Consequently we let $\pi_1(z)$, $\pi_2(z)$ and $\delta(z)$ be its vertical, horizontal and diagonal projections; these are intervals with respective endpoints noted $\pi_1^-(z)$, $\pi_1^+(z)$, $\pi_2^-(z)$, $\pi_2^+(z)$, $\delta^-(z)$, and $\delta^+(z)$. Typically we have

$$(t_1, t_2) \in z \quad \leftrightarrow \quad \begin{cases} \pi_1^-(z) \leq & t_1 & \leq \pi_1^+(z) \\ \pi_2^-(z) \leq & t_2 & \leq \pi_2^+(z) \\ \delta^-(z) \leq & t_2 - t_1 & \leq \delta^+(z) \end{cases}$$

with all constraints being tight. Note that under this representation diagonal constraints may no longer be integers. Due to the positive duration constraint for atomic predicates we also have to consider zones that are partly open, with the same canonical representation yet featuring strict inequalities.

Below we explain how the match-set of an expression is inductively constructed and prove that the outcome is always a finite union of zones. Since operations $\wedge$, $\langle . \rangle_I$ and $\cdot$ distribute over union, it is sufficient to prove closure of zones under their associated match-set operations and the closure of unions of zones will immediately follow. The closure is almost immediate for all cases except φ^* where we will compute the match-set by a finite number of concatenation. The convergence to a fixed point $\mathcal{M}(w, \varphi^{\leq k+1}) = \mathcal{M}(w, \varphi^{\leq k})$ can be intuitively understood due the finite number of zones definable using a finite number of constants in the constraints. One may show that non-redundant constraints, as opposed to tight ones are either integers or have a fractional part equal to that of some event in w. However a bound obtained from an argument along these lines would be overly pessimistic and we will use other proofs to compute better bounds on the number of iterations.

Empty Word.   Just notice that the match-set of ϵ is the diagonal zone

$$\mathcal{M}(\epsilon, w) = \{(t, t') \in \mathbb{T} \times \mathbb{T} : t = t'\}.$$

Literals.   When φ is a literal (p or $\bar{p}$) the match-set is a disjoint union of triangles touching the diagonal whose number depends on the number of switching points of the projection of w on p, see Fig. 2-(a).

Boolean Operations.   The match-sets for disjunction and conjunction satisfy

$$\mathcal{M}(\varphi \vee \psi, w) = \mathcal{M}(\varphi, w) \cup \mathcal{M}(\psi, w) \quad \text{and} \quad \mathcal{M}(\varphi \wedge \psi, w) = \mathcal{M}(\varphi, w) \cap \mathcal{M}(\psi, w)$$

and finite unions of zones are closed under Boolean operations.

Time Restriction. The match-set of the time restriction of an expression is obtained by intersecting the match-set with the corresponding diagonal band, that is,

$$\mathcal{M}(\langle \varphi \rangle_I, w) = \mathcal{M}(\varphi) \cap \{(t, t') : t' - t \in I\}.$$

This is just an intersection with a zone and the result remains a union of zones, see Fig. 2-(b).

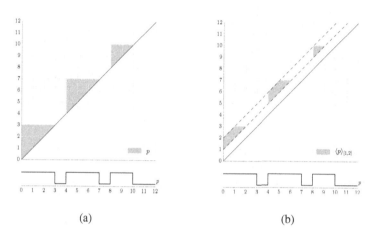

(a)   (b)

Fig. 2. (a) The match-set of a signal with respect to an atomic expression; (b) The effect of time restriction

Concatenation. Viewing $\mathcal{M}$ as a binary relation, the match-set for concatenation is nothing but a relational composition of the corresponding match-sets:

$$\mathcal{M}(\varphi \cdot \psi, w) = \mathcal{M}(\varphi, w) \circ \mathcal{M}(\psi, w)$$

as illustrated in Fig. 3-(a).

Lemma 1. *The composition of two zones is a zone.*

Proof. Let $F[t, t']$ and $G[t, t']$ be conjunctions of difference constraints defining zones z and z' respectively. Their composition $z'' = z \circ z'$ is defined by the formula $H := \exists t''. F[t, t''] \wedge G[t'', t']$. Eliminating t'' from H using the Fourier-Motzkin procedure we get an equivalent, quantifier-free formula H' which is also a conjunction of difference constraints and hence z'' is a zone.

Geometrically speaking, $z \circ z'$ can be seen as inverse-projecting z and z' into a 3-dimensional space with axes labeled by t, t' and t'', intersecting these two sets and projecting back on the plane t, t'. Another intuition in dimension 2 is given Fig. 3-(b).

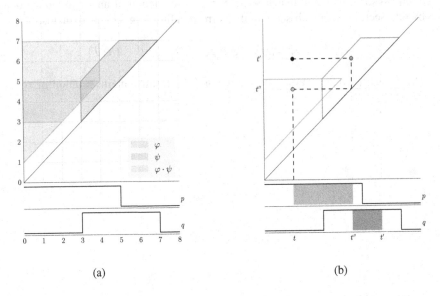

Fig. 3. (a) Match-sets of expressions $\varphi := \langle p \rangle_{[1,\infty]}$, $\psi := \langle q \rangle_{[0,2]}$ and $\varphi \cdot \psi$; (b) A point $(t, t') \in z \circ z'$ corresponds to a path from t to t' via some $(t, t'') \in z$, t'' on the diagonal, and $(t'', t') \in z'$

Star. We prove that the match-set of the star can be computed by a finite number of concatenations. An interval $[t, t']$ is said to be *unitary* with respect to w if $t' - t < 1$ and w is constant throughout its interior (t, t'). The following simple property of unitary intervals can be proved by a straightforward structural induction on φ.

Lemma 2. *Let $[t, t']$ be a unitary interval with respect to w. For all intervals $[r, r'] \subseteq [t, t']$ we have $(w, r, r') \models \varphi$ if and only if $(w, t, t') \models \varphi$.*

Let $\sigma(w)$ be the least k such that w can be covered by k unitary intervals, that is, there exists a sequence of intervals $[0, t_1], [t_1, t_2], ..., [t_{k-1}, d]$, all unitary with respect to w. A key property of $k = \sigma(w)$ is the following.

Lemma 3. *For any $n > 2k + 1$ if $(w, t, t') \models \varphi^n$ then $(w, t, t') \models \varphi^{n-1}$.*

Proof. Let $[0, t_1], [t_1, t_2], ..., [t_{k-1}, d]$ be a sequence of unitary intervals with respect to w. If $(w, t, t') \models \varphi^n$ then there exists a sequence of time points $t = r_0 \leq r_1 \leq \cdots \leq r_n = t'$ such that for any $i \in 1..n$

$$(w, r_{i-1}, r_i) \models \varphi \tag{1}$$

When $n > 2k + 1$, by the pigeonhole principle, among time points $r_0, ..., r_n$ there are three consecutive points, denoted by r_{i-1}, r_i, r_{i+1}, within the same unitary interval

$[t_{j-1}, t_j]$ of w. By Lemma 2 it holds that $(w, r_{i-1}, r_{i+1}) \models \varphi$, thus the time point r_i can be excluded from $r_0, \ldots, r_n$ still preserving (1). Hence $(w, t, t') \models \varphi^{n-1}$.

Corollary 1. *For any expression φ and any signal w with $\sigma(w) = k$ it holds that* $\mathcal{M}(\varphi^*, w) = \mathcal{M}(\varphi^{\leq 2k+1}, w)$.

From all this we conclude:

Theorem 1 (Match-Sets and Unions of Zones). *Given a finite variability signal w and a timed regular expression φ, $\mathcal{M}(\varphi, w)$ is a finite union of zones.*

Fig. 4 demonstrates the whole process of computing matches by zones for the expression $\langle (p \wedge q) \cdot \bar{q} \cdot q \rangle_{[4,5]} \cdot \bar{p}$ and signal of Fig. 1-(a) from the introduction. The result is indeed the rectangle $[1, 2] \times [6, 7]$.

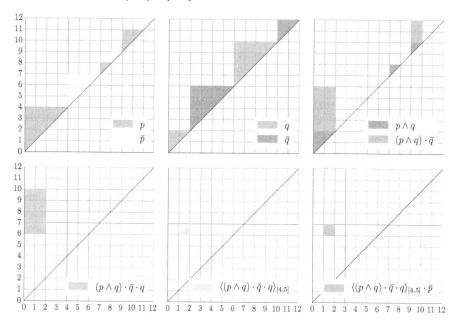

Fig. 4. The match-sets for all sub-expressions of $\langle (p \wedge q) \cdot \bar{q} \cdot q \rangle_{[4,5]} \cdot \bar{p}$ in the signal of Fig. 1-(a)

4   Computation

4.1   Algorithms and Implementation

The proof of Theorem 1 gives us a procedure for computing match-sets. This procedure, sketched in Algorithm 1, recursively calls a subroutine COMBINE that takes as arguments the topmost operator of the expression $\bullet \in \{\cdot, \vee, \wedge, ^*, \langle \rangle_I\}$ along with the match-set(s) of the subexpression(s) and applies the operation corresponding to the specific operator $\bullet$. All the operations on individual zones, including composition of two zones, see Lemma 1, are realized using calls to the zone library of the tool IF [BGM02] from our *Python* implementation.

Algorithm 1. ZONES(φ, w)

---

select (φ)
  case $\epsilon, p, \overline{p}$:
    $Z_\varphi := \text{ATOM}(\varphi, w)$
  case $\bullet \, \psi$:
    $Z_\psi := \text{ZONES}(\psi, w)$
    $Z_\varphi := \text{COMBINE}(\bullet, Z_\psi)$
  case $\psi_1 \bullet \psi_2$:
    $Z_{\psi_1} := \text{ZONES}(\psi_1, w)$
    $Z_{\psi_2} := \text{ZONES}(\psi_2, w)$
    $Z_\varphi := \text{COMBINE}(\bullet, Z_{\psi_1}, Z_{\psi_2})$
  end select
  return Z_φ

Our algorithm intensively performs various binary operations over sets of zones, that is, $Z \bullet Z' = \{z \bullet z' : z \in Z, z' \in Z'\}$. In addition to the operations defined in the expressions, in various stages we eliminate redundancy by checking *pairwise inclusion* of zones covering a match-set. For this we define a special *filtering* operation by $\downarrow Z = \{z \in Z : \forall z' \in Z. z \not\subset z'\}$, which consists in removing from Z all zones strictly included in other zones in Z. We define the general pairwise inclusion test $\sqsubseteq$ by $Z \sqsubseteq Z' \leftrightarrow \forall z \in Z, \exists z' \in Z'. z \subseteq z'$, that is each zone in Z is included in a zone of Z'. Note that the filtering Z is just taking the smallest $Z' \subseteq Z$ such that $Z \sqsubseteq Z'$.

A straightforward implementation of a binary operation on sets of zones with n elements will need $\mathcal{O}(n^2)$ operations. In practice, many of these operations yield an empty set and can be avoided by exploiting inherent ordering between zones. Such operations are very similar to the spatial join operation, studied extensively for spatial databases, see [JS07]. Spatial joins are usually performed using a *filter-and-refine* approach to avoid redundant operations, where two-dimensional objects in Euclidean space are first approximated by their *minimum bounding boxes* in a filtering stage and then actual operations are performed on filtered sets of objects. We implement this idea through the *plane-sweep* algorithm, used as is for intersection and filtering, and specialized for concatenation.

For intersection, Algorithm 2 keeps Z and Z' sorted according to π_1^-. It maintains two active lists Y and Y' consisting of candidates for intersection. Elements are successively moved to the active lists and are removed from them when it is clear they will not participate in further non-empty intersections. This happens for $z \in Y$ such that $\pi_1^+(z) < \pi_1^-(z')$ for every $z' \in Y'$ and vice versa. The filtering operation $\downarrow$ is performed using a similar algorithm. For concatenation, that is computing $Z'' = Z \circ Z'$, observe that $z \circ z' \neq \emptyset$ iff $\pi_2(z) \cap \pi_1(z') \neq \emptyset$. Hence we can apply an algorithm similar to Algorithm 2 where Z is sorted according to π_2^- and Z' is sorted according to π_1^-.

For the star operation, we tried two different approaches. In the *incremental* approach we compose the input set Z with an accumulating set Y initialized to Z. In the *squaring* approach we compose the accumulating set Y with itself. The squaring approach is more efficient for sets of zones that converge slowly to a fixpoint. Algorithm 3 depicts our implementation of this approach. In order not to compose the same sequence of

Algorithm 2. COMBINE($\wedge, Z, Z'$)   *assume Z, Z' sorted by π_1^-*

$Y := Y' := Z'' := \emptyset$
while $Z \neq \emptyset \vee Z' \neq \emptyset$ **do**
   $z := \text{first}(Z); \ell := \pi_1^-(z)$
   $z' := \text{first}(Z'); \ell' := \pi_1^-(z')$
   if $\ell < \ell'$ **then**
      Move z from Z to Y
      $Y' := \{z' \in Y' : \pi_1^+(z') \geq \ell\}$
      foreach $z' \in Y'$ **loop**
         $z'' := z \cap z'$
         $Z'' := Z'' \cup \{z''\}$
      end loop
   else
      Move z' from Z' to Y'
      $Y := \{z \in Y : \pi_1^+(z) \geq \ell'\}$
      foreach $z \in Y$ **loop**
         $z'' := z \cap z'$
         $Z'' := Z'' \cup \{z''\}$
      end loop
   end if
end while
return $\downarrow Z''$

zones twice, we maintain two sets X_k and Y_k such that at the end of iteration k we have $\cup X_k = (\cup Z)^{2^k}$ and $\cup Y_k = (\cup Z)^{<2^k}$. According to Corollary 1, we may stop at the first k such that $2^k \geq 2 \cdot \sigma(w) + 1$; however a fixpoint can be reached in less iterations. For performance reasons we use the pairwise inclusion test $X_k \sqsubseteq Y_k$ and give in the sequel an upper-bound on the number of iterations needed until this condition is met.

Algorithm 3. COMBINE($^*, Z$)

$Y := Z$
$X := \text{COMBINE}(\cdot, Z, Z)$
while $X \not\sqsubseteq Y$ **do**
   $Y := \downarrow (Y \cup X \cup \text{COMBINE}(\cdot, X, Y))$
   $X := \text{COMBINE}(\cdot, X, X)$
end while
return $Y \cup \{\varepsilon\}$

4.2   A Bound on the Number of Iterations

We show that for an input set of zones Z produced by our matching procedure, having $|Z|$ elements and covering $d = \lceil \max \{\pi_2^+(z') - \pi_1^-(z) : z, z' \in Z\} \rceil$ time units, the pairwise inclusion test is met before $k = \log(|Z| + d)$ iterations.

A sequence of zones $z_1, \ldots, z_n$ is said to be *redundant* if there exists $1 \leq i < j \leq n$ with $z_1 \circ \cdots \circ z_j \subseteq z_1 \circ \cdots \circ z_i$. Note that the star algorithm eliminates redundant sequences as for any such sequence $z_1, \ldots, z_n$ we have by transitivity $z_1 \circ \cdots \circ z_n \subseteq z_1 \circ \cdots \circ z_i \circ z_{j+1} \circ \cdots \circ z_n$. We first see that in a non-redundant sequence the maximal duration never decreases.

Lemma 4. *For any z, z' such that $z \circ z' \not\subseteq z$ we have $\delta^+(z \circ z') \geq \delta^+(z)$.*

Proof. The propagation of difference constraints gives us $\delta^+(z \circ z') = \min\{\delta^+(z) + \delta^+(z'), \pi_2^+(z') - \pi_1^-(z)\}$. Suppose $\delta^+(z \circ z') < \delta^+(z)$ and show $z \circ z' \subseteq z$. First note that $\pi_1(z \circ z') \subseteq \pi_1(z)$. By hypothesis $\pi_2^+(z') - \pi_1^-(z) < \delta^+(z)$, yet $\delta^+(z) \leq \pi_2^+(z) - \pi_1^-(z)$ so that $\pi_2^+(z') < \pi_2^+(z)$. This implies that $\pi_2(z \circ z') \subseteq \pi_2(z)$. Finally the hypothesis $\delta^+(z \circ z') < \delta^+(z)$ gives us $\delta(z \circ z') \subseteq \delta(z)$.

We call *repeated* a position i in the sequence $z_1, \ldots, z_n$ such that there exists $j > i$ with $z_i = z_j$. Now when appending a zone that may be repeated, the maximal duration increases by the corresponding amount.

Lemma 5. *For any z, z' such that there exists z'' with $z \circ z' \circ z'' \circ z' \not\subseteq z \circ z'$ we have $\delta^+(z \circ z') = \delta^+(z) + \delta^+(z')$.*

Proof. Suppose $\delta^+(z \circ z') < \delta^+(z) + \delta^+(z')$, take z'' a zone and show $z \circ z' \circ z'' \circ z' \subseteq z \circ z'$. Similarly to the proof of Lemma 4 it is sufficient to show that π_2^+ and δ^+ do not increase. On the one hand $\pi_2^+(z \circ z' \circ z'' \circ z') \leq \pi_2^+(z') = \pi_2^+(z \circ z')$, and on the other hand $\delta^+(z \circ z' \circ z'' \circ z') \leq \pi_2^+(z') - \pi_1^-(z) = \delta^+(z \circ z')$.

By a straightforward induction on the expression one may show that a zone z' such that $\delta^+(z') < 1$ always verifies $z' = \pi_1(z') \times \pi_2(z') \cap \{(t, t') : t' - t > 0\}$. Thus if such a zone z' was repeated it would make the corresponding sequence redundant; under the conditions of Lemma 5 we indeed have $\delta^+(z \circ z') \geq \delta^+(z) + 1$.

Theorem 2. *Let Z be a set of zones covering d time units; Algorithm 3 stops within $k = \log(|Z| + d)$ iterations.*

Proof. We first show that any non-redundant sequence of zones $z_1, \ldots, z_n$ with m repetitions verifies $\delta^+(z_1 \circ \cdots \circ z_n) \geq m$.

Let i be a position in the sequence. If z_i is repeated there exists $j > i$ with $z_i = z_j$. Factoring the composition of $z_1, \ldots, z_j$ into $(z_1 \circ \cdots \circ z_{i-1}) \circ z_i \circ (z_{i+1} \circ \cdots \circ z_{j-1}) \circ z_j$ we see by Lemma 5 that $\delta^+(z_1 \circ \cdots \circ z_i) = \delta^+(z_1 \circ \cdots \circ z_{i-1}) + \delta^+(z_i)$ and in particular $\delta^+(z_1 \circ \cdots \circ z_i) \geq \delta^+(z_1 \circ \cdots \circ z_{i-1}) + 1$, maximal duration increases of 1. Else z_i is not repeated and by Lemma 4 we ensure $\delta^+(z_1 \circ \cdots \circ z_i) \geq \delta^+(z_1 \circ \cdots \circ z_{i-1})$, maximal duration does not decrease. With m repeated zones the sequence $z_1, \ldots, z_n$ has maximal duration of at least m.

Now suppose the algorithm reaches iteration k, and take x a zone in X_k. There exists a sequence $z_1, \ldots, z_n$ such that $x = z_1 \circ \cdots \circ z_n$ with $n = 2^k \geq |Z| - d$. If such a sequence was non-redundant it would have at least $n - |Z|$ repeated zones, and maximal duration $\delta^+(z_1 \circ \cdots \circ z_n) \geq n - |Z| \geq d > \pi_2^+(z_n) - \pi_1^-(z_1)$ which is impossible. Therefore it is redundant so that there exists $y \in Y_k$ with $x \subseteq y$; we have shown $X_k \sqsubseteq Y_k$ thus if iteration k is reached the algorithm stops.

5   Experimentation

We test our implementation on several examples, focusing on performance aspects and investigating the sensitivity of our algorithms to various parameters such as signal variability, signal length, and the magnitude of time units in the expression.

Example: Performance of the Concatenation. In this example we define an expression $\varphi := p \cdot q$ on random Boolean signals p and q with length $\mathcal{L}$. We draw a number $\mathcal{E}$ of switching points from a uniform distribution between 0 and $\mathcal{L}$, and we define the variability of the resulting signal as $\mathcal{V} = \mathcal{E}/\mathcal{L}$. In Fig. 5-(a), we evaluate expression φ over such signals w with fixed variability and of increasing length to measure the execution time. This corresponds to the usual situation when monitoring various executions of the same system: there the algorithm performs in linear time with respect to signal length. Note that we use similar algorithms for concatenation, union, intersection and time-restriction operations; therefore, one can extend performance behavior of concatenation to others.

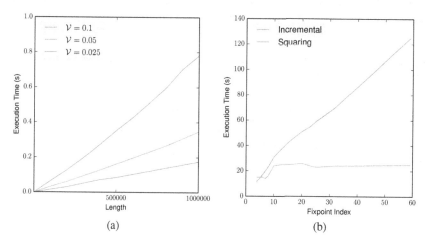

Fig. 5. (a) Performance of concatenation operation with respect to signal length; (b) Performance comparison of star algorithms with respect to fixpoint index

Example: Performance of the Star. In this example we use a family of expressions $(\langle p \cdot q \rangle_{[0,r]})^*$ on randomly generated Boolean signals p and q of fixed length and variability, taken as large numbers in order to stress our algorithms. Reducing r in the expression increases the fixpoint index n, defined as the minimum sequence length such that all longer sequences are included in a sequence of at most this length. We can compare incremental and squaring star algorithms as n changes and we plot the performance results in Fig. 5-(b). We see that the squaring performs better than incremental algorithm except cases where n is small. This can be explained by the fact that in the squaring approach, the effect of filtering is multiplied in the following sense. Every sequence that we discard may have appeared in several factorizations of longer sequences; squaring will reuse sequences as subsequences in many places which the incremental approach does not do. Another effect that we observe is that the number of zones covering sequences of length n does not explode but rather seem to stay constant over iterations. This is illustrated by the linearity of execution time with respect to fixpoint index in the incremental approach.

Example: A Complex Expression. In this example we keep expression φ fixed while modifying the signal. We have two Boolean signals p and q, and define an expression which is satisfied when they oscillate rapidly together for some amount of time:

$$\varphi := \langle (\langle p \cdot \bar{p} \rangle_{[0,10]})^* \wedge (\langle q \cdot \bar{q} \rangle_{[0,10]})^* \rangle_{[80,\infty]}$$

We generate input signals by segments, with a segment length of 400 time units. For each segment, we draw switching points in time using an exponential distribution over the segment to provide less switching at the end thus favoring the stabilization case. We tested the expression φ with varying signal length and variability. The results are depicted in Table 1. We also report the number of maximally uniform intervals in the signal $|w|$ along with the number of zones found $|Z_\varphi|$. These results are consistent with simpler examples, indicating that one can monitor complex expressions without facing a blow-up in computation time.

Table 1. Evaluation time of the matchset construction of φ as a function of the variability ($\mathcal{V}$) and length ($\mathcal{L}$) of input signal w

$\mathcal{V}$	$\mathcal{L}$	$|w|$	$|Z_\varphi|$	Time (s)
0.025	40000	1893	0	0.08
0.025	80000	3825	0	0.17
0.025	160000	7642	0	0.37
0.05	40000	3654	0	0.27
0.05	80000	7305	0	0.60
0.05	160000	14614	0	1.27
0.075	40000	5131	1	0.64
0.075	80000	10476	4	1.40
0.075	160000	21200	5	2.88
0.1	40000	6715	10	1.35
0.1	80000	13306	23	2.73
0.1	160000	26652	47	5.83

6 Future Work

We can already consider several direct or indirect extensions to the work presented here.

Longest or shortest match. There often exists several matches beginning at a given time or position. In that case string matching programs enforce the *greedy* policy of returning the longest match (containing all other matches), while hardware specification languages enforce the *lazy* policy of returning the shortest match (earliest violation). Both features are straightforward to implement within our framework.

Online matching. In the context of dynamic verification, it is useful to monitor a property during simulation so as to possibly stop early in case a violation. Making our algorithm work online would require to re-order the operations on zones according to some notion of time. The duration-restriction operator may also enjoy specific treatment so as to cancel matches passed the maximum duration.

New operators. Temporal operators can be useful to specify the intent of the regular expression; for instance a safety property should be monitored according to the semantics of a temporal *always* operator. This feature is available in hardware specification languages PSL/SVA, where a regular expression may be evaluated in the context of an arbitary temporal logic formula. Negation may also be introduced not as a Boolean operation on signals, but as a regular expression primitive. Looking for *absence* of a match requires to compute the complement of a matchset, which may be expensive to compute.

Events and delays. Standard assertions languages only handle events or actions. This also was the model of the timed regular expressions of [ACM02]. In our signals framework, we would like to handle events such as rise and fall of signals. Events only induce finitely many matches and can be represented by punctual zones. In the setting of events-based regular expressions, specification languages have concatenation operators allowing to wait a (non-deterministic) number of discrete time units between events; the generalization of SVA proposed in [HL11] shows that this concept easily translates in the real-time setting.

References

[ACM02] Asarin, E., Caspi, P., Maler, O.: Timed regular expressions. Journal of the ACM (JACM) 49(2), 172–206 (2002)

[AD94] Alur, R., Dill, D.L.: A theory of timed automata. Theoretical Computer Science 126(2), 183–235 (1994)

[AFH96] Alur, R., Feder, T., Henzinger, T.A.: The benefits of relaxing punctuality. Journal of the ACM (JACM) 43(1), 116–146 (1996)

[AGM⁺90] Altschul, S., Gish, W., Miller, W., Myers, E., Lipman, D.: Basic local alignment search tool. Journal of Molecular Biology, 403–410 (1990)

[BGM02] Bozga, M., Graf, S., Mounier, L.: IF-2.0: A validation environment for component-based real-time systems. In: Brinksma, E., Larsen, K.G. (eds.) CAV 2002. LNCS, vol. 2404, pp. 343–348. Springer, Heidelberg (2002)

[BM77] Boyer, R.S., Moore, J.S.: A fast string searching algorithm. Communications of the ACM (1977)

[CR02] Crochemore, M., Rytter, W.: Jewels of Stringology. World Scientific (2002)

[CVK04] Cohen, B., Venkataramanan, S., Kumari, A.: Using PSL/Sugar for formal and dynamic verification: Guide to Property Specification Language for Assertion-based Verification. VhdlCohen Publishing (2004)

[DBS12] Dluhos, P., Brim, L., Safránek, D.: On expressing and monitoring oscillatory dynamics. In: HSB, pp. 73–87 (2012)

[EF06] Eisner, C., Fisman, D.: A practical introduction to PSL. Springer (2006)

[Fri06] Friedl, J.: Mastering regular expressions. O'Reilly Media, Inc. (2006)

[FRM94]   Faloutsos, C., Ranganathan, M., Manolopoulos, Y.: Fast subsequence matching in time-series databases. In: Proceedings of the ACM SIGMOD Conference on Management of Data (1994)

[HL11]   Havlicek, J., Little, S.: Realtime regular expressions for analog and mixed-signal assertions. In: FMCAD, pp. 155–162 (2011)

[JS07]   Jacox, E.H., Samet, H.: Spatial join techniques. ACM Transactions on Database Systems (TODS), 70 (2007)

[Kle56]   Kleene, S.C.: Representation of events in nerve nets and finite automata. Automata Studies (1956)

[KMP77]   Knuth, D.E., Morris Jr., J.H., Pratt, V.R.: Fast pattern matching in strings. SIAM Journal on Computing, 323–350 (1977)

[Koy90]   Koymans, R.: Specifying real-time properties with metric temporal logic. Real-Time Systems 2(4), 255–299 (1990)

[Lau00]   Laurikari, V.: NFAs with tagged transitions, their conversion to deterministic automata and application to regular expressions. In: Proceecedings of the Symposium on String Processing and Information Retrieval (SPIRE 2000), pp. 181–187 (2000)

[MN04]   Maler, O., Nickovic, D.: Monitoring temporal properties of continuous signals. In: Lakhnech, Y., Yovine, S. (eds.) FORMATS/FTRTFT 2004. LNCS, vol. 3253, pp. 152–166. Springer, Heidelberg (2004)

[MNP05]   Maler, O., Nickovic, D., Pnueli, A.: Real time temporal logic: Past, present, future. In: Pettersson, P., Yi, W. (eds.) FORMATS 2005. LNCS, vol. 3829, pp. 2–16. Springer, Heidelberg (2005)

[MNP08]   Maler, O., Ničković, D., Pnueli, A.: Checking temporal properties of discrete, timed and continuous behaviors. In: Pillars of Computer Science, pp. 475–505 (2008)

[Pik87]   Pike, R.: The text editor sam. Software: Practice and Experience 17(11), 813–845 (1987)

[Spe06]   Spear, C.: SystemVerilog for Verification. Springer (2006)

[Ste94]   Stephen, G.A.: String searching algorithms. World Scientific (1994)

[Tho68]   Thompson, K.: Programming techniques: Regular expression search algorithm. Communications of the ACM, 419–422 (1968)

[VR06]   Vijayaraghavan, S., Ramanathan, M.: A practical guide for SystemVerilog assertions. Springer (2006)

[Wei73]   Weiner, P.: Linear pattern matching algorithms. Switching and Automata Theory (1973)

Interval Abstraction Refinement for Model Checking of Timed-Arc Petri Nets

Sine Viesmose Birch, Thomas Stig Jacobsen, Jacob Jon Jensen,
Christoffer Moesgaard, Niels Nørgaard Samuelsen, and Jiří Srba

Department of Computer Science, Aalborg University,
Selma Lagerlöfs Vej 300, 9220 Aalborg East, Denmark

Abstract. State-space explosion is a major obstacle in verification of time-critical distributed systems. An important factor with a negative influence on the tractability of the analysis is the size of constants that clocks are compared to. This problem is particularly accented in explicit state-space exploration techniques. We suggest an approximation method for reducing the size of constants present in the model. The proposed method is developed for Timed-Arc Petri Nets and creates an under-approximation or an over-approximation of the model behaviour. The verification of approximated Petri net models can be considerably faster but it does not in general guarantee conclusive answers. We implement the algorithms within the open-source model checker TAPAAL and demonstrate on a number of experiments that our approximation techniques often result in a significant speed-up of the verification.

1 Introduction

Formal verification of time-dependent systems has been an active area of research for the last two decades or so. There are two prominent models that involve timing: timed automata (TA) [1] and different time extensions of Petri nets like Time Petri Nets (TPN) [22] and Timed-Arc Petri Nets (TAPN) [5,15]. Both symbolic[1] and explicit time-representation techniques have been developed for these models. For TA and TPN, it is well known [4,25] that the explicit (discrete-time) semantics coincide up to reachability with the continuous (real-time) semantics on time models with closed (non-strict) clock guards. A similar result can be proved also for TAPNs. The state-space exploration techniques for continuous semantics usually rely on symbolic zone-based abstractions (using the DBM data structure [12]). On the other hand, the discrete state-spaces can be searched in a direct manner where the clock values are remembered explicitly. The explicit approach can successfully compete with the symbolic one, as long as the constants in clock guards are reasonably small [6,19,17,3,16]. As the sizes of constants grow, the models become increasingly more difficult to verify, in particularly in case of explicit verification techniques.

---

[1] Referring here to a symbolic way to represent clock values and not to symbolic techniques based on decision diagrams.

A. Legay and M. Bozga (Eds.): FORMATS 2014, LNCS 8711, pp. 237–251, 2014.

As a motivating example, consider a design of a task scheduling algorithm for an embedded system where timing constraints are obtained from real physical measurements given in nanoseconds. Here a worst-case and best-case execution time of a certain task can be in the interval from 117 to 185 nanoseconds, while having the period of 10000 nanoseconds (the timing is taken from the model of a LEGO Mindstorm scheduling algorithm [14] created by software engineering students at Aalborg University). If a model of the task scheduling algorithm is populated with a larger number of components at this precision level, checking for the schedulability becomes quickly intractable. However, we may instead of the measured values approximate that the task duration is between 1 to 2 time units with the period of 100 units, abstracting away the precise timing and hence extending the task execution window. In case we succeed to verify that the system is schedulable under this abstraction (as it is the case for the LEGO scheduler), the schedulability of the original system is established as well.

Our contribution is a methodology that allows us to perform automatically such abstractions. The technique is demonstrated on the model of timed-arc Petri nets. The main idea is that time intervals of the form $[a, b]$, where $a \leq b$ are nonnegative integers, can be divided by a given approximation constant r and become $[\lfloor a/r \rfloor, \lceil b/r \rceil]$ in case of over-approximation and $[\lceil a/r \rceil, \lfloor b/r \rfloor]$ in case of under-approximation. By doing this, the constants used in the net are reduced, resulting possibly in large (even exponential) savings in verification time and memory. However, over-approximated nets allow for more behaviour while the under-approximated ones contain less behaviour and this may result in inconclusive verification answers. We discuss the correctness of the approximation techniques in the continuous as well as discrete semantics and both for the reachability and liveness properties. The approximation algorithms are implemented in a publicly available, open-source model checker TAPAAL [10], including a suitable GUI support, and we demonstrate its applicability on a number of case studies, ranging from academic examples to real-world inspired scenarios. For example in the LEGO case study [14], it takes 3366 seconds (more than 56 minutes) to verify that all tasks meet their deadlines, while if we over-approximate the intervals by dividing them with $r = 10$ it takes 36 seconds and with $r = 50$ only 7 seconds, still providing conclusive answers.

Related Work. Abstraction techniques like over-approximation [9] and under-approximation [21,24] have been studied in the past, including a counter-example guided abstraction methodology [8] where spurious counter-examples are used to refine the current approximation. Our approach is inspired by these techniques but focuses exclusively on the refinement of timing information and efficient feasibility analysis of the generated traces. State equations [23] and linear programming are often used to over-approximate the reachable space-space of untimed Petri nets. This technique is efficient, however, the timing information is completely disregarded, resulting often in inconclusive answers for timed nets. The authors in [13] suggest an algorithm for under- and over-approximations of timed safety automata by approximating the union operation on zones. Our method is not based on zones and it is targeted instead towards explicit state-space

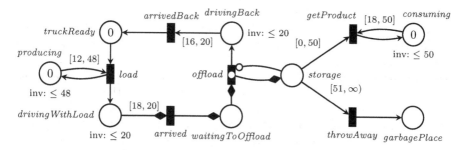

Fig. 1. Producer/consumer running example (intervals $[0, \infty]$ are not drawn)

exploration techniques where it can be combined with some recently introduced techniques and data structures like PTrie and Time Darts [16]. Finally, a time-relaxing method for a network of automata where events have interval-durations is described in [2]. The work proposes a pseudo-polynomial algorithm that enlarges delay intervals so that constants can be divided by a large greatest-common divisor (gcd). However, the division by gcd is, perhaps surprisingly, not a sound operation for liveness properties in the discrete semantics as we show in Section 3.2. Also, the method in [2] assumes that the network of automata satisfy the language intersection property (the language of the network is equal to the intersection of languages of the individual components). Our model of timed-arc Petri nets is more general as it supports also urgency, age invariants and inhibitor arcs (the language intersection property is not preserved anymore) and our approximation algorithm is simpler (with polynomial running time) and at the same time the experiments document a promising performance. Last but not least, another contribution of our work is the integration of the approximation algorithms into the tool TAPAAL.

2   Definitions

We start by informally introducing timed-arc Petri nets using a running example in Figure 1. The net consists of eight places (circles) and six transitions (rect-angles) and models a simple producer/consumer system where produced items are loaded on a truck, transported to an off-load storage and later processed by the consumer, while at the same time the truck returns to the producer site. The producer, consumer and the truck are represented by three tokens in the depicted marking, all having the initial age 0. In the initial marking the transition *load* is not enabled because its input places do not contain tokens of ages that fit into the time intervals on the input arcs of the transition (by agreement we will not draw intervals of the form $[0, \infty]$ that do not restrict the ages of tokens in any way). However, if we wait for between 12 to 48 hours (longer delay than 48 hours is not allowed due to the age invariant ≤ 48 associated with the place *producing*), the transition *load* can fire. The firing consumes the two tokens from the input places and produces two fresh tokens of age 0 into the places *producing* and *drivingWithLoad*. Now after another 18 to 20 hours the track arrives (by firing the transition *arrived*) to its destination. As the pair of arcs (with diamond-shaped tips) connected with the transition *arrived* are the so-called transport arcs, the token from *dirivingWithLoad* is transported into the place *waitingToOffload* and its age is preserved. Similarly once the transition *offload* is fired, the age of the token moved into the place *storage* now represents the total time the product was in transfer. Note that the transition *offload* has a special dot in the middle, meaning that it is urgent and once it is enabled, time cannot progress any more (though the transition does not have priority over other enabled transitions in the net). Moreover, *offload* cannot fire as long as there is a token in the place *storage* due to the inhibitor arc with a circle-shaped tip. Finally, the truck starts its journey back to the producer and the product can be consumed by the consumer. In case that the total amount of time the product was in transport exceeds 50 hours, it cannot be consumed any more and can only be thrown away while marking the place *garbagePlace*. The model can also contain weighted arcs (not depicted in our figure) that will consume/produce multiple tokens along the same arc.

We now proceed with a formal definition of timed-arc Petri nets (TAPN). Let $\mathbb{N}_0 = \mathbb{N} \cup \{0\}$, $\mathbb{N}_0^\infty = \mathbb{N}_0 \cup \{\infty\}$ and $\mathbb{R}^{\geq 0} = \{x \in \mathbb{R} \mid x \geq 0\}$. We define the set of well-formed time intervals as $\mathcal{I} \overset{\text{def}}{=} \{[a,b] \mid a \in \mathbb{N}_0, b \in \mathbb{N}_0^\infty, a \leq b\}$ and a subset of $\mathcal{I}$ used in invariants as $\mathcal{I}^{\text{inv}} = \{[0,b] \mid b \in \mathbb{N}_0^\infty\}$.

Definition 1. *A TAPN is a tuple $N = (P, T, T_{Urgent}, IA, OA, g, w, Type, I)$ where*

- *P is a finite set of places,*
- *T is a finite set of transition such that $P \cap T = \emptyset$,*
- *T_{Urgent} is a finite set of urgent transitions such that $T_{Urgent} \subseteq T$,*
- *$IA \subseteq P \times T$ is a finite set of input arcs,*
- *$OA \subseteq T \times P$ is a finite set of output arcs,*
- *$g : IA \to \mathcal{I}$ is a time constraint function assigning guards to input arcs,*
- *$w : IA \cup OA \to \mathbb{N}$ is a function assigning weights to input and output arcs,*
- *$Type : IA \cup OA \to Types$ is a type function assigning a type to all arcs, where $Types = \{Normal, Inhib\} \cup \{Transport_j \mid j \in \mathbb{N}\}$ such that*
  - *if $Type(a) = Inhib$ then $a \in IA$,*
  - *if $Type((p,t)) = Transport_j$ for some $(p,t) \in IA$ then there is exactly one $(t,p') \in OA$ such that $Type((t,p')) = Transport_j$ and $w((p,t)) = w((t,p'))$,*
  - *if $Type((t,p')) = Transport_j$ for some $(t,p') \in OA$ then there is exactly one $(p,t) \in IA$ such that $Type((p,t)) = Transport_j$ and $w((p,t)) = w((t,p'))$,*
- *$I : P \to \mathcal{I}^{inv}$ is a function assigning age invariants to places.*

The preset of input places of a transition $t \in T$ is defined as $^\bullet t = \{p \in P \mid (p,t) \in IA, Type((p,t)) \neq Inhib\}$. Similarly, the postset of output places of t is defined as $t^\bullet = \{p \in P \mid (t,p) \in OA\}$. Let $\mathcal{B}(\mathbb{R}^{\geq 0})$ be the set of all finite multisets over $\mathbb{R}^{\geq 0}$. A *marking* M on N is a function $M : P \to \mathcal{B}(\mathbb{R}^{\geq 0})$ where for every place $p \in P$ and every token $x \in M(p)$ we have $x \in I(p)$.

We use the notation (p, x) to denote a token at a place p of the age $x \in \mathbb{R}^{\geq 0}$. We write $M = \{(p_1, x_1), (p_2, x_2), \ldots, (p_n, x_n)\}$ for a marking with n tokens of ages x_i located in places p_i. A marked TAPN (N, M_0) is a TAPN N together with its initial marking M_0 with all tokens of age 0.

We say that a transition $t \in T$ is enabled in a marking M by the multisets of tokens $In = \{(p, x_p^1), (p, x_p^2), \ldots, (p, x_p^{w((p,t))})) \mid p \in {}^\bullet t\} \subseteq M$ and $Out = \{(p', x_{p'}^1), (p', x_{p'}^2), \ldots, (p', x_{p'}^{w((p',t))})) \mid p' \in t^\bullet\}$ if

1. for all input arcs except inhibitor arcs, the tokens from In satisfy the age guards of the arcs, i.e.
   $\forall(p, t) \in IA. Type((p, t)) \neq Inhib \Rightarrow x_p^i \in g((p, t))$ for $1 \leq i \leq w((p, t))$
2. for any inhibitor arc pointing from a place p to the transition t, the number of tokens in p satisfying the guard is smaller than the weight of the arc, i.e.
   $\forall(p, t) \in IA. Type((p, t)) = Inhib \Rightarrow |\{x \in M(p) \mid x \in g((p, t))\}| < w((p, t))$
3. for all input and output arcs that constitute a transport arc, the age of the input token must be equal to the age of the output token and satisfy the invariant of the output place, i.e.
   $\forall(p, t) \in IA. \forall(t, p') \in OA. Type((p, t)) = Type((t, p')) = Transport_j \Rightarrow (x_p^i = x_{p'}^i \wedge x_{p'}^i \in I(p'))$ for $1 \leq i \leq w((p, t))$
4. for all output arcs that are not part of a transport arc, the age of the output token is 0, i.e.
   $\forall(t, p') \in OA. Type((t, p')) = Normal \Rightarrow x_{p'}^i = 0$ for $1 \leq i \leq w((p, t))$.

A TAPN N defines a timed transition system where states are markings and the transitions are as follows.

- If $t \in T$ is enabled in a marking M by the multisets of tokens In and Out then t can fire and produce the marking $M' = (M \setminus In) \uplus Out$ where $\uplus$ is the multiset sum operator and $\setminus$ is the multiset difference operator; we write $M \xrightarrow{t} M'$ for this switch transition.
- A time delay $d \in \mathbb{R}^{\geq 0}$ is allowed in M if $(x + d) \in I(p)$ for all $p \in P$ and all $x \in M(p)$ and there does not exist any $t \in T_{Urgent}$ and any d', $0 \leq d' < d$, such that t becomes enabled after the time delay d' (by delaying d time units no token violates any of the age invariants and the delay can at most last until the first urgent transition becomes enabled). By delaying d time units in M we reach the marking M' defined as $M'(p) = \{x + d \mid x \in M(p)\}$ for all $p \in P$; we write $M \xrightarrow{d} M'$ for this delay transition.

We have just defined a *continuous semantics* of TAPNs where the possible time delays are from the domain of nonnegative real numbers. By restricting the delays only to nonnegative integers, we get the *discrete semantics* of TAPNs.

We write $M \to M'$ if either $M \xrightarrow{d} M'$ or $M \xrightarrow{t} M'$ for some delay d or a transition firing t. We write $M \xrightarrow{d,t} M'$ if there is a marking M'' such that $M \xrightarrow{d} M''$ and $M'' \xrightarrow{t} M'$. A *maximum* run of a net N from the initial marking M_0 is any infinite alternating sequence $M_0 \xrightarrow{d_0,t_0} M_1 \xrightarrow{d_1,t_1} M_2 \xrightarrow{d_2,t_2} \cdots$ or a finite alternating sequence $M_0 \xrightarrow{d_0,t_0} M_1 \xrightarrow{d_1,t_1} M_2 \xrightarrow{d_2,t_2} \cdots \xrightarrow{d_{n-1},t_{n-1}} M_n$ where either (i) for any delay $d \geq 0$ there is a marking M_d such that $M_n \xrightarrow{d} M_d$ or (ii) there is a delay $d \geq 0$ such that $M_n \xrightarrow{d} M_d$ and M_d does not allow any further nonzero delay and M_d does not enable any transition.

Let φ be a boolean combination of atomic predicates of the form $p \bowtie n$ where $p \in P$, $\bowtie \in \{=,<,>,\leq,\geq\}$ and $n \in \mathbb{N}_0$ (such predicates compare the number of tokens in a place p against the constant n), and the predicate *deadlock*. The satisfability of a formula φ in a marking M is defined by $M \models p \bowtie n$ if $|M(p)| \bowtie n$, and $M \models$ *deadlock* if there is no delay d and no transition t such that $M \xrightarrow{d,t} M'$. The extension to boolean operators is obvious. A formula φ is *deadlock-free* if it does not contain any proposition *deadlock*.

We can now define the reachability (EF) and liveness (EG) questions, as supported by the tool TAPAAL, for a given marked TAPN (N, M_0).

Definition 2 (Reachability). *We write $(N, M_0) \models EF\,\varphi$ if there is a computation $M_0 \rightarrow^* M$ such that $M \models \varphi$.*

Definition 3 (Liveness). *We write $(N, M_0) \models EG\,\varphi$ if there is a maximum run such that all markings M on this run satisfy $M \models \varphi$.*

If M_0 is clear from the context, we write only $N \models EF\,\varphi$ or $N \models EG\,\varphi$. The dual operators $AG\,\varphi \equiv \neg EF\neg\varphi$ and $AF\,\varphi \equiv \neg EG\neg\varphi$ are defined as expected.

Remark 1. If a query $EF\varphi$ is satisfied, the evidence for this fact is a finite run ending in a marking satisfying φ. The witness for the formula $EG\varphi$ is a maximum run invariantly satisfying φ. The maximum run is either finite (ending in a marking where we can delay forever or in a marking where no transition firing and no delay is possible) or infinite. If such an infinite run exists then there is also one that has a lasso shape (see e.g [3]) so that the sequence of the transition firings is of the form $t_1 t_2 \ldots (t_\ell \ldots t_n)^\omega$.

3   Interval Abstractions

Verification of reachability and liveness queries is a computationally hard problem because the size of the reachable state-space can be exponential compared to the size of the analyzed net. For timed systems, there are two sources of this exponential explosion. The first one is that Petri nets allow to model parallel activities that can have exponentially many different interleavings. The second degree of explosion stems from the addition of timing aspects. In this section, we shall see how the explosion caused by the timing constraints can be greatly reduced while still providing conclusive answers in many concrete scenarios. We suggest two approximation methods, one creating an over-approximation and the other one an under-approximation. Both methods rely on a given approximation constant r that determines the ratio by which the constants in the net are scaled. As constants in a net must be integers, we need to round the scaled values. For over-approximation, we enlarge the available intervals in the net, while for under-approximation we shrink them. A special care has to be given to inhibitor arcs as they inhibit behaviour. Hence for over-approximation we need to shrink the intervals on inhibitor arcs while for under-approximation we do the opposite.

Definition 4 (Interval abstraction by over-approximation). *Let* $N = (P, T, T_{Urgent}, IA, OA, g, w, Type, I)$ *be a TAPN, let* M_0 *be its initial marking and let* r *be a positive natural number (approximation constant). The over-approximation algorithm on an input* (N, M_0) *outputs a marked net* (N_r^{over}, M_0) *where* $N_r^{over} = (P, T, T_{Urgent}, IA', OA, g', w', Type', I')$ *such that*

- $IA' = IA \smallsetminus \{(p, t) \in IA \mid Type((p, t)) = Inhib, \lceil \frac{a}{r} \rceil > \lfloor \frac{b}{r} \rfloor$ *where* $[a, b] = g((p, t))\}$
- $g'((p, t)) = \begin{cases} [\lfloor \frac{a}{r} \rfloor, \lceil \frac{b}{r} \rceil] & \text{if } g((p, t)) = [a, b] \text{ and } Type((p, t)) \neq Inhib \\ [\lceil \frac{a}{r} \rceil, \lceil \frac{b}{r} \rceil] & \text{if } g((p, t)) = [a, b] \text{ and } Type((p, t)) = Inhib \end{cases}$

  for all $(p, t) \in IA'$,
- $w'(x, y) = w(x, y)$ *and* $Type'(x, y) = Type(x, y)$ *for all* $(x, y) \in IA' \cup OA$,
- $I'(p) = [0, \lceil \frac{b}{r} \rceil]$ *where* $[0, b] = I(p)$ *for all* $p \in P$.

The over-approximation clearly runs in polynomial time. Note that the over-approximation may remove some inhibitor arcs in case that the resulting interval is empty (meaning that the lower-bound is larger than the upper-bound).

Definition 5 (Interval abstraction by under-approximation). *Let* $N = (P, T, T_{Urgent}, IA, OA, g, w, Type, I)$ *be a TAPN, let* M_0 *be its initial marking and let* r *be a positive natural number (approximation constant). The under-approximation algorithm on an input* (N, M_0) *outputs a marked net* (N_r^{under}, M_0) *where* $N_r^{under} = (P, T', T'_{Urgent}, IA', OA', g', w', Type', I')$. *Let* $X = \{(p, t) \in IA \mid Type((p, t)) \neq Inhib, \lceil \frac{a}{r} \rceil > \lfloor \frac{b}{r} \rfloor$ *where* $[a, b] = g((p, t))\}$. *Then*

- $T' = T \smallsetminus \{t \in T \mid (p, t) \in X \text{ for some } p \in P\}$,
- $T'_{Urgent} = T_{Urgent} \smallsetminus \{t \in T \mid (p, t) \in X \text{ for some } p \in P\}$,
- $IA' = IA \smallsetminus X$
- $OA' = OA \smallsetminus \{(t, p) \in OA \mid t \in T \smallsetminus T'\}$,
- $g'((p, t)) = \begin{cases} [\lceil \frac{a}{r} \rceil, \lfloor \frac{b}{r} \rfloor] & \text{if } g((p, t)) = [a, b] \text{ and } Type((p, t)) \neq Inhib \\ [\lfloor \frac{a}{r} \rfloor, \lceil \frac{b}{r} \rceil] & \text{if } g((p, t)) = [a, b] \text{ and } Type((p, t)) = Inhib \end{cases}$

  for all $(p, t) \in IA'$,
- $w'(x, y) = w(x, y)$ *and* $Type'(x, y) = Type(x, y)$ *for all* $(x, y) \in IA' \cup OA'$,
- $I'(p) = [0, \lfloor \frac{b}{r} \rfloor]$ *where* $[0, b] = I(p)$ *for all* $p \in P$.

The under-approximation clearly runs in polynomial time. Observe that the construction of under-approximated net slightly differs from the over-approximated net. In particular, if an arc of a transition is removed because of an empty interval, then it is necessary to remove also the connected transition as otherwise the net might achieve more behaviour.

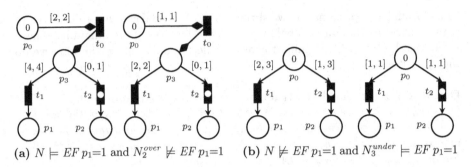

(a) $N \models EF\,p_1{=}1$ and $N_2^{over} \not\models EF\,p_1{=}1$ (b) $N \not\models EF\,p_1{=}1$ and $N_3^{under} \models EF\,p_1{=}1$

Fig. 2. Urgent transitions with timed input arcs

3.1 Approximation Correctness for Reachability

In order to argue about the correctness of the over-approximation for reachability queries, we wish to prove that if $N \models EF\,\varphi$ then also $N_r^{over} \models EF\,\varphi$ for any $r \geq 1$. For under-approximation, the implication should be the other way round. The correctness clearly does not hold if the formula φ contains any deadlock proposition as the approximations can both create new deadlocks and remove some existing ones. Moreover, the situation is a slightly more complicated than it may look, as urgent transitions with time-guarded input arcs may also influence the answer to reachability queries as demonstrated in Figure 2. This is caused by the fact that once the interval on an urgent transitions is approximated, it may disable a time delay that was possible in the original net. Hence for example the net N in Figure 2a can mark the place p_1 while this is not possible in the over-approximated net N_2^{over} because once the token of age 1 arrives to the place p_3, no time delay is allowed due to the urgency of t_2. This means that t_1 is never enabled in the over-approximated net. A similar situation can be observed also for the under-approximated net in Figure 2b.

We can now prove that the approximations are correct for any deadlock-free reachability objective, assuming that urgent transitions have only trivial guards on incoming arcs[2]. The following correctness theorem holds both for the continuous as well as the discrete semantics.

Theorem 1. *Let* $N = (P, T, T_{Urgent}, IA, OA, g, w, Type, I)$ *such that* $g((p,t)) = [0, \infty]$ *for all* $t \in T_{Urgent}$ *and let* φ *be a deadlock-free formula. If* $N \models EF\,\varphi$ *then* $N_r^{over} \models EF\,\varphi$ *for any* $r \geq 1$. *If* $N_r^{under} \models EF\,\varphi$ *for some* $r \geq 1$ *then* $N \models EF\,\varphi$.

3.2 Approximation Correctness for Liveness

Let us first notice that we cannot expect to prove under-approximation correctness for liveness queries as under-approximation can introduce additional deadlocks that can create non-existent maximum runs. For example, consider the net

---

[2] This restriction on urgent transitions also guarantees that DBM-based algorithms can be used in the TAPAAL continuous engine [11].

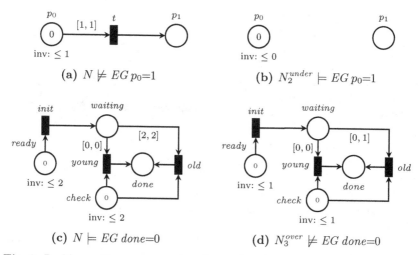

Fig. 3. Problem with over-approximation and under-approximation for liveness

N in Figure 3a that does not satisfy the query $EG\,p_0{=}1$ as any maximum run is forced to fire the transition t. On the other hand, the under-approximated net for $r = 2$ in Figure 3b clearly satisfies the query.

A less expected message is that the same problem is present also for the over-approximation as relaxing the net behaviour can remove some existing deadlocks. Consider the TAPN in Figure 3c that satisfies $EG\,done{=}0$ by the maximum run *delay 1, init, delay 1* that actually only uses integer delays. The over-approximated net for $r = 3$ in Figure 3d cannot deadlock in a similar situation as before as any maximum run will necessarily place a token into the place *done* (both in discrete and continuous semantics). Hence $N_3^{over} \not\models EG\,done{=}0$. For the discrete semantics we get already for $r = 2$ (greatest common divisor of all constants in the net) that $N_2^{over} \not\models EG\,done{=}0$.

To sum up, even though the over- and under-approximations are correct for reachability objectives, the correctness does not hold any more for liveness queries. Nevertheless, in the next section we show that we can still efficiently verify whether the maximal runs for EG queries in the approximated models are valid maximal runs also in the original ones.

4   Trace Validation

The aim of this section is to define the so-called trace net. A trace net guides the state-space search in the original net based on a given sequence of transitions (trace). The use of a trace net is to efficiently verify whether a trace proposed by a net approximation is executable in the original net or not (for each trace we construct a different trace net). Assume now a fixed untimed trace of the form $trace = t_1t_2\ldots t_n$ or $trace = t_1t_2\ldots(t_\ell\ldots t_n)^\omega$ where $t_i \in T$ for all i, $1 \le i \le n$. By $\#(t)$ we denote the number of occurrences of the transition t in *trace* (for an infinite trace only it its finite prefix $t_1\ldots t_n$). By $\#_i(t)$, where $1 \le i \le n$, we denote the number of occurrences of t in the prefix $t_1\ldots t_i$ of *trace*.

For the given TAPN N, we shall now construct a TAPN N^{trace} that restricts the behaviour of the net N so that transitions can be executed only in the order that follows the sequence *trace* (without imposing any concrete time delays), while at the same time making sure that along any computation in N^{trace} the proposition deadlock evaluates equivalently as it would in the original net N.

We shall modify the net N and its initial marking M_0 via the following steps until we get N^{trace} and the initial marking M_0^{trace}. The construction is depicted in Figure 4. In what follows,

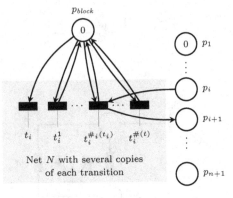

Net N with several copies of each transition

Fig. 4. Construction of the net N^{trace}

by a *simple arc* we mean a normal input or output arc of weight one; simple input arcs have the guard $[0, \infty]$.

- For each transition $t \in T$ we create $\#(t)$ additional copies of t, denoted by $t^1, t^2, \ldots, t^{\#(t)}$, such that every new copy t^j, $1 \leq j \leq \#(t)$, has an identical preset and postset as t (the same input and output places connected with arcs of the same type and with the same weight and containing the same time intervals as guards). The new copies of t are urgent if and only if t is urgent. Clearly adding these transitions does not have any effect on the behaviour of the net.
- We add new places $p_1, p_2, \ldots, p_n$ and a place p_{n+1} such that if *trace* is finite the p_{n+1} is a newly added place and if *trace* is infinite (of the form $t_1 t_2 \ldots (t_\ell \ldots t_n)^\omega$) then $p_{n+1} = p_\ell$. The added places have the age invariant $[0, \infty]$. There will be always exactly one token in the places $p_1, \ldots, p_{n+1}$, such that if the place p_i is marked then the only transition that can fire is some copy of t_i. In the marking M_0^{trace} the place p_1 contains one token and the places $p_2, \ldots, p_{n+1}$ are empty.
- For each i, $1 \leq i \leq n$, we add two simple arcs $(p_i, t_i^{\#_i(t_i)})$ and $(t_i^{\#_i(t_i)}, p_{i+1})$. In other words, the places p_i and p_{i+1} are connected via the next available copy of the transition t_i so that each copy is used only once in the sequence (note that the same transition can appear several times in *trace*). This construction imposes an order in which transitions can be fired, following step by step the sequence of transitions in *trace*. On the other hand, the modified net has a full freedom in choosing time delays as in the original net.
- Finally we add a place p_{block}, initially marked with a token, together with a pair of simple arcs (p_{block}, t_i^j) and (t_i^j, p_{block}) for each copy t_i^j of every transition t_i. We also add a simple arc (p_{block}, t_i) for every original transition t_i in *trace*. The purpose of p_{block} is to allow to deviate for one step from the transition sequence in *trace* so that every transition enabled in the original net N is enabled also in N^{trace}. However, once this step is taken (via firing some of the original transitions t_i), the token from p_{block} is consumed (and

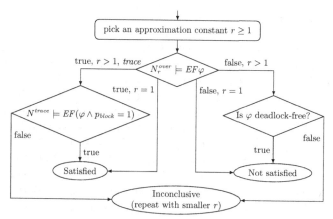

(a) Over-approximation flow diagram for $EF\varphi$

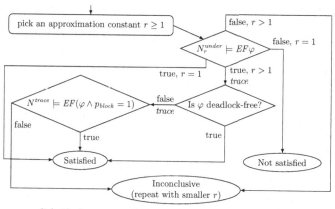

(b) Under-approximation flow diagram for $EF\varphi$

Fig. 5. Flow diagrams for over- and under-approximation reachability queries

the whole net N^{trace} terminates). This is to make sure that all enabled transitions in N are enabled also in N^{trace} in order to preserve the validity of the proposition *deadlock*.

Theorem 2. *Let N be a TAPN and let φ be a formula (possibly containing the proposition deadlock). If $N^{trace}, M_0^{trace} \models EF(\varphi \wedge p_{block} = 1)$ then $N, M_0 \models EF\varphi$. If $N^{trace}, M_0^{trace} \models EG(\varphi \wedge p_{block} = 1)$ then $N, M_0 \models EG\varphi$.*

Finally, we present the refinement process for approximation of reachability queries in Figure 5. The diagrams for liveness only differ in the point that a trace has to be always verified even for the under-approximation and in case a trace is not discovered in the approximated net, the answer is always inconclusive. The correctness of the flow diagrams follows from Theorem 1 and 2.

5   Evaluation

We discuss the case studies of *Patient Monitoring System (PMS)* [7] where the patient's pulse rate and oxygen saturation level is monitored and abnormal situations should be detected within given deadlines (constants scaled up to 250 seconds), *Business Activity with Participant Completion (BAwPC)* [18]—a web-service protocol from WS-BA where we verify its safety (avoidance of invalid states) using the fact that the original protocol is flawed while its enhanced variant is safe [18], *Train Level Crossing (TLC)*—a standard benchmark case study where trains are crossing a road and traffic lights should be controlled correctly, *Producer and Consumer Synchronization (PCS)*—our running example scaled by introducing more producers and consumers and *Plate Spinning Problem (PSP)* [20] where jugglers try to keep a number of plates spinning indefinitely. The greatest common divisor in all models is 1.

The approximations were implemented in the model checker TAPAAL available at http://www.tapaal.net/. The experiments, run on a Macbook Pro 2.7GHz Intel Core i7, were terminated once the memory usage exceeded 4GB (OOM) or the verification took longer than 5 minutes (☉). In the summary table we report on the running time using TAPAAL's discrete verification engine [16] and the column labelled with $r = 1$ corresponds to verification where no approximation is used. The rows marked with "no trace" correspond to EF or EG queries that are not satisfied (and hence no trace is returned). Only over-approximation is used here as under-approximation cannot reach conclusive results in this case. The rows marked with "trace" are satisfied EF and EG queries returning a trace that is verified by the trace net[3]. An inconclusive answer is prefixed by a question mark. We also note for each row whether we used depth-first search (DFS) or breadth-first search (BFS) when exploring the approximated nets.

In case of singleton intervals on arcs, under-approximation will remove such arcs (including the connected transitions). This may quickly result in a net where too many transitions are missing and the verification answers become inconclusive. Our experiments show that if we instead keep the arcs with singleton intervals (divided by the approximation constant r and rounded down), then we are likely to get more conclusive answers. Of course, we are not creating an under-approximation any more. However, this is not an issue as for liveness queries the trace returned by under-approximation must be always verified by the trace net (see Section 3.2) and we can do the same also for the reachability queries. Our experimental data use the variant of under-approximation described above.

The experiments show that both approximations frequently provide conclusive answers and significantly speedup the verification process. The general trend is that increasing the approximation constant r improves the verification times up to a certain point after which the improvements are not that significant and finally may result in inconclusive answers (like in PSP) or a timeout (in case of

---

[3] For the PMS case-study only under-approximation is reported as over-approximation was returning inconclusive answers; the size scaling in PMS is also different for the satisfied and unsatisfied query in order to provide measurable data.

Patient Monitoring System (PMS) — Reachability

	Size	r=1	r=2	r=3	r=5	r=7	r=10
no trace / over-approx / BFS	1	⏱	57.1 s	18.8 s	11.7 s	4.1 s	0.7 s
	2	⏱	102.3 s	25.4 s	38.6 s	5.6 s	0.8 s
	3	⏱	231.9 s	40.7 s	65.4 s	8.2 s	1.1 s
	4	⏱	⏱	67.4 s	135.0 s	56.0 s	1.5 s
trace / under-approx / BFS	1	39.3 s	5.0 s	? 2.1 s	1.2 s	? 0.5 s	0.5 s
	2	242.5 s	21.9 s	? 4.5 s	2.2 s	? 0.7 s	1.2 s
	3	⏱	39.7 s	? 3.9 s	3.2 s	? 0.9 s	1.4 s
	4	⏱	50.4 s	? 4.7 s	4.2 s	? 1.3 s	0.8 s

Business Activity Protocol (BAwPC) — Reachability

	Size	r=1	r=2	r=4	r=6	r=10	r=15
no trace / over-approx / DFS	1	⏱	88.6 s	16.4 s	7.8 s	3.1 s	2.3 s
	2	⏱	⏱	93.0 s	38.3 s	13.6 s	9.5 s
	3	⏱	⏱	⏱	136.5 s	41.1 s	31.7 s
	4	⏱	⏱	⏱	⏱	110.5 s	88.0 s
trace / over-approx / DFS	1	1.3 s	0.4 s	0.2 s	0.1 s	0.2 s	0.2 s
	2	155.9 s	24.5 s	4.9 s	2.6 s	0.2 s	0.2 s
	3	⏱	⏱	114.6 s	42.5 s	0.3 s	0.3 s
	4	⏱	⏱	⏱	⏱	0.4 s	0.3 s
trace / under-approx / DFS	1		0.4 s	0.2 s	0.1 s	0.1 s	0.1 s
	2		17.5 s	2.8 s	1.3 s	0.2 s	0.1 s
	3		⏱	51.1 s	14.6 s	0.2 s	0.2 s
	4		⏱	⏱	116.6 s	0.3 s	0.3 s

Train Level Crossing (TLC) — Reachability

	Size	r=1	r=2	r=3	r=5	r=7	r=9
no trace / over-approx / BFS	1	5.7 s	0.8 s	0.3 s	0.1 s	0.1 s	0.0 s
	2	⏱	21.4 s	5.0 s	1.0 s	0.3 s	0.2 s
	3	⏱	⏱	96.2 s	10.0 s	2.4 s	1.1 s
	4	⏱	⏱	⏱	80.7 s	14.4 s	5.4 s
trace / over-approx / BFS	1	4.1 s	1.9 s	1.6 s	1.4 s	1.4 s	1.4 s
	2	9.9 s	2.8 s	2.0 s	1.6 s	1.6 s	1.6 s
	3	12.0 s	3.0 s	2.1 s	1.6 s	1.6 s	1.6 s
	4	11.9 s	3.0 s	2.1 s	1.7 s	1.6 s	1.6 s
trace / under-approx / BFS	1		0.9 s	0.6 s	? 0.1 s	1.3 s	0.5 s
	2		1.9 s	1.0 s	? 0.7 s	1.5 s	0.5 s
	3		2.0 s	0.9 s	? 6.2 s	1.5 s	0.5 s
	4		2.0 s	0.9 s	? 50.4 s	1.5 s	0.5 s

Producer and Consumer Synchronization (PCS) — Liveness

	Size	r=1	r=2	r=3	r=4	r=5	r=6
trace / over-approx / DFS	1	0.8 s	1.0 s	1.0 s	⏱	? 171.1 s	⏱
	2	10.9 s	6.8 s	6.4 s	⏱	⏱	⏱
	3	126.0 s	30.4 s	27.5 s	⏱	⏱	⏱
	4	⏱	162.2 s	142.9 s	⏱	⏱	⏱
trace / under-approx / DFS	1		1.0 s	0.3 s	0.2 s	0.7 s	0.3 s
	2		6.7 s	1.2 s	1.1 s	4.2 s	1.0 s
	3		30.2 s	7.6 s	7.3 s	22.9 s	6.7 s
	4		157.2 s	47.1 s	50.3 s	120.3 s	43.4 s

Plate Spinning Problem (PSP) — Liveness

	Size	r=1	r=2	r=3	r=4	r=5	r=6
trace / over-approx / DFS	1	12.4 s	0.6 s	0.3 s	0.3 s	0.3 s	? 0.1 s
	2	41.3 s	1.5 s	0.4 s	0.4 s	0.4 s	? 0.1 s
	3	100.3 s	3.2 s	0.7 s	0.7 s	0.7 s	? 0.1 s
	4	213.2 s	6.3 s	1.1 s	1.1 s	1.1 s	? 0.1 s
trace / under-approx / DFS	1		1.7 s	0.5 s	0.6 s	⏱	0.3 s
	2		5.5 s	1.5 s	1.5 s	0.4 s	0.4 s
	3		12.8 s	3.2 s	3.2 s	2.2 s	0.7 s
	4		26.8 s	6.3 s	6.2 s	1.2 s	1.1 s

an over-approximation that suddenly allows too much behaviour like in PCS). Occasionally, inconclusive answers may appear for relatively small r values (like for PMS where $r = 3$ and $r = 7$) due to an unfortunate rounding of guards that produces infeasible traces.

As already mentioned, the reported experiments rely on the discrete-time engine. We also investigated how the approximation methods behaved in case of a continuous TAPAAL engine that performs a zone-based exploration (using DBM data structure). The general observation in most of such experiments is that the approximations do not significantly influence the verification times that usually differ by a constant factor only. This is caused by the fact that the continuous engine performs a symbolic exploration that is not that affected by the size of the constants like during the explicit exploration. The comparison of discrete vs. continuous verification is not in the scope of this paper and we refer to [6,19,16] for further discussion.

6   Conclusion

We provided a simple, yet efficient method for discrete-time verification of timed-arc Petri net. The approximation algorithms were implemented in the tool TAPAAL and the experiments document a high practical applicability, in particular for nets where the timing constraints are robust, meaning that small changes in the guard intervals do not change the validity of the properties in question. As a result, the designers of formal models do not have to consider so carefully the size of constants in their models anymore; in many cases the constants can be automatically lowered while still providing conclusive answers.

References

1. Alur, R., Dill, D.: A theory of timed automata. Theoretical Computer Science 126(2), 183–235 (1994)
2. Alur, R., Itai, A., Kurshan, R., Yannakakis, M.: Timing verification by successive approximation. In: Probst, D.K., von Bochmann, G. (eds.) CAV 1992. LNCS, vol. 663, pp. 137–150. Springer, Heidelberg (1993)
3. Andersen, M., Gatten Larsen, H., Srba, J., Grund Sørensen, M., Haahr Taankvist, J.: Verification of liveness properties on closed timed-arc Petri nets. In: Kučera, A., Henzinger, T.A., Nešetřil, J., Vojnar, T., Antoš, D. (eds.) MEMICS 2012. LNCS, vol. 7721, pp. 69–81. Springer, Heidelberg (2013)
4. Asarin, E., Maler, O., Pnueli, A.: On discretization of delays in timed automata and digital circuits. In: Sangiorgi, D., de Simone, R. (eds.) CONCUR 1998. LNCS, vol. 1466, pp. 470–484. Springer, Heidelberg (1998)
5. Bolognesi, T., Lucidi, F., Trigila, S.: From timed Petri nets to timed LOTOS. In: IFIP WG 6.1 Tenth International Symposium on Protocol Specification, Testing and Verification, pp. 1–14. North-Holland, Amsterdam (1990)
6. Bozga, M., Maler, O., Tripakis, S.: Efficient verification of timed automata using dense and discrete time semantics. In: Pierre, L., Kropf, T. (eds.) CHARME 1999. LNCS, vol. 1703, pp. 125–141. Springer, Heidelberg (1999)

7. Cicirelli, F., Furfaro, A., Nigro, L.: Model checking time-dependent system specifications using time stream Petri nets and UPPAAL. Applied Mathematics and Computation 218(16), 8160–8186 (2012)
8. Clarke, E., Grumberg, O., Jha, S., Lu, Y., Veith, H.: Counterexample-guided abstraction refinement. In: Emerson, E.A., Sistla, A.P. (eds.) CAV 2000. LNCS, vol. 1855, pp. 154–169. Springer, Heidelberg (2000)
9. Clarke, E.M., Grumberg, O., Long, D.E.: Model checking and abstraction. ACM Trans. Program. Lang. Syst. 16(5), 1512–1542 (1994)
10. David, A., Jacobsen, L., Jacobsen, M., Jørgensen, K.Y., Møller, M.H., Srba, J.: TAPAAL 2.0: Integrated development environment for timed-arc Petri nets. In: Flanagan, C., König, B. (eds.) TACAS 2012. LNCS, vol. 7214, pp. 492–497. Springer, Heidelberg (2012)
11. David, A., Jacobsen, L., Jacobsen, M., Srba, J.: A forward reachability algorithm for bounded timed-arc Petri nets. In: SSV 2012. EPTCS, vol. 102, pp. 125–140. Open Publishing Association (2012)
12. Dill, D.L.: Timing assumptions and verification of finite-state concurrent systems. In: Sifakis, J. (ed.) CAV 1989. LNCS, vol. 407, pp. 197–212. Springer, Heidelberg (1990)
13. Dill, D.L., Wong-Toi, H.: Verification of real-time systems by successive over and under approximation. In: Wolper, P. (ed.) CAV 1995. LNCS, vol. 939, pp. 409–422. Springer, Heidelberg (1995)
14. Drægert, A., Kaysen, A.C., Byrdal Kjær, J., Mikkelsen, F.B., Nduru, C., Petersen, D.S.: LEGO car safety systems. 5th Semester Software Engineer Project Report, Aalborg University (2014)
15. Hanisch, H.M.: Analysis of place/transition nets with timed-arcs and its application to batch process control. In: Ajmone Marsan, M. (ed.) ICATPN 1993. LNCS, vol. 691, pp. 282–299. Springer, Heidelberg (1993)
16. Jensen, P.G., Larsen, K.G., Srba, J., Sørensen, M.G., Taankvist, J.H.: Memory efficient data structures for explicit verification of timed systems. In: Badger, J.M., Rozier, K.Y. (eds.) NFM 2014. LNCS, vol. 8430, pp. 307–312. Springer, Heidelberg (2014)
17. Jørgensen, K.Y., Larsen, K.G., Srba, J.: Time-darts: A data structure for verification of closed timed automata. In: SSV 2012. EPTCS, vol. 102, pp. 141–155. Open Publishing Association (2012)
18. Marques Jr., A.P., Ravn, A.P., Srba, J., Vighio, S.: Model-checking web services business activity protocols. International Journal on Software Tools for Technology Transfer (STTT) 15(2), 125–147 (2013)
19. Lamport, L.: Real-time model checking is really simple. In: Borrione, D., Paul, W. (eds.) CHARME 2005. LNCS, vol. 3725, pp. 162–175. Springer, Heidelberg (2005)
20. Larsen, K.G., Behrmann, G., Skou, A.: Exercises for UPPAAL (2008), http://www.cs.aau.dk/~bnielsen/TOV08/ESV04/exercises
21. Lee, W., Pardo, A., Jang, J.-Y., Hachtel, G., Somenzi, F.: Tearing based automatic abstraction for CTL model checking. In: ICCAD 1996, pp. 76–81. IEEE Computer Society (1996)
22. Merlin, P.M., Faber, D.J.: Recoverability of communication protocols: Implications of a theoretical study. IEEE Trans. on Comm. 24(9), 1036–1043 (1976)
23. Murata, T.: State equation, controllability, and maximal matchings of Petri nets. IEEE Trans. on Automatic Control 22(3), 412–416 (1977)
24. Pardo, A., Hachtel, G.D.: Incremental CTL model checking using BDD subsetting. In: DAC 1998, pp. 457–462. ACM (1998)
25. Popova-Zeugmann, L.: On time Petri nets. Elektronische Informationsverarbeitung und Kybernetik 27(4), 227–244 (1991)

Author Index

Al-Bataineh, Omar   38
Andrychowicz, Marcin   7
Asarin, Eugene   222

Barkaoui, Kamel   53
Bartocci, Ezio   23
Baruah, Sanjoy   1
Berthomieu, Bernard   85
Bhaduri, Purandar   206
Bortolussi, Luca   23
Boucheneb, Hanifa   53
Brihaye, Thomas   69

Cleaveland, Rance   115

Dal Zilio, Silvano   85
David, Alexandre   100
Dziembowski, Stefan   7

Estiévenart, Morgane   69

Fang, Huixing   100
Ferrère, Thomas   222
Fontana, Peter   115
Frehse, Goran   176
French, Tim   38
Fronc, Łukasz   85

Geeraerts, Gilles   69

Johnson, Taylor T.   130
Jon Jensen, Jacob   237

Krishna, Shankara Narayanan   161
Kuřátko, Jan   146

Larsen, Kim Guldstrand   100

Maler, Oded   222
Malinowski, Daniel   7
Mathur, Umang   161
Mazurek, Łukasz   7
Minopoli, Stefano   176
Mitra, Sayan   130
Moesgaard, Christoffer   237

Nørgaard Samuelsen, Niels   237

Ratschan, Stefan   146
Reinkemeier, Philipp   206
Reynolds, Mark   38
Roohi, Nima   191

Sanguinetti, Guido   23
Srba, Jiří   237
Stierand, Ingo   206
Stig Jacobsen, Thomas   237

Trivedi, Ashutosh   161

Ulus, Dogan   222

Vernadat, François   85
Viesmose Birch, Sine   237
Viswanathan, Mahesh   191

Weslati, Karim   53

Zhang, Zhengkui   100